WINTER

WINTER

AN ECOLOGICAL HANDBOOK

JAMES C. HALFPENNY
ROY DOUGLAS OZANNE
ILLUSTRATED BY ELIZABETH BIESIOT

Johnson Books: Boulder, Colorado

First Edition
1   2   3   4   5   6   7   8   9

Library of Congress Cataloging-in-Publication Data
Halfpenny, James C.
    Winter : an ecological handbook / James C. Halfpenny and Roy
    Ozanne : illustrations by Elizabeth Biesiot. — 1st ed.
        p.   cm.
    ISBN 1-55566-036-3 : $16.95
    1. Winter—Popular works.   I. Ozanne, Roy.   II. Title.
QB637.8.H35   1989   88-81618
574.5'43—dc20   CIP

Printed in the United States of America by
Johnson Publishing Company
1880 South 57th Court
Boulder, Colorado 80301

Contents

Preface   vii

Acknowledgments   ix

1. Winter Ecology   1
    The Science Called Ecology   1
    The Science Called Winter Ecology   3
    History of Winter Ecology   4

2. What and Where is Winter   11
    The Sun and Winter   23
    Energy   25
    Snow   38

3. Life, Winter, and Adaptation   65
    Effects of Winter and Strategies for Coping   65
    Nivean Environment   73
    Temperature, Life, and Biochemistry   88
    Physiological Responses   108
    Energy and Mass Balance   118
    Animal Energetics and Nutrition   131
    Animal Populations   144
    Plants and Winter   163
    Insects and Winter   177

4. People and Winter   185
    Perceptions   185
    Humans and Cold   194
    Out in the Winter   198

5. Experiencing Winter   245
    Winter Field Experiments   246
    Ecology of Winter Symposium   262
    Research Equipment   262

Index   267

Preface

Each winter a blanket of white snow shrouds much of North America. We have developed a culture of hundreds of thousands of winter enthusiasts—naturalists, skiers, snowshoers, and snowmobilers—who live for the cold season. Still thousands of others experience winter as a requirement of residence in northern regions. Many people have questions about what they observe during the winter—the phenomena, the organisms, and the processes of existence. It is for these people that this book has been written.

Our knowledge of winter has developed slowly. Northern people, including Native American cultures such as Eskimos and Athabascans, have long endured harsh conditions and used the winter seasons to their advantage. They have lived in the snow, used ice for clear windows, and used the white surface for swift travel. An intuitive knowledge of winter has developed among them. Native peoples have their own terminology for the different types of snows blanketing their earth, and their languages are often richer in descriptive power of winter than the English language, reflecting a deep appreciation and understanding of snow.

Many of us now have the leisure time to explore and appreciate winter not as necessity of life but as a wonder of patterns and processes. In comparatively recent times science has turned its eye toward an understanding of winter and the interrelations between organisms and the cold environments.

Winter: An Ecological Handbook represents an overview of current knowledge about winter. It is designed to broaden your understanding of winter and to stimulate new ways to think about and relate to the fourth season of the year. Although we do provide many answers to questions you may have about winter, when the truth is known, our current knowledge of winter still provokes more questions than we can provide answers for. We hope this book will introduce you to the lifetime pursuit of understanding winter ecology.

Winter ecology, the formal science for the study of interactions among organisms and winter, is still in its infant stages; in fact, the general study of ecology has yet to become a truly mature science. As with most young sciences, knowledge and reports of studies are often fragmented. The literature is scattered in scientific journals, and a few articles have appeared in semipopular magazines. The wealth of scientific studies of snow as a material and its role in avalanches, for example, do provide important background material about the physical world, but further interpretation of snow as an ecological force is still needed.

We have written this book serve to three purposes:

1. To answer the questions of all who simply want to know more about winter,

2. To provide, in one book, an introductory compilation of knowledge about winter including information gathered from scattered literature sources and many new items, and

3. To share the joy and wonder that we have experienced in the winter wonderland.

We have designed this handbook to serve as a reference and have tried to present material in an accessible manner. Scientific jargon has been carefully defined and used in a limited manner, which we hope will enhance the enjoyment of all. Our audience is the educated layperson, but *Winter* can also be used for introductory college-level courses for juniors, seniors, and graduate students. Boldface type has been used to indicate key words in each discussion.

Although *Winter* has roots in several other winter ecology courses, this book is a direct outgrowth of the great times we have shared with our students at Teton Science School. For six of the last eight years we have jointly taught a two-week long, college-level program housed deep in the confines of Grand Teton National Park. At the start of each new year, while taking advantage of the pristine blanket of snow, we have shared the enjoyment of the winter environment with our students. These classes have been highly personal and exciting experiences. In this book, we try to convey our excitement about winter and science with a personable approach you will enjoy and understand.

Winter is designed to pique your interest and to encourage your participation in outdoor activities. To this end, we have included sections on winter equipment, travel, and camping and a chapter on experiencing winter. We have made suggestions for planning winter field trips and obtaining the equipment necessary to conduct scientific experiments during the winter.

Finally, a word about what *Winter* is not. We do not intend this introductory ecology handbook to replace the many excellent treatises or training programs on specific wintertime subjects. This is not a definitive work about first aid, skiing, winter camping, survival, nor avalanches. Instead, at the end of each section, we list books as Suggested Readings; we also recommend the excellent courses by organizations such as the American Red Cross, National Outdoor Leadership School, and the American Avalanche Institute.

Join us now in the wonder of winter.

Acknowledgments

Many people have contributed to this book in one fashion or another over the last decade. We wish to thank several people jointly, and others individually. First and foremost we thank our students who have shared the wonders of winter with us. Nancy Auerbach, Steve Beaupre, Pat Billig, Rich Bloom, Colleen Cabot, Margaret Creel, Jim Ebersole, Kim Fadiman, Jeff Hardesty, Frank Lowenstein, Paul Petzoldt, Warren Porter, Roger Smith, and Jennifer Tett have all played critical and pivotal roles in the development of this book and deserve our special gratitude. Audrey Benedict, Lisa Baietto, Karl Birkeland, Joyce Gelhorn, Anne Humphries, Charles Lennox, Pete Martinelli, Mardy Murie, and Greg Ziegler have each added to our efforts. Many people have reviewed early drafts of the text, including Dick Armstrong, Steve Beaupre, Scot Elias, Maryann Gaug, Nan Lederer, Mark Losleben, Mike McNierney, Tana Sholly, Brad Stelfox, Bruce Thompson, Rick Thompson, and Skip and Marilyn Walker. Rebecca Herr has helped to shape and finalize this book. We gratefully acknowledge these efforts and accept final responsibility for any remaining errors.

Permission to reproduce illustrations was granted by Joe Merritt (Carnegie Museum of Natural History), Pete Martinelli, Warren Porter (University of Wisconsin), Kathleen Salzberg (Arctic and Alpine Research), and the Denver Public Library, Western History Division, for photos from the 10th Mountain Division collection. Henry Diaz and George Kiladis were helpful in preparing figures on climate. We also wish to express our thanks to five institutions that have provided bases for our winter operations over the years: Cloud Ridge Naturalists, Institute of Arctic and Alpine Research, Mountain Research Station, National Outdoor Leadership School (NOLS), and Teton Science School (TSS).

I (JCH) wish to thank Ruth and Steve Bernstein for their early involvement in winter courses in Yellowstone, and Peter Marchand for his continued interest and support for winter ecology. Dale Gallagher, George Monsson, and Paul Petzoldt played important roles in my early development of winter skills and experience. In particular, I thank Paul Petzoldt and Rob Hellyer for their faith in allowing me to develop the NOLS winter branch in Yellowstone. Bill Broodigan, Rob Clark, Jack Niggermeier, and Dave Slovisky played very significant roles in the early Yellowstone programs. To the other NOLS and TSS staff who have helped, I also offer my gratitude. Thank you also to Greg Cook, Bob Gathercole, John and Pat Nix, Robin Ritger, Chuck Schaap, and Bob and Alice Stevenson for the development of Quiet Country Ski Tours in Grand Teton and Yellowstone National Parks. My thanks to my friends in the University of Wyoming Outing Club and the Wyoming Mountain Rescue for all the time we spent learning about winter. Ted Major and Pat Webber have played significant roles in providing institutional support for my programs through the years. Most of all though, I thank Larry Marlow, NOLS instructor, who has ventured to the far corners of the world with me and shared many a Yukon Jack at 40° below.

I (RDO) wish to acknowledge the NOLS for its programs. It was one of the winter trips lead by Pat Viani and Bill Webster in 1977 that turned me on to the experience of winter. Dr. Warren Porter, my former professor of ecology at the University of Wisconsin, is a forerunner in the biophysical approach to ecology that is reflected in this book. He was understanding and supportive of my outdoor excursions. Peter Hochachka's book on biochemical adaptations was the book that finally made sense out of winter for me. His excellent explanation of biochemistry gave me a better understanding of life's sensitivity to temperature than anything else I've come across. I wish to extend a very special thanks to Mark Losleben. Mark was the University of Colorado climatologist on Niwot Ridge when I did my studies there. He went up the mountain on foot to maintain equipment in all weather, all year long. He led me through incredible winter storms and taught me many practical "how-tos" of not just surviving winter, but enjoying the most absurd conditions imaginable. His spirit warmed and brightened up otherwise cold, lonely days on top of the ridge. Finally, I wish to thank my mother for her continued encouragement in my writing endeavors.

To anyone we may have missed, we express our thanks for your help in developing this book.

To my parents, Dorothy and Don,
for all their years of
support and caring

Jim

To my mom and dad

Roy

To my grandmother, Marie, whose
homestead in the North Woods of
Minnesota is where I first
experienced winter

Liz

Figure 1. *Winter ecology programs are taught at Teton Science School.*

1. Winter Ecology

You know what it's like in the Yukon Wild when it's sixty-nine below;
When the ice-worms wriggle their purple heads through the crust of the pale blue snow;
When the pine-trees crack like little guns in the silence of the wood,
And the icicles hang down like tusks under the parka hood;
When the stove-pipe smoke breaks sudden off, and the sky is weirdly lit,
And the careless feel of a bit of steel burns like a red-hot spit;
When the mercury is a frozen ball, and the frost-fiend stalks to kill—
Well, it was just like that that day when I set out to look for Bill.

ROBERT SERVICE

THE SCIENCE CALLED ECOLOGY

Ecology, the study of organisms and how they interact with the environment and other organisms, is a relatively new science. So new, in fact, that the word "ecology" was first used in 1866, and the study has only gained momentum during the twentieth century. We recognize that as a biological science, ecology is not an exact discipline. Nevertheless, it is still fraught with the excitement of newness. Since the 1970s, an ecological movement stressing the environment has grown within North America. New branches of ecology are still gaining recognition and one of these branches is winter ecology (Figure 1). For the moment, however, it may be helpful to dissect the science of ecology to provide a perspective for our winter studies.

We may visualize ecology as a five-tiered pyramid of scientific investigation

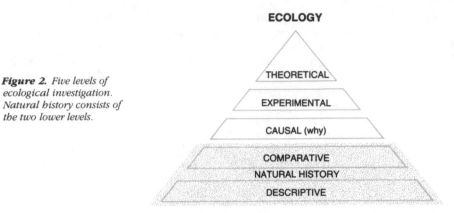

Figure 2. *Five levels of ecological investigation. Natural history consists of the two lower levels.*

(Figure 2). The base is formed by the broad realm called **descriptive ecology**. Descriptive studies are the earliest form of research. Our early ancestors saw nature and simply described their observations to their friends. Some of the earliest observers were the hunters providing for their families. Soon hunters began comparing notes. Hunters compared descriptions of animals and their behavior, in what we call **comparative ecology**. Spurred on by their comparisons, the hunters soon began to ask *why* different processes were occurring. The questions may have been as simple as why the hunters were more successful when hunting near the water hole. The questioning of biological activities and process represents the realm of **causal ecology**.

After the development of causal ecology came the need to test hypotheses formed to explain earlier observations. Biological science enters the realm of **experimental ecology** when researchers design studies to test different theories. In more recent times, ecology has developed into **theoretical ecology**, in which ecologists create theories about biological structure and function. Some of these theories are not possible to test, at least at the current time.

These five levels—descriptive, comparative, causal, experimental, and theoretical—compose the science we recognize as ecology. The bottom two levels, description and comparison, are distinctive in that they form the realm of science we know as **natural history**. Natural history is, perhaps, the oldest recognized biological science, but natural history is *not* ecology. It is only the two bottom layers of the ecological pyramid. We would, however, argue that natural history is the basis of all ecology. As such, any ecologist worthy of the title cannot, should not, be but a naturalist at heart. *Winter: An Ecological Handbook* explores the natural history of winter as a basis for understanding processes occurring during winter. It provides an overview of many natural phenomena detected by the casual observer.

Ecology has evolved past the point of descriptive study to the upper levels of scientific investigation. This book was thus written to immerse the reader in the exciting higher levels of ecology —causal, experimental, and theoretical. To do this, we have adopted an evolutionary approach that recognizes the need of organisms to adapt to the changing and often severe energy demands of winter. This is contrary to the often-used approach to the study of winter, the approach we call the "adaptation approach." In the adaptation approach, the study is of a list of adaptations and corresponding stresses. This approach misses the dynamic necessity of budgeting energy to meet the interlinked stresses of winter. More importantly, it overlooks the dynamic flexibility of organisms evolving into their niche in the winter environment.

Our approach to winter ecology is based on energetics. Winter is a seasonal period of decreased energy, including decreases in solar, thermal and nutritional energy. We recognize winter as an evolutionary challenge, in which successful organisms balance tradeoffs of their energy supplies with the necessity to live and reproduce. Our approach is to first study the stresses that winter places on organisms and how this determines their energy use. Next we will look at evolutionary solutions providing the balance needed to meet the energy demands of survival. Finally, we will look at specific examples of adaptations in organisms.

Ecology, by definition, includes the study of the functional relationship between the environment and the organism. The study of either the environment or the organism by itself is not ecology. Only when the link is made between the two does the study become ecology. For example, snowflakes are inherently beautiful and are a scientific curiosity. The study of snowflakes is not ecology, however, until we identify the interaction of the snowflakes with organisms. Therefore, at each opportunity, we stress the interactions between environments and organisms. We also stress that the human reader, as an organism, can experience these interactions. Many experiments are suggested in which you can use your own body to learn about winter.

For example, consider the question of what is the best way to keep your feet warm in winter. Does one loose, thick sock work better than two socks? Is one sock and an insole better than two socks? You can conduct a proper experiment in which you wear different combinations of socks on your feet. Remember to switch the combinations to the opposite foot during a second experiment the next day to control for differences in your feet. Use your body to test equipment every time you go to the field. As you go out into the winter, take the time to experience ecology by experimenting with your interactions to the stresses of winter.

THE SCIENCE CALLED WINTER ECOLOGY

Having defined the levels of ecological study, let us proceed to the realm of winter. Although large portions of North America are blanketed by snow annually, scientists did not recognize winter ecology as a formal branch of study until the 1940s. Perhaps this was because of the preoccupation of academic institutions with teaching inside classrooms during the winter season, and perhaps it was because of the problems associated with working outside during the harsh winter season. Since up to eight or nine months of each year can be spent locked in winter, however, it is appropriate to approach the science of winter ecology with a new-found determination to benefit from and understand the processes that are important to millions of people.

We will soon consider the question of what and where is winter. For the moment though, consider winter as a classroom, limited not by walls, but only by the imaginations of those who venture forth. We hope that by pulling together in one book the basics of winter ecology, we will tempt your imagination and spark your efforts at experiencing and learning.

HISTORY OF WINTER ECOLOGY

Let us first set the stage for our studies with an historical view of the development of winter ecology. This review is not designed as an all-inclusive overview, for we have not been able to survey all the necessary literature, especially on a worldwide basis. However, we do wish to list those people and works that have been important in North America and, in particular, important in our development as winter ecologists. Perhaps any deficiencies in this review will spark a more comprehensive work by an historian.

Although the peoples of the northern regions have long had an interest in winter, very little of their knowledge was written down. Early natural history books and ecology books fail to focus on the importance of winter snow cover as an ecological factor; only in 1957 did Pierre Dansereau in his chapter on bioclimatology hint that the mean annual snowfall was important in the distribution of sugar maples. However, nineteenth century naturalists were keen observers and reported on many specific happenings during the winter. **Snow flies** and **snow fleas**, insects that roam the snowy, winter environment, were of particular interest (Fitch, 1846; Folsom, 1902; Lugger, 1896).

With the introduction of the twentieth century, the word "snow" creeps into scientific writing. Naturalists were becoming interested in the effects of cold on life, and Ernest Thompson Seton (1925-1928), a foremost mammal ecologist of the time, wrote of animals, the rigors of winter, and hibernation. Hibernation became the major topic of interest into the 1920s and 1930s. Arthur Holmquist (1926, 1931) described the winter world of insects and of arthropod hibernation.

In 1926, William Peterson recognized the dramatic changes brought by the coming of winter. His work followed the seasonal succession of animals living in a cattail pond. Also in 1926, V.V. Stanchinski, a Russian scientist, recognized the importance of snow in the distributional ecology of animals. He wrote two papers: "On some climatological basis of rodent ecology" and "On some boundaries in distribution of birds in Eastern Europe." Both papers were written in the Cyrillic alphabet of the Russian language; their content is only readily available through the later work of A.N. Formozov (1964). G.E. Johnson provided an important summary of the knowledge of hibernation in 1931.

The year 1939 represents the hallmark for the inception of winter ecology. A most significant recognition of the influence of winter appeared that year when Ann Morgan wrote the *Field Book of Animals in Winter*. Morgan summarized winter activities, seasonal migrations, seasonal changes in animals and communities, and winter communities of land and freshwater animals. She provided an extensive review of animals, ranging from freshwater sponges to mammals, with considerable emphasis on the invertebrates. Morgan recognized the safety of small mammals living under the "blanket of snow." This book not only provides a summary of winter natural history of animals unsurpassed even today, but also provides an extensive review of the literature up to 1939.

Also in 1939, the Russian scientist Formozov first emphasized the importance of snow cover in the ecology of mammals and birds. Building on the earlier nonbiological work of V.I. Vernadskii (1933) who said:

> The presence of an ice and snow cover in the biosphere is, in its direct and indirect results, one of the most important factors in nature.

Formozov extended the observations to the biological world. Formozov's 1946 version of this paper, titled "Snow Cover as an Integral Factor of the Environment and its Importance in the Ecology of Mammals and Birds," was introduced into the English-speaking world through a 1964 translation provided by William Prychodko and William Pruitt.

The works of Morgan and Formozov together represent the beginning of the science now known as winter ecology. Since the appearance of these works, the science has grown by leaps and bounds into a major field of interest. This growth was no doubt enhanced by the growing recreational appreciation of winter following the 1932 Olympics and the return from World War II of the U.S. 10th Mountain Division troops (Figure 3). Following World War II, a few scientists began to investigate winter and even a few winter ecology teachers emerged.

In 1947, John Marr, fresh from the Mountain Troops, initiated a winter ecology course at the University of Colorado's Science Lodge. Through the years, many other winter ecology courses have been taught at the Science Lodge. The Science Lodge itself evolved into today's **Mountain Research Station**, and Marr's efforts led to the development of the University of Colorado's Institute of Arctic and Alpine Research. The **Boreal Institute for Northern Studies** at the University of Alberta provided a locus where William Fuller, Prychodko, and Pruitt worked to translate Formozov's paper.

During the 1950s and 1960s, William Pruitt became the leading advocate of winter ecology. Besides his numerous scientific articles, he produced movies that have introduced many young students to the wonders and studies of winter. Perhaps his single most important contribution was a 1960 *Scientific American* article, "Animals in Snow," which introduced the lay public to the importance of snow cover to the survival of wintering animals. Pruitt also stressed the knowledge acquired by native peoples living in snowy regions and emphasized that Eskimos and Indians had developed languages rich in descriptive words for the different kinds of snow.

The 1970s and 1980s saw a blossoming of courses, with five major centers developing an emphasis on winter ecology. In 1967, Ted Major formed the **Teton Science School**, located in Grand Teton National Park, with extended summer resident programs. In 1974, Ted and his brother, Jack Major, began resident winter ecology programs. After initial contacts with Pruitt, they established a program for middle and high school students, and also a program for college level students. Middle and high school students spent five days living at Teton Science School experiencing winter. College students participated in a two-week program originally accredited through the University of California at Davis. Bud Rice taught during the early years of the program and equipment was developed in conjunction with John Simms of Life Link. In 1980, James Halfpenny and Pat Billig took over the college winter ecology program at Teton Science School. Roy Ozanne joined the program in 1981.

Figure 3. Troops of the 10th Mountain Division practice at Camp Hale, Colorado (Drawn from a photo courtesy of the Western History Department, Denver Public Library).

Week-long residential programs for high school students are taught from January to April each year.

In 1973, James Halfpenny developed the Yellowstone Winter program at the **National Outdoor Leadership School**. This program consisted of two- and three-week long winter camping trips through Yellowstone National Park. Winter ecology is emphasized as well as camping and cross-country skiing.

Peter Marchand and the late Garrett Clough developed a winter ecology program in 1974 at the **Center for Northern Studies** at Wolcott, Vermont. Although it was a general winter ecology program, there was increased emphasis on invertebrates and freshwater ecology. Claire Buchanan and Joseph Merritt were instrumental in early program development. This highly successful college program has expanded from an initial two-week program to a four-week residential program under the direction of Gerard Courtin.

In 1974, John Gannon and Arlan Edgar developed a program at the University of Michigan **Pelton Biological Station**. Their program emphasized aquatic and terrestrial invertebrates and was also influenced in the early years by a visit from Pruitt. When Jim and Kathy Bricker joined the program, the audience shifted emphasis to primary and secondary school teachers and the program stressed in-service teacher training.

During the late 1970s, winter ecology courses continued at the **Mountain Research Station** in Colorado on a sporadic basis and were taught by a number of instructors including Ruth Bernstein, James Ebersole, Vera Komarkova, Patrick Webber, Roy Ozanne, and James Halfpenny. These programs were often resident at the Station and were accredited through the University of Colorado. Marchand currently teaches

the two-week resident program for college students.

In 1978, Gannon moved to the **University of New York at Oswego** and started a new program. This program was designed as an in-service training program primarily for high school science teachers. Through the combined efforts of Donald Cox, Alfred Stamm, Nathan Swift, Peter Weber, Suzanne Webber, and Gannon, major strides were made in winter science education, teacher training, and curriculum development. Their Winter Science Curriculum Project developed a report for the National Science Foundation called "Winter Activities for Middle and High Schools." This report may be published in the future for general usage.

All of the programs mentioned continue to provide excellent winter programs and serve as centers of focus for winter ecology. Two new programs include one offered by **Rocky Mountain Biological Laboratories** at Gothic, Colorado, originated by David Inouye, and one called **Winter Ecology of Interior Alaska** through the University of Alaska at Fairbanks, taught by Charles Lennox. There are, of course, many other programs—especially at nature centers throughout the United States and Canada. We do not mean to slight other programs, but limitations of space and lack of familiarity with all of these programs prevent their review here. (See *Winter Educational Programs* for detailed information.)

Several important publications have appeared over the last few decades and selected references will be found at the end of each section. However, we do wish to mention a few key papers here, as they are influential in the development of winter ecology in North America.

Donald Stokes (1976) wrote *A Guide to Nature in Winter: Northeast and*

North Central North America. Stokes covers aspects observed by a winter naturalist, including snow, trees, winter weeds, insects, bird nests, mushrooms, and tracks.

Two manuals provide information for teachers. These include the *Snow Ecology Guide* (Ted Major, 1979) and *An Annotated Bibliography for Curriculum Development in Winter Ecology* (Gannon and Jones, 1982). These manuals provide insight into the many materials and resources available for teachers wishing to start a winter ecology program.

The Secret Language of Snow (Williams and Major, 1984) provides a look into the world of the Kobuk Eskimos, their language of snow, and what snow means to living things. This book is an excellent introduction to winter for younger readers but will be a delight to all. *Winter Ecology of Small Mammals* (Merritt, 1984) provides a scientific look at winter. Although this is a technical book, it contains many of the new advances in winter ecology that will be of interest to many readers.

Peter Marchand's 1987 book *Life in the Cold: An Introduction to Winter Ecology*, is the first book to begin to bring together the scattered literature dealing with winter. The book provides a broad ecological view of winter. The sections dealing with plants and winter are excellent.

SUGGESTED READINGS

Dansereau, P. 1957. Biogeography: An Ecological Perspective. Ronald Press Co., New York.

Fitch, A. 1846. Winter insects of Eastern New York. Am. J. Sci. and Agr., 5:274-284.

Folsom, J.W. 1902. The identity of the snow flea (*Achorutes nivicola* Fitch). Psyche, 9:315-321.

Formozov, A.N. 1964. Snow Cover as an Integral Factor of the Environment and its Importance in the Ecology of Mammals and Birds. English translation. Boreal Institute for Northern Studies, University of Alberta. Occ. Paper. No. 1. Originally published in Material For Fauna and Flora of the USSR, New Series Zool., 5(XX)1946:1-152.

Lugger, O. 1896. The snow-fly. Univ. Minn. Agr. Exp. Sta., Ann. Rept., Ent., 2:230-231.

Gannon, J.E., and R.A. Jones. 1982. An Annotated Bibliography for Curriculum Development in Winter Ecology. State Univ. Res. Center at Oswego, NY, Spec. Rept. 1. 19 pp.

Holmquist, A.M. 1926. Studies in Arthropod Hibernation. Ecological survey of hibernating species from forest environments of the Chicago region. Ann. Ent. Soc. Am., 19:395-428.

Holmquist, A.M. 1931. Studies in Arthropod Hibernation. Temperatures in forest hibernacula. Ecology, 12:387-400.

Johnson, G.E. 1931. Hibernation in mammals. Quart. Rev. Biol., 6:439-461.

Major, T.N.D. Snow Ecology Guide. Thorne Ecological Institute, Boulder, Colorado.

Marchand, P.J. 1987. Life in the Cold: An Introduction to Winter Ecology. University Press of New England, Hanover, New Hampshire.

Merritt, J.F. (ed.). 1984. Winter Ecology of Small Mammals. Carnegie Mus. Nat. Hist., Spec. Publ., 10.

Morgan, A.H. 1939. Field Book of Animals in Winter. G. P. Putnam's Sons, New York.

Petersen, W. 1926. Seasonal succession of animals in a Chara-cattail pond. Ecology, 7:371-377.

Pruitt, W.O. 1960. Animals in the snow. Scientific American, 202:61-68.

Seton, E.T. 1925-1928. Lives of Game Animals. Doubleday, Page, and Co., New York.

Stanchinski, V.V. 1926. On Some Climatological Basis of Rodent Ecology. Collection BIZR, no. 7. *Also in:* Snow Covers as an Integral Factor of the Environment and its Importance in the Ecology of Mammals and Birds. A.N. Formozov. Boreal Inst. Northern Studies, Occ. Publ. 1. 141 pp.

Stanchinski, V.V. 1926. On Some Climatological Boundaries in Distribution of Birds in East Europe. Works, Smolensk Nat. Hist. Med. Sci., vol. 1. *Also in:* Snow Covers as an Integral Factor of the Environment and its Importance in the Ecology of Mammals and Birds. A.N. Formozov. Boreal Inst. Northern Studies, Occ. Publ. 1. 141 pp.

Stokes, D.W. A Guide to Nature in Winter: Northeast and North Central North America. Little, Brown, and Company, Boston.

Vernadskii, V.I. 1933. Story of minerals of the earth's crust. P. 1 *in* Snow Covers as an Integral Factor of the Environment and its Importance in the Ecology of Mammals and Birds. A.N. Formozov. Boreal Inst. Northern Studies, Occ. Publ. 1. 141 pp.

Williams, T.T., and T. Major. 1984. The Secret Language of Snow. Sierra Club and Pantheon Books, San Francisco.

Jim Halfpenny and students investigate a mound of dirt thrown up by a badger digging for hibernating ground squirrels.

Figure 4. *A cross-country skier skiing among the ghost trees of Yellowstone National Park. The ghost trees were produced by snowfall collecting on the branches and rime frost.*

2. *What and Where is Winter?*

Humans may perceive winter differently than other organisms. As humans, we know that when the blanket of snow drapes the landscape and the fire is burning in the fireplace, winter has arrived. We perceive the cold, heating bills, inconvenience on the road, beauty, or winter sports. Our exact perceptions, though, are often based on the weatherman on television telling us that the icebox of the nation was Fraser, Colorado, or Cut Bank or West Yellowstone, Montana.

Seldom do we question where weather statistics come from. The figures come from a continent-wide network of observers who maintain instruments in official recording stations known as **Stevenson** screens. A Stevenson screen is a white box standing three feet off the ground surface. The sides of the box are covered with down-sloping slats that prevent the entry of solar radiation but allow the circulation of air. Instruments housed in these shelters are routinely calibrated to ensure accurate readings. Thus standardized, temperature and relative humidity readings provide the official records of the weather bureau that can be used to develop a picture of winter across North America.

Let us characterize winter as we humans, including weathermen, perceive it. Winter is, first, a time of beauty. It is time when the hoarfrost crystals edge the open spots along the creek, when rime frost laces the trees, when cold temperatures hold the smoke-laden temperature inversions to the ground, and a time when the **ghost trees** shelter the small birds deep within their branches (Figures 4 and 5). But to the weatherman, these beautiful scenes are described in numbers reflecting climatic conditions. The human perception of winter occurs on two levels: sensuous and emotional perceptions, and weather patterns delineated by statistics and maps.

To us, winter is **cold**; to the weatherman it is **average** and **record low temperatures**. Official North American weather bureau records provide a perspective describing winter (Table 1). Record lows tend to be located in the high country of the western United States or in the northern regions of the continent. While -63°C (-81°F) may seem low, the world record at Vostoc, Antarctica (elevation 3,490 m, or 11,450 ft), tends to edge lower each year and is currently about -90°C (-130°F).

Large geographic areas may be affected by record low temperatures at a given time. The winter of 1978-79 may have been, in fact, the coldest North American winter in recorded history—certainly the coldest during the last 89 years (Figure 6). Even more unusual, the three winters beginning in 1976-77

Figure 5. Hoar frost forms an abstract drawing on grass blades in the early morning.

were all in the extremely cold category. Remember, the winter of 1988-89 brought record cold temperatures across much of North America. Besides affecting a large area, the cold lasted for an extended period of time.

It is cold, however, in more areas than those where the record lows have occurred. The distribution of cold is perhaps better understood by a map indicating the mean January temperatures (Figure 7). Notice in particular the -1.1°C (30°F) **isotherm** (line indicating the boundary of all equal tempera-

Table 1. Official record low temperatures for North America. Data compiled through 1976.

State or Province	Location	Elevation ft (m)	Temperature °F	Temperature °C
Yukon			-81	-63
Alaska			-80	-62
Montana	Rogers Pass	5,470 (1,667)	-70	-57
Wyoming	Moran	6,770 (2,063)	-63	-53
North Dakota	Parshall	1,929 (588)	-60	-51
Idaho	Island Park Dam	6,285 (1,916)	-60	-51
Colorado	Taylor Park	9,206 (2,806)	-60	-51
Colorado	Bennett	5,484 (1,672)	-60	-51

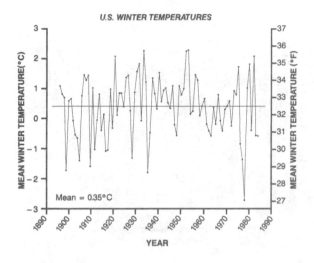

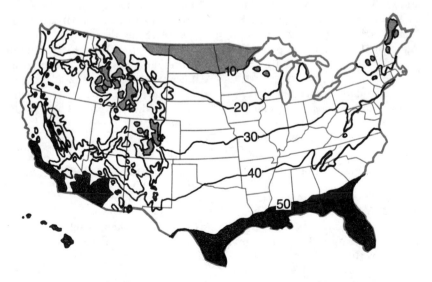

Figure 6. *Mean winter temperatures from the last 89 years for the contiguous United States (°C). The record winter of 1978-79 is apparent (Karl et al. 1984).*

tures), because we will use it for comparisons later in this section. In addition, extreme, life-threatening cold can occur in valley bottoms where it is caused by **temperature inversions**.

Winter is also **wind**. Winds affect organisms in many ways, including mechanical destruction, desiccation, and temperature depression. In Colorado, extreme gusts of wind blowing off the mountains of the Front Range often reach speeds greater than 45 m/s (meters per second, or 100 mph) with records on the high peaks of **Rocky Mountain National Park** reaching 92.5 m/s (207 mph). Winds at **Mt. Washington**, New Hampshire, have reached 103.3 m/s (231 mph). On the

Figure 7. *Map showing mean January temperatures (°F). In January, about half of the United States experiences temperatures below freezing.*

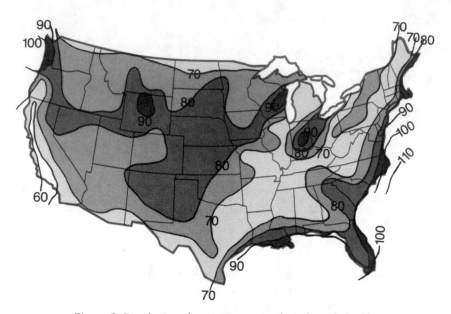

Figure 8. *Distribution of maximum expected wind speeds (mph).*

average, the **highest maximum winds** in the continental United States blow in the region of Wyoming, with very strong winds also occurring just off the Great Lakes and the coasts (Figure 8). Extreme gusts can be very damaging even to forests, as large expanses of trees are toppled in a "blow." Trees and other plants that are loaded with rime ice are particularly vulnerable to damage. Continuous winds cause extreme **windchills** that may drastically lower body temperatures and desiccate exposed parts of plants. Mechanical erosion by blowing snow particles may also occur.

Winter is **snow**. Dramatic **record snowfalls** include a 24-hour snowfall at Silver Lake, Colorado, where 183 cm (90 in) fell during a 30-hour storm. Places along the Pacific coast and in Yellowstone National Park receive over 600 cm (240 in) per year and even up to 800 cm (315 in) per year. Areas in

Newfoundland have snowfalls nearly as high. Mean annual snowfall provides a useful index of the impact of winter. On the map (Figure 9), note the location of the 40-cm (15.7 in) line (called an **isopleth**) for snowfall.

Winter is also **shorter days**. Shorter days resulting from the tilt of the planet earth provide considerably fewer hours of sunlight (Figure 10). The further poleward, the fewer the hours of daylight available. Once past the Arctic Circle, there are periods when the sun does not shine for days at a time. The regularity of annual changes in day length provides a **timing** device for organismal responses.

Winter is also **less sun**. During the winter, the northern hemisphere is further from the sun, and the earth receives less **insolation** (INcoming SOLar radiATION) (Figure 11). The higher the latitude, the less the amount of insolation for any given time and for

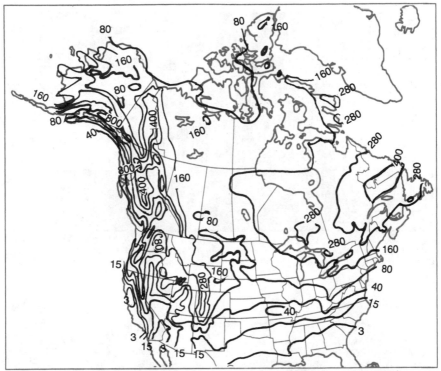

Figure 9. *Map showing mean annual snowfall (cm) (after Schemenaur, 1981).*

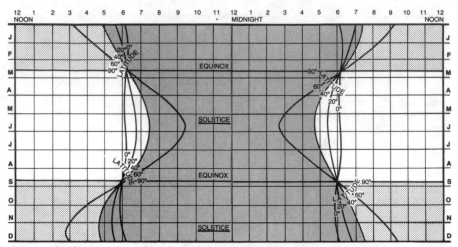

Figure 10. *The Hourglass of Darkness for the northern hemisphere. The emphasized period of darkness (heavier shading) is for 40° north latitude. From September 23 to March 21 at high latitudes the sun remains below the horizon for periods longer than 24 hours (lighter shading).*

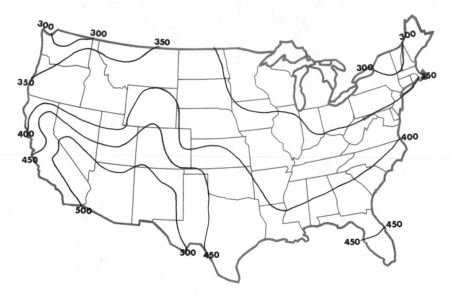

Figure 11. *Insolation for the continental United States (cal/cm²).*

any day. Less insolation has a reduced warming effect on organisms.

Our perception of winter, when molded by the weatherman, tends to focus on average and record values. The feelings of organisms, however, are not linked to the statistics of the television weatherman. They cannot sense that it is a record low temperature. but over evolutionary time (Figure 12), individuals adapting to winter must respond to many **selective criteria** for each environmental factor, including:

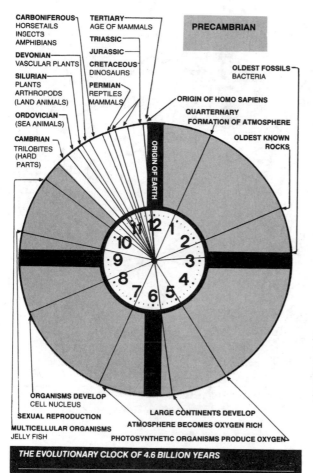

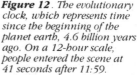

Figure 12. *The evolutionary clock, which represents time since the beginning of the planet earth, 4.6 billion years ago. On a 12-hour scale, people entered the scene at 41 seconds after 11:59.*

1. The mean value (for example, temperature) or total accumulation (for example, precipitation)
2. Extreme values
3. Timing of occurrence
4. Duration
5. Seasonality
6. Repeatability

The last four criteria may each exert selective pressure on an individual through different mechanisms that will be explained below.

The yearly date when the snowpack forms and disappears is of critical importance to organisms (Figures 13 and 14). Individuals must respond to the timing and duration of the snowpack. When cold temperatures occur in the fall before a protective mantle of snow has formed, many of the resident small mammals and plants can freeze or die of exposure. The **timing** of a late, heavy snowfall may kill overwintering deer or elk who have depleted their winter reserve of fat. The **duration** of winter snow cover determines survival rate of mountain pika who have cached their food for winter. A long-lasting snowpack depletes the food supply,

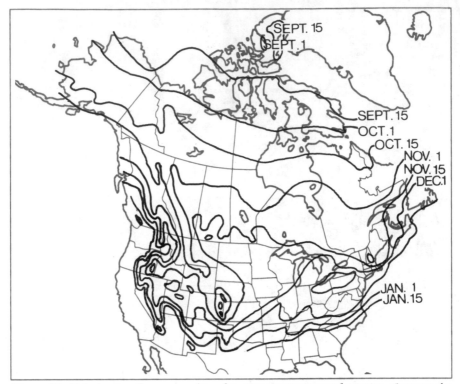

Figure 13. *Map showing the average date of continuous snowcover formation. Compare the locations of the boundary where snowpack formation occurs by December 12 to Figures 16 and 17 (after Schemenaur, 1981).*

causing overwintering animals to die and reducing the reproductive success for the following summer.

When great environmental differences occur between seasons (high **seasonality**), the selective pressure on organisms due to seasonality can be very high (Figure 15). For example, a broad range of temperatures to which an individual has to respond and the abruptness of the change between seasons may necessitate considerable energy expenditure. The opossum, a native of South America, has been extending its range northward in North America. Opossums have been very successful in environments with low **seasonality**, i.e., little change in temperature between seasons. In northern

regions, however, it is not unusual to see opossums missing parts of their ears and tails to freezing because of poor adaptation to the high seasonality of temperature change in winter climates.

The frequency of occurrence, or **repeatability**, of an environmental factor interacts with the life span of a species to determine the necessity for and type of adaptation for survival. Species with short life spans may not have to adapt to rare or low frequency events. Deer mice may not develop specific adaptations for -40°C (-40°F) record low extremes, which occur only every 20 years. Allocating energy to adaptations to the extreme but rare cold event is not the best course for deer mice popu-

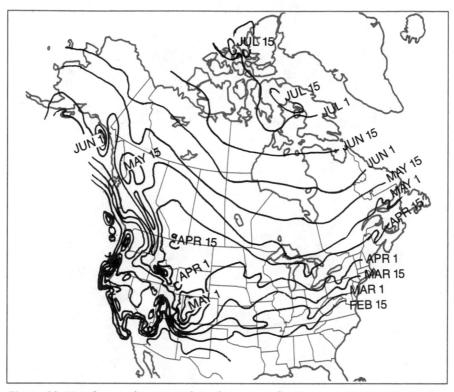

Figure 14. *Map showing the average date of snowcover disappearance. Compare the location of the boundary of the area where disappearance occurs after February 15 to Figures 16 and 17 (after Schemenaur, 1981).*

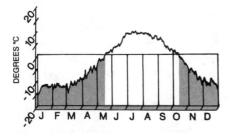

Figure 15. *The mean daily temperatures at the D-1 Weather Station (3,749 m, or 12,300 ft) on Niwot Ridge, Front Range, Colorado, show marked seasonality with large changes in temperature between seasons (adapted from Halfpenny and Clark 1988).*

lations; instead, recolonization following a severe cold snap may depend on the reproductive powers of the few surviving deer mice. Populations may, however, be nearly decimated by low-frequency events, and recovery may take years. Adaptation and energy allocations suitable to yearly extremes may differ considerably from those necessary to survive less frequent events with **return times** of 20 years. Frequent extreme events may require large energy allocations to assure the continuation of the species.

We humans may perceive winter by our interactions with snow or cold. Our perception may be further shaped by the statistics of the television weatherman, a perception that we intuitively

Figure 16. *Winter color phases exhibited by the long-tailed weasel in North America. In the northern region, weasels turn white in the winter. South of the shaded zones weasels stay brown, while within the shaded zone weasels of both color phases may be observed during the winter. The narrowness of the band in the west is a product of a small sample size and compressed vertical zonation due to the presence of high mountains (adapted from Hall, 1951).*

believe and understand. Humans can control their environment; they can mediate the effects of winter by living in a warm house, by wearing thick jackets, or by vacationing in Florida. Organisms other than humans also must interact with their environment, and they must respond to it. In order to respond, they must sense the environment in some way. For the moment, let us consider this sensing or feeling of the environment by organisms. The body of an individual feels the stimuli presented by winter and responds. Do other organisms sense winter the same way as humans? Do they "recognize" the selective winter criteria mentioned? Do patterns

of distribution of plants and animals indicate to us how they respond to winter? The answer to the last two questions is yes and that is what this book is about—the interaction of plants and animals with winter. How do organisms "sense" (in the broadest meaning of the word) the winter environment and respond to it?

For the moment, consider two examples in which the patterns of species respond to the environment. There are three species of weasels in North America: the short-tailed weasel, the long-tailed weasel, and the ermine. In the northern portions of their ranges, the coats of all three turn white during the

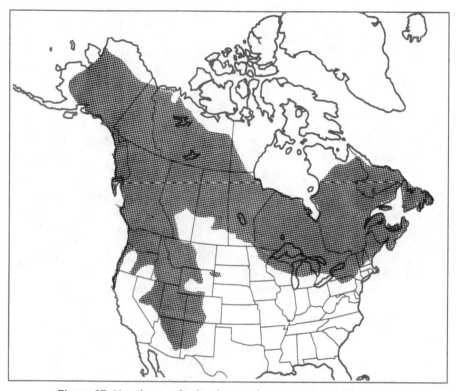

Figure 17. Map showing the distribution of spruce trees in North America.

winter. A weasel in its white color phase is commonly called an **ermine**. The distributional map of the **color phases** of the long-tailed weasel indicates a northern region where weasels turn white and a southern region where they stay brown during the winter (Figure 16). The regions are separated by a zone where weasels of both colors may be found. These traits appear to be genetically fixed; that is, a white-phase weasel taken to Texas would still turn white each winter even though the color would have little selective advantage in the south, and might in fact be disadvantageous to the individual.

Weasels have sensed winter and have responded to it. Those in northern regions expend energy to make two color changes each year. Southern weasels

may also perceive winter, but the selective pressures are low enough that they do not respond with a color change. The distribution map shows us the region where selective pressures are great enough to cause selective changes that we can observe in the animals. On the map, we see an ecological zonation of animals expressed by the response of animals to winter.

Plants as well as animals have adapted to conditions of winter. Consider the distribution of spruce trees in North America (Figure 17). The evergreen life form of the spruce is ready to photosynthesize at the first available moment each spring. The large surface area of all the needles, however, provides a collection area for winter snows that could potentially weigh the branches down and break them. Spruce trees, and in general conifers, differ from deciduous trees in that they have evolved branches which slope out and downward. As the snow accumulates, the weight presses the branches down, allowing the snow to fall off. Excessive weight from snow accumulations often breaks branches off deciduous trees, since the upright branches cannot shed their snow load. The distribution of spruce trees is an indication that individuals were able to adapt to winter and survive under the selective pressures of winter.

Many other examples could be given of species whose distribution shows adaptation to winter, but these two will suffice to show that organisms do sense winter, and over evolutionary time adapt to the rigors of winter.

Do the distributions of winter-adapted species correspond with human "perceived" distributions of environmental factors? The answer seems to be yes. Consider now some factors we have illustrated in the figures:

1. Mean January temperature of -1.1°C (30°F)
2. Maximum expected wind speeds of 37 m/s (80 mph)
3. Mean annual snowfall of 40 cm (16 in)
4. Mean annual insolation of about 375 cal/cm²
5. Continuous snow cover by December 12
6. Snow cover disappears after February 15

Compare these weather patterns to the distributions shown for the weasel and the spruce. Indeed, organisms sense environmental factors that, over evolutionary time, define ranges that researchers can correlate with winter weather patterns.

We may consider the above six factors as a working definition of **what and where is winter**, that is, the areas in which the influence of winter is significant enough to be a dominant evolutionary force. These weather patterns define the area where individuals will respond to the factors of cold, wind, and snow by developing specific adaptations. Individuals outside this area may also sense winter (for example, in the change in the length of day), but the factors do not affect survival and reproduction enough to result in dramatic evolutionary adaptations. Existing or subtle adaptations allow them to survive winter, which may include the occasional major influx of extreme conditions such as snow in Florida.

Before we consider the relationships between individuals and their environment, a detailed understanding of the nonbiological environment is needed. We will set the background for winter ecology by first looking at the sun, energy, weather, and snow.

SUGGESTED READINGS

Gray, D.M., and D.H. Male (eds.). Handbook of Snow: Principles, Processes, Management and Use. Pergamon Press, New York.

Halfpenny, J., and J. Clark. 1988. Climate calendars. BioScience, 38:399-405.

Hall, E.R. 1951. American weasels. Univ. Kansas Publ., Mus. Nat. Hist., 4:1-466.

Karl, T.R., R.E. Livezey, and E.S. Epstein. 1984. Recent unusual mean winter temperatures across the contiguous U. S. Bull. Am. Met. Soc., 65:1302-1309.

Kerr, R.A. 1985. Wild string of winters confirmed. Science, 227:506.

Keen, R.A. 1986. Skywatch: The Western Weather Guide. Fulcrum, Inc., Golden, Colorado.

Ludlum, D.M. 1962. Extremes of snowfall in the United States. Weatherwise, December: 246-278.

McKay, G.A. 1981. The distribution of snowcover. Pp. 153-190, *in* Gray, D.M. and D.H. Male (eds.). Handbook of Snow: Principles, Processes, Management and Use. Pergamon Press, New York.

Menzel, D.H., and J.M. Pasachoff. 1983. Stars and Planets. Houghton Mifflin Company Co., Boston.

Schemenaur, R.S., M.O. Berry, and J.B. Maxwell. 1981. Snowfall formation. Pp. 129-152, *in* Gray, D.M., and D.H. Male (eds.). Handbook of Snow: Principles, Processes, Management and Use. Pergamon Press, New York.

THE SUN AND WINTER

The sun provides the source of the energy supporting life on earth, but its influence is not constant. A variety of phenomena cause variations in the amount of solar energy received at any point on our planet. These phenomena include the elliptical orbit of earth around the sun, the tilt and wobble of earth on its axis, the interference of the atmosphere, and the length of day. The tilt of the earth results in the largest variation and causes the winter **season** (Figure 18).

The earth tilts on its axis at an angle of 23°27' (Figure 19). Different portions of the earth are nearer to the sun during its yearly orbit, because of the tilt. This results in different seasons in the northern and southern hemispheres. During the summer in the northern hemisphere, the north pole is closer to the sun, and during the winter the tilt is away from the sun. Winter occurs at opposite times of the year in the southern hemisphere, which is farthest from the sun in June.

In winter, rays of sunlight strike the earth at a lower angle, resulting in a glancing blow which imparts less energy to earth. A given amount of the direct beam of sunlight is spread out over a larger area, therefore providing less energy per unit area. A small reduction in **insolation** also results from the longer path that the beam must take through the atmosphere.

The effect of tilt on the distribution of radiation may be experienced by placing your hand near a fire or furnace. First, hold your hand so the palm is evenly exposed to the heat. Next tilt the top of your hand away from the flame. The effect of the tilt should be obvious as the lower portion of your

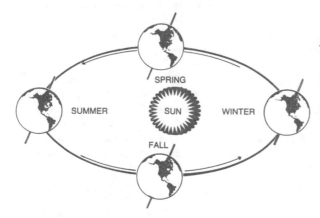

Figure 18. *The earth in its orbit around the sun. The tilt of the earth causes the seasons. During winter in the northern hemisphere, the north pole tilts away from the sun. Earth is closer to the sun in the winter.*

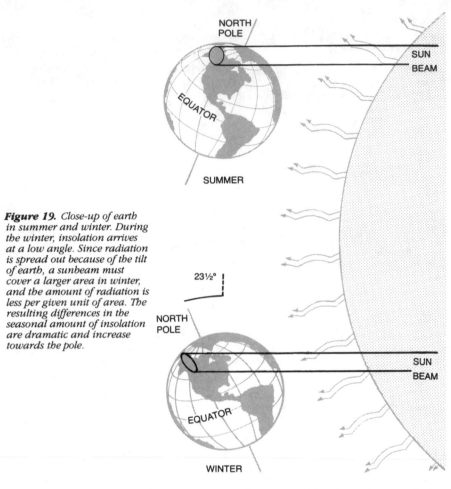

Figure 19. *Close-up of earth in summer and winter. During the winter, insolation arrives at a low angle. Since radiation is spread out because of the tilt of earth, a sunbeam must cover a larger area in winter, and the amount of radiation is less per given unit of area. The resulting differences in the seasonal amount of insolation are dramatic and increase towards the pole.*

hand is now warmer and the upper portion is cooler. This effect is analogous to the tilt of the northern hemisphere away from the sun during the winter. Similar patterns of insolation occur in the southern hemisphere; however winter occurs at opposite times of the year.

The **elliptical orbit** of the earth has little effect on winter. In fact, the earth's closest point (**perihelion**) in its journey around the sun, 56,792,699 km (91,398,990 mi), occurs in early January, while the farthest point in the journey (**aphelion**) occurs in early July, 58,725,661 km (94,509,790 mi).

The effect of the closer distance during the winter is masked by the effect of the tilt and atmospheric circulation, so that winters are not warmer even though the earth is closer to the sun.

An additional factor controls the amount of insolation. The **latitude** of a site determines both the length of the day and the angle of the sun (Figure 20). Both factors have obvious effects on the amount of radiation received. The shorter the day and the lower the sun is in the sky, the smaller the amount of radiation received.

The combination of all factors determines the total amount of radiation re-

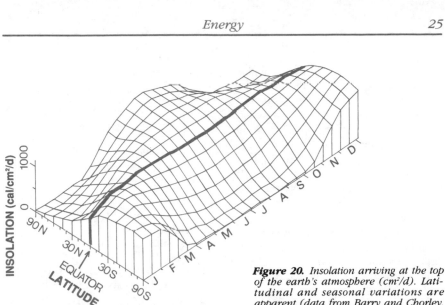

INSOLATION (cal/cm²/d)

Figure 20. *Insolation arriving at the top of the earth's atmosphere (cm²/d). Latitudinal and seasonal variations are apparent (data from Barry and Chorley, 1968).*

ceived during the winter. The net effect is that winter is a time of reduced insolation and this reduction greatly influences the environment and organisms. The land and its blanketing air mass cools, surface waters turn to ice, and precipitation freezes, covering the land with snow. The amount of energy available to organisms is lowered or may become negative because of reduced energy inputs. The organism may spend more energy than it receives. To do this it must borrow from fat stores accumulated during the summer. Organisms also must conserve what stored energy they have. Energy then becomes the crux of winter and of winter survival.

SUGGESTED READING

Barry, R.G., and R.J. Chorley. 1968. Atmosphere, Weather, and Climate. Methuen and Co. Ltd., London.

Reifsnyder, W.E., and H.W. Lull. 1965. Radiant energy in relation to forests. U.S.D.A. Forest Service, Tech. Bull. No. 1344. 111 pp.

ENERGY

Energy is the universal force that flows through the universe in many different ways. Energy is the ability to do work. It is the force that can make things happen. Often we know energy more by its properties than its definition. Energy is the agent of change, yet it is itself changing. Energy tends to move from where there is a lot of energy to where there is less of it. Energy can either be on the move or stored. When energy is in motion, we call it **kinetic energy**. When it is stored, we call it **potential energy**. There are many different forms of energy—**radiant energy**, **thermal energy**, **gravitational energy**, **chemical energy** (including nutritional energy), and **electrical energy**. Energy can neither be created nor destroyed, although it can be changed from one form to another form. How these forms of energy are transported, changed, stored, and utilized is of paramount importance to living organisms and their existence during the winter. Therefore, we need to develop a more detailed understanding of energy.

Understanding energy actually begins with the understanding of the two great opposites in the world: **motion** and stillness or a resting state. Objects tend towards a resting state, and they do so by giving away motion, that is, their energy. If the object touches something, it will give energy away by conduction. If nothing touches the object, it will send the energy off, a process we will call radiation.

We look at the sun. Our eyes sense something bright, and we call it light. Light is radiation and it has several different qualities. We know that our eyes can sense it. We know that having our skin exposed to it makes us warm and may even burn. Is that all the same stuff, that which our eyes sense, that which makes us feel warm, and that which burns our skin? Where does it come from?

Consider two examples, the sun (a ball of hot gas) and an electric light bulb. Similarities exist between the sun and the bulb. If you could look inside the sun or at the wire in the electric light bulb, you would see many rapidly moving molecules which appear as a bright glow. The glow represents molecular movement; things that are moving expel energy. We call this glow "hot." If you touch something hot, those hot molecules will make the molecules of your skin move very fast and your skin will then feel hot. If molecules are dangerously hot, they will move your skin so fast that it is injured—burned. But neither the sun nor the wire inside the light bulb are touching anything. They do not have an object to transfer their motion to by conduction, that is, by touching. So they get rid of their motion by sending it away. They send that motion away by express mail if you will, which we call **radiation**. One physical view is that they send that motion out in little packets of energy called **photons**. Another way of looking at it is that energy is sent off in **waves**.

Electromagnetic Spectrum

Energy travels in waves forming the **electromagnetic spectrum**. These radiant energy waves come in different lengths (measured from trough to trough or peak to peak), and each wavelength from gamma rays to radio waves carries a different amount of energy (Figure 21). The shorter the wavelength, the more energy it carries.

Different instruments can be constructed to detect each type of wave. The instrument that we are most familiar with is the human eye. The eye is capable of detecting wavelengths in the range we call visible light (0.4 to 0.7 μ). These are the waves that form the colors of the rainbow. We also feel infrared rays (0.7 to 4 μ) as heat on our skin, and ultraviolet rays (0.32 to 0.42 μ) tan our skin or cause sunburn and snowblindness (0.29 to 0.32 μ). Special antennas detect microwaves, television, and radio waves.

Different portions of the electromagnetic wave spectrum are known by different names. The portion up to 4 μ is generated mostly by the sun; these waves are known as **solar radiation** or the short wavelengths. The long wavelengths, starting at 4 μ, are referred to as **terrestrial radiation**. Solar radiation also is known as **shortwave radiation** and terrestrial radiation as **longwave radiation**. The earth radiates energy as does the sun. The earth and the sun exchange radiation. To see how this occurs it is easiest to consider radiation as photons.

Measuring Energy

Consider **photons**, those little packets of energy "seeking" something to move. The photons originate as radiation from hot molecules at the sun's surface. As a photon enters the earth's atmosphere, one of three things may happen. A photon may strike a molecule in the atmosphere. If so, it can transfer its energy by increasing the motion of the atmospheric molecule. The increased motion in the atmospheric molecule we would detect as an increase in temperature. This is how the heat of the sun is transported the tremendous distance to become heat of our own atmosphere. The photons from the sun interact with the molecules of our atmosphere and cause them to increase their activity, in essence causing the molecules to wiggle more, which we detect as increased temperature.

A second possibility is that when a photon strikes a molecule in the atmosphere, they are incompatible. For some reason the energy of the photon cannot be transferred to the molecule. The photon is bounced or reflected away and proceeds through the universe looking for something else to move. About 30 percent of the sun's radiation is reflected by the earth, its atmosphere, and clouds back into space.

Third, a photon may reach the earth's surface without colliding with a molecule in the atmosphere. The photon may also reach the surface after having been reflected by atmospheric molecules. At the earth's surface, the photon may be absorbed or it may be reflected. If it is absorbed, it will increase the movement or wiggling of the surface molecule that it hits, which we would note as an increase in its thermal

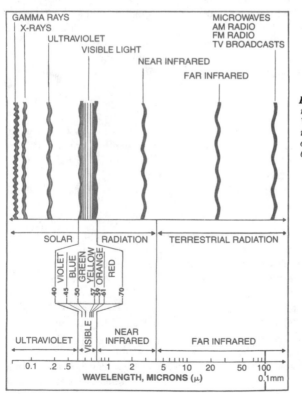

Figure 21. *The electromagnetic wave spectrum. Wavelengths are measured in microns (μ), which equal one millionth of a meter or 0.000001 m (0.00003937 in).*

energy. The photon would release its energy into the molecule of what it hits, whether it is an atmospheric molecule or a molecule in a rock, a plant, or an animal. This is what happens to us when we sit in the sun. The radiation striking our skin is changed into thermal energy.

Humans are good sensors of thermal energy. We have very sensitive sensors in our skin that detect heat, the increased vibrational movement of our molecules. If we touch something, we can tell how rapidly its molecules are moving. The more movement in the surface, the hotter it feels to us; the less movement, the cooler it feels. When we talk about movement here, we are speaking of the movement of individual molecules, not movement that we can see with our eyes. We sense that movement by noticing what the' effect is on our temperature sensors when we touch an object. This increased movement and increased warmth is **thermal energy.**

Another way that we measure thermal energy is to use a mercury thermometer. Stick the thermometer into a snowbank. As the snow molecules come in contact with the warmer glass of the thermometer, the thermometer transfers its energy from the mercury to the glass and into the snow. Eventually, the snow and the mercury molecules will have the same motion and that will be reflected by the decreased amount of space that mercury requires in its tube. The decreased amount of space results because colder molecules move slower, exerting less pressure therefore requiring less space. The thermometer is marked on the side and the level of the mercury in the thermometer shows the temperature of the snow in degrees centigrade or Fahrenheit. We read the lowered mercury level as a colder temperature.

Temperature relates directly to thermal energy. Even a snowball has thermal energy. If a snowball has a temperature of -6°C. we can ask how much thermal energy is in the snowball. To answer this question completely, we need to know how big the snowball is. In effect, we are asking how many molecules are there in the snowball. We also need to know when a molecule of snow has a certain temperature, how much energy it contains. A molecule of snow vibrating at a certain rate has a different amount of energy than a molecule of mercury vibrating at the same rate or frequency. This property is called the **specific heat** of a substance and represents the heat-holding capacity of the substance. The specific heat of the substance is usually represented by the amount of energy needed to raise the temperature of the object one degree centigrade. The specific heat of water is 1 cal/cm^3/°C; that is, it takes one calorie of energy to raise one cubic centimeter of water one degree centigrade. So the total thermal energy present in the snowball is equal to its mass times its specific heat (abbreviated **Cp**) times its temperature. Thermal energy includes both the kinetic and potential energy of the molecules within the object.

The colder something is, the less molecular movement exists. At absolute zero, all molecular movement stops and the object contains no thermal energy. The absolute temperature scale, known as the **Kelvin** temperature scale, starts at absolute zero: 0°K represents no molecular motion. Zero degrees on the Kelvin scale is -273.16 degrees on the **Celsius** scale (**Centigrade**). Therefore 0°C is equal to 273.16°K (see conversion charts on the inside front cover).

As long as objects have molecular movement—a temperature above absolute zero—they radiate energy; a black hole may be an exception to this rule. The book you are holding is now radiating energy at you, and you in turn, are radiating energy back to this book. The higher the absolute temperature (°K), the shorter the wavelengths radiated and the more energy per wavelength.

The Sun's Energy: Shortwave Radiation

Sunlight is made up of many wavelengths. For example, the things that we sense as different colors, the reds through the deep blues to the violets, are due to our perception of different wavelengths within the visible light. How do different wavelengths arise and what is their significance in terms of understanding winter?

The surface of the sun has a temperature of approximately 6,000°K (5,727°C or 10,341°F). That does not mean that every molecule in the sun and on its surface is moving with an energy equivalent to 6,000°K. As in any group of people you observe, there are some who move very fast and some who move slowly. If you watch over time, those that are moving fast will at some point most likely move a little slower and some of those who are moving slowly may start to move faster, especially as they are bumped by one of those who is moving very fast. This is also true of the sun's molecules. Some molecules are moving extremely fast, most are moving at a more moderate speed and a few are moving very slowly. A plot of the percentage of molecules that are moving fast, moderately, and slowly is a bell-shaped curve (Figure 22). As the temperature heats up, that plot will shift to the warmer end so that the peak shifts to a faster speed. As it cools off, the peak moves down to a slower speed.

Since the motion of the molecules on the sun's surface or on the surface of any object is not uniform, the wavelengths or the photon energies that are sent off are not uniform. Therefore, the radiant energy of the sun also assumes a distribution like a bell-shaped curve. A molecule which is moving very fast will send off a short wave that has lots of energy, that is, it is a very short distance from trough to trough or peak to peak (Figure 21). Or it will send off a photon that has potential for lots of motion in it. In other words, a molecule that is moving very slowly will send off a much more gentle, longer wave or a photon that is not as highly energized.

Figure 22. The distribution of the sun's radiant energy shown as the percentage of molecules moving at different speeds.

The distribution of wavelengths that leave a surface will be exactly that distribution of the motion of the molecules. The higher the absolute temperature (°K), the shorter the wavelengths radiated and the more energy per wavelength. Hotter surfaces will have more of the wavelengths in the shortwave region and cooler surfaces will have more of the wavelengths in the longwave region.

The energy emitted by a surface can then be calculated by knowing the temperature of its surface. For theoretical work, we consider objects as true **black bodies**, that is they absorb all the energy falling on them and in turn radiate out energy in direct proportion to the fourth power of their absolute temperature (°K). Slight changes in temperature, therefore, can make dramatic differences in radiative energy (see *Energy and Mass Balance*).

The amount of energy given off by the sun (E) is calculated according to the **Stefan-Boltzmann law**: $E = \sigma T4$, where σ is the Stefan-Boltzmann constant (5.7×10^{-8} W/m²/K4) and W stands for watts of energy. The sun, with a temperature of 6,000°K, gives off 8.4×10^7 W/m² at its surface. By the time it travels 148,800,300 km (93,000,000 mi) to earth's atmosphere it has spread out, reducing the energy to 1,360 W/m². This is the **solar constant** which remains relatively stable over time and is the amount of energy that reaches the earth's outer atmosphere. Most processes on earth depend on the amount of energy contained in the solar con-

stant. So we will look in greater detail at this 1,360 w/m² of energy and at it components.

Radiation from the sun (6,000°K) is emitted over a broad range of wavelengths with a peak intensity at a short wavelength of 0.5 μ (Figure 23). Photons traveling at a wavelength of about 0.5 μ have their energy stored at the frequency of green light. But to our eyes, the sun appears yellow because it emits wavelengths almost as strongly in the broader range we see as yellow. The planet earth, on the other hand, has a surface temperature of about 283°K and radiates at a peak energy of about 10 μ, a frequency too long for our eyes to sense as a color. We see the earth's surface as the colors of reflected sunlight, not in its own radiation (except for molten lava).

A few of the sun's molecules have a

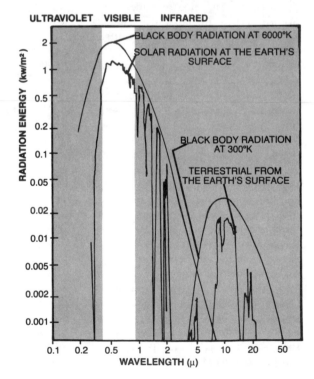

Figure 23. Radiation spectra for black bodies with the temperature of the sun (6,000°K) and a temperature near that of planet earth (300°K). The actual radiation spectra given off by earth differs from the theoretical value because of interference from water vapor and atmospheric gases.

much higher energy or a shorter wavelength, between 0.29 and 0.32 μ. These are the ultraviolet wavelengths that can burn our skin. Those between 0.32 and 0.7 μ may stimulate tanning but they do not cause as much injury as those wavelengths between 0.29 and 0.32 μ. On the other end of the spectrum, we get into the region we call infrared, consisting of wavelengths that are longer and have lower energy content. Other names for these longer wavelengths are **thermal wavelengths**, or **thermal radiation**. These wavelengths are felt by our skin as heat.

The various wavelengths or photons have different effects because of the way they interact when they collide with objects. The green wavelengths are small enough to enter a molecule inside the human eye and stimulate its chemical bonds in such a way as to cause a reaction which we interpret as green. An infrared wavelength or photon is too large to get into the tiny little space and interact inside the vision molecule. Instead, it shakes the entire molecule in a gross sort of way. The photon increases the vibration in the molecule it strikes. That vibration is felt as heat or thermal energy, rather than affecting the chemical nature of the eye.

The very short wavelengths are of such small size, and such intense energy, that they can actually break chemical bonds in molecules, causing injury to the organism. For example, certain chemical bonds maintain the elastin molecules in our skin. Damage to these bonds produces the skin injury called wrinkling. Some photons will collide with DNA, the genetic material of our cells, causing little nicks in the DNA. If those nicks are not repaired by the body, skin cancer may result. In our eyes, radiation can injure the muscle of the iris, burn the conjunctiva, or penetrate and injure the retina. The combination of these injuries is called **snow-blindness** since it usually occurs in the brightness of reflected sunlight from a snowy world.

The Earth's Energy: Thermal or Longwave Radiation

The sun is not the only object that emits radiation; any object that has molecular movement, a temperature above absolute zero, emits energy. This book, as mentioned before, is radiating. And again, just like the sun, the book emits photons in proportion to the energy of the molecule that is emitting the energy. This book is very much cooler than the sun and almost all of its molecules are moving at a slower speed. Most of its molecules emit wavelengths that are in the thermal range and almost no energy is emitted in the visible range. If you turn the lights off and the room is perfectly dark, you cannot see the book. You can only see the book because of reflected energy from a light source such as the sun or a light bulb.

Of course, the electrified wire inside a light bulb is at a much higher temperature, and it does emit wavelengths or photons with visible wavelengths so that we can see the light bulb even at night when the sun is not shining. Most objects on the earth's surface have temperatures somewhere between about minus 80°C to 100°C and most objects on the earth's surface emit radiation in the longwave or thermal band. Conversely most objects on the earth's surface emit very little radiation in the visible wavelengths and certainly very, very little in the ultraviolet range. We see objects not because of their own energy emissions, but because they reflect energy from an external source.

In nature, the external source is the

sun; the lack of the sun makes it dark at night since the earth does not emit in the visible color range. However, the earth's objects are emitting thermal radiation of substantial amounts, and we certainly can sense that with our skin. The important point is that all objects are emitting radiation; they are changing the thermal energy of their molecules into radiant energy at their surface and sending it elsewhere. Unless objects receive an equal or greater amount of energy from other sources in return, they will naturally cool off. At night, when we lose the input of the sunlight, we cool off at a much greater rate because we are radiating energy out under the night sky and not getting much radiation in return. If you are sitting in a warm room in front of a window on a cold winter night, you can feel your thermal energy take off for the stars.

From Solar Energy to the Winter Skier

Energy from the sun can pass into plants where it is transformed into a form of chemical energy that can be used by other organisms. The remarkable journey begins as the photon from the sun makes it through the atmosphere, through the surface of a green plant, and into a chloroplast and where it collides with a molecule of chlorophyll, the green pigment in the plant. A chlorophyll molecule is a very large molecule which acts as a workbench. It has a special **shape** which allows it to hold much smaller molecules of **carbon dioxide** and simple **sugars** in such a way that the photon can impart some of its energy to the rotation of an electron between the carbon of the carbon dioxide molecule and a carbon of the longer sugar molecule. Energy trapped in such a fashion we call

chemical energy. The energy stored between carbon atoms has the potential to make something happen—to do work or to make heat. Chemical energy can be released and can be felt as thermal energy. We get warm when we digest our food or when we burn wood. Chemical energy in the body is used to contract a muscle or to run **ion pumps** in our cells. It is the energy that makes our heart beat, and our brain function.

Chemical energy is stored whenever molecules are held close together. The amount of energy stored between two, three, or more atoms cooperating in this storage depends on the type of **bond** and the type of molecule involved. Physical chemists quantify the amount of chemical energy by measuring the amount of thermal energy that is released when a certain type of bond is broken. If we want to know the amount of chemical energy stored in a Snickers bar, for example, we need to know how much it weighs, how much of it is protein, fat, or sugar, and how many calories are in each food type. On a rather crude level, protein has about 3.1 **kilocalories** (kilocalories [kcal] are a measure of thermal energy) of energy in each gram, and fat has about 9.0 kcal per gram. Carbohydrates, including starches and sugars, have around 3.8 kcal per gram. Thus the chemical energy in the Snickers bar equals the weight of the bar times the food type (type of molecule) times the kilocalories (type of bond). This energy, which started out from the sun, can finally be converted into a snack for a human. The photon has completed its journey from the sun into a chemical form used by a winter skier.

Energy Transfers

We traced the transfer of energy from the sun to a winter skier. Now let's con-

Figure 24. *Energy is transferred away from the coyote by four mechanisms: radiation, conduction, convection, and evaporation.*

sider energy transfers in general. Energy transfers occur by four different modes: radiation, conduction, convection, and evaporation (Figure 24). **Radiation** is the movement of energy through a medium without influencing the medium. For example, sunlight travels as radiation through the window without heating the glass. If you hold your hand near the window it will feel warmer due to radiative heating by the sun.

Conduction is the transfer of energy by molecule-to-molecule contact. When you touch the glass, it feels cool. The

sensation of cold is due to the transfer of energy from your hand to the window glass. Molecules in the window glass are closely packed, and many molecules are available to accept energy. The contact of your hand thus quickly conducts energy to the glass.

Convection is the transfer of energy by movement of the medium surrounding an object. Blow across the back of your hand. The cool feeling is due to the movement of air away from your hand; the warm air molecules near the surface of your hand are convected away by the slight wind. The energy lost is that of **sensible heat**, that energy stored in the molecules of the air. Movement of large air masses (cold weather fronts for example) is a special type of convection known as **advection**.

Evaporation is the transfer of energy by the change in phase from liquid water to vapor in the air. Evaporation removes energy because additional energy is needed to complete the phase change. Wet the back of your hand with your tongue and blow on it. Blow on your other hand for comparison. The colder feeling on the wet hand is due to the additional energy loss by evaporation. Considerable energy is required to change the water in the skin to vapor in the air. This property of water is known as the **latent heat of vaporization**. Additional energy loss occurs as the sensible heat in the water molecules is wafted away. Evaporation losses are often hidden. As you breathe out on cold, dry winter days, the air circulating over the surface in your lungs causes considerable evaporative loss from your body. Both energy and water are lost during this process. Coping with water loss can often be critical to survival during the winter.

Since energy moves by warmer or active molecules transferring their motion to the slower moving cold molecules, the direction of energy transfer is always from hot to cold.

Insulation is the property of a material which slows or impedes the transfer of heat energy by conduction. **Dead air space** is the most effective way to stop conduction. To be considered a dead air space, the space must be small enough that effective convection currents are not set up within the space. In a down coat, the air trapped in the dead air space between the feathers is a good insulator. Many other materials are effective thermal insulators during

the winter because they trap dead air. These include feathers, fur, dacron, PolarGuard, wooden walls, and fiberglass. Also, snow is an effective insulator because it traps large amounts of air in small spaces.

Wind that is powerful enough to get into material and cause convection reduces the material's effectiveness as an insulator. Windproof outer layers of clothing are very important in maintaining the insulating value of clothing during the winter.

Space blankets (a very thin mylar or plastic sheet coated with a highly reflective silver-colored material) are often mistakenly thought to increase insulation. Space blankets themselves have no trapped air and add very little insulation! This is particularity important if the space blanket is used between a person and the ground. Conduction loss to the ground will still be effectively as high with the blanket as without. Since space blankets are windproof, they can prevent convective and evaporative loss, thereby maintaining the effectiveness of existing insulators. Space blankets may reflect some longwave radiation, but only highly polished (brand new) surfaces effectively stop much longwave radiation. The blanket may reduce radiant loss by the same mechanism as other layers. Space blankets are effective reflectors of shortwave radiation from the sun and can serve as solar collectors or signal mirrors.

Under different situations during the winter, any one of these four processes, (conduction, convection, radiation, or evaporation) may dominate the **energy balance** of an organism. When sleeping, conductive loss to the snow may be most important, but during the day evaporative loss might dominate. Convective loss to the wind can easily exceed evaporative loss but might be offset by solar radiation. It is the net balance of these four energy transfers that is important to each organism. In fact, the proper energy balance for the earth as a whole is essential for the existence of life on earth.

Energy Balance for Earth

Life on earth has evolved to live in a relatively narrow temperature range and were that temperature range to vary much, life would cease to exist. This narrow range of temperatures is maintained by the **energy balance** between the amount of energy earth receives from the sun and the amount of energy that earth radiates back to space. Each day earth receives and radiates energy, but over the course of the year, incoming and outgoing radiation are nearly equal. The yearly net **energy budget** of the earth is nearly zero; it can be neither negative nor positive for long or the earth would get colder and colder or hotter and hotter.

Seasonal energy budgets for a region, however, are either positive or negative. The winter energy budget is negative in the hemisphere where winter is occurring (Table 2). That negative balance is the driving force behind cold

fronts, snow, and wind. In other words, a negative energy balance is what causes winter!

Energy budgets can be constructed for any item, and later in the book we will look at energy budgets for both plants and animals. Life on earth is just like your financial budget—your checkbook cannot exist in a negative state for long without trouble developing. Neither can earth nor organisms living on it exist for long with a negative energy balance. Animals with negative energy balances starve before the winter is out. Over the long run, energy budgets must equal zero for the earth and be zero or positive for organisms. A positive balance shows as growth or reproduction, a negative balance as weight loss, illness, or eventual death.

Differences or changes in energy budgets are responsible for many of the processes that we observe in winter ecology. We will now look at one process in which changes in the energy budget can create a **temperature inversion** during the winter, resulting in extreme cold. Temperature inversions may develop in several ways, including inversions driven by radiative cooling.

A temperature inversion may be ob-

Table 2. The average energy budget for Teton Science School (northeast Wyoming) during December (presentation patterned after Reifsnyder and Lull, 1965) (units are cal/cm^2). Radiation expressed in different wavelengths.

Direction	Shortwave Radiation	Longwave Radiation	Radiation, all wavelengths
Downward from space (direct solar beam)	+12	——	——
Downward from the atmosphere (solar waves scattered by particles and reradiated by particles in the air)	+39	+582	+623
Upward from the earth's surface	-18 *	-621 **	-639
Totals	+33	39	-6

* = reflected from surface, ** = emitted from surface

served on a still, cold day when smoke, instead of rising from the warm air to colder air above as it usually does, stretches out, sometimes almost horizontally, as if trapped under a low ceiling. In fact, it is trapped under a ceiling of warmer air. Normally, air at higher elevations becomes successively colder, creating a gradient colder towards the top. With a temperature inversion, starting at some elevation, the normal relationship is reversed, and air is successively warmer at higher elevations. Smoke will not rise into warmer air, so it flattens out where the air begins to become warmer. The development of this temperature inversion by radiative cooling can be thought of as a four-step process (Figure 25).

In the first step, a normal, reclining temperature gradient occurs above the surface of the earth; temperatures taken at higher elevations are successively colder. During a clear winter day, insolation is high and the earth heats up. The earth emits longwave radiation, but the net energy balance is positive with insolation exceeding longwave radiation loss.

In step two, the sun sets and insolation is cut to essentially zero. The radiative loss from earth now becomes the dominant force in the energy budget and the energy balance becomes highly negative.

The ground becomes cooler because of excessive radiative loss in step three. The air is, however, slightly warmer than the ground. So the warmer air starts to transfer energy to the ground primarily by conduction. As the air loses energy, it continues to cool. The cooling is from the base of the air column, and energy is transferred from high in the relatively warm column toward the bottom, where it in turn is transferred to earth. The earth then radiates the energy to space. The cooling of the air column is shown in the temperature gradient where the bottom of the curve starts reversing itself. This draining of energy is cumulative, and the longer the period of radiative cooling, the greater the development of the temperature inversion. The temperature inversion is that portion of the temperature curve where temperature warms with increased elevation. The clearer

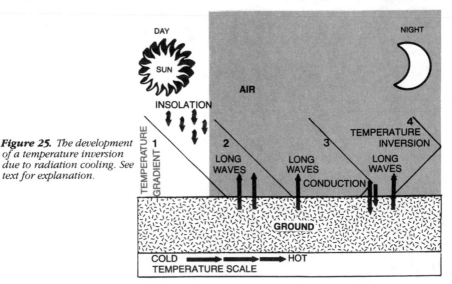

Figure 25. *The development of a temperature inversion due to radiation cooling. See text for explanation.*

and the colder the night, the greater the development of the temperature inversion due to the greater loss of long-wave radiation.

In step four, we see a well-developed temperature inversion. It is characterized by the appearance of a breaking point to a regular temperature gradient located high in the air column. Smoke normally rises up an air column from warmer temperatures to colder ones. However, in the temperature inversion, warmer temperatures are found at higher levels and the smoke cannot rise—it is trapped below the breaking point. We can see the presence of the temperature inversion in low-lying levels of trapped smoke.

It should be noted that air flow is not part of this mechanism forming the temperature inversion. Indeed, air flow would serve to disrupt the inversion. The radiative temperature inversion is common in mountain valleys and areas where extremely cold clear nights with no winds occur frequently. These temperature inversions cause bad pollution conditions by trapping polluted air, including wood and industrial smoke, close to the ground. This condition may last for days on end.

When the new day arrives, insolation heats the earth and starts to break up the inversion. However, since the energy budget is negative during the winter, the cooling effect at night exceeds the warming effect during the day. The net negative energy balance is cumulative during the cold winter season and each day's warming cannot catch up. The inversion then continues to strengthen until the arrival of a new front or windstorm to disrupt it.

Temperature inversions have a significant impact on life in the valley bottoms because they may trap extremely cold air down where the animals are wintering. It is not unusual to have air temperatures at the bottom of the inversion of -40°C (-40°F), while only a short vertical distance above, the temperature may be near freezing. The trapped cold air drives the animal's energy balance into a negative state, which requires the animal to use up valuable fat reserves. If conditions are too cold for too long, the animal will not live until spring.

Energy, or rather the lack of energy depicted in low energy balances, drives the factors controlling winter. Reduced radiation leads to colder temperatures, increased winds, and winter snows—in short, reduced energy input causes **winter weather**.

Winter Weather

Many of the factors that make winter *winter* have already been discussed, and each of us is familiar with the cold, the wind, and the snow that characterize winter. These weather factors result from the yearly change in global weather patterns as the energy balance becomes negative in the northern hemisphere. Reduced solar radiation in the fall drives the cooling of polar air masses over the arctic basin. As temperatures drop in the north, the winds of the jet stream transport cold air south, and winter temperatures and storms take hold of the continents. During the winter, the Canadian Arctic weather front shifts south towards the equator and cold weather sets in.

Snow is perhaps the single weather factor that most signifies the arrival of winter. As snow blankets the earth, its effects are observed in many ways: slick roads, sidewalks that need shoveling, camouflage for winter's white animals, insulation for the plants, and a radiation reflector to space. Snow is an incredibly complex material characterized by many different physical properties that affect winter and all life. Because of the intricacies and complexity of snow, we will consider snow in its various forms in detail in the next section.

SUGGESTED READING

Reifsnyder, W.E., and H.W. Lull. 1965. Radiant energy in relation to forests. U.S.D.A. Forest Service, Tech. Bull. No. 1344. 111 pp.

SNOW   *Snow:*

People, especially northern natives, have long recognized not only the importance of snow, but the many different types of snow. Although we can characterize snow by density measurements, numbers do not tell the whole story. Skiers recognize many types of snow, but have few words for describing them: powder, packed powder, corn snow, etc., but more detailed conversations rely to a large extent on numbers. Native peoples *Vocabularies* long ago developed vocabularies which described many types of snow (Table 3). They didn't use numbers, but their rich vocabularies allowed them to describe conditions that were critical to their way of life. Northern peoples knew and named different types of snow, such as snow on the ground and snow that collects on trees.

Snow Language

Snow: **Languages** of northern peoples, the **Inuit** and the **Chipewyan** Indians, described the snow conditions they knew. Those living in different areas where certain types of snow did not occur, did not have words for those snow conditions. Modern winter ecologists have

found it useful to incorporate many of these terms into their vocabulary to provide concise definitions for types of snow that would otherwise require many words to describe. For example, **qali** quickly and efficiently describes falling snow that collects on tree branches (Figure 4). Winter ecologists use other foreign terms, such as the Russian term **sastrugi**, to aid in describing the winter environment.

Even with the Inuit vocabulary, it is still necessary for modern snow scientists and winter ecologists to have **classifications of snow**. These classifications provide a standardized basis by which we can communicate. Through the years, many different systems have been proposed and used. We will discuss those in common usage.

Snow Classification

Strictly speaking, snow consists of ice crystals in the atmosphere which grow large and heavy enough to fall to the ground. However, in common language, the term "snow" often includes surface-generated ice features which are of great importance to ecologists. Practically we can define three general types of snow: falling snow (precipitation), snow on the ground (unmetamorphosed and metamorphosed), and surface-generated ice features (Table 4).

Falling Snow
Snowflakes that fall from the sky are composed of one or more ice crystals. **Crystals** form when water **vapor** freezes around a particle known as a **nucleating agent**. The resulting ice crystal grows when water molecules are transferred from water droplets in the air. Crystal type is determined by the temperature and available vapor supply during formation (Figure 26).

Snow language : terminology

Table 3. Inuit and Indian terminology for different types of snow.

English	Inuit Kobuk Valley Alaska	Dindye Fort Yukon Alaska
Falling snow	Annui	Za
Snow that collects on trees	Qali	De-za
Snow on the ground	Api	Non-kot-za
Depth hoar	Pukak	Zai-ya
Wind-beaten snow	Upsik	Seth(ch)
Fluffy taiga snow	Theh-ni-zee	
Drifting snow (smoky snow)	Siqoq	Za-he-ah-tree
Smooth snow surface of very fine particles	Saluma roaq	
Rough snow surface of large particles	Natatgonaq	
Sun crust	Siqoqtaoq	Za-es-(ch)a
Drift	Kimoaqruk	Za-ke-an-e-hae
Space formed between drift and obstruction causing it	Anmana	
Sharply etched wind-eroded snow surface (**sastrugi**)	Kaioglaq	
Irregular surface caused by differential erosion of hard and soft layers	Tumarinyiq	
Bowl-shaped depression in snow around the base of trees	Qamaniq	(zh)e-guin-zee
Snow deep enough to need snowshoes	Det-thlo(k)	
Spot blown bare of snow	Si(ch)	

How to pronounce Inuit (Eskimo) words

a = ah as in saw	u = oo as in tool
e = ey as in prey	au = ow as in now
i = i as in stick	ai = i as in hide
o = o as in bone	q = like a "k" gutturalized far back in the throat

Derived from works by Pruitt (1960, 1973), and Williams and Major (1984)

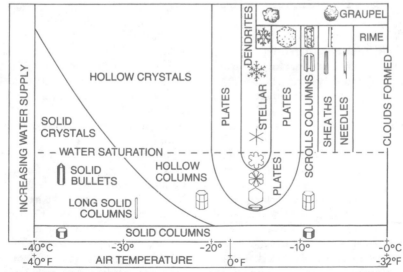

Figure 26. *Snow crystal type is determined by temperature and vapor supply (after Perla and Martinelli, 1976, and Magono and Lee, 1966).*

Table 4. Outline of types of snow and ice features and classification systems in use today.

I. Falling Snow (precipitation)
  A. Classification systems
    1. International Snow Classification
    2. Magono-Lee
  B. Types of snow

II. Snow on the ground (unmetamorphosed and metamorphosed)
  A. Classification systems
    1. Sommerfeld and LaChapelle
    2. Colbeck
  B. Types
    1. Dry snow
    2. Wet snow

III. Surface-generated ice features
  A. Classification systems
  B. Types
    1. Rime
    2. Hoar
    3. Needle ice
    4. Water ice
    5. Melt-freeze layers
    6. Ice layers
    7. Crusts
      a. Wind crust
      b. Sun crust
      c. Freezing-rain crust
    8. Runoff channels

One of the earliest and still very useful classifications of falling snow is known as the **International Snow Classification System** (Figure 27). This system divides precipitation into ten categories. The first six types are known as plates, stellar crystals, columns, needles, spatial dendrites, and capped columns. **Columns** are hollow crystals, **needles** are solid crystals, and **spatial dendrites** are three-dimensional crystals. The seventh category, irregular crystals, serves as a catchall unit. All too often, crystals are lumped into this category because they have not been carefully classified. Efforts should be made to avoid identifying too many crystals as irregular.

Ice crystals in the air may grow by another process called **rimming**, in which supercooled droplets of water collide with the crystal and freeze to it. When little rimming has occurred and the crystal retains its initial shape, it is referred to as a rimmed snowflake. However, when the rimming process is extensive, the crystal loses its identifiable shape, and is referred to as **graupel**.

Two other processes may form ice crystals. Water droplets which freeze on the outside are known as sleet. Those which have a solid core and grow by layering as they pass up and down through the clouds are known as hail.

Snow scientists may use a more detailed classification system developed by Magono and Lee (1966). This system has the advantage of providing more categories, making it easier to identify crystals without resorting to the irregular crystal category (Figure 28). However, this system does include a miscellaneous category. Several other useful distinctions can be made in this system, including the degree of rimming, the division of needles into subcategories, the addition of sideplanes as subdivisions of the irregular crystal category, the addition of a **germ** category for crystals in the first stage of formation, and the categories for broken branches.

At the current stage in the evolution of winter ecology, scientists have only begun to understand some relationships between falling snow and living organisms. We know, for example, that spatial dendrites form **qali** (snow resting on tree branches) more readily than other crystals, that snow composed of needles may easily avalanche, and that rimming may overload tree branches (causing breakage) or coat animals with ice (causing their death). For the most part, our knowledge is barely adequate to utilize the few categories of the In-

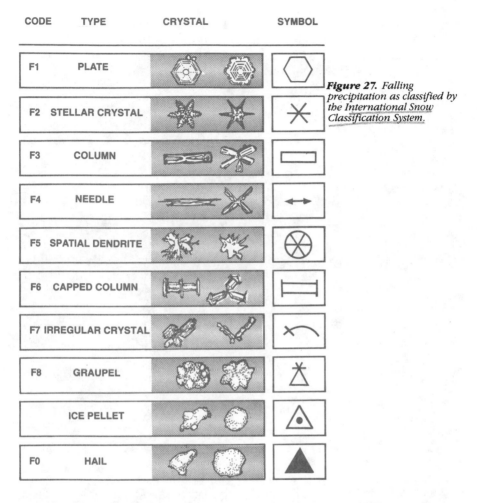

CODE	TYPE	CRYSTAL	SYMBOL
F1	PLATE		⬡
F2	STELLAR CRYSTAL		✳
F3	COLUMN		▭
F4	NEEDLE		↔
F5	SPATIAL DENDRITE		⊕
F6	CAPPED COLUMN		⊨
F7	IRREGULAR CRYSTAL		⌒
F8	GRAUPEL		⟁
	ICE PELLET		△
F0	HAIL		▲

Figure 27. Falling precipitation as classified by the International Snow Classification System.

ternational Snow Classification System and we are not yet able to use the finely divided Magono and Lee system. The future awaits our ability to learn to interpret the biological importance of the categories provided by Magono and Lee.

Snow on the Ground

Snow on the ground can remain unchanged for a period of time, but generally only a short period. Colder temperatures tend to promote the preservation of the original precipitation shape, and at temperatures below -40°C (-40°F), crystals change only very slowly. Wind can, however, mechanically change the crystals even at low temperatures. The falling-snow classifications can be used for crystals which have not been changed by the wind or through time.

Usually snow on the ground quickly starts to change (**metamorphose**) as water molecules move from the crystal points to the valleys between the crystal branches. Crystals in the snowpack can also grow as water vapor moves within the pack. A round shape results when the **surface free energy** is re-

Figure 28. *Classification of snow crystals according to Magono and Lee (1966).*

duced to its lowest point at any given temperature and water supply. Faceted crystals occur with rapid growth. Different metamorphic processes act to reach the equilibrium, and kinetic states and classifications have been developed which emphasize processes over morphological classifications of shape. The best-known classification system based on processes was proposed by Sommerfeld and LaChapelle and is shown in Figure 29.

The Sommerfeld and LaChapelle system recognizes four major categories of snow on the ground: unmetamorphosed, equitemperature, temperature-gradient, and firnification. In this system, wind-blown and fragmented snowflakes are classified in the unmetamorphosed category.

The first process changing snow crystals is known as **equitemperature (ET)** or **destructive metamorphism** because the newly fallen crystals are changed to form rounded ice grains. Under the idealized conditions of ET metamorphism, water vapor diffuses (evaporates and redeposits as a solid) from the sharp points of the crystals to new positions, creating rounded ice crystals in an equilibrium state. Grain size decreases because of water loss from crystals. During this process, the snowpack shrinks, resulting in a reduction of depth. ET metamorphism slows at lower temperatures and essentially stops at -40°C (-40°F).

In reality the temperature gradient in the snowpack is never equitemperature, and ET metamorphism actually occurs when the temperature gradient in the snowpack is relatively low. Under most conditions ET metamorphism will occur if the temperature gradient within the snowpack does not exceed 0.1°C/cm (also written as 10°C/m). This figure is only an approximate guide, however, and will vary slightly with the absolute temperature and the vapor pressure within the snowpack. ET metamorphism was originally known as **destructive** metamorphism because individual crystals are broken down.

Temperature-gradient (TG) or **constructive metamorphism** occurs when the temperature gradient in the snowpack exceeds 0.1°C/cm. Water vapor moves by a "hand-to-hand" process from warmer snow (higher **vapor pressure**) to colder snow (lower vapor pressure). Water molecules are transferred along the crystal branches, from crystal to crystal, and through the air between crystals. As the water **sublimates** (changes from ice to vapor or vapor to ice without going through a water stage), it moves to new crystals causing those crystals to grow in layers, ultimately forming large, cup-shaped crystals known as **depth hoar**. The process is known as **constructive** metamorphism because snow crystals grow in size.

Larger crystals form with larger temperature gradients and greater vapor pressure gradients. Greater vapor pressure gradients occur at higher temperatures that are found at the base of the snowpack. The largest crystals are therefore found at the base of the pack. Crystal growth often occurs just above ice layers in the snowpack, however, when the ice layer blocks water transport.

The mechanical strength of the snowpack is dramatically reduced since the crystals are only weakly bonded together and can easily collapse. A weak layer of TG crystals at the base of the snowpack is a potential release layer for avalanches. TG crystals are also important to those animals that live beneath the snow. Once the depth hoar layer forms each year, mammals easily burrow throughout the snowpack. This layer is often called **sugar snow**.

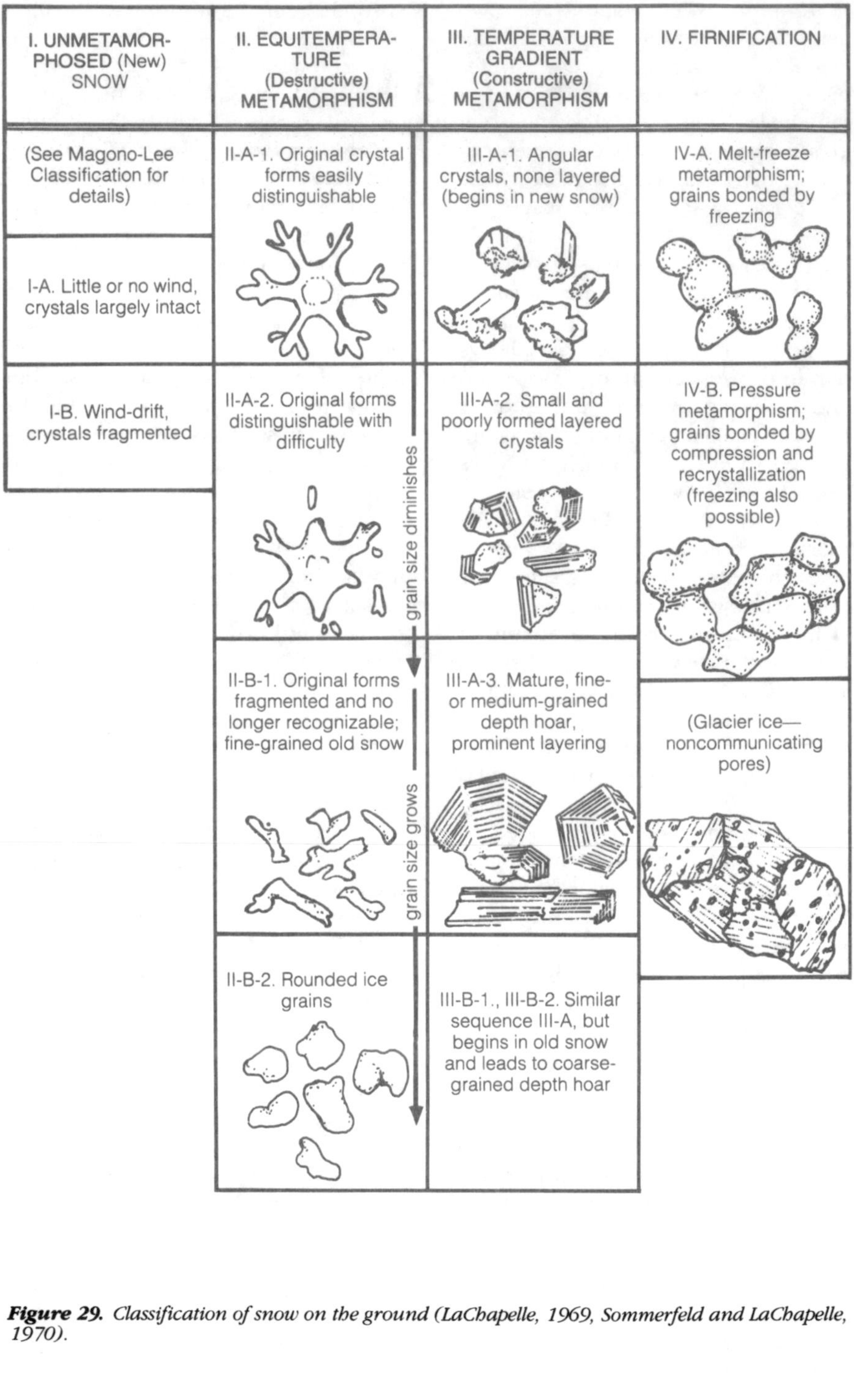

I. UNMETAMOR-PHOSED (New) SNOW	II. EQUITEMPERA-TURE (Destructive) METAMORPHISM	III. TEMPERATURE GRADIENT (Constructive) METAMORPHISM	IV. FIRNIFICATION
(See Magono-Lee Classification for details)	II-A-1. Original crystal forms easily distinguishable	III-A-1. Angular crystals, none layered (begins in new snow)	IV-A. Melt-freeze metamorphism; grains bonded by freezing
I-A. Little or no wind, crystals largely intact			
I-B. Wind-drift, crystals fragmented	II-A-2. Original forms distinguishable with difficulty	III-A-2. Small and poorly formed layered crystals	IV-B. Pressure metamorphism; grains bonded by compression and recrystallization (freezing also possible)
	II-B-1. Original forms fragmented and no longer recognizable; fine-grained old snow	III-A-3. Mature, fine- or medium-grained depth hoar, prominent layering	(Glacier ice—noncommunicating pores)
	II-B-2. Rounded ice grains	III-B-1., III-B-2. Similar sequence III-A, but begins in old snow and leads to coarse-grained depth hoar	

grain size diminishes

grain size grows

Figure 29. *Classification of snow on the ground (LaChapelle, 1969, Sommerfeld and LaChapelle, 1970).*

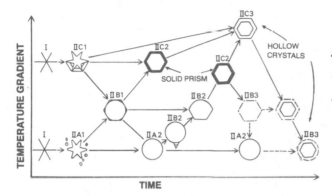

Figure 30. *A generalized configuration of dry snow formation showing the effects of temperature gradient and time (after Colbeck, 1986).*

Depth hoar formation occurs in cold regions where winter temperatures set up large gradients across relatively shallow snowpacks, such as in the Rocky Mountains of Wyoming and Colorado. Considerable depth hoar formation may occur early in the fall if air temperatures are unusually cold or if the snowpack is unusually shallow.

The final category, **firnification**, includes two processes: **melt-freeze** and **pressure metamorphism**. When melting occurs, water moves between crystals. Later freezing **sinters** (bonds) the crystals, increasing the strength and density of the snowpack. The weight of the snowpack can also force the crystals closer together, causing bonding by compression and recrystallization.

Problems exist with the Sommerfeld and LaChapelle system. First, there is a problem with terminology. Crystal growth is really controlled by temperature gradients whether or not the resultant form is identified as an ET or TG product. According to Colbeck (1986), "The equilibrium form (usually rounded) and the **kinetic** growth form (usually faceted) both appear in snow covers subjected to temperature gradients." The distinction between ET and TG metamorphism is thus an artificial one which does not exist in reality.

The Sommerfeld and LaChapelle system does not allow for the classification of snow containing liquid water—**wet snow**. In wet snow, crystals can grow without going through melt-freeze processes. Pressure can push crystals together but the effect of pressure contributes relatively little to crystal growth. In wet snow, it is the curvature of the crystal and not the pressure, that effectively sets the melting temperature. Because of these problems, Colbeck (1986) proposed a new classification system (Table 5).

The Colbeck classification of dry snow is best understood by referring to Figure 30, which shows one possible configuration that snow metamorphism might follow. Other configurations are possible depending on how the temperature gradient varies with time. At a low temperature gradient, newly fallen snow begins to round off (IIA1) and with time the crystal becomes well-rounded (IIA2). At medium temperature gradients (intermediate growth rates) crystals remain rounded but continue to grow (IIB1). As the temperature gradient increases, faceted crystals begin to form (IIB2). This may start with **spicules** (protrusions of ice) hanging down from the crystal and progress to crystals faceted on the growing or bottom half. The sublimating or top half is still rounded in shape. As the temperature gradient begins to decrease (warmer temperatures or additional

Table 5. Snow classification system.

I. Precipitation
II. Dry Snow
    A. Equilibrium (rounded) form
        1. Initial rounding of precipitate
        2. Fully rounded (may be faceted at low temperatures)
    B. Mixed rounded and faceted
        1. Intermediate growth rate
        2. Transitional as temperature gradient increases
        3. Transitional as temperature gradient decreases
    C. Kinetic growth (faceted) form
        1. Faceted growth on precipitate
        2. Solid crystals, usually hexagonal prisms
        3. Hollow crystals called depth hoar
III. Wet Snow
    A. Pure grain clusters
    B. Melt-freeze particles
    C. Slush
IV. Surface-generated features.

falling snow), faceted crystals begin to round off (IIB3). Fast growth occurs at large temperature gradients and results in the **kinetic** form of the crystal. Layering may occur on the newly fallen snow crystal (IIC1) but quickly progresses to solid crystals with hexagonal prisms (IIC2). Hollow crystals (**depth hoar**) form (IIC3) the "climax" crystal in this category. Note that reductions in the temperature gradient cause crystals to round off to the IIB3 form.

The Colbeck classification requires some knowledge of the history of the snow metamorphism. Several crystal types may be arrived at through different paths, but by knowing the history of crystal formation, important information is added to our knowledge of the snowpack. The requirement of additional knowledge before classification should not be considered a drawback but rather a chance to further our knowledge of the snowpack. The important lesson is to learn how to interpret the classified snow in ecologically meaningful terms.

Surface-Generated Features

Surface-generated ice features occur through many different processes and no one has thoroughly addressed the classification of all features. Both the Sommerfeld-LaChapelle and Colbeck systems consider surface features, but only in a cursory way. Surface-generated features are very important to living organisms and we are suggesting a slightly expanded classification that has direct implications for organisms. The classification suggested here considers the shape of features first and secondarily the processes by which these features are formed. The types of surface-generated features are:

    Rime frost
    Hoar frost
    Needle ice
    Water ice
    Melt-freeze layers
    Crusts
        a. Wind crust
        b. Sun crust
        c. Freezing-rain crust
    Runoff channels

Rime frost forms when **supercooled** water droplets (water below 0°C, or 32°F, but not frozen) contact an object and freeze in place. The water droplets are often in the form of a low-hanging cloud or fog. Rime accretions grow into the prevailing wind and the size of the formation is directly proportional to wind speed. Formations may look hummocky, feathery, or like slender needle-like spikes, but close examination will reveal a fine-grain granular structure lacking crystalline detail. The deposit may become very thick, threatening to break trees and shrubs where it accumulates. Rime accumulations mat down the fur of large mammals, reducing the insulation provided by the fur. The resulting exposure can cause death.

Hoar frost forms when water vapor **sublimates** onto a surface. It is the frozen equivalent of dew. Hoar frost shows a well-developed crystalline structure with considerable **layering** on the upper ends of the crystals (Figure 29). Crystals grow from small bases expanding to broad but flat feathers at the tips. Conditions leading to hoar frost formation include the movement of vapor within the snowpack, the presence of **supersaturated** air in crevasses, ice caves, and animal burrows, and the occurrence of clear evenings with high levels of outgoing longwave radiation. Vapor movement in the snowpack causes **depth hoar**, while hoar that forms in crevasses, caves, and on snow surfaces is known as **crevasse hoar**, **cave hoar**, and **surface hoar**, respectively.

Hoar crystals are the most spectacular of the surface-generated features. Ecologically, they are important for several reasons. The formation of surface hoar indicates extremely cold night temperatures and heavy loss of terrestrial radiation. Active rodent burrows and beaver lodges can be identified by the formation of hoar frost at the entrances or in the cracks between the logs in beaver lodges. Is it possible that predators can cue in on these small clues? A buried surface hoar frost in a snowpack can also serve as a weak zone on which avalanches may slide. Incidentally, when first buried the crystals would be classified as Colbeck IIB3 and eventually as IIA2.

Needle ice forms in soil with very high water content (Figure 31). The formation is due to repeated freeze-thaw cycles and occurs more often in the fall and spring before constant cold conditions have set in. At high latitudes and altitudes, needle ice formation is associated with **permafrost** (permanently frozen ground). Most often needle ice formation occurs where the ground is not covered by snow. Freezing initially occurs at the surface with subsequent freezing and accretion of additional ice occurring at the base of the needle ice. This stepped process pushes the needle ice from the ground. Smaller objects on top of the ice are lifted or torn from the ground. Each main melt-freeze cycle (not necessarily **diurnal**, day to night, cycles) defines a visible boundary or layer within the ice grain and cycles of formation can be easily counted.

Roots of plants and burrows of animals are destroyed by the cutting ice. In cold regions, buildings are torn from their foundations and concrete is broken as the ground heaves 30 cm (12 in) or more. Needle ice is extremely powerful. If the ground is denuded of vegetation by other processes, needle ice formation can keep it exposed to erosional processes. Plant recolonization is very slow.

Water ice or **verglas** is formed when water flows over a surface and freezes. Verglas surfaces on rocks are treacherous to mountain animals. The most common formation of water ice in the winter, however, is in stream bottoms. Since the earth is warm, water often flows in a stream below the snow

Figure 31. *Nancy Einarsen holds a well-developed example of needle ice from the Firehole River basin, Yellowstone National Park.*

during the winter. When a cold spell causes the ice to freeze to the bottom in spots, it forms dams. Water reaching these dams eventually increases in level until it finds a way out from under the ice and snowpack. Successive layers of water ice are then built up in the channel. When blocked, the water may find alternate ways around the existing channel, causing considerable damage to wildlife and surrounding land. Water ice dams, which do not form every year, also delay the spring meltoff.

Melt-freeze layers occur when the surface melt percolates down through the snowpack. This water is trapped by fine-grained layers of snow, where it freezes and increases the density of the layer. The layer is not a complete ice layer because it maintains some permeability. However, the layer can be strong enough to impede or stop the movement of small mammals within the snowpack. These layers are often called **lenses** where they do not cover large areas but are restricted to areas a few meters (yards) across.

Ice layers usually form at the ground-snow interface as the result of melting because of the warmer ground layer heat from the center of the earth. These layers can be nearly pure water ice and may restrict small mammal movement; they may also stop animals from grazing on the grass.

Crusts are generated in three ways. **Wind crusts** are the product of mechanical breakage of snow crystals. The resulting fragments are densely packed and **sintered** (frozen) together. Wind crusts can be very strong; when working above treeline on Niwot Ridge in Colorado we often need picks to dig snow pits to examine the snow.

Sun crusts (or **melt-freeze crusts**) form due to solar melting and refreezing. A specific type of crust called **firnspiegel** or **firn mirror** causes the rare but spectacular reflection referred to as **glacier fire**. The mirror surface is transparent and often acts as a greenhouse. Liquid and warmed water is present under the surface. **Snow algae** that live and grow in the snow thrive under the protective surface of the mirror. In Colorado, slopes with a southerly aspect at midelevations may be covered entirely with a sun crust. **Freezing rain** also forms a similar crust.

All crusts, when buried, become important potential sliding surfaces capable of causing avalanches.

Runoff channels form during warm spells or in the spring as meltoff begins. The general slumping of snow is probably a random but down-slope directed process. The snow surface develops shallow, somewhat parallel troughs aligned above surface water percolation. Melt water also percolates down through the snowpack drenching all creatures living below the surface. Wet animals can die of hypothermia or can simply drown during extreme warm spells.

Winter ecologists need to make better use of snow classification systems.

The challenge for the next decade is to try to improve our level of ecological interpretation to match the precision of existing classifications. Currently, the International Snow Classification System of falling snow is adequate for use by most ecologists. The Sommerfeld and LaChapelle classification system for snow on the ground is in widest use because of its popularity within the community of skiers and avalanche workers. As ecologists our efforts might be well served by increasing the use of the Colbeck system and learning to interpret the additional and corrected information that it contains. We hope that our classification of surface-generated features may spark additional research concerning their effects on organisms.

SUGGESTED READING

Colbeck, S.C. 1986. Classification of seasonal snow cover crystals. Water Resources Res., 22:59S-70S.

Colbeck, S.C. 1987. History of snow-cover research. J. Glaciology, Special Issue, pp. 60-65.

Commission on Snow and Ice of the International Association of Hydrology. 1954. The International Classification of Snow. National Research Council, Ottawa, Ontario.

LaChapelle, E.T. 1969. Field Guide to Snow Crystals. Univ. Washington Press, Seattle.

Magono, C., and C.W. Lee. 1966. Meteorological classification of natural snow crystals. J. Faculty of Science, Hokkaido University, Ser. VII (Geophysics), 11:321-335.

Perla, R.I., and M. Martinelli, Jr. 1978. Avalanche Handbook. U.S.D.A. Forest Service, Ag. Handb. 489. Revised. 254 pp.

Pruitt, W.O. 1958. Qali, a taiga snow formation of ecological importance. Ecology, 39:169-172.

Pruitt, W.O. 1960. Animals in the snow. Scientific American, 202:61-68.

Pruitt, W.O. 1973. Life in the snow. Manitoba Nature. Winter: 3-11.

Schaeffer, V.J., and J.A. Day. 1981. The Atmosphere. Houghton Mifflin Co., Boston.

Sommerfeld, R.A. 1976. Classification Outline for Snow on the Ground. U.S.D.A. Forest Service Res. Paper RM-48 1969. 24 pp.

Sommerfeld, R.A., and E. LaChapelle. 1970. The classification of snow metamorphism. J. Glaciology, 9:3-17.

Williams, T.T., and T. Major. 1984. The Secret Language of Snow. Sierra Club and Pantheon Books, San Francisco.

Snow Properties

Our fascination with snow, for its beauty and its uniqueness, is encompassed in its classification. However, snow is a substance that bends like warm tar, absorbs heat, reflects radiation, and insulates from temperature change. To understand the ecological role of snow, we must understand these inherent properties and many more. We must also understand how the properties of snow may interact with various organisms. We will now review the different physical and mechanical properties of snow.

Density

The snowpack on the ground is made up largely of air. Only a small portion of the snowpack actually consists of water in the form of snow. Glacial ice, in contrast, is mostly water and very little air. The **water content** of snow or ice is the measure of the amount of water it contains. We may refer to the water content by percent-age, with an imaginary block of water being pure water or 100 percent water. We may also define the water content of the block by its **density**, the weight of the water in the block divided by its volume. Different researchers speak of density in different units, but these units all relate to each other and to the percentage of water content (see Table 6). We will use grams per cubic centimeter (g/cm^3) to refer to the density of snow.

Age

Colloquially we speak of snow in terms of age. If you read directions on a tube of cross-country ski wax, it will recommend usage for new snow or for old snow. These terms refer to the amount of metamorphism that the snow has undergone. A crude correlation can be made between the type of snow and the density of the snow as it metamorphoses. In general, density increases with time on the ground (not true with depth hoar formation), correlating density with age. Newly fallen snow varies from 0.07 to 0.15 g/cc and old snow may vary from 0.20 to 0.45 g/cc. This is just a shorthand method of referring to snow and lacks accuracy. The terminology is useful, however, when we wish to speak generally.

Plasticity

Snow, though frozen, often behaves like water in slow motion. A snowpack moves and deforms under the pressure of gravity and the weight of the upper layers of snow. Snow is capable of flowing around objects without breaking. We refer to this movement and deformation without breaking as **plastic (or viscous) behavior**. The results of plastic movement are observed where the snow slowly curls under the edge of a roof (Figure 32). As the snow slides down the roof, the snowpack

Figure 32. *Robin Ritger observes the plasticity of snow that has slid off a roof in Yellowstone National Park.*

Table 6. Measurement of the water content of snow. Examples are of specific instances and will vary with different conditions.

Example	Water Content		
	Percent	g/cm³	kg/m²
Fluffy new fallen snow	8	0.08	80
Slightly metamorphosed snow	15	0.15	150
Depth hoar	20	0.20	200
Settled snow	30	0.30	300
Ice lens in snowpack	45	0.45	450
New glacial ice	70	0.70	700
Old glacial ice	90	0.90	900
Pure water	100	1.00	1000

g = gram, cm³ = cubic centimeter, kg = kilogram (2.2 lbs), m² = square meter

bends and curves around the eaves of the house.

Plasticity is important for small animals living under the snow. The snow that settles on a rock or a log gradually flows off the sides to the ground (Figure 33). In so doing, the snow does not fill the area directly next to the object, but falls to the ground a short distance from the object. This creates a hollow cavity along the sides of the object where rodents and insects may travel easily, protected from the outside environment.

Thermal Conductivity

Energy moves through snow in the form of heat. The rate at which energy is transmitted through the snowpack is known as its **thermal conductivity**. Snow has a very low thermal conductivity which makes it a good insulator; because of the low conductivity heat is not lost quickly through the snowpack. For comparison, rocks conduct 200 to 400 cal (cal = calorie) of heat per hour compared to 0.7 to 1.3 cal for newly fallen snow (Table 7). This value is comparable to the dry wooden walls (0.7 to 1.8 cal) which insulate our homes.

The amount of water that is present in a material affects its thermal conductivity. Wet material transmits heat about ten times faster than dry material. For example, wet sand transmits 7 to 21 cal, whereas dry sand conducts only 1.4 to 2.5 cal. The increased conductivity of wet material helps explain why our feet become so cold as our socks get wet from perspiration during winter outings. Older or denser snow also contains more water, which reduces its insulating value because dense snow may transmit about ten times more energy than newer or lighter snow.

Heat is transferred through snow by conduction, convection, evaporation, and sublimation. These processes are dependent on the density of snow, and thermal conductivity varies with density (Figure 34). Conductivity is not uniform over the full range of densities, but curves slightly at lower densities.

The transmission of heat through a material takes time. The lower the thermal conductivity (which is the same as saying the better the insulator) the slower the transmission of heat. This time delay results in two important phenomena in the snowpack: temperature gradients and thermal memory.

Table 7. Comparison of thermal conductivity in several materials (calories/hour/cm²/ for a thickness of one cm and a difference of 1°C)

Material	Thermal Conductivity	
Rock	193.3 – 416.3	
Glass	74.3 – 89.2	
Plastic	29.7 – 74.3	
Wet sand	7.2 – 21.6	
Ice	3.2 – 9.8	density 0.4 – 6.5
Wind-packed snow	1.3 – 3.1	density 0.2 – 0.35
Masonite	4.9	
Felt (thermafelt)	4.2	
Dry sand	1.4 – 2.5	
Newly fallen snow	0.7 – 1.3	density 0.1 – 0.2
Dry wood	0.7 – 1.8	

Note that thermal conductivity is shown here based on the energy conducted per hour rather than per second. This was done to award extremely small values and provide a more intuitive feel for the data.

The **temperature gradient** may be observed in a **snow pit** dug for the purpose of examining the snowpack (see Experiencing Winter). Once a pit has been dug, temperatures are taken in the side of the pit wall from the top to the bottom. These temperatures are graphed out to provide a **snow temperature profile** (Figure 35).

Generally snow profiles are warmest at the bottom. Excess energy from the sun is stored during the summer when

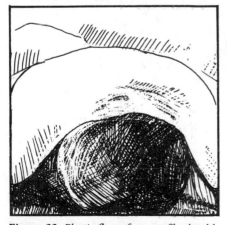

Figure 33. Plastic flow of snow off a boulder. Tunnels around objects are formed by snow slowly flowing off the boulders and creating spaces. Animals move freely within these spaces.

the flow (**heat flux**) into the ground is positive. During the winter, heat flux from the stored energy is from the ground to the air at about 20 to 30 cal/cm²/d. The contribution to heat flow from the warm center of the earth is minor, amounting to about 0.1 cal/cm²/d. Only in thermal areas, such as **Yellowstone National Park** would heat flow from the earth contribute significantly to warming the bottom of the snowpack. Since all snow (which is really ice) must be melted in the snowpack before the temperature can rise above 0°C, the bottom of the snowpack surface will seldom be above freezing during the winter. However, the soil temperature may rise several degrees above the freezing point. Contrary to common beliefs, the ground-snow interface is not necessarily at freezing (0°C). The temperature at the interface may in fact drop many degrees below freezing and freezing may progress deep into the ground. In cold regions, it is necessary to bury plumbing below the annual frost line to protect pipes from freezing. In **permafrost** areas, soil remains frozen all year; only the surface of the frozen ground melts each summer. In warmer regions, the

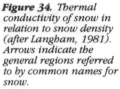

*Figure 34. Thermal
conductivity of snow in
relation to snow density
(after Langham, 1981).
Arrows indicate the
general regions referred
to by common names for
snow.*

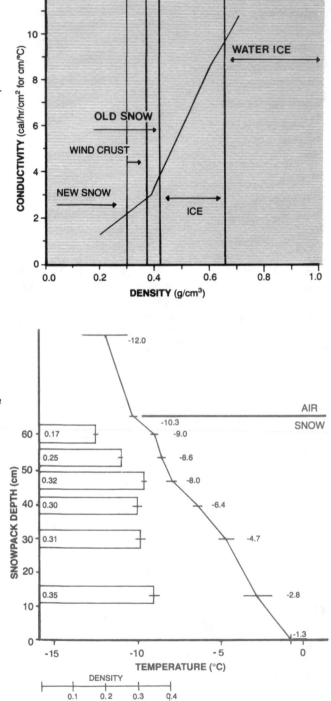

*Figure 35. Snow
temperature profile from
Teton Science School,
January 9, 1984. Data
gathered by Marsha
Benning and Leslie
Appling.*

ground-snow interface may be near freezing all winter. In any case, plants and animals living at the ground-snow interface, with a relatively constant temperature around freezing, may find it more conducive to survival than the harshness associated with life on top of the snowpack.

As long as the air temperature is cold, the snow temperature gradient may be very large. The greater the gradient of the profile, the faster the snow metamorphism is acting to produce **depth hoar** crystals. Shallow snowpacks and cold temperatures produce the greatest gradients through the snowpack.

The temperature profile can change dramatically during the day, especially with larger ranges of air temperatures during a 24-hour period. A large diurnal fluctuation in air temperature will start to cool the snowpack from the top, as energy is transported from the snow surface to the colder air. However, this transfer takes time. One January, students at Teton Science School followed the cooling wave down through the 53 cm (20.9 in) snowpack (Figure 36). The coldest air temperature occurred at midnight; the snow surface temperature was also coldest at midnight. By 1:00 AM, the coldest temperature of the day reached down another 2 cm (0.8) in) to 51 cm (20.1 in). The coldest temperature reached lower depths as follows: 46 cm (18.1 in) at 4:00 AM, 36 cm (14.2 in) at 8:00 AM, 18 cm (7.1 in) at 7:00 PM, and ground level at 8:00 PM. The passage of the cold pulse down the 53 cm (20.9 in) snowpack took 21 hours. The amount of temperature change (0.07°C) that reached the ground-snow interface was greatly reduced from the diurnal range of air temperatures (9.9°C).

The cooling or warming effect of diurnal changes often does not reach completely down to the bottom of the snowpack. For example, a long cold spell will lower the temperatures in the snowpack and will produce a reclining temperature profile (a in Figure 37). Then a warm day will increase the temperature near the snow surface (b in Figure 37). Although the air temperature may be above freezing, the snow temperature might still be far below freezing. This **thermal memory** results in a cold, lower layer that may cause a skier to suffer frostbitten feet on a day when the temperature is above freezing. In very cold regions, such as the Yellowstone Plateau, we have experienced daytime air temperatures above freezing when the middle of a one-meter snowpack was still -20°C (-4°F) or colder.

Each spring the warm weather begins to melt the snowpack from the top. Increasingly warmer temperatures from above and the warm earth impart energy to the snowpack, warming the snow (steps 1, 2, 3, and 4 in Figure 38). The temperature curve tends to flatten out and approach 0°C. As long as there is a snow-ice mixture, the temperature of the snowpack cannot go above freezing. Eventually the whole snowpack reaches the 0°C point, called the **isothermal** point (step 5 in Figure 38); this is the point where all the snow is just at freezing. At this temperature, liquid water is present throughout the snowpack. The isothermal period is a very important time for small animals, since they may die of hypothermia or even drown as gravity pulls the water down through the snow into their nests. Once reached, the isothermal condition of the snowpack begins to break down **depth hoar**, and the snowpack is temporarily stabilized against avalanches. With continued warming, the free water lubricates the snow and wet avalanches become a potential danger.

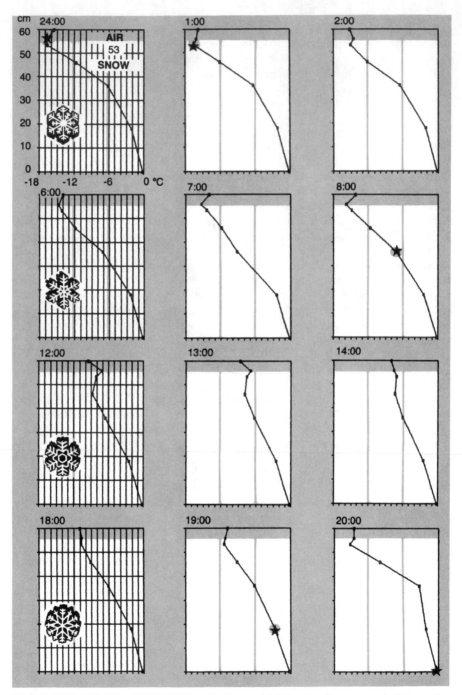

Figure 36. *A 24-hour series of snow temperature profiles showing the movement of the coldest temperature down the snowpack. Profiles were obtained by Marsha Benning and Leslie Appling*

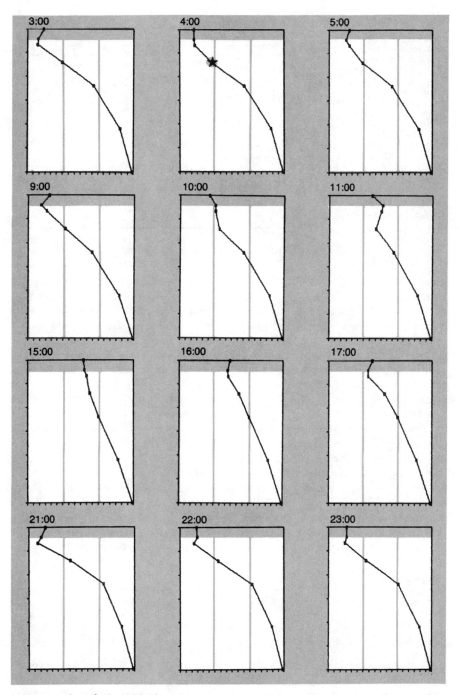

on January 9 and 10, 1984. The coldest temperature in the snowpack starts at the time of the coldest air temperature about midnight.

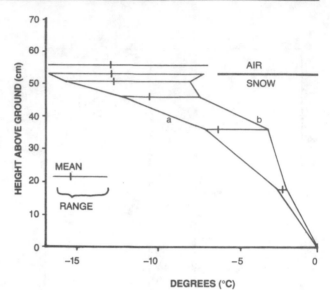

Figure 37. *A 24-hour snow temperature profile from Teton Science School for January 9 to January 10, 1984. The letter "a" marks the coldest temperature curve for the period and the letter "b" marks the warmest curve of the range in temperatures. Data gathered by Marsha Benning and Leslie Appling.*

Albedo

Most of us have experienced spring-time sunburns while skiing in March. During those episodes, the underside of the eye sockets, nostrils, and even the roof of the mouth can get burned. The direct rays of the sun burn us from above while the snow reflects rays back to burn us from below.

Snow is an excellent reflector of shortwave radiation from the sun. This property is referred to as **reflectance** or **albedo**. Albedo is defined as the percentage of the **insolation** which is reflected off a surface, in this case snow. Snow can reflect nearly 100 percent of the sun's rays. New snow (density about 0.1) easily reflects 85-90 percent or more of the insolation. New snow is

said to have a high albedo while older, dirty snow (density 0.5) has a low albedo and may reflect as little as 40 percent of the insolation (Figure 39).

Several other variables affect the albedo of the snow, such as snow grain size, sun angle, and surface roughness. Dirt and vegetation in the snowpack will reduce albedo. Increased water content (increased density) in the snow also reduces the albedo leading to increased absorption of solar radiation.

Attenuation

Even new snow cannot reflect all the insolation and older snow may reflect very little. The short wavelengths that are not reflected **penetrate** below the surface of the snow where they are

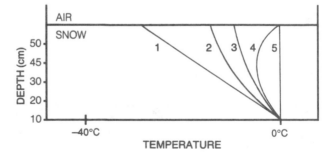

Figure 38. *The development of an isothermal snowpack is shown by the progression of the temperature profile from step 1 (coldest) through 5 (warmest). Progressive warming eventually causes the snowpack to have a 0°C (32°F) temperature throughout (indicated by line 5).*

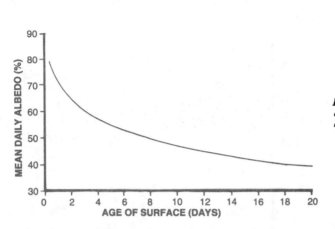

Figure 39. *Reduction of albedo as the snowpack ages.*

eventually trapped and absorbed. The **attenuation** (reduction of detectable radiation) of solar radiation as it is transmitted through the snowpack is very rapid. Below 30 to 50 cm (12 to 20 in) of low-density snow, most of the light is attenuated (Figure 40). Below this depth, a dark environment exists for plants and animals. Later in the spring season light will penetrate deeper into the dirtier and denser snowpack.

Transmission

Light **transmission** is measured in terms of an **extinction coefficient**, v, the Greek letter Nu. The extinction coefficient represents the reduction in light passing through the snowpack according to the following equation:

$$I = Io \ (e)^{-2}$$

Io represents the intensity of original radiation passing through a snowpack, e is a constant (2.718), and I is the remaining radiation. The larger the extinction coefficient, the less light that is transmitted through the snowpack.

The efficiency of light **transmission** through snow is primarily dependent on three factors: the grain size of snow,

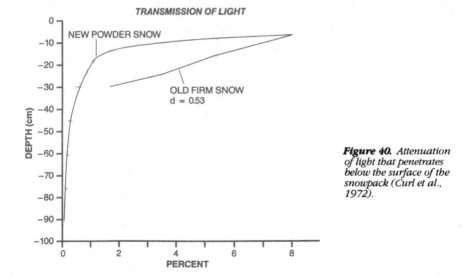

Figure 40. *Attenuation of light that penetrates below the surface of the snowpack (Curl et al., 1972).*

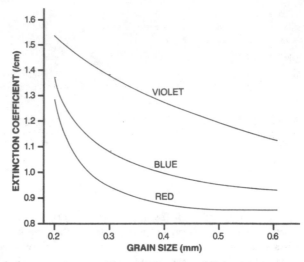

Figure 41. *Reduction in visible light transmission as a function of snow grain size (d = 0.45 g/cm³). The extinction coefficient indicates reduction of light that penetrates the surface of the snow and is usually reported in units/cm (after Mellor, 1965).*

the density of snow, and the wavelength of light. Extinction is inversely related to **grain size** and is dependent on the **color** of light (**wavelength**) (Figure 41). At small grain sizes (about 0.5 mm), extinction of all colors tends to converge and reach a maximum. At a grain size of about 2.0 mm extinction values again converge, indicating that larger grains transmit considerably more light. Shorter wavelengths (violet and blue) are more strongly affected than longer wavelengths (red).

The relationship of light transmission to **density** is more complex (Figure 42). Snow with a low or high density passes more light than does snow in the middle density range of about 0.5 to 0.56 g/cm³. The extinction coefficient is also dependent on the **color** of light, with shorter wavelengths (violet and blues) being more strongly affected than longer wavelengths (red). Light transmission is more sensitive to snow grain size than it is to density.

Two processes affect the extinction

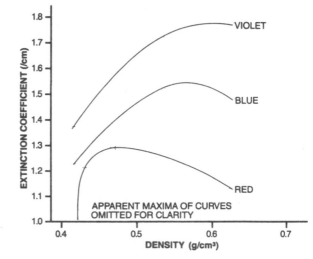

Figure 42. *Change in visible light transmission as a function of snow density (grain size = 0.2 mm) (after Mellor, 1965).*

of light as it passes through the snowpack: **scattering** and **absorption** of light. Scattering is most important in fine-grained snow and the extinction coefficient is lower at longer wavelengths. Absorption is more important in coarse-grained older or wetter snow. Absorption becomes stronger at the longer wavelengths removing more blues than reds. When density is considered, the transition from scattering attenuation to absorption occurs at about 0.50 to 0.56 g/cm³ for refrozen or wet medium-sized grains the transition may occur as low as 0.4 g/cm³. A density of 0.50 g/cm³ is considered the **critical density** in snowpack formation. Further densification can no longer occur from compaction, but must result from freeze processes. Sintering of grains and refreezing of melt water provides clear avenues for light transmission. Above 0.50 g/cm³, increased light transmission probably results from reduced pore space within the snowpack. Snow grain size increases by bonding between ice particles. Bonding reduces pore size, but develops continuous paths for light transmission within snow grains. Light

then is transmitted not only between crystals but within crystals. As density and grain size increase in the spring when the snowpack starts to melt, light is also transmitted deeper into the snowpack.

Different **colors** of light react differently to grain size and density and absorption is strongest in the long (red) wavelengths. The net effect is that the red color disappears and light passing through snow appears blue. As an experiment, stick a pipe into the snowpack during the day and look down into it at the snow. The pipe will cut out scattered light and only that light reflected back up the pipe will be visible. The snow will appear blue. The **visual spectrum** is strongly selected by the snowpack. Absorption reduces the intensity of light below the snowpack and **spectral selection** reduces the longer wavelengths (Figure 43).

The scientific literature is full of contradictory statements about transmission of light through snow. Some have suggested that transmission increases with increased snow density, while others have suggested that transmission decreases with increased density. Results

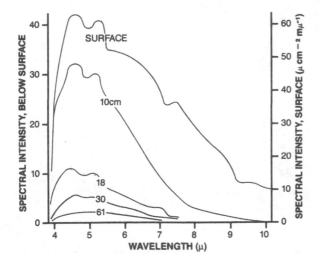

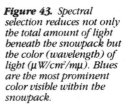

Figure 43. Spectral selection reduces not only the total amount of light beneath the snowpack but the color (wavelength) of light ($\mu W/cm^2/m\mu$). Blues are the most prominent color visible within the snowpack.

of scientific experiments often vary by several fold. Much of the contradictory evidence originates from equipment limitations, weak experimental procedures, simply different techniques, as well as from not accounting for density or grain size differences. Ecologists, in general, need to be more aware of the research of the physical scientists. The picture painted here appears to represent the current view by leading researchers. Several references are listed at the end of this section for those with more interest in this subject.

Absorption

While snow reflects nearly all of solar shortwave radiation that reaches its surface, snow acts like a **black box** (a theoretical object which absorbs all radiation) to terrestrial or longwave radiation and absorbs most of it. The differences in the manner in which snow reacts to shortwave and longwave radiation cause many interesting phenomena; three examples follow. In the springtime, as the snowpack starts to thin out and the sun climbs to a higher angle in the sky, shortwave radiation that is not reflected passes through the snowpack to dark objects below the snowpack. The shortwave radiation starts to heat up rocks and tree trunks. As temperatures increase within in these objects, they emit more longwave

radiation. Remember, longwave radiation is proportional to the fourth power of the temperature of the object. Therefore a small increase in surface temperature will result in a large increase in longwave radiation. The object then radiates longwave radiation back into the snowpack where it is readily absorbed by the snow. Warming of the snowpack close to the objects makes the snow soft and starts the melting process. The soft spots that occur around rocks in the high mountains are often called **elephant traps** by the hikers who fall into them.

In Antarctica, there are several lakes which are warmed by this process. The lakes, including Lake Vanda, have permanent ice on the surface. During the warm part of the summer the ice melts on the edge leaving a floating raft of ice still covering most of the lake. Shortwave radiation passes through the clear ice into the water below. Due to the greater density of the water compared to the ice, the shortwave radiation is readily absorbed. As the temperature of the water increases, energy is transferred to nearby water by conduction and longwave radiation. This warms a lens of water deep in the lake. This lens may be as warm as 21°C (70°F) even though the average yearly air temperature may be below freezing. The water does not turn over causing

Figure 44. The formation of a puddle of water on lake ice during the winter. Shortwave radiation passes through the snow and is absorbed by the ice. The warmed ice radiates longwave radiation back to the snow, where it is absorbed. This causes the snow and ice below it to melt, forming a puddle. This process is dependent on having a covering of snow.

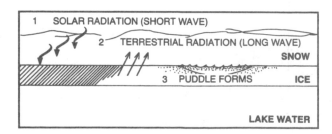

the lens of warm water to circulate, because of layering caused by different density salt solutions.

A similar process leads to the formation of water on ice surfaces of lakes (Figure 44). This process is dependent on the presence of a snowpack on top of the ice. Shortwave radiation passes through the snow to the ice surface. Since the water content in the ice is higher than in the snow, the ice absorbs more of the radiation. When the temperature of the ice begins to increase, it emits longwave radiation back to the snow surface. The snow readily absorbs the longwave radiation and eventually the snow at the ice-snow interface begins to melt forming a puddle under the snow. These puddles may form when the air temperature is far below zero. We have experienced them on the lakes in Yellowstone National Park at daytime temperatures of -30°C (-20°F). This is not the only mechanism that forms puddles under the ice; puddles can also be formed by cracking of the ice which allows lake water to flow out on top.

SUGGESTED READING

Armstrong, R.L. 1985. Temperature and Heat Flow Patterns in a Seasonal Snow Cover: The Role of Temperature Gradient Metamorphism. Unpubl. Ph.D. dissert., Univ. of Colorado, Boulder.

Armstrong, R.L. 1980. Some observations on snowcover temperature patterns. Proceedings of Avalanche Workshop, 3-5 November, 1980. Vancouver, B.C. Natl. Res. Council Canada Tech. Memo. no. 133, pp. 66-81.

Curl, H., Jr., J.T. Hardy, and R. Ellermeier. 1972. Spectral absorption of solar radiation in alpine snowfields. Ecology, 53:1189-1194.

Everden, L.N. and W.A. Fuller. 1972. Light alteration caused by snow and its importance to subnivean rodents. Canadian J. Zool., 50:1023-1032.

Gold, L.W. 1958. Influence of snow cover on heat flow from the ground. Int. Assoc. Sci. Hydrol. Publ., 46:13-21.

Gray, D.M., and D.H. Male (eds.). 1981. Handbook of Snow: Principles, Processes, Management and Use. Pergamon Press, New York.

Halfpenny, J.C. 1984. Variation in Snow Test Pit and Mount Rose Sampling Data. Abstracts and Program, International Snow Science Workshop: A Merging of Theory and Practice. Aspen, Colorado. October 24-27, 1984. 42 pp.

Kingery, W.D. (ed.). 1963. Ice and Snow. M.I.T. Press, Cambridge, Massachusetts.

Langham, E.J. 1981. Physics and properties of snowcover. Pp. 275-337, *in* Handbook of Snow: Principles, Processes, Management and Use. D.M. Gray and D.H. Male (eds.). Pergamon Press, New York.

Marchand, P.J. 1984. Light extinction under a changing snowcover. Pp. 33-37, *in* Winter Ecology of Small Mammals. J.F. Merritt (ed.). Carnegie Mus. Nat. Hist., Spec. Publ., 10.

Marchand, P.J. 1987. Life in the Cold: An Introduction to Winter Ecology. University Press of New England, Hanover, New Hampshire.

Mellor, M. 1964. Properties of Snow. Cold Regions Research and Engineering Laboratory, Mono. III-A1. Hanover, New Hampshire. 105 pp.

Mellor, M. 1965. Optical Measurements on Snow. Cold Regions Research and Engineering Laboratory, Res. Rpt 169, Hanover, New Hampshire. 19 pp.

U.S. Army Corps of Engineers. 1956. Snow Hydrology. Portland, Oregon. North Pacific Div., Corps of Engineers.

Warren, S.G. 1982. Optical properties of snow. Reviews Geophys. Space Physics, 20:67-89.

Elk crossing crested snow. When the crust fails to support their weight, the elk break through, causing injury to their legs.

3. Life, Winter, and Adaptation

EFFECTS OF WINTER AND STRATEGIES FOR COPING

We all can attest to the effects of winter on human life: aching muscles from shoveling walks, frozen pipes, cars that don't start, high heating bills, and so on. But all life in the snow world is influenced by the changes winter brings. Many major effects of winter are obvious—**hypothermia, frostbite,** and **starvation**—while subtle effects such as **biochemical changes** and winter **hardening** are less obvious. However, all effects relate either directly or indirectly to lowered or negative **energy balances**. Winter is an energy bottleneck, a constraint on the lives of organisms. Reduced solar radiation during the winter leads to a plethora of forces that act harshly on plants and animals, reducing their chances for survival.

Vectors of Winter

Less radiation is received from the sun during the winter because of its lower angle in the sky, and this reduced radiation leads to colder temperatures. Precipitation arrives in the form of snow. Winter air masses bring not only snow, but windy conditions. For those animals that remain active during the winter, locating food often becomes problematic. Less chemical energy is available to stoke the internal furnace of each animal. These forces, the **vectors of winter**, combine to make survival difficult. Five vectors—**snow, cold, radiation, energy, and wind**—form a powerful factor, the **SCREW** factor, that shapes the direction of evolutionary response to winter. In the general sense, the SCREW factor encompasses all the influences of the environment on organisms during the winter.

Acclimation and Adaptation

Each individual, plant or animal, undergoes several processes during its life, which include collection of energy, maintenance, growth and development, acclimation, reproduction, and aging, resulting finally in death of the individual. The SCREW factor of winter impacts directly on life processes. Snow and wind can reduce access to food supplies. Lowered ambient temperatures may increase metabolic rates and induce biochemical changes. Less available energy may further inhibit maintenance by reducing the ability of the body to repair itself or the ability of the animal to defend itself. Even reproduction, which may occur outside the winter season, can be affected by the rigors of winter. Animals that suffer a hard winter may not successfully bear previously conceived young in the spring or they may not have enough energy remaining to suckle or to breed.

Organisms must expend **energy**, the currency of life, in order to respond to the rigors of winter. Over the course of a winter, an individual may **acclimate** to the SCREW factor. That is, it may go through short-term physiological or behavioral changes that allow it to survive environmental changes. Genetically, the range of possible acclimation is fixed and perhaps small relative to environmental forces. The animals that do not respond sufficiently within the range for acclimation must die. The range of responses to the SCREW factor may be enlarged on a long-term basis, as the species evolves increased genetic capability to meet the demands of environmental factors. Specific **adaptations** evolve over evolutionary time and increase the ability of organisms to survive and reproduce. Short-term acclimation must occur within the bounds set by evolutionary adaptations. Acclimation occurs over short time periods of days to months during the lifespan of an organism; adaptations take several generations to evolve.

For example, conifers have adapted to life in cold regions by evolving certain biochemical processes to survive cold temperatures. Each fall, the conifers must **harden** to survive winter. The hardening process is a short-term physiological acclimation to winter. A cold snap occurring before the trees have had time to harden will kill the trees, but following hardening the trees can survive cold temperatures. Genetically, some trees can harden only down to -40°C (-40°F) and acclimation is limited to the range of that existing adaptation.

The evolution of an adaptation may not have been specific to the winter environment, but may have secondarily proved effective in allowing winter survival. Often, we cannot tell what was the original purpose of an adaptation. For example, does a moose have long legs to allow it to feed in a deep pond during the summer, or to move through deep snow in the winter? Whatever the purpose of the original adaptations, those that work well for winter conditions provide a selective advantage allowing organisms to survive winter. Some adaptations certainly appear to be specific to the winter environment, however, such as ptarmigan turning white.

Responses to Winter

A wide range of possible **responses** to the SCREW factor exists. At a general level, these responses may be visualized as a **decision tree** of adaptation and acclimation (Figure 45). Some animals avoid winter by migrating. If, however, over evolutionary time an organism has adapted to be present in an area, the question of avoiding or tolerating the winter environment must be answered. Some plants and insects avoid winter by dying; that is, they produce seeds or eggs that overwinter while the adult dies.

Those organisms that remain in a winter environment may encounter winter in an active or inactive state. Inactive encounters occur along a continuum of biological processes from cold-induced torpor to hibernation. Active encounters occur either above or below the snow. In either case, the organism must select a maintenance strategy in which the body temperature can remain high or else perhaps be lowered for a time. Moose, for example, lower their body temperatures during the winter (without going into a torpor), thereby reducing **basal metabolism** and reducing food requirements. Some animals that display an active mode of encounter may temporarily go into an inactive torpor. Badgers, for instance, will lower their body temperatures and go into short periods of torpor when temperatures remain very low for extended periods of time.

Take a moment to study the **Winter Response Tree** (Figure 45). Select different plants and animals and visualize the strategy they use to survive the winter. Are all strategies successful under abnormally severe conditions?

When a strategy is not wholly successful, at least a few members must survive to continue the existence of the species in that area. Over evolutionary time, the SCREW factor has proven severe enough that some species have become extinct. One example is the caribou of Western Greenland.

In the fall of 1899, large herds of caribou existed along the western coast of Greenland. These caribou had been there for as long as we have records. When the Scandinavian fishermen returned to the coast in the spring of 1900 all of the caribou were gone. During the winter, conditions were so harsh that all of the caribou along about 960 km (600 miles) of coast had died. It has been suggested that a late fall rain froze all available food. Lacking food, the caribou all migrated out onto the sea ice where they perished, leaving no sign. Or alternatively they tried to migrate over the ice cap, again perishing and leaving no sign. The exact reason for their extinction is unknown, but to this day caribou do not exist in western Greenland. The take-home message: winters can be severe enough that even well-adapted species can be driven to extinction.

The SCREW factor of winter affects all levels up the ladder of biological organization: molecules, cells, organs, organ systems, organisms, populations, communities, and even ecosystems. Throughout the rest of the book we will look at effects on each of these levels. First, we will provide an overview of strategies used for coping with winter. Then we will explore life in an environment dominated by snow. The roles of biochemistry, energy balance, nutrition, and population biology will be examined and specific cases of wintering plants and animals will be analyzed. Finally, we will look at humans and their responses to winter.

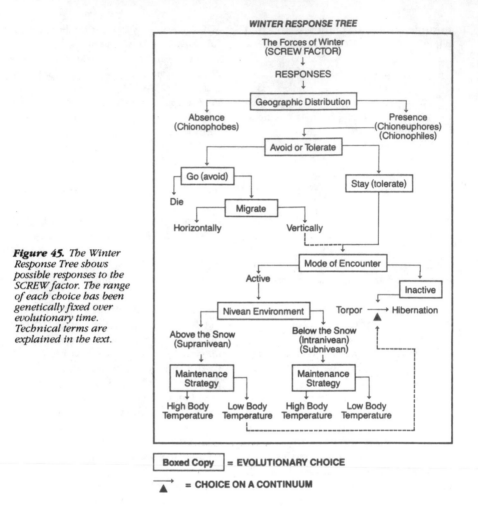

WINTER RESPONSE TREE

The Forces of Winter
(SCREW FACTOR)
↓
RESPONSES
↓

Geographic Distribution

Absence
(Chionophobes)

Presence
(Chioneuphores)
(Chionophiles)

Avoid or Tolerate

Go (avoid)

Stay (tolerate)

Die

Migrate

Horizontally

Vertically

Mode of Encounter

Active

Inactive

Nivean Environment   Torpor ──→ Hibernation

Above the Snow
(Supranivean)

Below the Snow
(Intranivean)
(Subnivean)

Maintenance
Strategy

Maintenance
Strategy

High Body   Low Body   High Body   Low Body
Temperature   Temperature   Temperature   Temperature

| Boxed Copy | = EVOLUTIONARY CHOICE

──→
▲   = CHOICE ON A CONTINUUM

Figure 45. The Winter Response Tree shows possible responses to the SCREW factor. The range of each choice has been genetically fixed over evolutionary time. Technical terms are explained in the text.

Strategies for Coping

There appears to be a limited number of strategies that organisms can use for coping. Each strategy is constrained, in turn, by the evolutionary heritage of the organism. We will explore some basic strategies and their influence on acclimating to winter, a period of decreased solar, thermal, and chemical energy.

Winter is coming. What are the options of a living organism? In some cases, it can leave. If it stays, there are other options. From the energy standpoint, it can conserve energy by shutting down, giving up certain activities. The alternative option is to remain fully functional. It can encounter winter. If the organism is active, it may try to maintain its temperature above the cold environmental temperature or it may allow its internal temperature to lower, at least for periods of time. Understanding which groups of plants and animals use which options provides a basis for interpreting ecology during the winter.

Size often serves as a constraint determining which options are available. For instance, size limits the length of possible migrations. For birds in the far north, the only really feasible option is to fly at least one-quarter of the way around the globe. In order to fly that far, the bird needs to be large enough to have the necessary energy to complete the trip. For most small birds, that is not feasible. The size constraint also works on very large animals, because they have not evolved to fly. Thus, long-distance migration is available to the body size of most of birds.

Body size also determines the micro-habitat in which an organism can live. Small rodents have the option of staying underneath the snow, and avoiding some of the effects of the SCREW factor. The same is true for many insects, which crawl under the bark of trees, bury themselves under ground, or spend the winter buried in the fur coat of a large mammal. Staying under the snow is not an option available to a buffalo. A moose, with its long legs, can move through deep snow, while a mule deer, a smaller animal, cannot make it through such deep snow. Size dictates that the deer have to move out of areas of the deepest snow. Size plays a significant role in determining residence and migration patterns.

Size is important in determining what temperature options are available. To maintain a temperature warmer than the environment, the organism must produce heat, and must not lose that heat too rapidly into the environment. Heat is produced by the bulk of body tissues, muscles, and metabolic tissue like the liver. The larger the organism, the more heat-production capacity it has. Heat is lost to the environment from the surface of the organism. The greater the surface, the greater the heat loss. Temperature stability depends on the ratio between the capacity for heat production, which is determined by volume, and the potential for heat loss, which is determined by surface area. A big, bulky animal has a greater capacity to stay warm than does a small animal. A large animal has a high heat-production capacity in relation to its surface area, whereas a small animal has a large surface area in proportion to its lower heat-production capacity.

The size ratio of **surface to volume** is critical to heat retention. Consider two blocks, one that is one centimeter on a side and another that is two centimeters (Figure 46). The area of one face of the small block is 1 cm² (1 x 1) and the total surface area is 6 cm². The volume of the small block is 1 cm³ (1 x 1 x 1), for a surface-to-volume ratio of 6. The large block has a surface area of 24 and a volume of 8, so its surface-to-volume ratio is 3 (24/8). The big block has eight times more volume for generating heat than the small block. Conversely, the small block has twice the surface area for dissipating heat, rela-

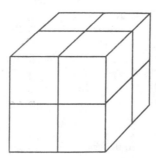

Figure 46. Comparison of two blocks, differing by only one centimeter along each side. See text for the discussion of the surface-to-volume ratio.

tive to its volume (6:1), compared to the large block (3:1). The small block would lose heat at a dramatically higher rate than its big relative. The same is true for surface-to-volume ratios of organisms.

The **temperature transient** determines how rapidly objects or organisms cool off or heat up in different environments. Temperature transient relates directly to the surface-to-volume ratio and the material composition of an object. Small objects have a short transient; they cool off or heat up quickly. If a butterfly is placed into a freezer at the same time as an entire moose, the butterfly will cool off more quickly than the moose. The butterfly has a shorter temperature transient.

Size relationships in reference to climate were recognized by ecologists, who developed two rules. **Bergmann's rule** states that geographic races of a species possessing larger body size are found in the cooler parts of the range. **Allen's rule** states that tails, ears, bills, and other extremities are relatively shorter in the cooler parts of a specie's range than in the warmer parts. Small, compact extremities have a reduced capacity to radiate heat.

Let's consider the options organisms have and their overall strategies for coping depending on their **body size**. Let's wander through the world of creatures, from tiny to small to moderate to big, looking at the physical attributes and limitations determined by body size, and considering temperature and chemical or food energy alternatives.

Tiny living creatures range from one-celled organisms up to more complex insects. Tiny organisms have a very difficult time migrating. They either cannot fly or cannot fly very far, because they simply do not have enough fuel. Most tiny organisms do not have the option to migrate in winter. Keeping

their body temperatures above the air temperature is not a viable option, since they have little or no heat-production capacity and a great capacity to lose heat to the environment. Their surface area is large compared to their volume. Few have any type of insulation. If they use external heat, such as the sun, to warm up, they may still lose this heat very rapidly to the air. They can avoid exposure to cold air temperatures, however. They can hide underneath snow, inside bark, in the soil, or in water. Because of their small size, they will take on the temperature of their immediate surroundings. Unless they choose an extremely warm microenvironment, they have to let their body temperatures drop to that of the environment by adjusting biochemically. Perhaps the main challenge to tiny organisms is to adjust their biochemistry to survive winter, yet avoid the problems of freezing.

Most tiny organisms will maintain their bodies at a low temperature, which reduces energy use to metabolic processes. Tiny organisms do not need much energy during winter. Because of their small size they cannot support large stores of energy. Instead they shut down almost completely, using only a very small amount of stored energy to get them through winter. An example of this strategy is the larvae of an insect that stays inactive through winter. Some spiders stay active through winter, but they do not need a tremendous energy intake, as they are operating at a relatively low temperature. Some social insects, such as bees, swarm to stay warm in the winter. Communal activity provides energy for warmth. Small organisms can function, but some use the option of shutting down their metabolism and going into cold storage to tolerate freezing temperatures. If they can find a good microclimate, a place where they will be safe until spring, a reasonable option is to become dormant. To be dormant, however, it may be necessary to spend energy to make antifreezes to prevent damage from freezing. There is an energy cost even to being dormant.

At the next level of the size hierarchy, we find reptiles, amphibians, and small mammals and birds. Reptiles and amphibians adopt a passive strategy, not maintaining a distinction between their body temperature and the temperature of the environment. Small mammals and birds take a more active role, maintaining high body temperatures. Reptiles conserve more energy; small birds and mammals expend more chemical energy in winter.

On the physiological level, the reptile's body tends to function as a single unit in terms of body temperature—that is, the body is at one temperature. Small mammals and birds maintain two temperatures: an inner core and an outer layer. To maintain two temperatures, small mammals and birds have insulation, and the outer layer, including the extremities, may be allowed to cool to near freezing. Reptiles and amphibians choose a microclimate for hibernation that does not freeze: the bottom of ponds, streams, or deep in the ground.

Small birds and mammals have a very interesting dilemma. They have the potential to generate enough heat to raise their core temperature above the air temperature as long as they have some insulation. They can allow their outer core and their extremities to be below their inner temperature. The dilemma is that they cannot store enough energy to run their furnace for very long. If it gets very cold, they usually cannot maintain that gradient between the required inner body temperature and the outer environment. Small

birds and mammals do not have the capability, as do reptiles, to shut down metabolically for long periods of inactivity, although exceptions do occur. Why most of these animals are not able to shut down is an interesting, unanswered question. It may relate to the complexity of the nervous system.

To resolve the dilemma—small birds and mammals cannot run their furnace fast enough, long enough, to keep warm the entire winter, yet they also cannot shut their bodies down and stay cold the entire winter—they make a compromise, called **heterothermy**, meaning variable body temperature. For short periods they maintain a warmer body temperature, and then for longer periods, from a few hours to a day or so, they let their body temperatures drop.

In winter there is not enough chemical energy to be used both for **thermal regulation**, that is, for maintaining a warm body temperature, and for **growth** or **reproduction**. For most small birds and mammals, reproduction is timed to occur in the summer when it is warm enough that most food intake is not needed for heat production, and an adequate energy supply is available to produce young. In the winter the reproductive system is shut down. Food that is available is used almost entirely for thermal regulatory needs.

Small birds and mammals also use behavioral strategies to cope with winter. They change their posture as the temperature changes. In warm temperatures, they spread out, exposing their undersides, which have less fur, so they can lose heat from that surface. In the winter they do the opposite by curling up, hiding the underside surface, and exposing more of their fur on the backside of their bodies. This provides a very significant savings in heat. Often they take this strategy even further by huddling together, which in effect increases the body size and decreases the surface-to-volume ratio.

Moderate-sized animals include those with smaller surface-to-volume ratios, which means they are able to store fat and carry it around. They have good insulation consisting of fur and feathers and a large furnace capacity. At this size, they still have short legs relative to snow depth. Moderate-sized animals include cats, dogs, foxes, coyotes, and the large birds, such as ducks and geese.

The host of options available to animals in this size range include leaving. The birds, for example, are large enough to fly great distances during migration. Even the mammals can make short vertical migrations to more favorable microhabitats at lower elevations. For those that stay, air temperature is a major determinant of their heat loss. Moderate-sized animals do not get a lot of heat from sunlight without losing a fair amount to the air. Some are small enough to burrow and to avoid the extremes of air temperature by getting underneath the surface of the snow or living underground.

In terms of energy sources, moderate-sized animals use fat for a significant portion of their energy supply. **Carnivores** function all winter, but many **herbivores**, such as ground squirrels and marmots, shut down by becoming **dormant**. Many patterns of dormancy exist to allow a continuum from **torpor** (short periods of dormancy) to **hibernation** (long periods of dormancy). Patterns of dormancy vary from small-sized to large-sized animals and will be discussed in the next section. Birds, interestingly enough, do not hibernate; an interesting speculative question concerns why no winter-hibernating birds have evolved. A few do go into torpor for short periods, but they do not shut down for long periods.

Large creatures include the biggest land mammals, the furless two-legged human animal, and the swimming types such as whales. These animals have the smallest surface-to-volume ratio. They may store large amounts of fat because of their great body size. They also can store heat for significant amounts of time. They tend to have good insulation, which they grow themselves or manufacture. In short, their big furnaces and long temperature transients allow them to easily maintain a constant body temperature.

Because of their size, large animals have several options for leaving. They may make vertical migrations down the mountain to lower elevations and milder temperatures, swim halfway around the world to warmer waters, or fly south to the Caribbean. For those that stay, the major source of warmth is internal heat, generated by digesting foods or metabolizing fats. They are mostly too big to burrow, except for the bear, who hibernates. Significant choices of microclimate are still possible to prevent environmental losses of energy. In general, the strategy of large animals is to stay warm and active throughout the winter. Notable and interesting exceptions occur. Humans modify their environment to overcome the effects of winter, for example. Bears, the largest carnivores, hibernate.

Body size is one of the main determinants of which strategies animals use for coping with the vectors of winter. Body size determines storage capacity for energy and the costs of maintaining body temperature. Body size also determines the ability to migrate. The larger the body size, the more options the animal has. Tiny creatures may be able to tolerate freezing temperatures. Small creatures tolerate freezing and hibernate. Moderate-sized creatures tolerate, hibernate, and migrate. Of course, exceptions to these generalities exist at all sizes.

Coping strategies exist at many levels in organisms: biochemical, physiological, morphological, and behavioral. The basis for coping strategies depends upon how organisms relate to cold, and that in turn depends on body size. As we explore life in the world of snow, continue thinking about how size determines the strategies with which animals cope with winter.

SUGGESTED READING

Degerbol, M. 1957. The extinct reindeer of East Greenland. Acta. Arctica, Fasc. 10:1-66.

NIVEAN ENVIRONMENT

Most organisms pass the winter season living in some contact with the snow. Snow may be the key to survival or it may be the worst enemy of the organisms that have to survive in the snowy world. This snow world is known as the **nivean environment**.

The nivean environment can be divided into three categories: the supranivean, the intranivean, and the subnivean. The **supranivean** environment refers to that area at and above the snow surface, the **intranivean** is the area within the snowpack, and the **subnivean** is the interface between the ground and the snow. When speaking in general terms, the term "subnivean" is often used to refer to both the intranivean and subnivean environments.

Ecological Classification

Central to the question of adaptation to the winter environment is the question of how organisms perceive the winter environment. Certainly nonhuman organisms must experience this environment differently than humans, and there must be dramatic differences in the ways that plants and animals experience the environment. In order to look at the way organisms experience the environment, we need a classification based on their perspective. We might consider this classification an ecological classification because it deals with the way organisms are related to their environment. Such an ecological classification was developed by A.N. Formozov (1964).

The Formozov classification has only three categories, but these categories deal with how organisms experience winter and how they have adapted to winter over evolutionary time. The names of the three categories are based on the Greek word for snow, **chion**. The three categories are chionophobes (literally, "snow fearers"), chioneuphores ("snow tolerators"), and chionophiles ("snow lovers").

Chionophobes are those organisms that have been unable to adjust to life in the nivean environment. These organisms tend to live in warmer regions and are not usually found in those regions that are severely impacted by winter. Some possible examples of chionophobes are the black vulture and the ocelot. The opossum might also be considered a chionophobe. Although you might find opossums in a winter environment, they have not developed any specific adaptations to counter the rigors of the winter environment.

The opossum represents a chionophobe that succeeded in expanding its range north into the winter environment. The expansion was possible because of its high reproductive rate and its ability to exist in many habitats. However, the opossum's lack of adaptation to winter is clearly evident each

spring when we find opossums that have lost the tips of their tails and ears to frostbite. The opossum is truly a chionophobe adapted to life in the warmer regions. In general, however, chionophobes tend not to be found in winter regions; the more severe the winter conditions, the fewer the species of chionophobes that occur.

Chioneuphores are those organisms that have adjusted their life to winter and can survive although they have not developed any special adaptations for survival. These organisms can survive in the winter environment because they are able to take advantage of the environment. Chioneuphores may live under the snow or find favorable microclimates conducive to survival. The selection of specialized conditions allows the chioneuphore to live in winter environments. In severe winters, however, the number of chioneuphores that do not survive the winter may be high. Examples of chioneuphores include the shrew, red fox, vole, and elk.

Chionophiles are those organisms that possess definite adaptations for life in a winter environment. Generally, the geographic distribution of chionophiles is limited to the winter-dominated regions. Some examples of chionophiles include the snowshoe hare, lemming, ptarmigan, and weasel. Several species become white in the winter, an obvious adaptation to the presence of snow.

These categories may also be used to describe organisms other than mammals and birds. For example, the palm tree is a chionophobe because it has not been able to adapt to the winter environment and is now found only in the tropics. On the other hand, the spruce tree (Figure 17) has evolved adaptations to the winter environment and can survive conditions of extreme snowfall. The spruce would be considered a chionophile.

The classification by Formozov is a simple means by which we can identify levels of adaptation to the winter environment that organisms have achieved. Let us note that this classification considers adaptation to life under winter conditions. The hummingbird has adapted to *winter* by migrating far to the south, but it has not adapted to living under *winter conditions*. It, therefore, is a chionophobe.

Sometimes an organism's adaptations to winter may serve other purposes and the original evolutionary advantage may not be identifiable. The moose is such a creature. It has very flexible legs and can lift each front leg out of the snow and move it nearly horizontally above the level of the snow before setting it down for another step. This flexibility allows the moose to move in chest-deep snow, snow in which elk and deer would not be able to move. The same adaptation, though, is useful for wading in deep streams and exiting to the high streambanks. In chionophiles, however, we might expect the development of anatomical features and behavioral patterns to evolve specifically as adaptations to snow.

Supranivean Environment

Let's explore life in the nivean environment starting with some of the problems of living in the supranivean environment. Once snow has blanketed the ground, it may serve either to impede or to assist the movement of animals. Several inches of snow will slow down a deer or stop its movement. When it becomes necessary for the deer to bound over the top of the snow or to use its chest to plow through the snow, the cost in terms of available energy quickly exceeds the benefits of moving, and deer **yard up**, or stay in one place. The Canada lynx, however, may be able to move swiftly on top of the same snowpack. Its large feet act as snowshoes, distributing its weight on top of the snow.

The ability of an animal to move on top of the snow is related to the weight each foot places on the snow. Many factors, including weight, speed, type of location, and behavior, are involved in determining the actual weight an animal places on each foot. We may estimate foot load (snow load) assuming each foot supports one-fourth of the body's weight (in reality, while walking, the front feet support up to 70 percent of the body's weight). **Foot load (or snow load)** is the amount of weight per surface area of each foot. One-fourth the weight of the animal is divided by the surface area to estimate the force that the foot places on the snow (Figure 47).

Foot load generally increases with body size (Figure 48) and we may represent the average foot load for animals with a line drawn through the data. Species that carry more weight per foot than average in relation to the surface area of their feet appear above the line, while those with less weight appear below the average line. Mammals with a light foot load are often adapted for living in snow conditions. The lynx, an animal that evolved in the far northern regions, has a low foot load. The lynx's extremely large feet disperse the downward force of the animal's weight over a larger area of the snow, allowing the animal to move effortlessly over the snow. It is interesting to note that the main food species for the lynx, the

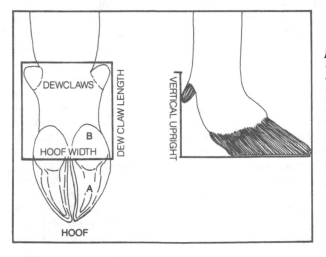

Figure 47. *Surface area of an elk foot. When an elk steps on the snow, the lower portion of the leg up to the dew claws as well as the hoof support weight. To calculate a better estimate of the supporting area of the foot, the area inside the rectangle marked "B" was added to the surface area of the hoof (after Telfer and Kelsall, 1984).*

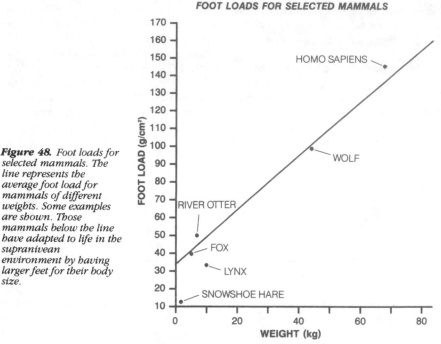

FOOT LOADS FOR SELECTED MAMMALS

Figure 48. Foot loads for selected mammals. The line represents the average foot load for mammals of different weights. Some examples are shown. Those mammals below the line have adapted to life in the supranivean environment by having larger feet for their body size.

snowshoe hare, has evolved an even lower foot load. In the evolutionary race to adapt to the supranivean environment, the snowshoe hare still leads the lynx.

Humans, compared to chionophiles, place more weight on their feet than average. Natives of northern regions developed snowshoes and skis to offset this disadvantage. The use of these devices increases the surface area on the snow and decreases the foot load.

Although foot loading provides an index of adaptation to the snow, a better understanding of an animal's ability to live in the supranivean world can be obtained by analyzing both anatomical and behavioral adaptations. E.S. Telfer and J.P. Kelsall (1984) developed the **snow-coping index** to indicate the ability of animals to survive in the supranivean environment. The index includes both anatomical (morphological) and behavioral features. They com-

bined **chest height** and **foot load**, key factors in the ability to cope with snow, into a morphological index (Table 8).

Species that have evolved in the northern regions, such as caribou and moose, ranked highest, indicating high levels of adaptation to snow. Bison and pronghorn, dwellers of the great plains, ranked lowest. Different combinations of features allowed a species to rank high on the list. Moose have a low foot-loading index but this is compensated for by the moose's long legs. The caribou ranked high because of its large feet. Mammals with large feet, such as sheep and white-tailed deer, have an advantage when walking on **snow crusts** because the snow may support their weight, preventing them from sinking in.

It is interesting to note that the predators all ranked about the same. In part, this might be the result of a small sample of predators. However, it may

Table 8. Morphological index of the snow-coping abilities of selected North American mammals. The morphological index combines values for chest height and foot load. The foot-load index has a maximum of 100, which would be the best possible adaptation.

Species	Mean Chest Height (cm)	Foot-load Index (unitless)[1]	Morphological Index (unitless)
Caribou	73	81	154
Moose	105	35	140
Dall sheep	54	67	121
Elk (wapiti)	85	33	118
Bighorn sheep	50	64	114
White-tailed deer	61	51	112
Bison	67	28	95
Pronghorn antelope	53	28	81
Wolf	50	85	135
Coyote	47	86	133
Wolverine	41	94	135

[1]The foot-load index is calculated as follows: 100 - ([foot load]/10) where foot load (g/cm^2) is one-fourth of the body weight divided by the surface area of the foot.

also represent an optimum combination of anatomical features for predators. Predators all ranked high because of their relatively large feet. It is possible that the evolution of larger feet is more energy-efficient than the evolution of larger body size to facilitate taking larger prey.

The moose and wolf have similar morphological indices, indicating that they may be similarly matched in their ability to cope with deep snow. This may be the reason that moose often stand their ground and fight when they are attacked by wolves rather than running. The wolf, with similar snow coping abilities, might easily catch the moose.

The behavior of mammals also affects their ability to cope with snow. Telfer and Kelsall identified six important behavioral traits: trail making, selection of soft and/or shallow snow, feeding above the snow, digging for forage, migration, and specialized techniques for locomotion (Table 9). Trail making includes both the repeated use of old trails, and following behavior—

often called **trailing**—in which many animals follow in the trail made by a strong lead animal. Digging behavior includes not only pawing with feet but swinging of the head by bison to clear broad swaths of snow. Examples of specialized locomotion include moose pulling their feet out of the snowpack and deer bounding in deep snow.

Ungulates were rated in each of these six categories (Table 9). Caribou and white-tailed deer showed the highest level of behavioral adaptation to snow conditions. Caribou showed important adaptations for making well-defined trails, digging for forage, migration, and locomotion. Antelope and bison, on the other hand, were the least behaviorally adapted to the nivean environment.

Since morphological and behavioral adaptations together form the complete picture of animal adaptation to the nivean environment, the authors combined the two indices into the **snow-coping index** (Table 10). Caribou showed the highest overall adaptation to winter (snow-coping index = 0.82),

Table 9. Behavioral adaptations of mammals for survival in the supranivean environment. Each ungulate was ranked subjectively from 1 to 5, with 5 indicating maximum adaptation to snow.

Species	Trail making	Selection of soft and/or shallow snow	Feeding above the snow	Digging for forage	Migration	Techniques of locomotion	Behavioral index
Caribou	5	4	2	5	5	5	26
Moose	2	3	5	1	3	5	19
Dall sheep	3	5	1	2	4	2	17
Elk (wapiti)	1	4	3	3	5	2	18
Bighorn sheep	2	5	1	2	4	2	16
White-tailed deer	4	5	5	1	3	3	21
Bison	4	3	1	4	3	1	16
Pronghorn antelope	2	3	2	2	3	1	13

Table 10. Snow-coping index based on the morphological and behavioral indices. The closer the snow-coping index is to a value of one, the better the mammal is adapted to life in the snow (Telfer and Kelsall, 1984).

Species	Morphological index/200[1]	Behavioral index/30[1]	Snow-coping index
Caribou	.77	.87	.82
Moose	.70	.63	.67
Dall sheep	.61	.57	.59
Elk (wapiti)	.59	.59	.59
Bighorn sheep	.57	.53	.55
White-tailed deer	.56	.70	.63
Bison	.48	.50	.49
Pronghorn antelope	.41	.43	.42

[1]The morphological and behavioral indices have been divided by their maximum value to give each equal value in determining the snow-coping index.

being far better adapted than their nearest competitor, the moose (snow-coping index = 0.67). The pronghorn showed the lowest combined level of morphological and behavioral adaptation to snow (snow-coping index = 0.42).

The supranivean environment places numerous stresses on animals. In addition to the amount of energy necessary to move through deep snow, crusts may physically injure animals as they **break through**. During the Wyoming winter, strong winds form crusts that may only partially support pronghorn antelope during their search for food.

When pronghorn break through, the crust cuts the leading edge of their legs. Pronghorn mortality during the winter increases because the loss of blood and open wounds allow infection.

Survival in the supranivean environment is aided by finding favorable topographic locations. In these locations, the impact of the weather or the snowpack is reduced. Animals successfully seek out locations with shallow snowpacks or places where crusts have not formed. Deer will be found on south-facing slopes with shallower snowpacks and warmer conditions. There are even sexual differences—the larger bull elk form separate herds that winter in areas with deeper snows than the areas where the cows and calves spend their time.

Intranivean and Subnivean Environments

Life in the intranivean and subnivean environments may be sheltered from some of the rigors of winter, but it has its own special limitations. The impact of wind and cold are reduced, but moisture, carbon dioxide, oxygen, and light assume more important roles because of limitations they may impose. Limitations imposed by these stresses reduce the number of individuals that survive to summer. High rates of mortality have been noted during periods of the fall, winter, and spring, and individuals must survive these critical periods if they are going to reproduce during the coming year.

Critical Periods

We recognize three **critical periods** in relation to surviving in the subnivean environment: fall, overwinter, and spring. The **fall** period brings dramatic changes in the environment. There is a point when daily air temperature falls below the daily ground temperature. This point is referred to as the **autumnal thermal overturn** and it signifies the beginning of the time when animals find conditions below ground warmer than out in the open.

About the time the autumnal thermal overturn is occurring, the winter snowpack begins to build up. Snows are usually shallow initially, and the small creatures, such as mice and voles, continue to forage on the snow surface. Eventually the snowpack deepens and the animals retreat beneath the snow for safety during the remainder of the winter. Generally, about the time the snowpack reaches 15 to 25 cm (6 to 10 in), we cease to find the small mammals venturing forth to the surface. This depth is referred to as the **hiemal threshold**.

As the hiemal threshold is reached, many things have been happening in the subnivean world. Foraging for food has become restricted to the ground-snow interface. Runways have become established, especially if cold fall weather conditions have led to the development of a depth hoar layer. And, perhaps most importantly, the increasing thickness of the snow has insulated the soil against fluctuating ambient air conditions. Under the blanket of snow, plants may avoid frost damage and desiccation from the winter winds.

The formation of the hiemal threshold represents a critical time period for plants and animals. If the threshold is reached early, before the autumnal overturn or before substantial cold temperatures have occurred, then plants and animals are protected for the winter. However, if either cold temperatures or the autumnal overturn occurs before the hiemal threshold is reached, a **freezeout** may occur. During a freezeout small mammals may die from exposure or plants may be killed by frosts. Even the works of man may suffer, as we find early deep frosts freezing our pipes; a deep snowpack is critical to protecting plumbing in the colder regions.

Fall is a critical period when populations may be substantially reduced without the protection of a snow layer. Interactions between decreasing temperatures and increasing snowpack depths are critical to survival. Many organisms are governed by an internal **biological clock** that triggers developmental stages at set times each fall. If the biological events do not correlate with the environment, the plants and animals suffer. If a weasel turns white before the snow has fallen, it becomes a more conspicuous prey for larger carnivores. If cold temperatures hit before the plants have gone through their **winter hardening**, the plants may die without the protection of the snow.

The **overwinter period** is often characterized by stable but slowly decreasing population levels. Sometimes, however, it is not possible to predict overwinter survivorship. Small mammals often successfully reproduce under the snowpack and populations of lemmings and voles may reach dramatic highs. Overwinter survival is a product of many things, including the impact of the climate and the availability of food. Snowpack conditions may also affect survivorship. The formation of **ice lenses** (layers of water ice in the snowpack caused by melting) within the snowpack may restrict small mammals to areas where they cannot find enough food to survive.

While it is not possible to characterize every overwinter situation, the overwinter period in the subnivean environment is often the least critical period for plants and animals. They are sheltered from fluctuating weather conditions by a roof of insulating snow. Conditions in the supranivean environment may be harder on organisms that bear the full brunt of winter there.

Spring is another critical period for life in a subnivean environment. A **vernal overturn** occurs when the air temperature again reaches a point higher than the ground temperature. This period is accompanied by **ripening** of the snowpack. During ripening, increasing daytime temperatures warm the snowpack to its **isothermal point** of 0°C (32°F). At the isothermal point, the snowpack contains liquid water, which percolates down to the ground.

Water running through the snowpack can cause **flooding**, and animals may drown or die in their nests from hypothermia. Young born in nests under the snowpack are particularly vulnerable, as they lack locomotion and the ability to effectively regulate their body temperatures. Refreezing during the isothermal period can create **ice lenses**, trapping animals away from a food supply.

Eventually, melting reaches the point where the **spring runoff** starts. During the runoff, small streams may flow under the snowpack, further flooding winter homes. Flooding may also erode plants from their secure footing. During both the fall and spring overturns, the presence of large amounts of water during daily freeze-thaw cycles may lead to **needle ice** formation. Needle ice can sever plant roots and destroy animal burrows.

Spring may be more critical to the survival of subnivean animals than the other two periods. During the spring, food supplies have dwindled and fat reserves are gone. The snowpack is losing its insulating power and free-moving water quickly conducts available heat away from the body. The margin for survival is simply at its lowest and minor changes may prove fatal. A vole might survive a dunking in a stream in the fall that may be fatal in the spring.

The ground-snow interface is warm relative to the air during the winter, and life in the subnivean environment exists under somewhat mild temperature conditions. However, cold temperatures can and do affect the subnivean zone. The passage of a cold front can chill the subnivean environment, and perhaps the most important aspect of the snowpack is its ability to buffer temperature changes at the bottom of the snow.

Survival is simpler if organisms live

in an environment with reduced daily variations; the snowpack filters out the extremes of the ambient air temperature. The key questions are: how effective is the snow at stabilizing ground temperatures, and how stable is the temperature beneath the snowpack?

Temperature

Let's first define the temperature stability of the subnivean environment. A stable subnivean zone experiences only a small temperature change when there is a large change in air temperature. Mathematically, we define this ratio as:

$$\frac{\Delta T_{subnivean}}{\Delta T_{air}} = \text{Temperature stability ratio}$$

where ΔT signifies change in temperature (T). If the air temperature changed 10°C in 24 hours (the difference between the maximum and minimum temperatures) and the subnivean temperature changed an equal amount (10°C), the ratio would be 1 and there would be no effective buffering. However, if there was only a 1°C temperature change in the subnivean for a 10°C change in the air temperature, the ratio would be 0.1 and the subnivean environment would be effectively stabilized against the air temperature change.

Two indices of temperature stability in the subnivean environment have been developed. While the Thermal Index of Marchand (1982) is the most appropriate to use, we will briefly review both because they are mentioned in the literature. Pruitt (1970) developed the **Stability Index** (SI) where

$$SI = C \left(\sum T_{(i)} D_{(i)} \right)$$

and C is the percentage of the ground covered by snow, T is the thickness of the snowpack in cm, and D is the density in g/cm³ of each layer (i). All layers are summed for a total value. The ability of the snowpack to stabilize temperature depends essentially on its insulating properties. As Marchand (1982) has pointed out, the SI does not correctly reflect the insulating effect of snow. Insulation would increase as snow thickness increased but would decrease as snow density increased. The relationship of the SI to density should therefore be inverse. Since it is not an inverse relationship, confusing answers may result as follows:

40 cm of snow at a density of
0.1 g/cm³ = SI of 4
20 cm of snow at a density of
0.2 g/cm³ = SI of 4

Clearly the shallow, dense snowpack will not provide insulation equal to the 40-cm snowpack.

Marchand (1982) proposed an alternative index to alleviate the problems with SI. His index, the snow **Thermal Index**, is

$$TI = \sum_{i=1}^{n} \frac{T_i}{P_i}$$

In this relationship, the thickness of each layer (i) is divided by its density and all layers are summed for total value. Single layers of our previous example then would yield TI values of 400 (40/0.1) and 100 (20/0.2), which seem appropriate for those snow conditions.

Extensive sampling of snowpacks demonstrated the relationship between actual subnivean stability and the TI. Under real snowpacks, temperatures stabilize at TI values of about 150 to 200. This is the level at which increased thickness or density does little to increase temperature stability under a snowpack. TI values may go much higher than 200, but there is little increase in thermal stability beyond this value.

For a moment now, consider some examples of snowpacks (Table 11).

Table 11. Relationship of thickness and density to thermal index.

Thickness	Density	Thermal Index
10 cm	0.1 g/cm³	100
15 cm	0.1 g/cm³	150
20 cm	0.1 g/cm³	200
25 cm	0.1 g/cm³	250
20 cm	0.2 g/cm³	100

Falling snow often has a density of about 0.1 g/cm³. New snow at this density would stabilize the subnivean environment when it reached a depth of 15 to 20 cm (TI = 150 to 200). It is interesting to note that recent studies quantified the depth needed to reach stability at the value observed by the early naturalists who defined the hiemal threshold (also at 15 to 20 cm). Small mammals evidently perceive temperature stability when the hiemal threshold is reached. At that time, animals continue their activities, but mainly in the subnivean environment.

The snowpack acts as a shield protecting the organisms below it. The shield slows the loss of energy and stabilizes temperatures in the subnivean environment. It may also impede the movement of light and the gases oxygen and carbon dioxide (Figure 49). These factors play major roles in the survival of life in the subnivean.

Light

Plants are particularly sensitive to the light penetrating the snow. This light may serve as a cue, "telling" the plants when the sun has reached a certain angle in the sky as it journeys to its highest angle in the summer. The critical angle may be a signal for the plant to start growth for the year. In Greenland and in the Snowy Range of Wyoming, plants have been recorded growing under 50 cm (20 in) of snow in the spring. Often snowbank buttercups (*Ranunculus adoneus*) grow and flower through the remaining snow and even ice in the high mountains. **Spring ephemerals** are plants that often start growth under the snow, flower and set seed immediately after snow melt. Many of these plants have large bulbs with stores of food that provide energy for the growth under the snow.

Evidence also suggests that **protochlorophyll** can be changed into **chlorophyll** beneath the snow. If the winter scientist digs down through the snow in the spring, plants covered by more snow have less chlorophyll (Figure 50). Synthesis of chlorophyll appears to be a function of the timing and amount of light penetrating the snow. It is also significant that some plants remain green all winter under the snowpack. These **winter-green** plants must either take advantage of the first snow-free days or else photosynthesize in the subnivean.

Seeds have been shown to germinate with up to 2 m (6.5 ft) of snow above them. Some of these seeds appear to be dependent on light penetration for germination.

For mammals living in the subnivean, the overwintering status of plants is very important. First, plants serve as a food source. Spring beauties (*Claytonia*), spring ephemerals with large bulbs, tend to continue to lose sugars and starch while overwintering in the subnivean (Figure 51). Although during March an unexplained increase in carbohydrates has been detected, the general depletion in food reserves during the winter may serve as an additional stress on hungry animals in the subnivean.

Second, plants may play a role in the chemical cueing of the initiation of re-

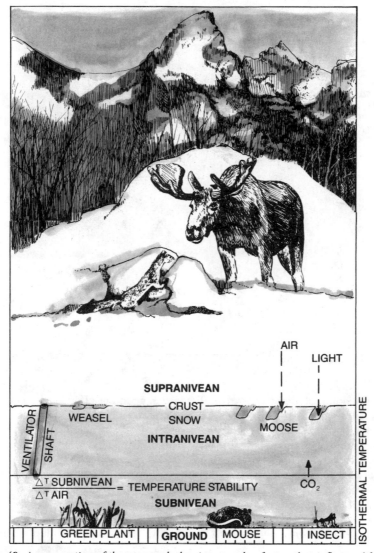

Figure 49. *A cross-section of the snowpack showing some key factors that influence life in the nivean environment. Plants, mice, and insects live in the subnivean world where light, CO_2 exchange, and air are critical. Ventilator shafts may help in gas exchange. Temperatures are relatively stable in the subnivean environment. Animals in the supranivean environment must travel on the snow where the crust may or may not support their weight.*

production in small mammals. A group of chemical compounds, known as phenolics, have been identified that stimulate reproductive activity in voles (*Microtus montanus*). These compounds, when introduced experimentally to field populations during the winter, trigger the formation of sperm and eggs. The phenolic compounds are present in actively growing grasses and perhaps other plants. These chemicals seem to be able to override the normal timing of reproduction which is tied to **photoperiod** (length of day).

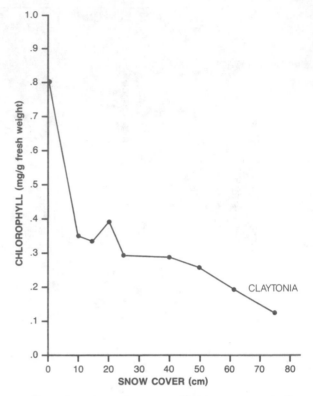

Figure 50. _The chlorophyll content of spring beauty (Claytonia) decreases under increasing amounts of snow (modified from Salisbury, 1982)._

The initiation of plant growth and chlorophyll production then becomes a critical issue for mammal reproduction. It is possible that unusually early plant growth caused by a shallow spring snowpack might trigger mammal reproduction in the subnivean. Indeed, in years of population eruptions of lemming and voles there is often considerable reproduction beneath the snow.

Atmospheric Gases

The snowpack may act as a barrier to the flow of atmospheric gases, causing **carbon dioxide** (CO_2) to accumulate beneath the snow. Higher concentration of carbon dioxide in the subnivean zone may possibly influence physiological functions of plants and animals. For example, small mammals, including voles, decrease their oxygen consumption, heart rate, and body temperature in an apparent effort to compensate for excessive carbon dioxide. These lowered body functions might in turn cause a reduced ability to find food or avoid predators.

Scientists, however, have not been able to fully define the ability of snow to concentrate carbon dioxide. Ice is quite permeable to carbon dioxide and many studies have failed to find increased levels of carbon dioxide beneath the snow. Several recent studies, however, have detected increased levels of carbon dioxide in the subnivean, especially during the spring months. This discrepancy in study results may be a product of several factors. Low levels of photosynthesis by mosses and other plants beneath the snow could reduce levels of carbon dioxide. Photosynthesis can occur at the low temperatures and low light levels occurring be-

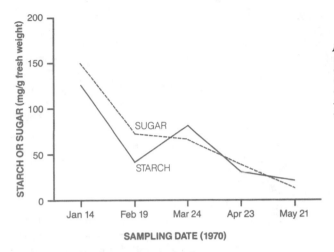

Figure 51. *The decrease in carbohydrate content of spring beauties (Claytonia lanceolata) overwintering in the subnivean (from Salisbury, 1982).*

neath the spring snowpack. Algae have been shown to photosynthesize when trapped in ice. All subnivean habitats may not accumulate carbon dioxide and even in a given habitat there may be microtopographic differences in accumulation points beneath the snowpack.

Several possible sources of carbon dioxide exist beneath the snowpack, including respiration by plants and animals. Masses of fungi beneath the snow have been shown to double in the spring at the same time carbon dioxide concentrations reach levels twice that found in the atmosphere (levels of CH_4 and CO also increased). Winter wheat plants sometimes receive considerable damage from **snow mold**, indicating fungal activity under the snow.

When carbon dioxide is detected beneath the snow, areas of concentration do vary with plant communities and with topography. Recent studies at the Taiga Biological Station, 280 km (448 mi) northeast of Winnipeg, Canada, have detected consistent spring concentrations of carbon dioxide in stands of black spruce, aspen, and an alder-ridge ecotone, but not in alder-tamarack bogs and jackpine stands. Areas of rocks and

thin soils had lower concentrations of carbon dioxide than did areas with thicker soils. Carbon dioxide began to increase in January and sustained concentrations were maintained until snowmelt allowed mixing with the atmosphere.

At the Taiga Station, red-backed voles (*Clethrionomys gapperi*) were shown to move from areas where carbon dioxide began to increase and also to avoid areas with increased concentrations of carbon dioxide. Movements occurred at concentrations below 0.12 percent (for comparison, atmospheric concentration at the study area was 0.02 percent). Small mammals have been shown to respond physiologically at concentrations varying from 0.14 to 0.50 percent. It is possible, however, that concentrations were even higher in the nests used by the voles.

Early naturalists noted tunnels through the snow down to the ground and speculated that these were **ventilator shafts** that allow the subnivean animals access to clean air. The number of tunnels were reported to increase each spring, which could be a direct response to the increases of levels of carbon dioxide in the spring. It has also been suggested that these tunnels provide access for the animals to detect changes in day length and subsequent setting of their internal clocks for the timing of spring reproduction. We have detected a third use for tunnels: that of a radiation warming room during extremely cold nights. A mouse running on the snow surface can burrow a quick tunnel into the snow where it warms itself following radiation loss to the open sky.

We are not aware of any studies of oxygen concentrations beneath the snowpack and suggest this as a topic for future studies.

Subnivean Food Web

In spite of increased carbon dioxide, life does go on in the relatively hospitable subnivean environment. Many creatures are active beneath the snow and many plants have stored their food in forms available to winter scavengers. Scientists have postulated a possible ecological food web for **winter-active** subnivean animals (Figure 52). Even though we represent the relationships as a simple pyramid, we recognize that the structure is a complex web with many interlinked components. For instance, spiders many feed on flies, springtails, and aphids. Spiders, in turn, are fed on by shrews and mice, and perhaps even weasels.

Our web is a five-tiered pyramid, and the primary producers of food are plants and fungus. Dead plants, rotten logs, and old fungal mats serve as detritus for the **detritivores** (organisms that feed on detritus). Fungal mats feed springtails and flies, while a host of **herbivores**, including aphids and leaf hoppers, feed on **winter-green** plants. All these organisms form the primary consumer layer. Primary consumers are, in turn, fed on by secondary consumers, also known as the primary

predators. Secondary consumers may even be parasites.

The main members of the tertiary consumer layer are the shrews, which devour anything that moves. The incredible metabolism of the shrews requires that they eat up to twice their body weight each day. Once thought to feed mostly on dormant insect larvae, it is now known that the shrews probably prey mostly on the large number of winter-active insects beneath the snow. We have shown shrews to exist on top of Mt. Evans in Colorado, at elevations of greater than 4,270 m (14,000 ft). Since shrews are not known to hibernate or become dormant, these voracious little creatures must be able to find winter-active insects even under the harsh winter conditions at that elevation. Mice and voles are also members of the tertiary level and, though primarily herbivores or **granivores** (seed eaters), they will not turn down a juicy protein meal if an insect runs across their path. Conversely, shrews may, at times, take up to 50 percent of their winter diet in the form of conifer seeds or beechnuts. They have even been known to hoard these items by making food caches.

The subnivean world is a complex place, being both benefactor and death trap for those living beneath the snow. The subnivean may serve its small members as an hospitable escape from the rigors experienced by the larger organisms consigned to living in a supranivean environment. In the subnivean, temperatures are relatively warm, fluctuations minor, and winds nonexistent. Plants and animals can pass the winter without evolving energy-costly mechanisms for life under extreme weather conditions. There are dangers though—increased carbon dioxide, flooding, ice layer formation and predators in well-constructed tun-

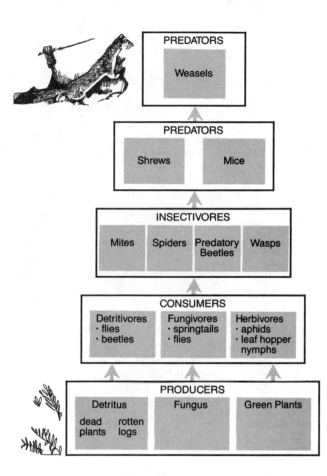

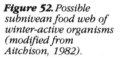

Figure 52. *Possible subnivean food web of winter-active organisms (modified from Aitchison, 1982).*

nels. Many of the dangers exert their greatest force in the critical periods for survival, spring and fall. During the spring and fall, subnivean populations may suffer dramatic reductions; conversely, in some years, incredible spurts of reproduction may produce so many young that the vegetation is devastated.

SUGGESTED READINGS

Aitchison, C.W. 1984. A possible subnivean food chain. Pp. 363-372, *in* Winter Ecology of Small Mammals (J.F. Merritt, ed.). Carnegie Museum Nat. Hist. Spec. Publ. No. 10, Pittsburgh.

Berger, P.J., E.H. Sanders, P.D. Gardner, and N.C. Negus. 1977. Phenolic plant compounds functioning as reproductive inhibitors in *Microtus montanus*. Science, 195:575-577.

Formozov, A.N. 1964. Snow Cover as an Integral Factor of the Environment and Its Importance in the Ecology of Mammals and Birds. English translation. Originally published in Material For Fauna and Flora of the USSR, New Series Zool., 5(XX)1946:1-152.

Fuller, W.A. 1984. Demography of a subarctic population of *Clethrionomys gapperi*: Can winter mortality be predicted? Pp. 51-57, *in* Winter Ecology of

Small Mammals (J.F. Merritt, ed.). Carnegie Museum Nat. Hist. Spec. Publ. No. 10, Pittsburgh.

Halfpenny, J.C. 1970. Distributional ecology of algae in the Dry Valleys, Antarctica. Unpubl. M.S. Thesis, University of Wyoming, Laramie.

Kelsall, J.P., and E.S. Telfer. 1971. Studies of the physical adaptation of big game for snow. Proc. Snow Ice Relation Wildl. Recreation Symp., Iowa State Univ, Ames, Iowa, 134-146.

Marchand, P.J. 1982. An index for evaluating the temperature stability of a subnivean environment. J. Wildl. Mgmt., 46:518-520.

Negus, N.C., and P.J. Berger. 1977. Experimental triggering of reproduction in a natural population of *Microtus montanus*. Science, 196:1230-1231.

Oedekoven, O.O., and F.G. Lindzey. 1987. Winter habitat use patterns of elk, mule deer, and moose in southwestern Wyoming. Great Basin Nat., 47:638-643.

Penny, C.E., and W.O. Pruitt, Jr. 1984. Subnivean accumulation of CO_2 and its effects on winter distribution of small mammals. Pp. 373-380, *in* Winter Ecology of Small Mammals (J.F. Merritt, ed.). Carnegie Museum Nat. Hist. Spec. Publ. No. 10, Pittsburgh.

Pruitt, W.O., Jr. 1970. Some ecological aspects of snow. Pp. 83-99, *in* Ecology of the Subarctic Regions. Proc. Helsinki Symp. United Nations Scientific Cultural Org., Paris, France.

Salisbury, F.B. 1984. Light conditions and plant growth under snow. Pp. 39-50, *in* Winter Ecology of Small Mammals (J.F. Merritt, ed.). Carnegie Museum Nat. Hist. Spec. Publ. No. 10, Pittsburgh.

Telfer, E.S., and J.P. Kelsall. 1984. Adaptation of some large North American mammals for survival in snow. Ecology, 65(6):1828-1834.

TEMPERATURE, LIFE, AND BIOCHEMISTRY

Of the elements of winter included in the **SCREW** factor, probably the most prominent one in the minds of people when they think about winter is **cold**. We understand cold on a physical level. It makes us tense, we feel uncomfortable, it will even cause pain if it is severe enough. Physiologically, it can cause severe injury and death. On an emotional level, the word "cold" can have a pretty strong negative connotation. On an intellectual level, what is cold? Why does cold cause such tremendous problems? And how are these problems circumvented by the plants and animals that survive through the winters?

Living systems function at many different levels, from spiritual to the psychological level down to the internal level and finally the physiological and biochemical levels. We will eventually examine these other levels, but we wish to start at the biochemical level for two reasons. First, temperature is defined at the molecular level. **Temperature** is a measure of molecular motion. The less **thermal energy** in a substance, the less molecular motion it has. The scale from cold to hot really represents the amount of molecular motion or thermal energy from low to high. It is this movement or lack of movement that strongly influences biochemical molecules. Second, we start at the biochemical level because living systems are biochemical machines. At the most basic level, organisms accomplish what they do by manipulating molecules. It is the biochemical entity that is so temperature sensitive.

A knowledge of the biochemical level is critical to understanding why temperature has its obvious effects on living systems. We will briefly review biochemistry to provide the basis for understanding the effects of temperature on life. Then we will examine the interactions of cold and biochemistry.

Introduction

Biochemicals are molecules constructed by a living system. For instance, plants use carbon dioxide and water to make sugars, a biochemical. Humans ingest food and break it down into fats, proteins, and carbohydrates. Nucleic and amino acids are assembled into **DNA** (deoxyribonucleic acid), a biochemical that contains the genetic program telling cells how to function. **Hormones**, combinations of fats and proteins, act as biochemical messengers, taking messages throughout the body. These elements compose very large molecules (**macromolecules**) compared to a molecule of water. Macromolecules are affected by temperature changes, as is water.

The biochemicals are very carefully organized within the body. Inside the body are large units: the organs, the heart, muscles, liver, kidneys, bones, and so on. Inside the organs are smaller individual units, the cells. The cells in turn contain smaller units called **organelles**, including the nucleus. The cells also contain water, and dissolved in the water are mineral salts such as sodium, potassium, calcium, magnesium, and manganese, as well as sugars, proteins, and various small molecules that act as messengers. Living systems stay relatively neatly organized. Everything is packaged away in one compartment or another. The walls or **membranes** of these packages are made of fats or **lipids**. The membranes are useful in that they are like walls with shelves with many things stacked on them, including fats, proteins, and certain hormones.

Temperature affects the **organization** of the body. Butter, a fat, changes consistency with changes in temperature. Similarly, membranes composed of fats are extremely sensitive to temperature. As the temperature changes, the fats can become either too stiff or too permeable. As they get too stiff, the function of proteins and enzymes on the shelves within the membrane walls is impeded. As the temperature decreases, proteins within the membranes start clumping together. Instead of having a smooth covering for the entire wall, there will be big holes in the membrane. Holes cause leaks, and substances pass in and out of the cells that shouldn't.

Water appears much the same at one temperature or another unless it is boiled or frozen. However, significant changes take place in water with any change in temperature. Water changes viscosity, pH, and electrostatic charge as the temperature changes. The viscosity indicates how "liquid" it is—how easily it flows, and how easily things move about in it. The **pH** of water indicates its **acidity**, and the electrostatic charge indicates how strongly water is attracted or repelled from ions. For both lipids (fats) and water, significant changes result from small changes in temperature. These changes have significant effects on the biochemical functioning of living systems.

Temperature-induced effects cascade up the living system from inside the cell to the entire organisms. Life processes, such as breathing, thinking, moving, digesting, and eating, are dependent on biochemical reactions. Muscles contract because proteins slide over each other in a biochemical reaction. Messages pass throughout the body along our nerve cells, releasing messenger chemicals in biochemical reactions that generate small electrical fields. Oxygen is transported from our lungs to where it is needed within the cells by a large biochemical called **hemoglobin**. Hemoglobin picks up oxygen molecules in a biochemical reaction and releases the oxygen molecule through another reaction. The processes of the body are dependent on biochemical reactions, and these reactions, in turn, are dependent on temperature.

The next section on the basics of biochemistry provides background material. If you have a familiarity with biochemistry, you may wish to skip directly to *Temperature Effects on Biochemistry*. However, this section does provide a useful review that highlights the aspects of biochemistry that are particularly sensitive to cold temperature effects.

Basics of Biochemistry

One rather important property of living things is **shape**. We know living things from their shape. Grass has thin, tapering green blades, and a skunk is a small creature with short legs, a pointed snout, and covered with black and white fur. Shape is maintained throughout all types of movement and different conditions. We also know that we are made of atoms of carbon, oxygen, hydrogen, nitrogen, and other chemicals. How is it that our atoms are stuck together to give us our shape and what does this have to do with temperature?

Bonds in Biochemical Compounds

A universal property of all things, no matter what their size, is that they are subject to attractive and repulsive forces. At the scale of atoms, the forces of attraction tend to be such that most atoms are not single isolated atoms—most atoms tend to hold on to other atoms. Atoms **bond** by sharing electrons. For instance, **carbon** shares four of its electrons with other atoms. The other atoms may be other carbons and the bonds create complex carbon macromolecules. **Oxygen** shares electrons too. Oxygen is often found in molecules where there are two bonds, such as water. **Hydrogen** shares one electron. Bonding is central to the maintenance of shape, and many different types of biochemical bonds exist.

Energy Storage in Bonds

An important property of bonding is that significant amounts of **energy** are held within bonds. When there is a good fit between atoms or molecules, there is a lot of energy in that bond and separation is not easy. To separate the molecules, a lot of energy is required, and a lot of energy is released.

Chemists have studied and measured the energy involved in different types of bonds—for instance, the bond between a carbon and an oxygen atom, or between an oxygen and a hydrogen atom, as in water. Bonding is more complex than we have described. Energy stored within biochemical bonds is referred to as **chemical energy**.

Energy originating from the sun is

processed and stored by plants. **Photosynthesis** captures the energy of the sun and turns it into simple carbohydrates, or sugars. Plant **chlorophyll**, an enzyme with a special shape, holds carbon dioxide and water to facilitate production. The energy of the sunlight activates the carbon dioxide, causing it to bond with water, forming sugars. This process accomplishes two things. It forms long chain sugar, and it fixes the energy of the sun into that sugar. This energy is then available as chemical energy to living things. Humans remove simple sugars from plants and turn them into food products such as a **Snickers bar**. Another process, using enzymes, splits the carbon-carbon bond and releases the sun's energy stored in the Snickers bar. The Snickers bar (61.2 g or 2.16 oz) contains about 290 kcal of chemical energy bound by biochemical bonds. Biochemical bonds are important to life because of their property of storing energy until it is needed. Incidentally, we will often use the Snickers bar because it is an intuitive unit of energy that people understand. While 2,900 kcal is hard to visualize, 10 Snickers bars are not.

Bonds are the energy source, the **energy storage** form for living activities. It is this ability to store energy that allows living things to function during times when sunlight is not available. We can use this energy throughout the long winter. Stored chemical energy is used to do the work of living systems—to digest food, to synthesize more tissue, to make muscles contract, and to make hearts beat. This energy is needed for thinking, for protecting ourselves from infection and illness, and for reproducing.

Bonding creates groups of similar biochemical compounds: carbohydrates, proteins, fats. Complex compounds are built from the simpler compounds. **Fats** are energy-rich and contain about 9.3 kcal/g compared to 3.79 kcal/g for **carbohydrates**, and 3.12 kcal/g for **proteins**. Each of these compounds possesses different amounts of stored chemical energy because of different numbers and types of bonds. An understanding of the types and numbers of bonds is necessary to comprehend energy storage in biochemical compounds.

Types and Numbers of Bonds

Consider three substances: a piece of wood, some butter, and some ice that are outside at -40°C (-40°F). When they are brought inside, the ice begins to melt and forms a pool of water, the butter softens and begins to sag, and the wood keeps its original shape. The different reactions occur because of different types of bonds. Bonds are categorized into two main groups: strong and weak bonds. Understanding their behavior is the key to most temperature-related questions.

Strong bonds, also known as **covalent bonds**, are formed by sharing electrons between atoms (Figure 53). Carbon atoms are covalently bonded to each other in sugars. Covalent bonds are relatively stable with respect to temperature changes. However, covalent bonds do form and break at specific temperatures. **Enzymes** (molecules that increase rates of reactions) may increase the rates at which covalent bonds form or break.

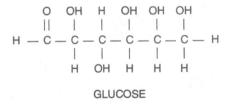

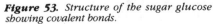

Figure 53. *Structure of the sugar glucose showing covalent bonds.*

Covalent bonds are important in **cellular respiration**, the breakdown (or **oxidation**) of food molecules by cells. Cellular respiration is also known as **metabolism**. During cellular respiration, oxygen combines with various carbon compounds in the food to release carbon dioxide and energy. At each step in the cycle, bonds are made and broken. When bonds are broken, energy is released as heat or carried to other chemical reactions in molecules of **adenosine triphosphate** (**ATP**). ATP is the currency of energy in living systems and acts as the carrier of energy from carbon-containing, energy-storage molecules to energy-requiring reactions.

Fats are interesting compounds in that they may contain more than one covalent bond between carbon atoms. Fats with only one bond between carbon atoms are known as **saturated fats**. Those fats with more than one bond are referred to as **unsaturated fats**. Unsaturated fats tend to be oily liquids and are more common than saturated fats in plants. The amount of saturation determines the **melting point** of fatty acids, or conversely the temperature at which they become stiff when it gets colder. Unsaturated fats tend to have lower melting points and do not become as stiff when they are cold.

Weak bonds do not have the strength found in covalent bonds (Figure 54). Among these weak bonds are ionic, polar, hydrogen, hydrophobic, and nonpolar bonds. Weak bonds are temperature-sensitive and slight changes may break weak bonds, affecting structure and function. Weak bonds are easily changed. As the temperature increases, the weak bonds holding ice together begin to break and the structure changes to a pool of water. The weak bonds of butter change slowly with temperature increases, so that its

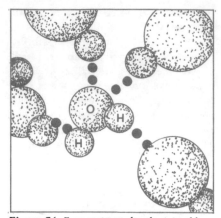

Figure 54. *Four water molecules joined by a weak bond (the hydrogen bond) form the crystalline structure found in ice.*

consistency changes gradually. If a protein is heated, it changes constituency because of changes in the weak bonds. We say the protein has become **denatured**. This is what happens when you heat egg whites or cook meat.

Additionally, weak bonds are energy-poor. They do not contain a lot of stored energy. This is especially true when weak bonds are compared to covalent bonds. For every one to two kcal of weak bonds, covalent bonds contain 30 to 100 kcal. The significance of this is that weak bonds can be easily altered, whereas covalent bonds are difficult to alter.

Biochemicals

Organisms bond together elements to form complexes of **biochemicals**: sugars bond to form complex sugars and carbohydrates, amino acids into DNA, fatty acids into fats, and minerals into bones and teeth. To set the stage for studying temperature effects on biochemistry, let's briefly review some biosynthesized chemicals.

Sugars are simple compounds consisting of carbon, hydrogen, and oxygen. All the carbohydrates contain energy and react with oxygen to release simpler carbohydrates, carbon dioxide, water, and stored energy. Digesting the **glucose** (a sugar) in a Snickers bar yields about 136 kcal of energy for your body. Sugars, and their temporary storage form in the body, **glycogen**, are important sources of energy for winter. Long-term energy storage in the body is in the form of **fat**.

The building blocks of **proteins** are **amino acids**, small chemical compounds of carbon, hydrogen, and oxygen to which a nitrogen atom has been added. Proteins are the workhorse—or more accurately, the caretaker—of the body. Almost everything that needs to get done, gets done by a protein. Proteins exist for many different functions: transportation, movement, structural integrity, facilitating chemical reactions, and information transfer.

Proteins **transport** many things around the body, either large distances through the bloodstream, or over very small distances across membranes—for example, from outside a cell to inside a cell, or from the outside of a nucleus to the inside of a nucleus. Oxygen is taken into the body through the lungs. Oxygen moves from the air sac of the lung into the blood, into a red blood cell where it is picked up by a protein called **hemoglobin**. Hemoglobin moving in the blood transports the oxygen to the tissues of the body, where the oxygen is released. The oxygen then diffuses from inside the red blood cell to the body cell. Finally, the oxygen is used to break down a carbohydrate. There are many other transport proteins in the blood.

The food we eat is broken down in our intestines then transported across the intestinal wall, usually by proteins. Fats that are absorbed from the intestine are transported to the liver carefully bound in globules formed by protein and fats, **lipoproteins**.

Proteins are imbedded on the surface and in the membrane of the cell. Their function is to transport substances across the cell membrane. One of the major protein functions, known as **ion pumping**, moves **sodium** and **potassium** across the cell wall. This protein continually moves sodium from the inside of a cell to the outside and potassium from the outside of the cell to the inside. The ion pump serves a vital function in living things. For cells to live, most of the potassium must be on the inside and most of the sodium on the outside of the cell surface. Ion pumping is one of the major energy-consuming functions of living things. At times as much as a quarter of our energy is used by ion pumps maintaining the proper balance of potassium on the inside and sodium on the outside of cells.

Muscle movement is another task of proteins. Most living things move in one fashion or another. That movement is usually accomplished by **contractile proteins**. These are proteins that have the ability to shorten or lengthen, depending upon signals received from the nervous system. Skeletal muscles contract and expand, causing joints to move a limb. Heart muscles contract rhythmically, pumping blood through the body. The walls of blood vessels themselves contract and expand, adjusting the flow of blood from one part of the body to the other. Movement is also a very energy-consuming activity.

Other proteins provide **structure** for the body. These proteins are coiled in very special ways that provide elastic-like properties, giving the skin an elastic feeling. This protein is called **elastin**. Connective tissue is largely made of **collagen proteins**. Connective tissue forms tendons, ligaments, and the sheet-like material that separates organs and muscles, allowing them to slide over one another.

Proteins serve an **informational** function. The genetic information passed from parents to their offspring is contained in proteins. The best known of the informational proteins are **DNA** and **RNA** (ribonucleic acid).

Finally, proteins are also the craftsmen of the body, putting together large molecules, including constructing proteins themselves. Proteins are at work wherever **biosynthesis** is taking place. Here, proteins assemble small units of **biochemicals** into macromolecules that are used in structuring living tissues. Proteins also facilitate and speed up chemical reactions.

Fats similarly are made of simple units, called **fatty acids**, which are connected together by a **glycerol** molecule to make what we call long chain fatty acids or fats (Figure 55).

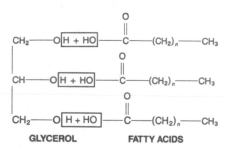

GLYCEROL   **FATTY ACIDS**

***Figure 55.** Chemical make-up of a fat. Three fatty acids are connected to a glycerol molecule.*

Some fats are soft solids at room temperatures and others are liquid. For example, consider butter, olive oil, and safflower oil when taken slightly chilled from the refrigerator. The butter is rather firm, the olive oil is transparent but thick and hardly pours. Yet the safflower oil is still very liquid. When warmed to room temperature, the safflower and olive oil become liquid and look much the same, yet the butter still

looks like butter. If we heat all three, they all look liquid and clear. They behave differently with increased temperatures because they have different amounts of saturation, specifically **hydrogen saturation**, or the number of hydrogen atoms attached to the carbon atoms. Double bonds between carbons reduce the number of positions where hydrogen can attach. Butter, olive oil, and safflower oil differ in their degree of hydrogen saturation—the number of double bonds present.

When molecules are fully saturated with hydrogen, they are smooth, and they can fit close together (Figure 56). As fat molecules get very close to each other, the fat congeals and begins to look hard. When heat is applied, the greater energy content of the molecules prevents them from fitting closely and the substance begins to be more liquid. Its weak bond, a hydrophobic bond, is disturbed.

An unsaturated bond, a double bond, causes a kink in the fat molecule (Figure 56). The unsaturated molecule cannot lie as close to the next molecule as it could if it were fully saturated. It is like trying to line up a whole bunch of sticks when one has been broken and has a kink—the sticks do not fit as tightly any more. Neither do the unsaturated fat molecules. If there is one unsaturated bond, cooling it down to refrigerator temperature will take away enough energy so that the fat will start to become solid. But if two or more bonds occur, such as in safflower oil, the refrigerator temperature is not cool enough to get it to congeal. At what temperature does safflower oil congeal? You might want to do an experiment to find out.

What about **animal fats**, such as beef fat? How saturated or unsaturated do you think beef fat is? At room temperature, beef fat is fairly solid. So beef

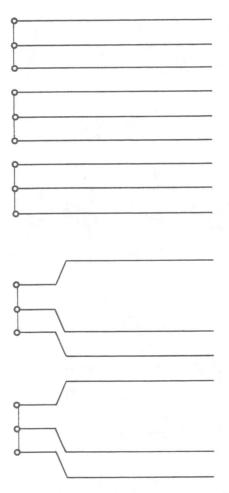

Figure 56. *Diagrammatic representation of the alignment of a saturated fat (a) and unsaturated fat (b). More saturated fats can be packed into a given space than unsaturated fats, allowing the saturated fats to congeal and become hard at high temperatures. Unsaturated fats remain liquid at low temperatures.*

fat is mostly saturated. In fish, the fat is more unsaturated, and remains liquid at room temperature. In fact we don't speak of fish fat, we speak of **fish oil**. This makes sense, because fish function with their bodies at lower water temperatures and their "fat" must not stiffen up. Cattle tend to maintain their bodies at a warm temperature at which fat is

soft, approaching a liquid state. Wolves and caribou have unsaturated fats in their feet, so that the feet do not become hard at cold temperatures.

Plants and seeds have more **unsaturated fat** than animals, so at colder temperatures their fats remain soft or liquid. Olive and sesame oils are from the tropics and are composed of saturated fats. Corn, which is a more temperate zone plant, contains more unsaturated fat.

Fats represent energy in long-term storage in the body. In general, fats yield about 9.3 kcal/g of energy when metabolized. Metabolizing 1.0 kg (2.2 lbs) of fat would yield 9,300 kcal, or over three times the daily requirement of calories for a moderately active adult.

Structure and Shape in Living Organisms

Structure is hierarchical, with each level of complexity building on the level below it. The structure of protein **DNA** and **hemoglobin** molecules illustrates four levels of biochemical hierarchy: primary, secondary, tertiary, and quaternary (Figure 57). At the primary level, covalent bonds link amino acids (carbon compounds with attached nitrogen atoms) to form a long string. At the secondary level, twisting occurs because of hydrogen (weak) bonding; in DNA, a double helix is formed. At the tertiary level, proteins fold back on themselves to form complex globular proteins. Two or more of these folded chains combine to form large globular proteins such as hemoglobin. Weak bonds are responsible for holding together the higher levels of structure within proteins. Weak bonds are also very temperature-sensitive. A temperature-induced change of weak bonds causes major disturbances to structure and resulting physiological functions.

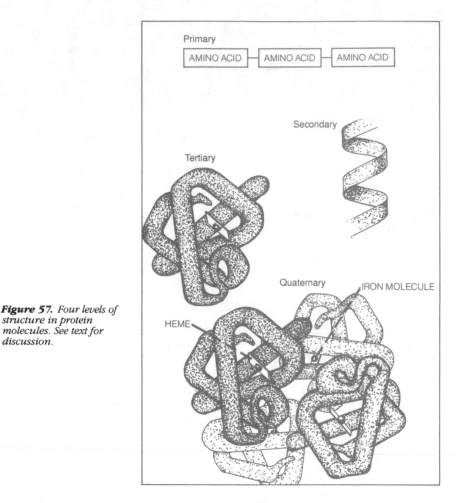

Figure 57. *Four levels of structure in protein molecules. See text for discussion.*

Another type of structure is that involved in the composition of membranes. **Membranes**, the units which separate cells in organisms, are made up largely of lipids and proteins. **Lipids** are a general group of substances that include fats. The lipids involved in structural functions are phospholipids. They are composed of three chains of **fatty acid** linked to **glycerol**, a three-carbon molecule. The first two carbons of glycerol are linked to fatty acid, while the third carbon is linked to a **phosphate** molecule. The phosphate molecule has an electric charge and is soluble in water. The fatty acid portions are **hydrophobic** and tend to cluster. As a result, lipids form **bilayer membranes** with the phosphate "heads" facing outward and the hydrophobic "tails" forming the inner portion of the membrane. Large proteins bridge one or both layers of the membrane (Figure 58).

Reaction Rates and Enzymes

Chemical reactions require energy to start (Figure 59). This energy is known as **activation energy**—the amount of energy that must be added to com-

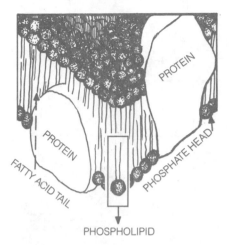

Figure 58. *Model of a cellular membrane. The lipid bilayer membrane is composed of fatty acids and proteins.*

PHOSPHOLIPID

PROTEIN

PROTEIN

FATTY ACID TAIL

PHOSPHATE HEAD

pounds to get them to react together. Striking a match to a paper provides the activation energy to start the paper burning. Some compounds require little energy to react (for example, acid and a book). Other actions, such as breaking down carbohydrates in the body, may require considerable activation energy.

Reactions can be made to proceed with a lower activation energy or at a faster rate by the addition of a catalyst (Figure 59). **Catalysts** are substances that regulate the rate of reactions but remain unchanged themselves. Since extra energy to start reactions is at a premium and costly to organisms, it is not surprising that living systems have developed biochemical catalysts. These catalysts, called **enzymes**, are globular proteins. Enzymes are effective in small amounts because they are used over and over again. Reactions can occur at lower temperatures because enzymes reduce the amount of activation energy that is necessary to start a reaction. Enzymes also speed up the rate of interactions.

Enzymes are large proteins which are folded into extremely complex shapes. The shape of the enzyme is very important for the task of making or breaking a covalent bond. By controlling enzymes, the body controls very important properties of living things. Enzymes are extremely temperature sensitive, because their shape and function depend upon weak bonds that are alterable by temperature changes.

Temperature Effects on Biochemistry

Biochemistry and the structure and function of living things are complex. We have already hinted that temperature interacts with biochemistry to interfere with the functioning of an organism. Now we will look at why cold causes such tremendous problems with living systems.

Bonds and Cold

The temperature of an object relates to how much motion or energy there is in the object. At the temperatures found on the earth's surface, most molecules have only enough energy to break and form **weak bonds**. However, there is not enough energy to break, or form readily **covalent bonds**. Covalent bonds are stable at normal temperatures. If the temperature changes slightly (e.g., from summer to winter) structure that is dependent on covalent bonds will not change very much. Wood stays as wood, and skin holds itself together as skin in summer and in winter. However, weak bonds may be drastically affected by seasonal changes in temperatures that occur with winter.

Most living activities involve making and breaking covalent bonds. Energy to do many tasks comes from breaking the covalent bonds of stored energy

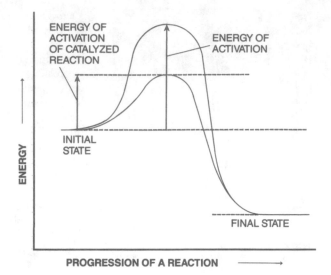

Figure 59. Graph of the progression of a chemical reaction. The reaction will not start until the required amount of activation energy has been added to the chemicals. Enzymes lower the amount of activation energy that is necessary.

sources. Building our proteins, building our fats, repairing our body tissue, sending messages throughout the body, contracting our muscles—all of these activities involve making and breaking covalent bonds at an extremely rapid rate. Yet covalent bonds are very stable.

Although relatively stable, covalent bonds are sensitive to temperature. As the temperature cools, covalent bonds become more and more stable. As they become stronger, it becomes more difficult to get energy from any of the energy storage forms. Since the rate of the chemical reaction is proportional to the number of molecules with enough energy to react, decreasing the internal temperature of an organism just a couple degrees slows chemical reactions markedly, making it more difficult to break covalent bonds, energy must be added to break the bond (Figure 60). But energy is a scarce commodity during the winter.

Weak bonds are more sensitive to temperature change than are covalent bonds. Slight decreases in temperature may break existing weak bonds or cause new ones to form. New bonds

forming under decreased temperatures may be at unusual places, causing changes in structure and function. The extreme sensitivity of living things to temperature is mainly due to the effect of temperature upon the weak bonds, which are so important to the structure and function of everything that happens in living organisms.

Shape and Cold

The shape of macromolecules is very sensitive to changes in temperature. Not only must proteins have a specific shape to work effectively, they must be able to change their shape to complete required tasks. Macromolecules must move, and they must bend. However, shape, movement, and bending are all dependent on weak bonds, which are temperature-sensitive. Altered weak bonds cause changes in shape that affect many functions, including protein synthesis, membrane permeability, structure of DNA and RNA, gene expression, and hormone receptor mechanisms.

Transport by proteins is also temperature-sensitive because of a shape-

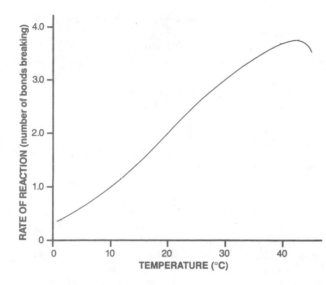

Figure 60. *Rate of chemical reaction. The rate of a chemical reaction is temperature-dependent. Dropping the temperature 10 degrees cuts the rate at which the reaction proceeds about in half, because it is more difficult to break chemical bonds at lower temperatures.*

related process. **Hemoglobin**, which carries the oxygen in our blood, consists of four subunits and a small central molecule called the **heme**, which has iron bound in it (Figure 57). As an oxygen molecule touches the heme, it causes the four subunits to shift slightly —in essence closing themselves over the oxygen, locking it in place. The four units come together in a shape that allows the hemoglobin to pick up oxygen and hold it tightly. One tiny oxygen molecule fits in the very center of a very large hemoglobin molecule.

The internal environment changes by the time the blood reaches the capillaries of an extremity. In the periphery of the body there is more acid, and in the presence of acid the hemoglobin molecule opens up. It cannot hold the oxygen any more and the oxygen moves off the hemoglobin.

The transportation process depends on two key elements of protein: first, hemoglobin has a specific **shape** which allows the oxygen molecule to come in contact in a very special way. Second, the protein is **flexible** and can exist in two different shapes, open or closed.

(There are other factors that affect the opening and the closing, but we do not need to go into them here.) The fact is that hemoglobin opens and closes, and this opening and closing is affected by temperature. If the hemoglobin molecule is too cold, even by just a couple of degrees, it is difficult for the hemoglobin molecule to open up and release its oxygen in the human body.

Cold acting on hemoglobin accounts for an interesting phenomenon that we have all observed: Someone who is cold has a red nose. Cold air cools the nose. Blood, which is filled with oxygen and therefore red, comes into the nose. Even though there is acid present, the nose is too cold for that hemoglobin molecule to open and release the oxygen. Normally, the blood would release the oxygen and turn a bluish color, leaving the nose with a normal skin color. But in the cold, the hemoglobin cannot let go. It holds onto the oxygen and stays red. Therefore, the nose appears red; that is, the nose has the color of oxygen-rich blood. The tissues of the nose are depleted of oxygen and it is easier for frostbite to occur.

Rates and Cold

Activities inside a cell within a living being are highly coordinated. Synthetic processes, such as making a hormone like insulin, involve many steps. Each step includes breaking and forming covalent bonds. Bonds are made and broken at the same rate all through the process to prevent ending up with a lot of intermediate, useless pieces. If one step goes too fast, the material is blocked up at that stage. Instead, reactions are closely linked so that, for example, each molecule is turned into an insulin molecule in the proper fashion.

This intricate coordination happens because the rates of our chemical reactions are highly controlled. Now, **rates** are very **temperature dependent**. As temperature alters, the rates at which these bonds are made and broken alter in a chaotic fashion. For most living systems, coordination occurs only within a narrow range of temperature. As the temperature gets further and further from the optimum temperature for the organism, the processes do not stay coordinated, and we find some processes going too fast and others going way too slow. Coordination will get out of sync, and chaos will result.

One of the big problems organisms face in winter is that the rates of reactions are jeopardized; in general **reactions** slow down, become irregular and uncoordinated. The rate of a reaction is proportional to the number of molecules that have enough energy to react. A decrease in temperature creates a disproportionately large decrease in the number of reactive molecules (Figure 61). When temperature is near the activation level, a decrease of a couple of degrees can nearly halt reactions because most molecules become nonreactive. Living systems, if they are going to survive changes in temperature, must compensate for changes in reaction rates.

Phase Changes
Resulting from Cold

Temperature controls the physical **phase** of chemical substances. As temperatures decrease, water goes from vapor to liquid to ice. The process is not strictly a stepped function between phases, but may be gradual. For example, over part of the temperature range,

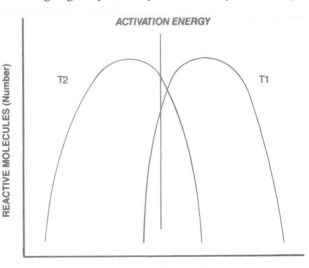

Figure 61. *Plot showing substantial decrease in the number of reactive molecules because of a small decrease in temperature. At time T1, most molecules have more energy than the amount needed to activate the reaction. At time T2, very few molecules have the energy necessary to react.*

ACTIVATION ENERGY

T2

T1

REACTIVE MOLECULES (Number)

TEMPERATURE (°C)

water changes from thin liquid to thick liquid. Phase changes with decreasing temperatures have dramatic effects on living organisms.

Water undergoes phase changes because its weak bonds are altered by temperature. **Hydrogen bonds** and another type of weak bond, called **electrostatic bond**, change so that water **viscosity** (that is, its thickness) alters. Like motor oil, the viscosity of water increases with decreasing temperature. The acidity (**pH**) and **ionization** (a measure of the number of atoms ready to bond) of water also change. These changes will affect substances dissolved in water.

The phase change from liquid water to ice has dramatic impacts in living organisms. People and other animals suffer **frostbite**, and may lose fingers, toes, legs, hands, ears, and noses due to freezing. Considerable damage is done to plants (including crops) if they freeze when they are not ready.

Dropping of temperature toward freezing is a very difficult phenomenon for living things to handle. Much of the trouble attributed to freezing comes just with the dropping of temperature. Changes in structure and functions

occur well before freezing. Additional damage happens at freezing, as ice crystals begin to form inside tissues.

Consider **ice formation** in a tissue (Figure 62). Space exists between the cells. Water forms solutions both within the cell and in the space between the cells. Inside the cells there are usually more salts and sugars, which lower the freezing point of the cell, allowing the water inside the cell to remain liquid at lower temperatures. The inside of the cell will not freeze as soon as the space between the cells. When the water between the cells reaches its freezing point, ice crystals start to form. Free water molecules clumping to the new ice crystals reduce the number of liquid water molecules between the cells.

Since water moves from high liquid concentrations to low liquid concentrations, water moves from inside the cell to the intercellular space where ice is forming. At this stage, damage occurs to the cells not from ice formation, but from **dehydration**. The cell walls can collapse, and the cell may not function any more because it is dried out. Although some of the injury to plants in winter is dehydration damage, dehydra-

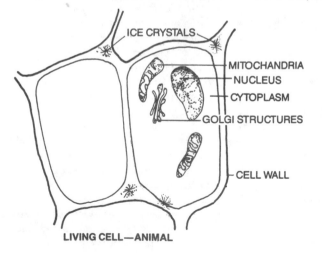

ICE CRYSTALS

MITOCHANDRIA
NUCLEUS
CYTOPLASM
GOLGI STRUCTURES

CELL WALL

LIVING CELL—ANIMAL

Figure 62.
Diagrammatic representation of ice formation in a tissue. Large ice crystals may puncture the cell membrane.

tion can also be beneficial. As water leaves the cells, the cells become drier, less likely to freeze. Dehydration is, in part, a protective mechanism for those cells that can tolerate the dehydration problem.

Sharp ice crystals forming between the cells can puncture internal cell membranes. Ice crystals forming secondarily within the cells can cause additional dehydration damage. The reason to avoid rubbing areas of **frostbite** damage as part of the treatment is that remaining ice crystals may damage membranes, or weakened membranes may be ruptured by additional pressure. All frostbitten areas should be treated extremely gently. All plants and animals whose internal temperatures go below freezing have to face the problems of how to handle the dehydration of cells and how to avoid damage from ice crystals.

Plants, incidentally, can tolerate freezing better than animals because they have both a cell wall and a cell membrane. The cell wall protects the membrane from ice crystals forming between cells. Animals only have a cell membrane. (For more information on this, see the section on *Plants* in this chapter.)

The insides of cells are mostly water. Living activities take place either dissolved in water or in fats. Both of these substances undergo drastic phase changes with decreases in temperature.

Fats congeal as they cool, causing many problems. **Membranes** are composed of fatty compounds, a **lipid bilayer**. There are many proteins in the lipid bilayer, **ion pumping** sodium to the outside and potassium to the inside of the cell. The pumps must move thousands of ions per nanosecond. Because of the speed of this process, the protein macromolecule must bend rapidly, changing shape as it moves from one side of the greasy membrane to the other side. The pump sort of slides the ions through the membrane. But what happens to fat as it gets cool? It gets thick, it gets stiff. The speed at which ion pumps work, and the speed at which they can move things through the lipid layer is very temperature-dependent. If the temperature decreases just part of a degree, the lipid bilayer begins to stiffen and the rate at which substances can move through the layer slows down.

A different type of protein functions as a **valve** in the lipid membrane. Most of the time a pore in the wall is plugged by this protein. The pore can be opened easily by the body, and as soon as it is opened, **potassium** ions can go streaming out and **sodium** ions come in. When a nerve cell needs to communicate, it opens the pore. This controlled mechanism transmits messages, and the more pores open, the faster the transmission.

As the temperature cools, the proteins in the membrane start to clump together, leaving their pores open. Just a slight decrease in temperature causes clumping in the membrane, leaving big gaps and leaky holes, so substances can start moving through these holes. The functioning of a cell is hampered when all of its contents start leaking to the outside or when some of the substances that belong on the outside start leaking to the inside. Again, this is a **temperature-dependent** process. Small changes in temperature, of a degree or less, can start causing damage.

Remember, too, that there are other membranes besides cell walls—for instance, around the **nucleus** and **chloroplasts**—and all membranes are affected by cold.

In summary, cold causes strong bonds to become too stable and causes weak bonds to break or form in disrupting manners. Bonding, in turn, affects the structure of macromolecules, influencing their ability to flex, to support, to carry information, and to facilitate chemical reactions. Rates of chemical reactions are decreased and retrieving stored energy becomes harder. Shapes of proteins change, altering many structures and functions. Phase changes alter the chemical composition of solutions within the cells and the cell membrane structure. Membrane structure breaks down, altering internal chemical balances. The formation of ice may dehydrate or mechanically damage a cell. Living organisms must find mechanisms for adapting to all these problems.

Strategies for Combatting Cold

Changes in environmental temperature seem to happen on about four different **time scales**. First is a long, slow change—for instance, that accompanying the coming or going of ice ages. Second is the seasonal change in temperature, characteristic of the coming of winter. Third is a daily change in temperature from night to day. Fourth is a very short time scale, that of seconds or minutes, as when an person falls into cold water. Living systems have adapted successfully to all four of these time scales. It will be interesting to note whether the same type of adaptation is used for each time scale or if there are different ways of adapting.

All four time scales are relevant to winter. Many of the **adaptations** that are used on a seasonal basis may have come about as evolutionary response to the coming of ice ages. These adaptations were maintained, to draw upon on a seasonal basis. The shorter time scales of daily cycles are very important in winter. The temperature regime of a calm sunny day is very different for a large animal than what it faces at night. On a calm sunny day, a large animal can actually be gaining heat from its environment and have a problem ridding itself of excess heat. At night, however, it can have a rather significant heat-loss problem. A small insect may spend the daytime on the sunny side of a tree. With the sun on it, this protected, dark-surfaced environment may be well above freezing during the day, but at night the surface temperature may fall below freezing.

The shortest time scale, of seconds or minutes, is also relevant. All living things may undergo these quick changes to some degree. For instance, consider human beings. When outdoors, our hands can get down to 15°C (59°F), yet our heart is up at 37°C (98.6°F). Consider then the different temperature regimes. The muscles in the hands are functioning at a cold temperature and the muscles in the heart at a warm temperature. The blood that cycles between them has cells and substances in it that must function at both temperatures, a temperature difference of 22°C (42.6°F). This is a tremendous change—22 degrees in just seconds. It poses a very significant short-range problem of response. So all of these different time scales are relevant to consider.

Quantitative Responses

Response to cold must address three problems: change in rates, change in structure, and resulting changes in function following structure change. Responses to cold-induced problems might fall into three categories: quantitative, qualitative, and modulation strategies. The **quantitative response** involves adding more of the same **enzyme**. This would solve only the rate problem but wouldn't address altered structure and function. There would also be a limit to how much enzyme could be added to a cell; at very low temperatures this solution would not work. However, this solution appears to be hypothetical, as currently no organisms are known that use quantitative strategies to counter cold-induced problems.

Qualitative Responses

A **qualitative response** could involve manufacturing new, better **enzymes** or improving existing enzymes. The question is whether cells should contain many different enzymes that will work over a broad range of temperature so they are always available, or should they alter their enzymes so that at each temperature they use the most efficient enzyme? Can cells do this? How long would it take to alter enzymes? Do all living things use the same method?

Consider **warm-blooded** animals (or **endotherms**), such as bear, elk, eagles, or humans. Endotherms tend to keep their body temperatures at a very steady state in warm or cold temperatures. Do they need enzymes that work over broad temperature ranges? In con-

trast, consider frogs, fish, insects—animals whose body temperatures fluctuate a bit more with the environmental temperature. What sort of solution will they find to this problem?

Living systems seem to do almost everything imaginable, but they do not fill their cells with large quantities of one enzyme. This makes sense. The space inside a cell is limited. There are many reactions taking place, involving many enzymes. It seems as though there is not enough space inside the cell to keep copies of enzymes. In the fall, many organisms start changing the types of enzymes in their cells. Cells take apart the enzymes that were used in the warm, steady summer temperatures and replace them with enzymes that will work in colder temperatures. New enzymes are synthesized. This process may take hours or days to accomplish, so it is not a process that can be used instantly to get results throughout the entire organism. It is usually a seasonal process.

There is nothing sacred about 37°C (98.6°F) in the body. The enzyme that is used at 37°C was made to be just the right enzyme to complete a reaction at

that temperature. At a lower temperature, living systems can make an enzyme with slightly different shape so that the new enzyme can carry out the reaction at almost the same rate as the original enzyme. At a colder temperature, the process will not go quite as fast, but it can be very close.

For example, consider two related **fish** species, one tropical and one polar. Their metabolic rates are about the same even though the tropical fish is in water of 30°C (86°F) and the arctic fish is in water with temperatures down to -3°C (about 27°F). Activities go on at almost the same **rate**, because the polar fish has enzymes that work at colder temperatures. There are other problems this fish has had to compensate for, but the problem of manipulating covalent bond reactions at different temperatures can often be handled by altering the shape of the enzyme involved.

Enzymes that do the same job under slightly different conditions—in different temperatures, for instance—are called **isoenzymes**. They catalyze the same reaction, but they work best under different conditions. Isoenzymes are used by living systems to compensate for other changes and conditions. For instance, when the pH varies, some isoenzymes will work under more acid conditions and others work in more basic conditions.

Modulation

Slightly altering an existing enzyme so that it works under varying conditions is another useful strategy. This avoids the problem of using energy for synthesizing and getting rid of the old enzyme. Altering an enzyme may be a quicker solution and might work for short-term response. As the temperature decreases, the enzyme needs to have a slightly different shape (or it

may have gotten out of shape and needs get back into the proper shape). Shape can be altered by changing the pH of the environment slightly, for example. As the cell cools, the body allows itself to be slightly more acidic. At a lower pH (more acidity), the same enzyme might work better, or it might secrete a small molecule that would make the necessary adjustment in shape. Alteration of the internal environment to make the enzyme work better is known as **modulation**. Modulation occurs with the transport of **oxygen** by **hemoglobin**. The adjustment of pH causes the secretion of a small molecule that causes hemoglobin to work in a normal fashion.

Of course, there is another option, and that is to do nothing at all, and let the body processes slow down. Many animals take this option by hibernating or by letting their metabolic rate vary greatly with temperature.

Protection against Freezing

Organisms need protection against freezing. Often this protection takes the form of chemical **antifreezes**. The **wood frog** found near Alberta, Canada provides an excellent example. Most frogs burrow into either the soil or a lake bottom to avoid freezing. The wood frog, however, buries itself only a few centimeters deep, where the ground often freezes. Wood frogs recovered during the winter are frozen as solid as a rock. Although the frogs look like lumps of colored ice, when warmed inside they start jumping. When placed back outside, the frogs again freeze. Rewarming brings the frogs back to an active state. The wood frogs appear to freeze solid and not suffer any injury.

The wood frog does amazing things with sugar. Wood frogs store large amounts of **glycogen** (the short-term storage form of **glucose**) in their livers until they are about to freeze. When **ice crystals** start to form in the frog's feet, in the space between the cells, the liver pours a tremendous amount of glucose into the blood and starts packing cells full of glucose. The blood level of glucose goes from about 0.00004 g/ml (grams/milliliter) up to over a thousand. (People would die at about 400 or 500.) With all this sugar in the cells, the cells are not very likely to freeze. Ice formation between the cells starts to draw water out of the cells. The water between the cells freezes, but water trapped inside is too saturated with sugar to freeze: the inside of the cell is protected.

When the frog thaws out, it transports the glucose back out of the cells to the liver, where it is stored as glycogen and later used for other processes. If it is needed again as freeze protection, it gets pumped back out to the cells. In this way, the wood frog, unlike most frogs, actually can let its body temperature drop below freezing. It keeps cells from freezing by packing them with sugar.

Some plants use a similar process. As cool weather comes on, simple sugars or alcohols are produced and transported into leaves or stems, the parts of the plant that need protection from freezing. This lowers the freezing point. It is essentially putting an **antifreeze** into the water so that it will not freeze. A common antifreeze made by plants is **glycerol**. Glycerol is also used by some insects and probably some fish.

Chemical antifreezes can protect living things from freezing. Antifreezes apparently work by preventing water molecules from getting close together. If water molecules cannot get close, they cannot freeze at a certain temperature; it must get much colder in order for them to freeze. Antifreezes work in

proportion to their concentration—the more antifreeze, the lower the temperature before freezing. To get a significant protective effect, cells must contain a lot of antifreeze. High concentrations do not leave room for other active processes to go on; thus the organism must become dormant. Active organisms cannot use antifreeze to protect from low temperature.

An interesting solution to the antifreeze problem occurs in some arctic fish. They have evolved a protein, called a **glycoprotein**, which functions like an antifreeze but at a much lower concentration. Glycoproteins work somewhat differently than other antifreezes. Glycoproteins allow the freezing process to begin. Tiny **ice crystals** form, but the glycoprotein interrupts the growth of the ice crystal into a big crystal, thus preventing damage. We will classify glycoprotein for our purposes as an antifreeze, even though it merely inhibits the growth of larger ice crystals. Thus we have two types of antifreezes: glycoproteins that work in very small concentrations, and sugars and alcohols that work at much higher concentrations.

Deep-sea polar fish function in below-freezing waters, where other fish would normally freeze, but use no antifreeze to protect themselves. If these fish are brought to the surface, they freeze immediately. These fish make use of **supercooling**: internal water is cooled below freezing but does not freeze until something triggers **ice crystal formation**. The water molecules will freeze if they are disturbed or jostled a certain amount. Freezing can be caused by a **ice nucleation center**, a speck of dust, or the presence of some particle for crystals to form around. If no nucleation centers or crystals of other types are present, freezing will not start until the internal water is quite cold—then freezing starts spontaneously. An organism that can isolate itself from movement and rid itself of disturbing crystals can use supercooling to avoid freezing. Only recently has supercooling been discovered in mammals. Arctic ground squirrels can allow their body core temperatures to drop to -2.9°C (26.8°F) to avoid freezing. The squirrels are capable of spontaneous arousal from these low core temperatures. No evidence has been discovered to indicate the presence of antifreeze molecules in their bodies.

Supercooling is used by many plants and insects (see the sections on plants and insects in this chapter). In fact, many of the plants and insects that tolerate the greatest amount of freezing at the lowest temperatures use a combination of defenses.

Consider the **goldenrod insect gall**. This is caused by **gall moths** (*Gnorimoschema gallaesolidaginis*) or flies (*Eurosta solidaginia*). The gall is a thickening of the goldenrod caused by the irritation from the insect. In the fall, as freezing begins, the insect is protected inside the gall from the first light freezes, which do not penetrate deeply. The insect is slightly protected from colder freezes by another process. As the goldenrod material itself begins to freeze, it gives off some heat during the freezing process. The heat liberated by the gall as it freezes will keep the insect above freezing for up to about twelve hours—extra hours that allow the insect to make it through to the warmer morning. At that time the metabolic processes of the insect are turned on, so they start to make **antifreeze alcohols** in a very rapid fashion. The alcohol protects the insect down to perhaps -15°C (5°F). Below that, the insect may depend upon supercooling to prevent irreparable damage.

Stored **fats** can also freeze in the winter or simply stiffen up. Consider the feet of long-legged herbivorous mammals such as the moose. Moose will often stand inactive with their feet in contact with the very cold ground. To compensate for the cold, they have more **unsaturated** fat in their feet. In fact, we call it **neatsfoot** oil. The oil in the hooves is a highly unsaturated fat that will stay liquid at cooler temperatures. The feet of wolves and huskies also contain concentrations of unsaturated fats.

Biochemistry is extremely sensitive to decreasing temperatures and damage may result quickly. In short, cold causes many different problems, but organisms have evolved mechanisms for responding. Biochemical defensive mechanisms operate at the molecular, cellular, and tissue level. Different combinations occur in different organisms. It is a safe bet that scientists have not yet discovered all the mechanisms nor all the combinations. Biochemical adaptations promise a rich field for future research.

SUGGESTED READINGS

Barnes, B.M. 1989. Freeze avoidance in a mammal: body temperatures below 0°C in an arctic hibernator. Science, 244:1593-1595.

Blank, J.L., and C. Des Jardins. 1985. Metabolic and reproductive strategies in the cold. Pp. 373-382, *in* Living in the Cold: Physiological and Biochemical Adaptations (H.C. Heller, X.J. Musacchia, and L.C.H. Wang, eds.). Proc. Seventh Internat. Symp. Natural Mammal Hibernation. Fallen Leaf Lake, California, October 6 - 11, 1985. Elesevier, New York.

Campbell, G.S. 1977. An Introduction to Environmental Biophysics. Springer Verlag, New York.

Carey, C., and R.L. Marsh. 1981. Shivering finches. Nat. Hist., 90(10):58-63.

DeVries, A.L. 1980. Biological antifreezes and survival in freezing environments. Chapter 33, *in* Animals and Environmental Fitness (R. Gilles, ed.). Pergamon Press, New York.

Heller, H.C., X.J. Musacchia, and L.C.H. Wang (eds.). 1985. Living in the Cold: Physiological and Biochemical Adaptations. Proc. Seventh Internat. Symp. Natural Mammal Hibernation. Fallen Leaf Lake, California, October 6 - 11, 1985. Elesevier, New York.

Hochachka, P., and G. Somero. 1973. Strategies of biochemical adaptation. W. B. Saunders Co., Philadephia.

Storey, K.B. 1985. Freeze tolerance in vertebrates: biochemical adaptation of terrestrially hibernating frogs. Pp. 131-138, *in* Living in the Cold: Physiological and Biochemical Adaptations (H.C. Heller, X.J. Musacchia, and L.C.H. Wang, eds.). Proc. Seventh Internat. Symp. Natural Mammal Hibernation. Fallen Leaf Lake, California, October 6 - 11, 1985. Elesevier, New York.

PHYSIOLOGICAL RESPONSES

The science of physiology entails the study of how cells, organs, and organisms function. As such, physiology bridges the gap between the biochemical and behavioral levels of biological functioning. In this section, we look at physiological functions of organisms as they cope with winter.

Keeping Warm

For many organisms, keeping warm is central to existence. Central to the ability to stay warm is the ability to produce heat. Two types of heat production are important to the body: acute (short-term) and chronic (long-term). The first type, **acute heat production**, answers the sudden demand for increased heat, in situations such as a

sudden cold storm in the summer, or an individual falling into cold water; also during winter an organism may experience a short-term demand for more warmth. Several mechanisms exist for the rapid production of heat. First, more food may be eaten, since digestion produces heat. Sugar provides quick energy and heat, while fats take longer to warm the body. (If you awaken cold during a winter camping trip, eat some candy for quick warmth.) Usually in the cold there is a stimulus to increase the appetite and eat more food. Second, heat may be produced by muscular activity, either voluntary exercise or involuntary shivering. Finally, heat production may occur in nonmuscular tissue through a process called **nonshivering thermogenesis** (**NTG**). Nonmuscular tissues that produce heat include digestive tissue and the liver.

The body produces heat when shivering breaks down adenosine triphosphate (ATP) bonds, releasing energy. Shivering is a good method of generating heat but it does deplete body energy. Nonshivering thermogenesis produces heat through repetitive, or futile, cycles. Muscle proteins contract but slide over each other without grabbing. No useful contraction takes place, but heat is released. In the cycle, glucose molecules are broken and put back together again to produce heat. Heat is produced because two enzymes, the enzyme for splitting glucose and the enzyme for forming it, are present at the same time in the same cell. Normally this is not the case; usually the enzymes are separated so that futile cycles do not happen. Another futile cycle occurs when cell membranes leak sodium to the outside of the cell and allow potassium to leak in. The ion pump can run at a great rate, moving the ions to their proper position, but in so doing ATPs are used to produce heat.

To produce heat quickly, extra effort is needed from muscles or nonmuscular tissues, and sometimes they must work beyond their normal limits. Acute heat production is accomplished by stress reactions within the body. Under stress, the nervous system stimulates the adrenal glands to release more **epinephrine** and cortisol. **Cortisol** is a hormone that mobilizes fuel into the bloodstream, and stops other fuel uses such as immune surveillance or protein synthesis. Epinephrine stimulates the **mitochondria** (organelles in the cells active in energy transfer during metabolism) and the muscles to work close to their absolute capacity.

Limits to heat production do exist. The amount of heat that can be produced at any one time is determined by the number of "furnaces" in the body, and their condition. The furnaces of the body are the mitochondria, where fuel, such as fats, proteins, or carbohydrates, is turned into energy in the form of ATP and heat. The mitochondria are the furnaces for shivering and nonshivering thermogenesis. There is a limited number of mitochondria and they can only operate so fast. With repeated stimulus, the numbers of mitochondria and their rate of work can also be increased, but for quick heat production, their limits are set.

Mitochondria are not just producing heat, but also produce ATP, an energy form used for most body functions. Production of ATP ceases when concentrations of ATP in the cell are high. Heat production also ceases when the production of ATP stops. To continue heat production, the body must dispose of the extra ATP. Shivering helps, by removing ATP.

There is also a limit to the fuel supply. In the body of an average human, there are approximately 135,000 kcal of fat, 24,000 kcal of protein, and only about 1,200 kcal of carbohydrates. Short-term heating of the body is limited by the amount of carbohydrate fuel available to the mitochondria. When that is used up, production in mitochondria stops. This is true for either acute or chronic responses, but the difference is the rate at which carbohydrate will get used up in these two cases.

If we exercise extremely hard, we get exhausted much more quickly than if we work at an easier pace. At the slower pace, we can sometimes go and go and go, eventually burning a lot of calories. We cannot go at the maximum rate as long, and thus we don't use as many calories at the maximum rate. As long as mitochondria are working at less than 60 percent of their capacity, they burn a relatively large amount of fat and a small amount of carbohydrate. At greater than 60 percent of their capacity, mitochondria burn more and more carbohydrate in relation to the fat metabolized. It is this mixture that determines how long the mitochondria can function at any given rate. At high rates, the body carbohydrate reserve is depleted more quickly than it can be replenished. Soon heat production will start to fall. In outdoor situations, this is when a person starts to become hypothermic.

There are still other limits on acute heat production. The amount of oxygen that can be transported by the blood to the muscles limits activity rates. Muscle activity, although it generates more heat, may not be efficient if movement through cold air loses more heat than the muscles can generate.

Long-term or **chronic heat production** also occurs in organisms. Animals acclimating to colder temperatures and people exposed to repeated cold stress increase the number of mitochondria, which increases the capacity to burn fat while conserving carbohydrates. Besides increasing the number of mitochondria, there is an increase in appetite to bring in more food reserves. Overall, the nonshivering heat-producing capacity of the body increases and sustains longer periods of heat production.

Another interesting mechanism for increasing the heat production by mitochondria bypasses the formation of ATP. This chemical reaction occurs in **brown adipose tissue** (**BAT**), an amazing tissue whose specialty is to produce heat. BAT is found in almost all mammals in at least one stage of their life. It is usually present during infancy, when muscular activity has not developed and newborns need some way to produce heat. In many mammals, including humans, BAT is lost soon after birth, as soon as other means of heat production become functional. In animals that hibernate, BAT remains in the body, and is one of the main tissues used during arousal from hibernation.

BAT gets its name from the high concentration of mitochondria in the cells and the large amount of fat present as fuel for the mitochondrial furnaces; the fat molecules of BAT are stored in tiny globules that are easily processed rather than in white storage fat, which is formed in less accessible large globules. When white fat is metabolized normally, it has to be taken from the fat cells and shipped to the liver, where the fatty acids can be burned. In BAT, there are large concentrations of mitochondria with special proteins that short circuit the production of ATP. The proteins essentially allow a hydrogen ion to escape the mitochondria rather than binding it in the normal production of ATP. Thus, the animals burn

brown fat to produce heat, not ATP.

Several characteristics make BAT an ideal tissue for heat generation. It has an excellent blood supply, and is located in strategic locations—usually in the thorax and neck—where heat produced by BAT specifically heats key organs, such as the heart and brain. BAT is also found around the kidneys. BAT accounts for 20 to 80 percent of nonshivering heat production.

Small animals—those of less than ten kilograms—mainly depend upon nonshivering thermogenesis for warmth and BAT for heat production. This size limit appears to apply to any stage of life, and newborn babies of most mammal species have and utilize BAT. The BAT is lost as the animal increases in size.

Small **goldfinches** provide a model demonstrating the dynamics of heat production. A summer-caught goldfinch put into very cold conditions of perhaps -60°C (-76°F) can produce enough heat to maintain its body temperature for a short period of time, perhaps minutes. Soon the body temperature begins to fall and the bird must be removed from the test situation. A winter-captured bird under the same temperature conditions can keep itself warm for several hours. The difference results from the number of mitochondria present and the amount of fat that is being burned in relation to carbohydrates. The summer-caught bird runs out of its carbohydrate stores very quickly and it does not have enough enzymes to burn fat at a great rate. The winter-caught bird has changed its enzyme composition and is able to break down fat at a greater rate. It has more mitochondria, so presumably it is burning at less than 60 percent of its capacity and can burn much more fat in relation to its carbohydrates. The winter-caught bird has stored more fat in its body, so that it can run its mitochondria at a fast rate for several hours. This type of acclimation allows these daytime feeders to survive through the winter nights when they are not able to forage for food.

The goldfinch uses many other strategies to combat winter. It increases the number of feathers covering its body by almost double as winter approaches. During winter, it stays in protective roosts and forages for shorter periods of time. This behavior provides about a 30 percent savings in energy. A goldfinch stores an extra 2 g (1/14th oz) of fat during the winter. At night, its body temperature may drop, producing a 20 percent savings in metabolic costs. It also has the capacity to increase its heat production up to about five times normal and to sustain that production for several hours. In the winter, the goldfinch may shiver all night long.

Heat Production in Humans

Humans are mammals, with many of the same capacities just outlined. We do lose our BAT at a very early age, but we still posses the other attributes for heat production. It is interesting that when we start to become hypothermic —when our heat production is almost zero, though we still have plenty of fat in our bodies, we are still working within our oxygen capacities and have the ability to breathe harder or exercise more—we still get cold. If we have even a small piece of chocolate (or a Snickers bar), that process can be readily reversed.

Hypothermic victims (excluding cases caused by immersion in cold water) have depleted their carbohydrates, but still have fat reserves available. To use fat reserves, carbohydrates must be added to the system and chocolate seems to do wonders. Chocolate has both sugar and a **theophylline** chemical substance called **theobromine** that helps stimulate the mitochondria as well as the fuel delivery to the mitochondria. (Chocolate has only small amounts of fat in it, which may be a slight disadvantage, but it tastes good besides working.) Hot tea with a fair amount of honey also contains sugar and theophylline. For those on macrobiotic diets, we suggest amazaki, a carbohydrate made from rice.

Heat production is increased by acute methods and by more chronic changes in humans. Acute methods include a complex of reactions. For example, indirect changes occur because the effects of cold will increase appetite. The more food that is eaten, the more heat will be produced by means of digestion. A more direct effect comes from the cold center of the brain; the **hypothalamus** increases shivering and the sympathetic **adrenal system** stimulates nonshivering heat production. Nonshivering thermogenesis is mediated by the hormones **epinephrine**, **norepinephrine**, and **cortisone**. These hormones mobilize fuel by breaking down fat and glycogen stores. More fuel is sent to the cells that need it. The hormones also induce constriction of peripheral blood vessels, lowering the skin temperature and reducing heat loss from the extremities. Hormones increase the activity of BAT and the **thyroid adrenal system** is stimulated. The thyroid hormone seems to act as an amplifier of active hormones. The more active the thyroid, the stronger the body's response to norepinephrine and epinephrine in terms of increased heat production.

Chronic changes mostly involve an increase in nonshivering thermogenesis. Less shivering occurs at low temperatures because heat production is taken over by nonmuscular tissue. On a longterm basis, there is an increase in overall peak metabolic rates, and better regulation of blood flow in the body.

Winter Dormancy

Another important strategy for energy conservation during winter is letting the body temperature drop. This drop saves energy, which is in short supply during the winter. Body temperatures drop during periods of dormancy and a continuum of dormancy to escape the hardships of winter exists. Terminology has often been used in conflicting manners when referring to different periods of dormancy. Some animals may be dormant for short periods (**torpor**); other animals may be dormant for long periods, sometimes approaching nine months (often called **hibernation**). We often use the word hibernation in its broadest sense to refer to periods of dormancy, no matter what the length, but will refer to short periods (such as days) as torpor. Dormancy conserves energy through various processes, including reductions in body temperatures, breathing rate, and basal metabolic rate.

Body size determines the fuel-storage capacity in terms of fat and size determines the heating costs—the cost of maintaining body temperature. Consider hibernators from small to large size. In the smallest hibernators, including the jumping mouse (*Zapus*) and the bats, body temperatures are lowered to near freezing. They have relatively long periods of torpor with short periods of awakening (about one hour). Their arousal is timed to coincide with the availability of green plants. In moderate-sized mammals, such as marmots, temperatures are lowered, but not quite as much. They awake more often and remain awake for longer time periods, about a day. In the spring, marmots seem to gamble. They come out of hi-

bernation at a specific time each year, trusting that food will be available. If spring is late, marmots must rely on stored fats until green plants arrive. In the largest hibernators, the bears, body temperatures are lowered only slightly. During the winter they may awaken for periods of several days, but they do not eat any food until spring.

The annual budget of energy differs for a hibernator and a nonhibernator (Figure 63). For the ground squirrel, a hibernator, energy expenditure is high during spring, which is the time of peak reproduction activity. In summer, expenditures begin to fall off and available food provides abundant energy. Toward fall, the extra food is stored as fat for hibernation. Winter is a period of reduced food availability and yet, for a mammal, it can be a period of high energy expenditure due to the cost of keeping warm. The ground squirrel beats these energy costs by hibernating. The lowered body temperature reduces metabolism to a minimum and burns few calories. The thirteen-lined ground squirrel decreases its energy expenditure to 1/50th of its normal costs. The Richardson ground squirrel decreases its costs to about 1/90th. Evaporative water losses are decreased to about 1/80th. Lower energy expenditures from hibernation do not exceed the available food reserves. For nonhibernating mammals, the cost of maintenance may exceed available food reserves and they may go into energy deficit.

Energy savings from hibernation are tremendous. Savings are so great that energy is rarely a limiting factor. Often when larger hibernators are aroused in the spring, they have enough energy left so that they do not have to eat for extended periods of days after arousal.

Timing of the hibernation cycle is critical, and for mammals it appears to

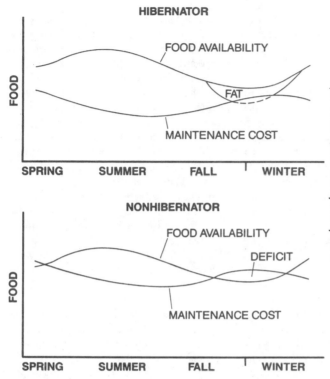

Figure 63. *Animal budget of available food and maintenance costs. The upper graph is for a hibernator and the lower graph for a non-hibernator. Hibernators store extra food from summer as fat. Most years they do not use all their fat reserves because they are in hibernation. Nonhibernators also store food as fat, but in most winters they must use up much of the fat to maintain their bodies.*

be a two-level system. At the first level, there is an internal cycle completely separate from environmental cues. Animals removed from environmental cues continue to have cycles of reproduction, storage, and hibernation. However, these cycles will not be timed on a yearly basis. They tend to drift and become spread over a much longer period of time. The internal cycle provides a gross timing mechanism.

The second level, that of fine-tuning the timing, is accomplished by synchronization with environmental clues. Some years fall may arrive earlier or later than usual. The length of the day is a constant for a given date each fall and signals when to start preparations for winter. Temperature changes later in the fall complete the fine tuning, which is exquisite. In the spring, the finely tuned timing allows individuals

who live on north slopes to come out of hibernation at different times than those that live on south slopes, or those that live under forest conditions to come out at different times than those in meadows or the alpine. Internal differences in the cycles allow for differences in timing related to age, sex, and different physiological states. Males tend to go into hibernation earlier than females; adults usually go into hibernation earlier than juveniles. These patterns also hold for emergence from hibernation; adults and males usually come out earlier than the females.

All animals seem to arouse during hibernation. Sometimes this occurs because the environment gets too cold, but animals simply do not seem to be able to "sleep" all winter without waking up. During **arousal**, metabolic rates usually rise above normal. Animals often move, become alert and functional before going back into hibernation. Animals fit into one of two categories during arousal: feeders and nonfeeders. Feeders have cached food before hibernating and eat when aroused. But even nonfeeders arouse themselves periodically, once a day to once a week depending on size. Larger hibernators, such as bears, arouse less frequently and may not feed at all. The cost of arousal is the main energy expenditure during winter. Periodic arousal accounts for up to 90 percent of the energy use.

Proteins appear to be one of the limiting factors during hibernation because of a complex set of chemical interactions. Unlike lipids, proteins are not stored in the body. Animals go into hibernation with extra fat, but they do not have extra protein or the other major body fuel, carbohydrates. Fats supply about 90 percent of the energy used during hibernation, whereas burning proteins supplies only 10 percent. Proteins, fats, and carbohydrates have different uses in the body. To some extent, the body can convert one compound into the other. Fats can be made out of protein and sugars, but it is not easy to turn fats back into sugars. Significantly, the main fuel for the brain is glucose, and the glucose in the body and during hibernation comes from proteins. There are small glucose needs throughout the body during hibernation, but the major use is for the brain. If the brain were to function at normal rates during hibernation, the glucose would need to be metabolized from protein, which would mean breaking down the muscle tissue to a great extent, and body muscle degeneration must be avoided.

But there is another fuel that the brain can use: chemical compounds called **ketones**. Ketones are made from

fat in the liver. During hibernation, brain metabolism shifts to ketone fuels in most hibernators. Ketones do not metabolize as cleanly as pure glucose and the resulting byproducts are not healthy. Elevated ketone levels may be one of the triggers causing animals to arouse. When they are aroused, the body can change excess ketones into glucose, which it does not do during hibernation.

The disposal of wastes, specifically urine, could be another problem during hibernation. One of the major wastes produced by the kidneys is **ammonia**. When proteins are metabolized, ammonia and bicarbonate are released as byproducts. Both of these, especially the ammonia, are toxic chemicals. Normally the ammonia and bicarbonate are combined by the liver into a substance called urea, which is less toxic. The urea is excreted into the kidneys for urination.

The formation of urea during hibernation would be a problem because urea requires water, and the loss of water would cause dehydration. Hibernators cycle urea to prevent its buildup. During hibernation urea is produced in the liver, released into the blood, and excreted in the saliva, which the animals swallow. When the urea reaches the intestine, bacteria convert it back into bicarbonate and ammonia. Other bacteria convert the ammonia into protein. The ammonia is completely recycled. The bacteria, as a byproduct, produce hydrogen ions, which form acids. The acid combines with the bicarbonate to produce carbon dioxide gas and water. The water is of course reabsorbed, and the carbon dioxide accumulates in the blood or may be passed from the body.

Water loss during hibernation is also important. Several mechanisms help maintain water balance. The low metabolic rate results in less breathing and thus less water loss through the lungs. Animals can further decrease evaporative water loss by curling into a ball and breathing through their fur, which traps some of the moisture and humidifies the air coming into the lungs.

Sufficient water for the needs of the animal through the winter is provided by metabolizing a mixture of fat and protein to supply water. In essence, just as the calories for hibernation are stored in fat and protein, so is the water. Water is stored in the chemical bonds of fat molecules and as free water surrounding the protein. Fats and proteins are burned in a ratio that liberates enough water to meet needs during hibernation. Urea recycling allows the kidneys to almost shut down, so there is low urine loss.

Delicate control exists over the hibernation process. The bodies of mammals do not freeze; body temperature is stabilized at some point. For Arctic ground squirrels (who supercool), body temperature is just below freezing; for other ground squirrels, just above freezing; for marmots, it is quite a bit above freezing; and for bears, only slightly below normal body temperature. Whatever the appropriate temperature, it is a closely regulated temperature. If the animal is too cold, it will produce a little more heat, and if it gets too warm, metabolism decreases. Most importantly, if the animal is threatened with freezing, it will arouse itself.

There are many questions about the control of hibernation that scientist haven't yet answered. How do animals go into hibernation? How do they shut down their furnaces and cool off to hibernate? How do they maintain their body temperature while they are hibernating, while their furnaces are shut down? How do they arouse themselves

periodically? And finally, how do they arouse themselves at the right time and become active in the spring?

Part of the answer seems to lie within the functioning of the body furnace itself. The furnace is controlled by breathing. It seems that before animals go into hibernation or as they are going

into hibernation, the breathing rate is decreased to as low as a few beats per minute. Breathing appears to be controlled by small protein hormones found in the brains of hibernating animals. The ratio of two peptide hormones controls the use of food and possibly the breathing rate as well. When the ratio increases, food metabolism and breathing decrease. Another hormone, called **hibernation induction trigger** (**HIT**), has been found in the brains of hibernators. HIT causes the pulse to drop about 50 percent, as well decreasing the appetite and body temperature, causing the animal to enter hibernation.

As breathing slows, the blood becomes more acidic. Carbon dioxide in the blood shifts the pH toward a more acid position. As the blood becomes more acidic, the heat-producing tissues, especially the BAT, decrease their activity. Many things are affected by the change in pH, including an enzyme called **phosphofructokinase** (**PFK**). PFK controls the release of glycogen, the carbohydrate storage form that is used to power shivering. PFK is also important in the arousal process. As the pH drops, PFK breaks into pieces. Before an animal wakes, its breathing increases. As the breathing rate increases, carbon dioxide is exhaled from the lungs, taking with it hydrogen ions that reduce the acidity of the blood. With a pH approaching normal, PFK reassembles and activates shivering. This process takes about one hour to activate or deactivate the enzyme.

Arousal is a controlled, sequential process. During rewarming the face is warmed first, which gets the nervous system going. Then the rear of the body is warmed. Initially, the animals depend on their BAT and probably their ion pumps to produce heat. In the latter stages of warming there is an act of shivering by the muscles.

In summary, let's look at the biggest hibernator, the **bear**. Confusion exists about hibernation in bears. We all grew up "knowing" about hibernation of bears, but when scientists started actually measuring the body temperature of bears, they were quite surprised. Measuring the body temperature of a hibernating bear was an interesting process in itself, involving sneaking into a bear den and putting a thermometer in the rectum of a bear, and then finding out that the hibernating bear was really not so sound asleep. A number of scientists were chased out of dens as they learned that bears hibernate at what seems to be a relatively shallow level, and keep their body temperatures quite warm, around 30°C (86°F).

The quick arousal and high body temperatures suggest the question: do bears hibernate or are they just sort of resting in some other physiological state? What is going on with the bear during the winter? After about ten years

of study, there is quite a bit known about the physiological state of black bears in the winter. It seems clear that what goes on deserves to be called hibernation. Bears may go three to seven months without ingesting any food or any water. Their body temperature will range from 30 (86°F)1°C to 35°C (95°F), and they metabolize 4,000 kcal each day. They don't urinate or defecate.

One of the keys to this period of fasting is that bears are able to burn mostly fat for fuel and save their protein supplies. Small rodents, on the other hand, must burn 10 percent of their protein. In bears, glycerol from fat is turned into glycogen, which can be used by the brain. The small amount of protein that does get converted to glucose leaves some nitrogen wastes in the form of ammonia, which are recycled by the process mentioned earlier. A bear goes through the period of hibernation using mostly stored fat for fuel and comes out of hibernation with about the same amount of lean body mass (that is, the same amount of muscle) as it had when it entered hibernation. During hibernation, it only exchanged oxygen, carbon dioxide, water, and heat with its environment. It has ingested no food or water. There has been no urine and no feces.

Certainly a period of dormancy that is this efficient qualifies as hibernation. The only difference between the bear and the small rodents is that the body size causes the bear to have a higher body temperature during hibernation. Its pattern of hibernation certainly includes keeping energy losses to a minimum for a period when energy is scarce; in fact the bear takes in no energy at all during that period. This is hibernation.

SUGGESTED READINGS

Barnes, B.M. 1989. Freeze avoidance in a mammal: body temperatures below 0°C in an Arctic hibernator. Science, 244:1593-1595.

Carey, C., and R.L. Marsh. 1981. Shivering finches. Nat. Hist., 90(10):58-63.

Chaffee, R.R., and T.C. Robert. 1971. Temperature acclimation in birds and mammals. Ann. Rev. Physiol., 33:155-202.

Dawson, W.R., and C. Carey. 1976. Seasonal acclimatization to temperature in Cardueline finches. I. Insulative and metabolic adjustments. J. Comp. Physiol., 112:317-333.

Evans, K.E., and A.N. Moen. 1975. Thermal exchange between sharp-tailed grouse (*Pedioecetes phasianellus*) and their winter environment. Condor, 77:160-168.

French, A.R. 1988. The patterns of mammalian hibernation. Amer. Scientist, 76(6):568-575.

Irving, L. 1964. Terrestrial animals in cold: birds and mammals. *In* Adaptation to the Environment, Handbook of Physiology, Sec. 4.361 (D. B. Dill, ed.). Amer. Physiol. Soc., Washington.

Kenagy, G.J. 1985. Strategies and mechanisms for timing of reproduction and hibernation in ground squirrels. Pp. 383-392, *in* Living in the Cold: Physiological and Biochemical Adaptations (H.C. Heller, X.J. Musacchia, and L.C.H. Wang, eds.). Proc. Seventh Internat. Symp. Natural Mammal Hibernation. Fallen Leaf Lake, California, October 6 - 11, 1985. Elesevier, New York.

McNab, B.K. 1970. Body weight and the energetics of temperature regulation. J. Exp. Biol., 53:329-348.

Mitchell, D. 1974. Physical basis of thermoregulation. Pp. 1-32, *in* Environmental Physiology (D. Robertshaw, ed.). MTP Internat. Review Science,

Physiol. Ser. One, Vol. 7. Butterworth, London; University Press, Baltimore.

Pulliainen, E. 1973. Winter ecology of the red squirrel (*Sciuris vulgaris*) in northeastern Lapland. Ann. Zool. Fennici, 10:487-494.

Rogers, L. 1981. A bear in its lair. Nat. Hist, 90(10):64-70.

Roseman, M., P. Morrison, and P. Feist. 1975. Seasonal changes in the metabolic capacity of red-backed voles. Physiol. Zool., 48:303-310.

Schmidt-Nielsen, K. 1981. Countercurrent systems in animals. Scientific American, 244(10):118-129.

Scholander, P.F., R. Hock, V. Walters, and L. Irving. 1950. Adaptation to cold in arctic and tropical mammals and birds in relation to body temperature, insulation and basal metabolic rate. Biol. Bull., 99:259-271.

Sealander, J.A. 1952. Behavior of small mammals in the cold. Ecology, 33:63-71.

Underwood, L.S. 1979. Comparative Mechanisms of Cold Adaptation. Academic Press, Orlando, Florida.

Wang, L.C.H., and J.W. Hudson. 1978. Strategies in Cold, Natural Torpidity and Thermogenesis. Academic Press, Orlando, Florida.

Webster, A.J.F. 1974. Physiological effects of cold exposure. Pp. 33-69, *in* Environmental Physiology (D. Robertshaw, ed.). MTP Internat. Review Science, Physiol. Ser. One, Vol. 7. Butterworth, London; University Press, Baltimore.

Webster, A.J.F. 1974. Adaptation to cold. Pp. 71-106, *in* Environmental Physiology (D. Robertshaw, ed.). MTP Internat. Review Science, Physiol. Ser. One, Vol. 7. Butterworth, London; University Press, Baltimore.

Wunder, B.A. 1984. Strategies for, and environmental cueing mechanisms of, seasonal changes in thermoregulatory parameters of small mammals. Pp. 165-172, *in* Winter Ecology of Small Mammals (J.F. Merritt, ed.). Carnegie Museum of Nat. Hist. Spec. Publ. No. 10, Pittsburgh.

ENERGY AND MASS BALANCE

One of our basic understandings about **energy** is that it neither suddenly appears nor disappears; if we start with a certain amount of energy and keep track of it, we can account for it all. The energy may change forms but it will still be present in the system. Einstein showed us that energy relates to mass (the weight of a material) through the equation $E = MC^2$. Energy and mass, however, are not exactly the same, and an accounting of a biological system must keep track of both energy and mass.

The totality of this energy must be partitioned among critical life functions within each organism: maintenance, activity, growth, storage, and reproduction (Figure 64). **Maintenance** of the body has priority over other uses of energy. When food is scarce, the other vital processes may receive little to no energy. The principle **activity** of an organism, of course, is to gather more energy, and use of energy for activity has nearly the priority level relegated to maintenance. Sometimes, as will be apparent in later sections, it is more energy efficient not to try to gather more energy and, instead, to avoid all activ-

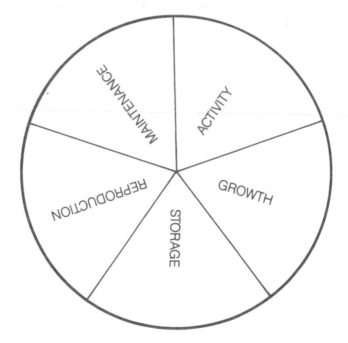

Figure 64. *The pie of life. Available energy is divided among five critical life functions and often the slices are not equal.*

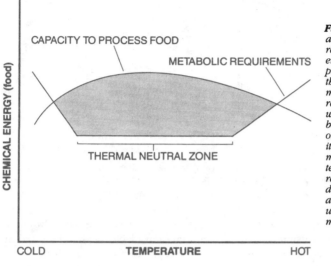

Figure 65. *Energy availability and body requirements. Chemical energy is provided by processing food. In the thermal neutral zone, metabolic requirements remain the same, but when temperatures become cold or hot, the organism must increase its use of food to maintain body temperature. The shaded region is the discretionary energy available for biological uses other than maintenance.*

ity. When available, energy is allocated to **growth** and development processes, and remaining energy is placed in **storage** or devoted to **reproduction**.

The relationship between available **chemical energy** (stored as food) and the requirements of the body can be shown graphically in reference to temperature (Figure 65). **Metabolism** is the process of chemical burning of food or stored energy for use by the body, and the basic metabolic requirement is enough energy to keep an organism functioning at a minimum level. **Discretionary energy** is that energy available after metabolic needs have been met. It represents the difference between the capacity to process available food and the amount of energy needed to keep the body temperature within an acceptable range. Discretionary energy can be used for activity, growth, storage, or reproduction. At colder temperatures, the amount of discretionary energy is limited. At extremely cold temperatures, energy requirements for basic metabolic needs exceed the ability to process food, and

energy costs must be made up by taking energy from storage in the body.

Mass Balance

In the context of balancing the energy checkbook of an organism, food taken into the body must equal what leaves or is stored in the body because energy neither increases nor disappears. The chemical energy from food can be stored in the body as fat, protein, or carbohydrates, it can be excreted in feces and urine, or it can be converted to other forms of energy as it does work or is burned to produced heat (Figure 66). The equation for this balance is: food taken in equals that which leaves the body plus that which is stored. This balance, over time, is always zero. If more food is eaten, then there is more available to be stored as fat, burned metabolically, or excreted. If there is less food taken in, something on the other side of the equation must be decreased. There will either be less fat stored or less energy metabolized or less waste excreted.

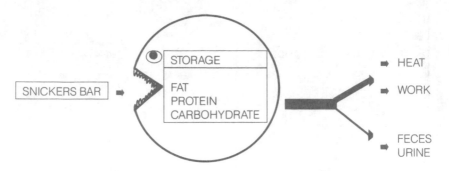

Figure 66. *The chemical budget of a generic organism. Food going in must equal food stored, converted to heat, used for work, and excreted as feces and urine.*

The equation below shows the budget of food for an organism; we call this the **mass budget**. In simplest form, it is written as:

$$Mass_{in} = Mass_{out} + Mass_{stored}$$

For a better understanding of the mass budget process, a longer form of the equation may be written (here M = Mass)

$$M_{in} = M_{metabolized} \\ + M_{feces} \\ + M_{urine} \\ + M_{storage}$$

Mass metabolized refers to the mass converted to thermal energy or work. The mass budget can be divided into wet and dry budgets to accommodate the food eaten or water imbibed. The water budget is

$$H_2O_{in} = H_2O_{evaporation} \\ + H_2O_{feces} \\ + H_2O_{urine} \\ + H_2O_{storage}$$

Evaporation refers to loss from the lungs during breathing. Evaporation losses increase during the winter, since cold requires more heat production and cold, dry air absorbs the water from the lungs during breathing.

In winter, metabolic needs for non-hibernators are increased, but the amount of available food is the same or less than at other times of the year. Usually energy reserves are depleted. The question often becomes, can the mass stored support the organism for the entire length of a severe winter?

In biochemical terms, when energy is metabolized, stored chemical energy changes form. **Covalent** bonds are changed to thermal energy, either in the form of increased motion of molecules or in the form of longwave radiation. Some of the covalent bond energy may be stored in other bonds or as thermal energy in the cells. The amount of thermal energy must also balance out and we account for thermal energy through heat balance equations.

Heat Balance

In the same way that we can account for mass energy, we can account for **thermal energy** in the heat budget. Thermal energy taken in must equal thermal energy put out plus thermal energy stored. Thermal energy is represented by the letter "Q," which you may think of essentially as heat. In the shortest form:

$$Q_{in} = Q_{out} + Q_{stored}$$

Heat inputs come from a variety of

sources. Metabolic heat is produced when stored energy is burned. Radiant heat arrives from two sources: from the sun as shortwave radiation and from other objects as longwave radiation. Energy may also be transferred to the organism by conduction and convection, although in winter this is rare unless the organisms are huddling together, as mice do in a nest.

Heat losses from the body include conduction, convection, longwave radiation, and evaporation losses from the lungs. Thermal energy that is not lost is stored in the body as chemical bonds or as increased molecular motion, which is measured as increased body temperature. Eventually, increases in body temperature must be shed through radiation or the organism will die from **heat exhaustion**.

The simple thermal balance equation may be expanded to increase our understanding of how the energy balance is achieved.

$$\begin{aligned}
& Q_{met} && Q_{IR\text{-}out} \\
& + Q_{sol} && + Q_{cond\text{-}out} \\
& + Q_{IR\text{-}in} \quad = \quad && + Q_{conv\text{-}out} \\
& + Q_{cond\text{-}in} && + Q_{evap} \\
& + Q_{conv\text{-}in} && + Q_{stor}
\end{aligned}$$

where met is metabolism, sol is incoming solar radiation, IR is longwave radiation, cond is conduction, conv is convection, evap is evaporation, and stor is storage. During the winter, incoming conduction and convection are usually near zero and often these terms are included only as net values on the right side of the equation.

We have an intuitive understanding of the concept of thermal balance because it is something that we live by. We are constantly adjusting our thermal balance; moving from places that feel a little too cold to places that feel warmer; if too warm, we make adjust-

ments to feel cooler. We adjust our posture, put on clothes, take them off, and get out of the wind. Often we are not even aware of why we are moving or shifting our posture, but it may be because our bodies are paying close attention to the thermal energy balance. Along the surface of the skin, very sensitive nerves determine whether the skin is gaining or losing heat. Sensors also monitor the heat content of the inside of the body, especially the blood going to and from the brain, to determine the amount of heat stored in the body. Our rate of breathing from exercising also signals metabolic changes in heat production. All these signals are used by the body to keep tight control over the thermal energy balance.

The storage term in this equation is very important, for it represents the body temperature. Total stored heat equates to body temperature. Reactions to changes in the thermal balance help keep the storage factor constant. Since all biochemical systems are sensitive to the temperature of the body, this one term of the equation is closely regulated. If an organism senses that the storage term is decreasing, it may react to increase inputs or decrease outputs. It may try to get more heat from radiation, either longwave or shortwave, or it may increase the rate of metabolism, firing the internal furnace. Conversely the organism may try to decrease heat losses by decreasing conduction, convection, radiation out, or evaporation. As humans we do those things by moving to a warmer spot, by moving out of the wind, by putting on more clothes, or if we are wet, by drying off.

Mass and Heat Budgets

Mass and heat budgets are closely linked. When food (mass in) or fat (mass stored) is burned, the thermal balance changes because metabolic heat increases. If thermal conditions change, such that there is an increased need for metabolism, it affects the mass energy balance so that more energy must be obtained through either stored proteins, fats, carbohydrates, or increased food intake. Conceptually, we show a simple model linking the two budgets:

$$
\begin{array}{l}
\text{H} \\
\text{E} \\
\text{M A S S} \\
\text{T}
\end{array}
$$

An expanded form of this conceptual equation provides insight into the intricate linkage between mass and thermal (or heat) balances in organisms (Figure 67).

Metabolic heat (Q_{met}) is related to all the other factors in the heat balance equation. If all the other terms are known for a given environment, we can then predict the heat from metabolism required to maintain a given body temperature. And since the heat from metabolism comes from the burning of food or stored energy, we know how much food must be metabolized under these conditions to maintain an optimum body temperature. This relationship allows us to use the equations as a predictive model to understand food requirements necessary to maintain body temperature in different winter environments. Conversely, if food availability is limited during the winter, the equations show the options, changes of thermal environments, and other factors that can be adjusted by an organism to stay in balance.

Next, we will explore thermal balances in a quantitative fashion by writing equations for each of the terms. These equations will then be used to determine contrasting thermal budgets for a mouse and a moose. Important

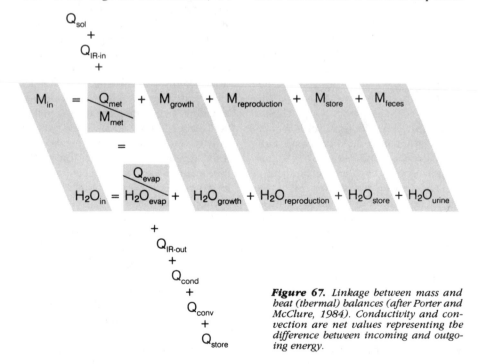

Figure 67. *Linkage between mass and heat (thermal) balances (after Porter and McClure, 1984). Conductivity and convection are net values representing the difference between incoming and outgoing energy.*

principles of thermal transfer are explained in the next section, but the reader wishing to avoid the mathematical treatment may skip to *Animal Energetics and Nutrition.*

Thermal Transfers

If we know the actual processes by which thermal energy is exchanged between plants and animals and their environment, we can begin to understand strategies that are used by different plants and animals to maintain their thermal energy budget. Heat is gained from the environment in three ways: from food, solar radiation (shortwave), and longwave radiation from objects in the local vicinity.

The properties of longwave and shortwave radiation differ considerably. **Longwave radiation** is almost completely absorbed by skin, fur, or clothing. It is not likely to be reflected after striking a surface. Higher energy, **shortwave radiation** from the sun, is more likely to be reflected after striking a surface. A significant amount of sunlight may be reflected from skin. For instance, a lizard can change the reflectivity of its skin by changing the amount or the position of **melanin** (pigment) in its skin.

Radiation is absorbed through skin. The more surface exposed to the source of radiation, the more heat absorbed. The warmer the object transmitting the radiation, the more heat absorbed. In addition, the closer the transmitting object, the more heat absorbed. These principles may be expressed in two equations:

$$Q_{sol} = A_s \, \alpha \, I_s$$
and
$$Q_{IR} = \varepsilon \, A_{IR} \, \sigma \, T^4$$

Solar radiation (Q_{sol}) is equal to the surface area (A_s) exposed to the sun (m^2) times its solar **absorptivity** (α = value of ability to absorb) times the intensity (I_s) of the sun (W/m²). **Longwave radiation** (or infrared, Q_{IR}) is equal to the **emissivity** (ε = value indicating ability to emit or absorb infrared radiation) times the fraction of the total area (A_{IR}) exposed, times the **Stephan-Boltzman constant** (σ) times the temperature (T, in °K) to the fourth power. Values for absorptivity and emissivity must be obtained from the *CRC Handbook of Chemistry and Physics* (Weast, 1988).

These equations demonstrate a couple of important points. First, area of the body is critical to radiation inputs. If an animals curls up in a ball, it receives less radiation from the sun than if it sprawls out. The orientation of the surface makes a difference. If the radiation strikes directly, more energy is received than if surface is at an angle to the source. You can feel the difference if you place your hand in front of a warm object (a light bulb, radiator, or fire) and hold it perpendicular to the object. Next, tilt your hand away from the object and compare the feeling of reduced warmth. Quantitatively, the amount of radiation absorbed equals the area exposed to the radiation times the intensity of radiation. In an area of one square meter exposed to the intensity of radiation from the sun at noon in the winter, about 600 watts is absorbed.

The strongest source of radiant energy in our natural environment is, of course, the sun. In the human environment, however, we create various sources of heat, like fires and radiators, but in the outdoors, next in strength would be radiation coming from another warm body. The next warmest source of radiation would be an object such as the side of a tree or a rock heated by the sun. Objects emit longwave radiation in direct proportion to their temperature raised to the fourth power. A small increase in the temperature of an object makes a very, very large increase in emitted radiation. Have you ever felt a road, a rock, a concrete surface, or a tree after the sun sets? The warmth felt from outgoing longwave radiation is dramatic. For animals in the winter, it is advantageous to be near radiation-emitting objects such as trees.

There is a great difference between the amount of radiation that comes from the trees versus that which comes from the night sky. The night sky is cold, because it has very little longwave radiation coming from it. For an animal to be warmer at night, it makes sense, then, to stay under trees. Deer and elk spend their nights underneath trees, so they will receive some radiation from the trees rather than receiving very little from the night sky.

Distance from the radiation source makes a large difference. The stars, radiating objects in the night sky, are far away and the total radiation from the sky on a clear night may be less than 5 watts of energy. On a cloudy night, incoming longwave radiation increases to maybe 100 watts, because the clouds are warmer and nearer. Clouds receive and absorb radiation leaving the surface of the earth. Once warmed by the earth's radiation, the clouds reradiate back to the earth. Even on a clear night, reradiation from the canopy of trees might contribute 150 or more watts of energy coming down for each square meter of canopy exposed.

For a moment consider yourself. Radiation from your skin is directly proportional to the skin temperature to the fourth power. When we get overheated, lots of blood flows to the surface of our skin. Skin temperature increases and the radiant heat loss increases, cooling our body. When it is cold, the body can

reduce radiation loss by reducing blood flow to the skin, and effectively lowering the radiation by lowering skin temperature. Our skin is fairly sensitive to radiant heat exchange. Test your skin as a radiation sensor. Move your hands over warmer and cooler parts of your body and sense the differences that you feel.

Where our skin is covered by clothing, the outside surface of the clothing radiates heat into the environment. The cooler the clothing surface, the less heat radiated. So the more insulation provided by clothing, the lower its surface temperature, and the less heat we will lose by radiation.

Other modes of energy transport usually have a net effect of taking energy away from organisms. The other modes include conduction, convection, evaporation, and, from the core of the body, blood flow and tissue conduction. **Conduction** transports heat to other solid objects. An animal and the objects it touches pass thermal energy to each other. The net exchange will be from the warmer object to the colder object. In fact, the thermal transfer will continue until the two objects have the same temperature. If the cold object is very large or very cold, this equalization may never happen. As long as there is a heat source inside the organism, it may keep sending heat to that cold object.

Thermal conduction is described by the following equation:

$$Q_{cond} = k\ (A_c/t)\ (T_{surface} - T_{ground})$$

where k is **conductivity** (W/m^2), A_c is the contact area (m^2), t is the thickness of insulation (often hair) between surfaces (cm), and T refers to the temperature of the surface of the skin and the ground (°C). Heat transfer through conduction depends on the temperature difference between the skin of an animal and the surface being touched. Conduction also depends on the type of material touched; how readily that surface conducts heat away. If we touch a metal object, we lose heat to it quickly because it passes the heat quickly between its densely packed molecules. It continues to feel cold to us for a long time. If we are touching a piece of wool, however, heat transfer is slow and the wool surface feels warm. In effect, the wool acts as an **insulator** by slowing heat transfer.

Conduction is inversely proportional to the thickness of the area between the heat source and what it touches. More hair, more fat, more wool—in short, more insulation—all lead to reduced heat loss from conduction. Better insulation (lower thermal conductivity) will also reduce conduction loss. It is better to have a felt liner than a leather boot of the same thickness, because felt has a low conductivity.

Heat is lost through convection when a medium, such as air or water, passes over the skin. We all know how quickly flowing water will transmit heat away from our bodies, and how much cooler a windy day is than a still day.

Convection is described by the following equation:

$$Q_{conv} = \frac{k(V)^{1/3} \ A \ (T_{surface} - T_{air})}{D^{2/3}}$$

where k is the conductivity (W/m^2), V is velocity (m/s), A is surface area, D is diameter (m^2), and T refers to the temperature of the surface, the air, or water (°C). Since convection is directly proportional to thermal **conductivity** of the medium, it is easy to understand why water, which has a high conductivity, causes greater convection loss than does air. Also convection loss is directly proportional to wind speed; the higher the wind speed, the greater the convec-

tive loss. The greater the difference in temperature between the surface and the air, the greater will be the heat loss to convection.

Friction between the liquid or gas medium and the object that medium is flowing past tends to reduce convection. As air flows over our body or across any surface, the air molecules at the surface tend to stick. If you put your finger close to the ground, you do not feel a strong wind. That is because the air close to the ground is being slowed by friction. Moving your finger away from the ground, you will encounter the free air stream, that is, the zone where no frictional effects from the ground occur. There is a thin layer of almost stationary air on top of all objects in our atmosphere due to friction. That thin layer of stationary air is called the **boundary layer**.

The larger an object, the larger the surface area, and thus the greater the friction and the thicker the boundary layer. A tiny twig will barely slow down the wind around it, and will have a very thin boundary layer. A tree trunk is a much larger object that slows the wind more and has a larger boundary layer. The surface of the earth has the largest boundary layer, our atmosphere. The importance of a boundary layer is that it acts as an effective insulator, reducing the tendency of the wind to take heat away by convection. A tiny object with a small boundary layer loses heat to the air through convection much more quickly than does a large object.

The boundary layer effect is also present in water. If you get into a hot bathtub, at first the water feels hot but then cools as a boundary layer builds up around your body. As soon as you move, though, you move out of the boundary layer and the water feels hot again. For this reason, individuals who fall into cold water should not move unless it is to facilitate their escape or rescue. Let the warmer boundary layer build up in the cold water.

The faster the wind blows, the more it will scour into the boundary layer and thin it out. The boundary layer is not static, but is very dependent on the speed of the wind and also the turbulence of the wind. If the wind is flowing smoothly, it will not gouge as deeply as when the wind is tumbling roughly along and gouges in some places and skips others. Turbulent wind flow, which is the normal process outdoors, will take away more heat than smooth wind flow.

Evaporation from the skin is described by the following equation:

$$Q_{evap} = Lh_d \, A \, (\rho_{surface} - \rho_{air})$$

where L is the **latent heat of evaporation** (energy necessary to change water to vapor in J/kg), h_d is the convective mass transfer value (W/m² °K), A is area (m²), and ρ is **vapor density** (the amount of water vapor at the surface or in the air). Important in this relationship is the amount of energy necessary to change water to vapor, 596 cal per gram of water. It is easy to understand why sweating is such an effective means of cooling down. The greater the difference between the amount of moisture on the surface and that in the air, the greater will be the heat loss by evaporation. Sweating on a hot, dry day causes a cool feeling, but sweating on a hot, muggy day does little good.

In winter, the air is very dry and evaporation proceeds at a fast rate from warm skin into the dry air. Evaporation also occurs from the lungs; the surfaces of the lungs are extremely wet and warm. Evaporation proceeds at a very high rate in the lungs, and then the warm moist air is exhaled, transferring body heat in our breath to the atmosphere. Most animals have rather impermeable skin in terms of water loss by evaporation, especially those animals covered by fur. So, in winter, when sweating mechanisms are shut down, water loss occurs mainly through the lungs through the act of breathing and energy transfer occurs by means of evaporation.

Wind is important in the evaporation process. The faster the wind is blowing, the more rapidly it will pull water vapor away. Evaporation is similar to convection in terms of its relationship to a boundary layer that traps the water molecules and prevents the wind from scouring it away. Animals prevent water and energy losses by placing their noses in sheltered humid locations. An animal will curl into a ball and hide its nose in stomach fur, or retreat down into a warm, moist burrow, thus reducing evaporative loss.

Energy is lost from the core of the body to the surface of the skin by **conduction** and **blood flow**. The equations for these losses follow:

$$QT_{cond} = \frac{k}{d} \, (T_{core} - T_{surface})$$

and

$$Q_{BF} = (Flow) \, C_p \, (T_{core} - T_{surface})$$

where k is conductivity, d is diameter (cm), Flow is speed times volume, C_p is the specific heat of blood (J/kg °K), and T refers to temperature of the core and the skin surface. Significantly, conduction through tissue is inversely proportional to the diameter (thickness) of the body. In other words, the thicker the fat layer, the more slowly heat is conducted through body tissue. This is one reason heavier people seem to tolerate cold better.

The picture of an organism's response to the environment can be expanded with our enhanced understanding of thermal and mass balances. Earlier (Figure 65), we diagrammed how metabolic requirements and food processing capacity varied with temperature. Energy and mass balance equations demonstrate that there are many factors besides air temperature that control metabolic and food requirements. In energy budget calculations, radiation often dominates the other forms of energy transfer. Combining radiation, both shortwave and longwave, with temperature provides a more complete picture of the energy budget of an organism (Figure 68). Study the diagram for a few minutes to ascertain how different factors interact. Metabolic requirements vary in a complex manner dependent on both radiation and tem-

perature. This is why it may feel warm on a sunny day when the temperature is very cold.

An understanding of the complex picture of the energy budget, including all forms of energy transfer, is necessary to determine metabolic requirements for organisms. Computers are often used to solve all of the coupled equations. Insights gained by means of graphs (Figure 68) and mathematical answers help winter ecologists understand energy drains during winter.

Radiation and convection are the two dominant forms of heat transfer for most terrestrial creatures. Let us look at energy requirements resulting from size differences between a moose and a mouse. A mouse is a very tiny creature,

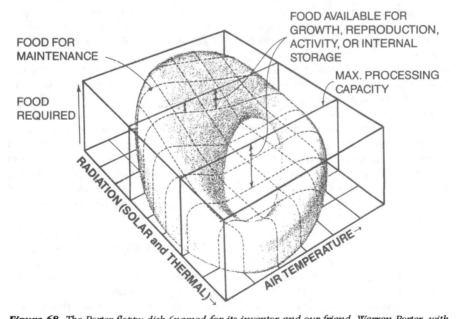

Figure 68. *The Porter floppy dish (named for its inventor and our friend, Warren Porter, with permission from the Carnegie Museum of Natural History). Graphical solution of the coupled equations in Figure 67 yields the floppy dish and lid, illustrating mass of food required for maintenance as a function of radiation and temperature (Porter and Jaeger, 1982; Porter and McClure, 1984). The top of the diagram (the lid) represents the maximum food processing ability of the organism. The surface of the dish represents the amount of food necessary for maintenance. The difference between the top of the dish and its lid represents food available for growth, reproduction, or storage. A cross-section parallel to the air temperature axis would produce a graph such as the one illustrated in Figure 65.*

and as such, has a very small boundary layer surrounding it. Due to this, the mouse is poorly insulated. The moose, on the other hand, is a large creature and has a large boundary layer. Consider what happens if both creatures sit in the sun on a cold day with a slight wind blowing. They will both absorb solar radiation. The moose may fare better on this day. The mouse has a large surface area in comparison to its body weight, but it also has a thin boundary layer. As the mouse absorbs solar radiation, much of the radiation leaks off into its boundary layer and then is scraped away by the wind, before it can be absorbed into the body. The moose has a relatively thick boundary layer. It absorbs sunlight and is insulated from the wind blowing past by its boundary layer. A moose is large enough that it can take advantage of solar radiation gains on a slightly windy day, whereas a mouse would have a much more difficult time absorbing radiation from the sun on a windy day.

In general, there are two environmental temperatures outdoors, the **radiant or sky temperature**, and the **air temperature**. During the day in the winter, the radiant temperature from the sun will be warmer than the air temperature. Animals can try to use that radiant temperature to increase their skin temperatures above that of the air. The ability to raise the skin temperature depends on the thickness of the animal's boundary layer. With a thick boundary layer, large animals are insulated from the air. They can move toward that radiant heat source by moving out into the open on a south-facing slope, for example. The skin temperatures of small animals with a very thin boundary layer, however, remain close to the air temperature. Any energy gained from radiation is quickly lost through the thin boundary layer. The

radiant environment has a greater impact on larger creatures than smaller creatures because energy gains are protected by thicker boundary layers. The wind conditions and air temperature, however, are relatively more important for smaller creatures than for the larger creatures. These patterns are apparent for the overall energy balance for a moose and a mouse in different environments (Table 12). Note, in particular, the effects of the changes in temperature, solar and thermal radiation, and wind-induced convection.

On a warm, winter day on a south-facing slope with a wind speed of 2 m/s, the moose actually gains energy (0.001 Snickers bars/kg/hr), while the mouse loses energy (-0.391 Snickers bars/kg/hr). Even when the wind becomes calm (0.2 m/s), the mouse still loses energy (-0.069 Snickers bars/kg/hr), while the moose is gaining. Comparison of the calm situation to light wind shows that the mouse suffers more from wind effects than does the moose. The loss of inputs at night from solar and thermal radiation places the moose into a negative heat balance (-0.003 Snickers bars/kg/hr) and plunges the mouse even further in debt (-0.253 Snickers bars/kg/hr). Moving into the trees at night also places the moose into a negative energy balance (-0.002 Snickers bars/kg/hr), but the effect is less than being out in the meadow (-0.003 Snickers bars/kg/hr). The increased thermal radiation (200 compared to 60 W/m^2) provided by the trees is not enough to offset the lower temperature (-5.4°C) for the mouse, and its loss is still equal to being out in the open at night (-0.253 Snickers bars/kg/hr). The mouse, though not the moose, can offset the deleterious effects of wind, surface temperature, and night time radiation by retiring beneath the snowpack (-0.069 Snickers

Table 12. Energy balances for a mouse (0.02 kg or 0.7 oz) and a moose (455 kg or 1000 lb). Data were gathered at Teton Science School. By reading down the columns indicated by the headings, differences resulting from wind speed and radiation regimes are indicated. Radiation regimes include the difference between day and night, and between open meadows and forests. Results for a moose are shown in the upper portion of the table, those for a mouse in the lower portion. The cost for different environmental situations is shown in Snickers bars; a negative value indicates an energy cost to the mammal. The cost for the mouse was calculated for above and below the snow. For this example conduction and evaporation were assumed to be negligible because the animals were standing still.

Comparisons	**Wind** versus **calm**			
		Day versus **night**		
			Open cover versus **trees**	
Wind speed	**wind**	**calm**	calm	calm
Time	day	**day**	**night**	night
Cover	meadow	meadow	**meadow**	**trees**
Large mammal: Moose				
Environmental inputs				
Radiation				
Solar (W/m^2)	850	850	0	0
Thermal (W/m^2)	100	100	60	200
Temperature (°C)				
Animal height	2.2	2.2	2.2	- 5.4
Surface	2.0	2.0	2.0	- 6.0
Wind speed (m/s)	2.0	0.2	0.2	0.2
Animal losses				
QIR-out (W/m^2)	1885.3	1885.3	1885.3	1885.3
Convection (W/m^2)	362.5	104.5	104.5	104.5
Snickers bars				
(/kg/hr)	0.001	0.002	- 0.003	- 0.002
(/moose/hr)	0.628	1.938	- 1.566	- 0.311
Small mammal: Mouse				
Environmental inputs				
Radiation				
Solar (W/m^2)	850	850	0	0
Thermal (W/m^2)	100	100	60	200
Temperature (°C)				
Animal height	1.0	1.0	1.0	- 5.4
Surface	2.0	2.0	2.0	- 6.0
Wind speed (m/s)	2.0	0.2	0.2	0.2
Animal losses				
QIR-out (W/m^2)	2.3	2.3	2.3	2.3
Convection (W/m^2)	4.3	1.2	1.2	1.2
Snickers bars (/kg/hr)				
Above the snow	- 0.391	- 0.069	- 0.253	- 0.253
Below the snow	- 0.069	- 0.069	- 0.069	- 0.069

Solar input appears high because of reflection from newly fallen snow.
For conversions: 1 Snickers bar was used as 290 kcal
    1 kcal = 1 Cal (nutritional calorie) = 1000 cal
    1 kcal = 4185 J (joules)

bars/kg/hr), where its energy balance is a constant low negative value; the mouse does have to constantly supplement its food supply in the subnivean to offset this loss. When the mouse retires to a nest or deep burrow, its energy balance will be positive.

The moose gains considerable energy on the south-facing slope during the day, but loses energy at night. The loss resulting from remaining in the meadow is the equivalent of 1.57 Snickers bars/hr or about 22 Snickers bars per 14-hour night. By moving into the trees and receiving the thermal radiation from the trees, the moose need expend only 0.31 Snickers bars/hr or about 4.4 Snickers bars per night, a considerably savings thanks to the trees. Although the moose's energy balance is positive during many days, its total energy budget for the winter is negative and the critical question is, does the moose have enough energy stored to survive until spring?

The four modes of energy transfer—radiation, conduction, convection, and evaporation—interact in complex ways to control the energy balance of an organism. No mode acts independently of the others, but all progress and interact at the same time. Energy transfer through the skin and fur of an elk provides an example of the complexity of energy transfer (Figure 69).

The temperature of the skin and the air differ substantially, and a temperature gradient exists through the fur. The outermost end of a hair is colder than its innermost end. Heat is conducted from the skin along the fur fibers. Some heat is radiated from the surface of the skin out toward the outside environment. Heat at the outside end of the hair is conducted into the air above the fur. If there is any wind, convection also carries heat away. Some of the heat radiated from the skin does not reach the atmosphere, but is intercepted by the fur. Radiation from the skin warms the hair temperature and increases the heat that is being conducted to the surface. In turn this warmed fiber radiates the additional heat. Little evaporation occurs from hair-covered skin, so we will omit evaporation from consideration now. If the skin or fur is wet, however, evaporation further complicates the picture.

Energy also comes to the elk, especially if the sun is shining. Solar radiation penetrates into the fur. Some radiation is absorbed right at the surface of the fur, some is absorbed partway down the shaft of the hairs, and some is absorbed at the skin. If radiation hits the fur fiber, it will be absorbed. The fur fiber can then either conduct the new heat toward the skin surface or out toward the air, or it can radiate

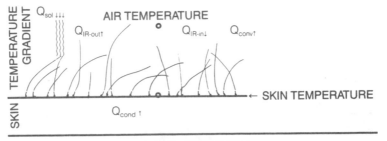

Figure 69. *Cross-section of the skin and fur of an elk, showing the complex interactions associated with energy transfer.*

some of that heat. All of these possibilities for energy occur for solar radiation and also for longwave radiation. In this small layer, which is perhaps one, two, or four centimeters thick, thermal energy is being exchanged between the skin and the outside in a very complex arrangement.

The quality of fur as an insulator depends upon the length of the hairs, their density, diameter, and color, and how erect they stand. All of these things affect the relative amount of heat that is transmitted by conduction, convection, or radiation. Longwave and shortwave radiation respond differently to hair color. The absorption of longwave or thermal radiation is little affected by hair color; all hair colors absorb about the same. The absorption and reflectivity of shortwave or solar radiation varies dramatically depending on hair color; this variation is most evident between black and white hair.

Contrary to popular belief, black or dark fur may not always be the warmest fur to have. Black fur is a good absorber of solar radiation, absorbing most of the **insolation**. Absorbed solar radiation is converted into longwave radiation and much of the heat is reradiated back to the environment. This effect blocks solar energy from reaching the skin. In contrast, white fur reflects some of the sunlight back out, but it also reflects some of the sunlight down into the fur layer and, in fact, white fur reflects some of the sunlight down to the skin layer. Depending upon the thickness of the fur fibers, their density, and how they are folded over each other, white fur can act to "escort" sunlight down to the skin where it can be absorbed as heat. Some winter-adapted animals that have white fur do absorb more sunlight at their skin surface by having white fur rather than dark fur. Dark skin at the base of white hair increases the absorption by the skin. Black hair is a good absorber of shortwave radiation, while white hair is a good reflector.

SUGGESTED READINGS

Gates, D.M. 1980. Biophysical Ecology. Springer Verlag, New York.

Hardy, R.N. 1972. Temperature and animal life. Institute of Biology Studies in Biology, No. 35. Edward Arnold, Ltd., London.

Porter, W.P., and D.M. Gates. 1969. Thermodynamic equilibria of animals with environment. Ecol. Monogr., 39:237-244.

Porter, W.P., and J. Jaeger. 1982. Impact of toxicants, disease, and climate on growth and reproduction using *Peromyscus maniculatus*. Pp. 126-147, *in* Environmental Biology State-of-the-Art Seminar (P.A. Archibald, ed.). Office of Exploratory Res. Publ. EPA-600/9-82-007.

Porter, W.P., and P.A. McClure. 1984. Climate effects on growth and reproduction potential in *Sigmodon hispidus* and *Permyscus maniculatus*. Pp. 173-181, *in* Winter Ecology of Small Mammals (J.F. Merritt, ed.). Carnegie Mus. Nat. Hist., Spec. Publ., Pittsburgh.

Pruitt, W.O., Jr. 1957. Observations on the bioclimate of some taiga mammals. Arctic, 10:130-138.

Weast, R.C. 1988. CRC Handbook of Chemistry and Physics. CRC Press, Inc., Boca Raton, Florida.

ANIMAL ENERGETICS AND NUTRITION

The vectors of winter, **SCREW** (snow, cold, radiation, energy, and wind), combine to affect the energy that an animal has available to combat winter. Available nutrition and nutritional requirements may change considerably during the snow season and a variety of strategies may be deployed to meet energy and nutritional needs. Any aspect of an animal's life might be optimized to provide the necessary energy to survive until spring. Important ways to optimize energy expenditures during the winter include maintaining a lower body mass, changing social structure, switching activity schedules, and selecting favorable wintering microhabitats and food. We will explore these topics, including examples detailing the energy use patterns of animals during the winter.

Lowered Body Mass

In many species, **body weights** of individuals are lower during the winter. Fewer calories are required to support a smaller mass, creating less drain on the energy budget for the entire winter. However, a smaller mass is less effective in retaining heat. There may be a trade-off in determining how much an animal's weight can be lowered during the winter while still being able to provide an energy savings, without increasing losses of energy to the environment due to lower heat retention. It is sometimes difficult to determine whether a reduction in body mass is the result of decreased availability of food or a strategy to save energy.

The decrease in winter weight for **moose** (*Alces alces*) reflects a deficit in nutrition and a continual state of **malnutrition** over the winter. Each year during May, moose begin to gain weight as they feed on succulent summer forage, and they continue to gain until early fall. Moose eat about 11 kg (24.2 lbs, dry weight) of high-quality food daily during the summer. Daily consumption drops to 5 kg (11 lbs) in the winter and consists of bitterbrush,

willows, fir trees, and green algae (Figure 70). Lower food intake is the result of the increased time necessary to digest woody browse materials. This food is also of lower nutritional quality, requiring increased **fermentation time** for bacteria to digest the cellulose-rich branches in the rumen. The decrease in quantity and quality may amount to 30 percent less energy than is required to support body maintenance. To compensate for this nutrient-poor diet, moose metabolize their stored fat and protein, causing a continual decrease in weight until spring.

Lower food intake during the winter may result from other causes. Depleted winter range, congregating moose, and increased snow depths can further restrict food intake. Where winter browsing has been heavy, moose can no longer find the succulent new growth from summer and must switch to stems that grew the previous year, now about 18 months old. Eighteen-month-old willow twigs have about 50 percent less crude protein and 25 percent more crude fiber than six-month-old willow twigs. The fiber provides little nutrition. Decreased foraging activity during severe weather conditions may further reduce food intake.

Scientists have long believed that small mammals reduce their body weight as a strategy to reduce caloric needs during winter, but the universal application of this strategy has been questioned in recent years. Mice and voles (*Peromyscus, Microtus, Clethrionomys*) are notable for records of reduced weights during winter. However, few studies are available that follow individual mice during the winter season. Most studies use a mean weight for the whole population. A decrease in mean weight might result from the loss of older, larger animals from the population, **recruitment** (the addition of

Figure 70. *Moose browsing on willows in Grand Teton National Park.*

young animals) of lighter weight animals, cessation of growth in younger animals, or a decline in individual weight. Recent work following individual animals suggests that under certain conditions the red-backed vole (*Clethrionomys*) may show a 30 percent weight reduction during winter. In these animals, **resting metabolic rates** decrease about 8 percent, a caloric savings of up to .03 cal/hr. However, other populations of the red-backed voles did not show decreases in winter weights, suggesting that, although the weight decrease might be real, it could be the result of nutritional deficiencies rather than an actual strategy. For subnivean mice, foraging might be limited by snow conditions and ice layers, or food quality might be reduced during the winter. Since many mice are **omnivo-**

rous (they will eat almost anything), it is unlikely that they are limited by the quantity of food often. It is more likely that mice are limited by some sort of quality factor, which might reflect different biochemical compositions of food during the winter.

Social Structure

Whether decreased body weight is a strategy or the result of nutritional deficits, animals may offset reduced body weight and volume by social interaction, including gathering together in a mutual nest. **Winter aggregation** allows small mammals to form a ball—a mass of larger volume—thereby gaining the advantage of a higher **surface-to-volume ratio**, which reduces heat loss. **Winter-social** species are those that tend to aggregate in the winter. Species of voles that normally live in colonies form winter aggregations. Noncolonial species may also aggregate. These animals usually remain separated during the rest of the year because of territoriality, foraging strategies, or high aggression levels. During the winter, forces separating individuals tend to break down, allowing them to aggregate harmoniously.

Even more interesting are those species that are noncolonial and form aggregations with individuals of other species. Notable for this trait are two species of deer mice (*Peromyscus maniculatus* and *P. leucopus*). Deer mice may be highly aggressive during the breeding season, but barriers break down to the point that the deer mice allow members of other species to join them in communal nests during the winter. When these nests are uncovered, the mice will be found huddled in tight little balls, gaining the collective advantage of all members of the group.

Conversely, some species are **winter-solitary**. These species, which tend to be small and **insectivorous**, are not known to form groups. Most members of this group are shrews, but a species of lemming (*Lemmus lemmus*) and the grasshopper mouse (*Onychomys leucogaster*) are also included. The grasshopper mouse is largely insectivorous. Perhaps the reason the lemming, a rather large rodent, is winter-solitary is that it breeds during the winter, and this keeps aggression levels high. Only one shrew species, the least shrew (*Cryptotis parva*), is known to be winter-social.

Energy requirements appear to drive the social system of winter aggregation. Many factors promote winter aggregation, including high population density, high intergroup relatedness, low temperatures, thin snowpack, scarce overwintering sites, and clumped food resources (Figure 71). A uniform dispersion of individuals and a solitary lifestyle is dictated by low-quantity food or high-quality food with a low renewal rate and even dispersion. Winter-social animals tend to use clumped food sources of lower quality but higher quantity.

Activity-Schedule Switching

Energy expenditures may also be optimized by switching activity schedules during the winter. Energy expenditures are often estimated by observing the amount of time that an animal expends for each activity. Time allocation is then recorded as a time budget and estimates of energy expenditures are made for each category of activity in both kcals and Snickers bars (Table 13).

The time an elk allocates to various activities changes during the winter. Foraging time decreases due to difficulties in obtaining food and perhaps increased time is needed for ruminating poor-quality food. Time spent bedding increases dramatically and much less time is spent traveling. Switching activities creates an energy savings amounting to over 800 kcal per day. The savings is critical because energy needs exceed energy availability during winter.

Two possible **energy allocation strategies** have been suggested for compensation of energy deficits during the winter. An elk could increase foraging effort or it could decrease energy expenditures. Many factors interact to determine which of these strategies may be beneficial at a given time. When green leaves from summer are gone, plants are covered by snow, and travel through the snow is difficult, the value of increasing foraging efforts decreases. Reducing the energy costs of locomotion and capitalizing on the

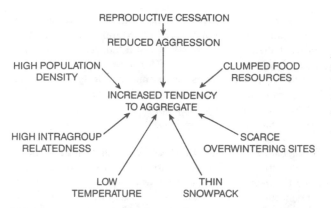

Figure 71. *Factors promoting aggregation of small mammals during the winter (after West and Dublin, 1984, with permission from the Carnegie Museum of Natural History).*

Table 13. Time budget for activities and estimated energy expenditures for a 236 kg (519 lb) female elk (after Craighead et al., 1972; Moen, 1973; Thomas and Toweill, 1982).

Activity	Winter Energy expended			Summer Energy expended		
	hours spent	kcal	Snickers bars	hours spent	kcal	Snickers bars
Foraging	9.2	1172	4.04	9.7	1236	4.26
Bedding	13.5	0	0.00	9.8	0	0.00
Ruminating	6.0	340	1.17	6.0	340	1.17
Traveling	0.9	301	1.04	3.1	1036	3.57
Standing	0.4	7	0.02	1.3	23	0.07
Standard metabolic rate		4215	14.53		4215	14.53
Totals	24.0	6035	20.81	23.9	6850	23.62

Note: This is a simplified time budget and assumes that the same amount of time is needed for ruminating food gathered in slightly less time during the winter. More time may actually be required than is indicated, because of the poor quality of winter food. It is also assumed that the same energy expenditure rates apply during both seasons, while in actuality, it may cost more energy during the winter for movements such as traveling.

benefits of microhabitats favors inactivity. One important factor in determining whether to forage or to remain inactive is the trade-off between heat generated by activity versus the extra loss of energy from exposure to the elements during standing activity.

A **thermoregulatory penalty** occurs from standing in the cold. The penalty results from an increase in surface area due to a less compact body configuration and also the loss of protection from the microhabitat. Energy costs rise because of increases in sur-face area, blood circulation, body core temperature, convection, and evaporation. The penalty is paid in increased energy expenditures for standing.

Increased activities such as traveling and foraging may also suffer a thermoregulatory penalty if the energy these activities generates is less than the cost of the activity. In other words, if traveling generates 100 kcal of heat but costs 150 kcal of heat, a thermoregulatory penalty is paid. On many occasions during the winter, a thermoregulatory penalty does exist for standing, traveling, or foraging. The cost of activity may be double the cost of lying in a bed. On these occasions activities should occur only when the value of the food exceeds the cost of the penalty for standing, traveling, and foraging. Since food quality is so poor in the winter, it is often better to remain inactive than to forage. Deer and elk often **yard up**, staying in protected microhabitats without even moving to forage. **Foraging cessation** is an extreme case of activity-switching, when the foraging activity is dropped from the daily schedule. During severe weather spells, many days may go by when ungulates do not even attempt to forage.

Selection of Wintering Sites

The selection of the best microhabitat available plays an important part in optimizing energy expenditures and conserving the energy necessary to survive a late spring. At least three factors may be important in the selection of a microhabitat: habitat, location within the habitat, and available food sources. Once selected, an animal may then improve the site by nest preparation.

Site Selection of Habitat

Habitat selection is critically important to bald eagles on the Nooksack River, Washington, where **winter kill** due to starvation and cold stress does occur. Bald eagles utilize three habitats: gravel bars for feeding, and deciduous forests or coniferous forests for roosting. Considerable differences occur in the microclimates of the three habitats (Table 14).

During the day, warmer temperatures on the gravel bars make these areas the favored habitat, followed by the deciduous forest where the eagles perch for a clear, high view of the river and gravel beds so that they can spot dead or dying fish. They may then fly down to feed on any food that becomes available. At night, warmer temperatures and a more favorable longwave radiation balance (considerably less outgoing radiation) make the coniferous forest the desired habitat. Rainfall and wind speeds are lower there; overall, the coniferous forest provides a buffering influence and better microclimate for the eagles.

The bald eagles on the Nooksack River feed primarily on salmon, consuming 94 percent of the salmon that become available as carrion along the river banks. Energy requirements for the various daily activities vary only for roosting; less energy is needed for roosting in the coniferous forest (Table 15). Energy savings within the coniferous forest habitat are particularly great

Table 14. Microclimatological data for three habitats used by bald eagles on the Nooksack River, Washington (after Stalmaster and Gessman, 1984). Values represent the means of December, January, and February.

Habitat	Diurnal Temp (°C)	Nocturnal Temp (°C)	Rainfall (cm/d)	Wind (m/s)	Long-wave radiation			
					Diurnal		Nocturnal	
					up (W/m²)	down (W/m²)	up (W/m²)	down (W/m²)
Gravel bar	3.7	-0.2	0.52	1.14	326	289	308	274
Deciduous	3.0	0.1	0.46	0.60	322	300	309	287
Coniferous	2.3	1.5	0.20	0.11	319	316	315	312

m/s = meters per second   W/m² = watts per square meter

Table 15. Daily energy requirement for a 4.5 kg (9.9 lbs) bald eagle adjusted for the percentage of time spent at each location or activity (after Stalmaster and Gessman, 1984).

Activity	Energy (kJ/bird/d)	Salmon (g/bird/d)	Snickers bars (bars/bird/d)
Feeding/waiting	26	6	0.03
Perching	601	137	0.72
Roosting			
Deciduous habitat	1,385	326	1.65
Coniferous habitat	1,314	307	1.57
Flight	110	30	0.13
Subtotals			
Deciduous	2,153	503	2.54
Coniferous	2,051	484	2.45
Difference between habitats	102	19	0.09

kJ = kilojoules

at night and total savings amount to 102 kJ, or 19 g of salmon per day.

Coniferous habitats are located farther from the gravel bars than the deciduous forests. The extra cost of flying to and from the coniferous habitat amounts to about 31 kJ (5.8 g of fish) per day. Eagles that adopt the strategy of flying greater distances to the habitat that is more conducive to energy conservation realize a net energy savings of about 71 kJ (13.2 g of fish) per day. While this may not seem like much, over the 90-day winter it amounts to 6,390 kJ, 1,196 g of fish, or 5.64 Snickers bars per winter. Five and a half Snickers bars is a considerable energy savings, one that might affect behavior and survival.

In terms of habitat selection, eagles often select old-growth coniferous forests for roosting, and adult eagles will displace juveniles from the most desirable roosts. Eagles spend 73 percent of their roosting time in coniferous forests. The time roosting in locations other than in the coniferous forest may represent periods of less severe weather.

Other behaviors are associated with maximizing energy resources. These in-

clude **kleptoparasitizing** (adults taking food from the juveniles by combat), **group feeding** (where juveniles learn to locate food by following adults), selection of nonfrozen fish, selection of undecayed carcasses, and adults feeding only once per day at high-quality food sources (young must fly to several food sources). Nonfrozen fish require less energy to eat and undecayed carcasses retain all their nutritional value. The juvenile eagles are at a disadvantage in this whole process, being forced from the best roosting and feeding sites. As a result, in times of food scarcity, juveniles die. Only those young that are successful at learning how to locate food survive to adulthood.

Site Selection for Location

Locations within major habitat types may confer considerable energy savings to their occupants. Microhabitats offer advantages of insulation, shelter, elevation, or special features to protect the inhabitants.

Insulation provided by the snowpack reduces energy loss. On Niwot Ridge in Colorado, differences in snowpack boundaries for different years determine the location of pocket gopher and vole burrows and nests during the winter. The winter of 1987-88 had a deeper snowpack than recent years. Under this deeper snowpack, gophers expanded activity into areas where they had not been in recent times and vole activity expanded in size. Perhaps it was coincidental, but the deeper snowpack in the spring of 1988 also covered a vole population eruption of greater magnitude than had been observed in perhaps 30 years.

In areas where snow cover is not continuous or of uniform depth, location of nests and burrows may reflect snowpack depth. The **thermal index** provides a means of quantifying the benefits of life in the subnivean zone. An interesting project would be to determine the relationship between snowpack and the spatial distribution of small mammal activity in the subnivean. A map could be developed showing the distribution of thermal index values in a field or small valley. This could be done quickly using a **Mt. Rose sampler** (a coring device used by the Soil Conservation Service) and calculating one thermal index value for the entire snow column. Then, as the snow melted in the spring, the distribution of vole nests and burrows could be mapped to determine the controlling influence of snow depth.

Elevated spots under the snowpack may also be at a premium. When the snow goes **isothermal** in the spring and water starts to drain down through the snow, lower nest sites become wet. Energy loss increases dramatically from wet nests and is worse yet for wet animals. Under extreme conditions, animals will die in their nest from hypothermia, or they may even drown. Those individuals on higher ground may remain dry and relatively warm.

Advantages of wind-sheltered spots for larger animals are obvious, and as with the Nooksack eagles, spots with favorable radiation balances may provide shelter of another type—shelter from radiation loss. Areas where losses of longwave radiation to the winter sky are offset by incoming radiation from relatively warmer trees or rocks (or even snowpack for a subnivean animal) are preferable.

Special habitat features may offer unusual opportunities for energy savings by animals. Yellowstone National Park is a classic example where thermal features provide warm ground to lie on and even green plant growth during the winter. Plants also sprout early during the spring. Oftentimes, the activities of humans may inadvertently supply energy-saving situations; plowed roads may provide easier travel routes and access to plants and seeds along the road edges, and certainly the shelter provided by buildings make winter easier for many animals.

Site Selection for Food

Much of the time, animals select their wintering location because of the availability of food. Nearby or clumped food resources require less energy expenditure for traveling and foraging. Selection for availability of food resources was observed in bald eagles along the Snake River in Jackson Hole, Wyoming during the unusually cold winter of 1978-1979 (Figure 72).

The January mean temperature of -26.3°C in the 1978-79 winter was ten degrees lower than normal. The Snake River froze from the **Yellowstone National Park** south past **Grand Teton National Park** and the **National Elk Refuge**. With the river frozen, fish were locked beneath the ice and no longer available as a source of carrion for the bald eagles, which had to rely on other food sources. Field surveys from Jan-

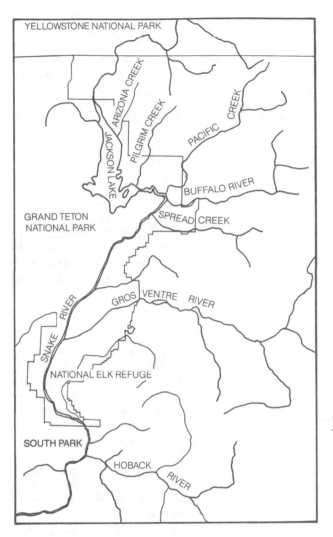

Figure 72. *Map of the Jackson Hole, Wyoming, region.*

uary 14 to 17, 1979, revealed 29 to 32 eagles (including five subadults) using the Snake River with three aggregations: one group of seven eagles at the National Elk Refuge, one group of five to eight eagles at South Park, and one group of five eagles at Astoria. Other eagles were scattered throughout the Snake River Valley.

Bald eagles switched to mammal carrion for food, and concentrations of eagles were found near winter ungulate populations at the three sites mentioned. At the Elk Refuge, 97 dead elk provided an estimated 17,620 kg (38,764 lbs) of carrion for 7 eagles. At Astoria, dead animals numbered 29 mule deer, 12 elk, and 3 moose, for an estimated carrion availability of 4,296 kg (9,451 lbs) for 5 eagles.

The 7 eagles at the Elk Refuge in 1978-79 represented an increase of one to five from recent years, indicating clumping because of available food. The amount of available elk carrion increased on the Elk Refuge because of severe winter conditions. Distribution of eagles all along the Snake River coincided with wintering elk and therefore carrion supplies. Eagles tended to be within 3.2 km (2 mi) of the carrion source. Food sources became scarcer downstream from the Elk Refuge and the subadults tended to winter further downstream. The eagles were selecting wintering sites based on food availability and younger birds were relegated to regions with smaller food supplies.

Preparation of Sites

Once wintering sites are selected, animals will often improve the site itself, creating additional energy savings. Brown lemmings, for example, build nests in the subnivean. Females tend to build bigger nests than males and the biggest nests belong to the breeding females. The larger nests (25 cm compared to 12 cm diameter [9.8 to 4.7 in]) cut heat loss in half. Reducing heat loss is important because **neonates** (newborn animals) do not have the ability to regulate their core temperatures and may lose heat rapidly. Females with young in larger nests can then be absent from the nest for longer periods, which allows them the necessary time to forage. Even so, the energy drain of raising young pups beneath the snow appears to be about the same for three pups in the winter as for six pups in the summer.

The advantage of larger nests is apparent at a secondary level. Weasels foraging under the snow tend to prefer the larger nests. They will kill a female lemming and her young. The weasel then lines the lemming nest with the fur of its victims, increasing its insulating value. For a period of time, the weasel then forages out from the improved nest, killing other lemmings and bringing their bodies to the home nest. As the lemmings are eaten, fur is added

to the lining and a pile of bones accumulates outside the nest. These fur-lined nests can be found in the spring when the snow melts. The same phenomenon occurs in areas with voles and deep winter snowpacks. Search grassy fields in the spring for these signs of life in the subnivean.

Food Selection

Food is obviously central to any consideration of optimizing energy for life in the winter. Several factors influence the selection of food during the winter. We have mentioned travel time to food, and dispersion of food sources. Here we will explore diet switching, determining quality foods, and plant defenses against foraging.

Diet Switching

Diet switching during the winter occurs largely because of changes in available food resources. Many animals migrate away from the lush summer ranges before winter arrives. Deer, elk, moose, and bighorn sheep migrate to lower ranges. On the winter ranges, entirely different food may be available. Even where similar foods are present, they may be covered by snow and thus unavailable. Grasses and **forbs** (herbaceous, nonwoody plants) are usually not easily obtained, reducing **grazing** opportunities and requiring animals to switch to **browsing** on shrubs and trees (Figures 73 and 74).

Elk, like other **ruminants** (mammals with four-chambered stomachs), are adapted to foraging on coarse, woody material. The first of their four stomachs, the **rumen**, serves as a storage chamber which they fill during bouts of extended foraging. Once they are bedded, they regurgitate and chew this food (a process known as **rumination**) more extensively. The rumen contains

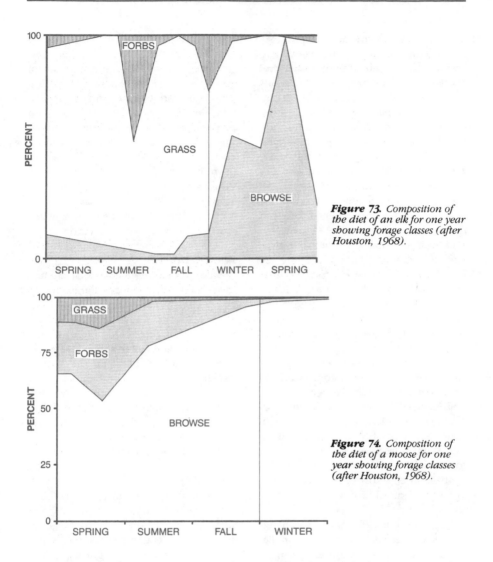

Figure 73. Composition of the diet of an elk for one year showing forage classes (after Houston, 1968).

Figure 74. Composition of the diet of a moose for one year showing forage classes (after Houston, 1968).

an ecosystem of its own, composed mostly of **bacteria** and some **protozoans**. Bacteria are capable of digesting complex chemical compounds, such as cellulose and starch, from which they synthesize large quantities of volatile **fatty acids**. The fatty acids are absorbed by the elk directly from the rumen and constitute a major source of energy for the elk.

At times during the winter, elk and moose must rely almost exclusively on woody plants, which are poor-quality foods because of their high cellulose content. The poor-quality foods increase the time necessary for ruminating and decrease time available for foraging.

During severe winters, deer and elk are often observed **yarding up**, lacking the food resources for survival. Public outcry demands that local officials feed the starving animals, but **supplemental feeding** is controversial and does not always serve the desired purpose. From a management standpoint, in areas such as **Yellowstone National Park**, supplemental feeding goes against the role of nature in maintaining natural population balances. Under natural conditions, when winters are severe, more elk die. More important, supplemental feeding may not save the elk. The bacteria in the rumen are adapted to digest the food of a current diet. The bacteria take time to adapt the capacity to digest the new food, and quick switches from native range materials to feedlot hay does not allow the bacteria time to adjust to digesting the hay. It is possible for elk to die with a stomach full of undigested food. Ruminants should be gradually switched to artificial diets and if possible, hay diets should continue to be only a supplement to plants from the native winter range. Gradual introduction and partial supplementation is the procedure used on the **National Elk Refuge**. Another consideration is that supplemental feeding may encourage elk to stay on crowded, stressful, depleted winter range when they should be moving out to other food sources or beginning migration in the spring. Crowded and weakened animals are more susceptible to disease.

Ungulates often increase the percentage of coniferous browse in their diet during the winter. Conifers contain many **terpenes**, chemical compounds from which the commercial product turpentine is derived. Terpenes are abortive agents (drinks made from pine needles were used by some American Indian tribes to induce abortion). A small proportion of coniferous material in the diet is probably not harmful, but a high proportion during the fall and early winter may be harmful to pregnant females. This time period would correspond to the first trimester in the human pregnancy cycle, a period of known sensitivity to chemicals. It is possible that browsing large amounts of conifer materials at this time might induce **spontaneous abortions**. Around Boulder, Colorado, it has been observed that following severe early winters, when the deer herd must feed on conifers early, the number of fawns born in the spring is reduced and twinning is also low. Diet switching at an early date in the winter may be more harmful than later in the winter, when it is less likely to induce abortion.

Food Quality

Some evidence suggests that animals may selectively feed on higher quality parts of plants during the winter. **Grouse** have been observed to select buds over the internode portions of the stem—but more interestingly—they select the buds containing the female **catkins** over those containing the male catkins. The female catkins contain **endosperm**, nutrient-rich material that supplies food to the developing embryo. The endosperm-rich female catkin is a high-quality food source.

Plant Defenses

Herbivory may not simply be a one-way street controlled by the animals, as plants tend to evolve defenses that reduce foraging pressures. Selection of food sources by animals, in fact, may be in negative response to **chemical defenses** developed by the plants. Those plants or parts of plants high in certain chemical compounds may be less palatable to herbivores. **Phenol** and **triterpene** chemical compounds have been implicated as **feeding deterrents**.

Snowshoe hares tend to reject **foliar** (leaf) **buds** and **staminate** (male) catkins of alders in favor of internodes on the stems. These buds and catkins contain high levels of nutrients and carbohydrates and low levels of fiber, which would appear to make them desirable food sources. However, they also contain **pinosylvin methyl ether**, a phenolic compound that deters feeding. Similar defense against snowshoe hares has been observed in Scots pine. In birch shrubs, the defensive compound against hares appears to be **papyriferic acid**, a triterpene.

Plant defense systems seem to be two-tiered. Not only are certain parts of plants defended, but also certain growth stages. Juvenile stages appear to be better protected by more phenols and high **lignin** (tough fibrous material) content than are adult stages. Mature willows that are heavily browsed by hares revert to the juvenile form of stump sprouts with twigs that are unpalatable. The **browsing-induced resistance** may last three years, until the plant again reaches taller stature and greater maturity. Adult forms have lower levels of chemical compounds, but appear better able to resist winter browsing.

Plants show **compensatory growth** in response to browsing pressure by animals. When moose browse on birch, the browsed birch trees produced larger shoots with larger leaves containing more **chlorophyll**. Buds also do not develop into long stems, but develop at the same height on the plant. The compensatory growth is advantageous to the moose in that it maintains shoot biomass, keeps more annual growth within browsing range, and increases shoot size. However, browsing decreases the amount of calcium, magnesium, and fat in new shoots.

Meeting the nutritional energy requirements of winter is critical. Only two sources of nutrition are available to wintering animals: eating or mobilizing stored fats. It is desirable to save the stored fats for as long as possible; therefore activities that conserve energy should be maximized. Energy conserving strategies include a variety of im-

portant tactics, many of which we have discussed. Natural selection favors those animals that have adopted maximized strategies of conserving energy. Even with conservative strategies, however, animal populations will decline during the winter. Old animals and weak animals succumb to the rigors of winter each year. In the next section, we will follow several populations from the benign summer through the course of one winter.

SUGGESTED READINGS

Bryant, J.P., G.D. Wieland, P.B. Reichardt, V.E. Lewis, and M.C. McCarty. 1983. Pinosylvin methyl ether deters snowshoe hare feeding on green alder. Science, 222:1023-1025.

Bryant, J.P., G.D. Wieland, T. Clausen, and P. Kuropat. 1985. Interactions of snowshoe hare and feltleaf willow in Alaska. Ecology, 66:1564-1573.

Craighead, J.J., G. Atwell, and B.W. O'Gara. 1972. Elk migrations in and near Yellowstone National Park. Wildl. Monogr. No. 29. The Wildlife Society, Washington, D.C.

Danell, K., K. Huss-Danell, and R. Bergstrom. 1985. Interactions between browsing moose and two species of birch in Sweden. Ecology, 66:1867-1878.

Davenport, D.R., and J.L. Weaver. 1982. Wintering bald eagles in Jackson Hole, Wyoming. N.W. Science, 56(2):79-82.

Gates, C.C., and R.J. Hudson. 1979. Effects of posture and activity on metabolic responses of wapiti to cold. J. Wildl. Manage., 43(2):1979.

Martin, A.C., H.S. Zim, and A.L. Nelson. 1961. American Wildlife and Plants: A Guide to Wildlife Food Habits. Dover Publications, Inc., New York.

Merritt, J.F. (ed.). 1984. Winter Ecology of Small Mammals. Carnegie Mu-

seum Nat. Hist. Spec. Publ. No. 10, Pittsburgh.

Moen, A.N. 1973. Wildlife Ecology. W.H. Freeman and Co., San Francisco.

Stalmaster, M.V., and J.A. Gessman. 1984. Ecological energetics and foraging behavior of overwintering bald eagles. Ecol. Monogr., 54:407-428.

Thomas, J.W., and D.E. Toweill (eds.). 1982. Elk of North America: Ecology and Management. Stackpole Books, Harrisburg, Pennsylvania.

West, S.D., and H.T. Dublin. 1984. Behavioral strategies of small mammals under winter conditions: solitary or social? Pp. 293-299, *in* Winter Ecology of Small Mammals (J.F. Merritt, ed.). Carnegie Museum Nat. Hist. Spec. Publ. No. 10, Pittsburgh.

ANIMAL POPULATIONS

Very little is known about the biology of animal populations during the winter. Collecting data on large groups of animals is difficult even in the summer, and scientists have not been able to thoroughly investigate processes that influence numbers of animals during the winter. We will look briefly both at preparations for the winter that animals make during the fall, and processes affecting their survival during the winter. Important processes affecting whole populations include seasonal changes such as migration and hair color changes, and year-round processes such as foraging, starvation, predation, and scavenging. Collectively, many of the forces acting on animals during the winter produce a phenomenon known as **winter kill**, in which a number of animals die. We will follow mammal populations from the Rocky Mountain states through a winter to gain an understanding of what happens to their numbers.

Let's look first at **populations** at the end of the summer and then at how the populations change (usually decreasing) during the winter. It is very difficult to obtain figures for entire populations during the winter. Each autumn, however, the Wyoming Game and Fish Department estimates numbers of resident large mammals throughout the state (Table 16). We can use these numbers as a starting point to understanding the magnitude of possible herd reductions during the winter.

Table 16. Census figures for Wyoming large mammals. These figures represent the average of fall censuses from 1960 to 1969 for the entire state of Wyoming.

Mammal	Wyoming Fall Population Census
Deer	316,600
Elk	60,105
Moose	5,900
Black bear	2,150
Grizzly bear	200?[1]
Pronghorn antelope	152,204
Bighorn sheep	3,600
Mountain goats	60
Bison	700

[1]The grizzly is an endangered species and because of its rarity exact counts are not possible.

Wyoming is rich in wildlife and, in 1989, the numbers of some species were probably higher than presented here. For comparison, Wyoming has a population of 470,000 people. There is one deer for every 1.5 people in the state and one elk for every 7.8 people. Animal populations are high in the fall and the animals are healthy. Summer has been a time of plenty and animals were able to grow fat in preparation for winter. Many young were born. During the fall, the animals begin to change and acclimate for winter. As winter nears, the number of animals starts to decrease also.

Hunting

First, around September 1, the high country comes alive with people shrouded in orange (Figure 75). The hunting season begins. Whether one agrees with hunting or not, it does make a decided impact in terms of the number of animals that will survive through the winter. Hunting may be a useful management tool, allowing herds to be reduced to a level that can be supported by the **winter range** or to a lower level that will reduce the

Table 17. Hunting reductions in Wyoming large mammals. Numbers are averages from the 1960-1969 time period.

Mammal	Wyoming Fall Population Census	Hunting Harvest	Percentage of Herd Harvested
Deer	316,600	89,562	28
Elk	60,105	11,743	20
Moose	5,900	793	13
Black bear	2,150	282	13
Grizzly bear	200[1]	0	0
Pronghorn antelope	152,204	28,860	19
Bighorn sheep	3,600	105	3
Mountain goats	60	4	7
Bison	700	0	0

[1]The grizzly is an endangered species, and because of its rarity, exact counts are not available.

Figure 75. *A successful hunter in the Wyoming high country.*

spread of contagious **diseases**, such as pinkeye in bighorn sheep.

Large reductions are made in the herds (Table 17). From 3 to 28 percent of each species is harvested during the fall. Studies have shown that hunters, on average, act like predators, taking the slower and weaker animals (although designated male-only seasons direct the harvest to the male segment of the herd). Hunting selection will vary by area, but often tends to reduce younger (less experienced animals) and older (trophy and weak animals) segments of the population more than other portions of the herd. The animals removed during the hunt will not compete for winter range and will not spread diseases. They also will not be among the number of possible survivors through the winter to spring.

Migration

During the fall many other changes are also occurring. These seasonal changes prepare the animals for winter. Those animals that cannot survive in their summer ranges **migrate** to surroundings with conditions more conducive to survival during the winter. Migrations may be either vertical, toward lower altitudes, or horizontal, to the southern hemisphere, to the tropics, or simply to farther south than the summer range. Some birds make truly remarkable migrations; the arctic tern makes perhaps the longest (Figure 76). The tern migrates from a summer range above the Arctic Circle to another summer range (southern hemisphere summer) above the Antarctic Circle, a distance of over 16,000 km (10,000 mi).

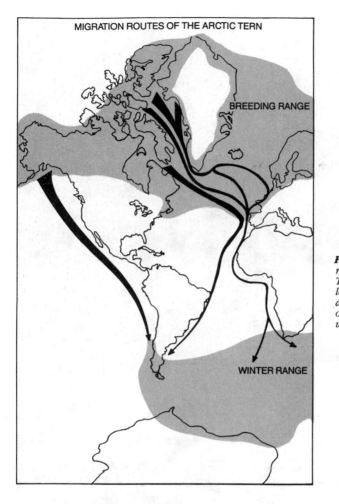

MIGRATION ROUTES OF THE ARCTIC TERN

BREEDING RANGE

WINTER RANGE

Figure 76. *Migration routes for the Arctic tern. The tern is perhaps the longest migrator of all animals, traveling well over half way around the world each year.*

Some birds simply migrate short distances farther south. Canada geese move from the Arctic circle down to Wyoming to winter. This short migration into the inhospitable winter climate of Wyoming hardly seems worthwhile. It must, however, provide the advantage that is needed, since the geese have selected these **wintering grounds** over **evolutionary time**. Further evidence of the suitability of these areas for wintering is found in the fact that some Canada geese spend the entire year in Wyoming. Other geese however, do migrate farther south.

Some mammals—mostly bats—do make horizontal migrations similar to birds. For most mammals, the migration routes are more of a vertical nature, dropping to altitudes lower than the summer ranges or dropping into favorable areas of microclimate. The advantage of a vertical migration is illustrated by an examination of the location of **treeline** (Table 18). Treeline occurs at progressively lower altitudes at more northern locations. Biogeographers use a rough rule-of-thumb to determine the lowering of treeline at more northerly latitudes: for every 500 km (300 mi) to

Elk in Wyoming migrate to the low valley bottoms where shallower snows provide better access to winter food supplies.

the north, the treeline will occur about 300 m (1,000 vertical feet) lower. Conversely, a decrease in altitude of 300 m (1,000 ft) will be the equivalent of traveling to the south about 500 km (300 mi).

Table 18. Altitudinal limits of treeline at selected points on a transect from Colorado to Alaska.

State	Treeline	
	m	(ft)
Colorado	3,350	(11,000)
Wyoming	3,140	(10,300)
Montana	2,130	(7,000)
Alaska	0	(0)

In Wyoming, seasonal vertical migrations often result in drops of 1,200 m (4,000 ft), with animals reaching weather conditions equivalent to migrating 2,000 km (1,200 mi) to the south. The advantages of moving 2,000 km to the south can be realized in some mountainous areas by migrating as few as 16 km (10 mi). In other areas, migrations may be hundreds of kilometers long.

The elk of the southern Yellowstone herd migrate 60 to 110 km (40 to 70 mi) south, to the **National Elk Refuge** in Jackson Hole, Wyoming to winter (Figure 77). The elks' summer range consisted of open parks and alpine ridges near treeline. Browsing in the open meadows and in the alpine tundra was easy during the summer months, but deep snows and windswept ridges do not provide suitable conditions for winter survival. A relatively short migration south provides conditions with shallower snows, relatively warmer temperatures, and access to the summer crops of grasses in the valley bottoms. Each autumn from 7,000 to 11,000 elk migrate to the elk refuge. Caribou in northern regions have to migrate hundreds of kilometers

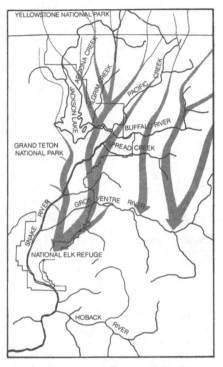

Figure 77. *Migration routes of the elk wintering in the National Elk Refuge. Many of the elk are from the southern Yellowstone herd.*

to achieve similar suitable wintering conditions.

Other mammals in the Jackson Hole region make shorter migrations that drop them into suitable winter grounds. Moose migrate from the upper forest meadows down 15 to 20 km (24 to 32 mi) to the willow-lined stream bottoms (Figure 78). Bighorn sheep migrate similar distances down to the ecotone between lower treeline and sagebrush flats. The bison also leave the higher regions of Yellowstone and migrate to the lower valleys. Pronghorn antelope find conditions in Jackson Hole too harsh for the winter and migrate out over passes in the Gros Ventre mountain range down into the Green River valley and drier desert regions.

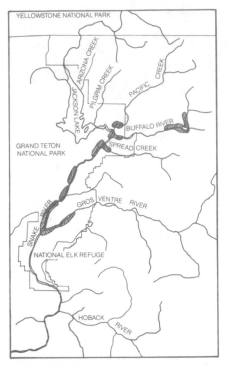

Figure 78. *Winter ranges of moose (after Houston, 1968).*

The timing of the migration is critical. If animals do not migrate early enough, perhaps because of a mild autumn, it is possible that heavy snows later on may trap them away from the wintering grounds. Snow depth is the main factor inducing the start of migration. Generally, animals tend to start their migration when the snow depth reaches mid-calf height. Animals in the higher regions start migration sooner, since deep snows accumulate earlier in the fall at higher altitudes. Size of mammals is an important factor determining timing of the migration; broadly speaking, deer migrate first, followed by elk, and then moose. The elk migration starts when one old cow leads long lines of animals of her herd out of the high mountains. Moose migrate later when snows at the 2,400 m (8,000 ft) level reach a depth of about 60 cm (24 in).

Not all animals migrate at the same time, and some animals migrate more quickly to and from the wintering grounds (Table 19). Migrations of the

Visitors use horse-drawn sleighs to observe wintering elk at the National Elk Refuge.

Table 19. Timing of the migration of the Piceance Basin deer herd to its winter range in Colorado.

Date (1981)	Leave Summer Range (percentage)	Arrive Winter Range (percentage)
September 17 - 23	0	0
September 24 - 30	4	0
October 1 - 7	41	4
October 8 - 14	51	0
October 15 - 21	4	77
October 22 - 28	0	19
October 29 - November 4	0	0

Table 20. Comparison of summer and winter diets for selected ungulates in the northern, mountainous United States. Main items are indicated by percentage of diet.

Species	Summer Diet	Winter Diet
Elk	Grasses (mostly)	Snowbrush (*Ceanothus*) (5-10) Pine (5-10) Willow (5-10) Mountain mahogany (2-5) many different grasses
Mule deer	Serviceberry (10-25) Grasses (5-10)	Sagebrush (10-25) Pine (5-10) Aspen (autumn) (2-5) Douglas fir (2-5) Snowbrush (2-5) Rabbitbrush (2-5) Bitterbrush (autumn) (2-5)
Moose	Aquatic plants (large amount) Forb (many types)	Aspen (5-10) Grasses (5-10) Willow (5-10)
Pronghorn	Sagebrush (25-50) Rabbitbrush (10-25) Grasses (2-5) Mountain mahogany (2-5)	Sagebrush (25-50) Rabbitbrush (10-25) Grasses (2-5)
Bighorn	Needlegrass (2-5) Mountain mahogany (2-5) Sedge (2-5)	Fescue grass (10-25) Wheatgrass (5-10) Sagebrush (5-10) Ricegrass (2-5) Muhlygrass (2-5)

deer of the Piceance Basin, Colorado, have been followed by radio collar. Their departures from the summer range extended over a four-week period, but their arrivals at the winter range was mostly synchronized to a two-week period. The actual migration took about two weeks. Migrations tend to be slow when the weather is mild and rapid when the weather is harsh.

Some animals tend to migrate very late and a few elk arrive at the National Elk Refuge as late as January each year.

Diet Switching

Migrations often result in **diet switching** as different items are added to the winter food list (Table 20). Elk include more woody shrubs and trees in their diet. Moose switch from a high percentage of aquatic plants to more willows and aspen. Bighorn sheep utilize different grasses and add a high percentage of sagebrush to their diet. The diet of pronghorn antelope does not vary much between summer and winter. Therefore, it is important for them to migrate out of Jackson Hole, with its deeper snowpack, to the Green River valley where the snowpack is shallow enough that the grasses and sagebrush are still exposed.

As mentioned earlier, most of the winter food items may lack the nutritional value of the summer diet. Although conditions on the new wintering range may be more conducive to winter survival than those that would be encountered by remaining on the summer range overall, the winter diet is probably lower in nutritional value than the diet found on the summer range. In many areas of the west, and around Jackson Hole in particular, the winter range has been drastically reduced or destroyed by the encroachment of civilization. Fences and roads serve to isolate traditional ranges. In many areas, the diet of wintering ungulates is supplemented by federal or state agencies. At the National Elk Refuge, elk are fed in all but very mild winters. This results in **supplemental feeding** during about nine out of every ten years.

The refuge elk are fed alfalfa pellets at a rate of 1 kg (2.2 lbs) per 45 kg (100 lb) of elk weight per day. This means that a bull elk (295 kg, 650 lbs) will receive 5.9 kg (13 lbs) of supplemental feed, a cow (250 kg, 550 lbs) will receive 5 kg (11 lbs), and a calf (118 kg, 260 lbs) will receive 2.4 kg (5 lbs). Under this regime, **winter survivorship** is excellent, with only about one percent of the herd dying on the refuge each winter.

Supplemental feeding often is visual-ized as the answer to protecting wild ungulates during the winter. When conditions become harsh, the general public raises an outcry for local officials to implement supplemental feeding. As mentioned in the previous section, however, there are many practical problems associated with supplemental feeding. At the Elk Refuge, elk are gradually introduced to the artificial diet, and native grasses are available as part of their diet during the whole winter. Abrupt supplemental feeding is not the answer to short harsh periods of weather during the winter.

While some populations prepare for winter by migrating, others prepare by going through physiological or morphological changes such as shedding antlers and changing colors. Here we would like to consider the ramifications these changes have on animal populations.

Preparation for Winter

Antlers appear to have evolved not only for defense, but also for display purposes in attracting females. In some species, antlers reach enormous size; those of elk weigh over 12 kg each (26.4 lbs) and those of the moose may reach 30 kg each (66 lbs). Carrying the weight of such large antlers over the course of a winter represents a serious energy drain, which might reduce the odds of surviving. It may well behoove the animal to **shed** (**cast**) its antlers as early in the winter season as possible. Early casting would reduce energy losses, and different species have evolved different schedules of casting their antlers.

Moose, with the largest antlers of the North American ungulates, cast their antlers in December in the Rocky Mountains. (By January, only small-antlered bulls will still have their antlers, and these they may retain for several more months.) Mule deer will cast shortly thereafter. However, elk may retain their antlers until May. Occasionally, elk with the last year's antlers may be observed during the month of May grazing next to elk showing new growth. Elk may even carry the last year's antlers back toward the summer range.

Different selective pressures appear to control the adaptation for the timing of antler casting. Moose and deer take advantage of the energy savings gained by early shedding of antlers. The moose winters in relatively small groups where antlers may not be important in obtaining food—the main purpose of large antlers for the moose is the increased ability to obtain a mate. Deer also winter in small groups where the energy cost of maintaining antlers may not offset the enhanced ability of the deer to obtain food. Elk, however, winter in large herds where, even after the mating season, the antlers appear to provide an advantage in maintaining dominance. When a **dominant** bull loses its antlers, it immediately becomes submissive to previous **subdominants**. With a lower status in the social hierarchy, that bull may receive less food. Thus the longer a bull maintains its antlers during the winter, the greater its apparent food-gathering ability and the greater its chances of survival.

The use of antlers for protection and food gathering might provide selective pressures leading to the retention of antlers all winter. However, the use of antlers for protection against predators does not appear to have exerted enough selective pressure to cause deer, elk, or moose to keep their antlers all winter. Each of these animals is capable of putting up a good fight against predators simply by striking out at them with its front hooves. For elk,

and perhaps deer, wintering as a herd provides protection against predators. Deer, elk, and moose do not make significant use of their antlers in food gathering during the winter. Caribou, the only members of the deer family in which both sexes possess antlers, do use their antlers to scrape away snow to get at forage.

Some animals begin their preparations for winter by undergoing a **color change**. The coats of weasels, ptarmigan, and snowshoe hares change from shades of brown to white for the winter. Hair color changes may be accomplished in different ways. For instance, the hairs of the weasel turn white along the entire length of the hair (see Figure 16). This color change involves a complete **molt** in which each hair is lost and a new, white hair replaces the brown hair. The white **pelage** (covering of hair) is a beautiful and efficient camouflage during the snow season. It is so beautiful that people prize the ermine pelt and many ermine are taken by trappers each winter. Ermine fur is favored by British royalty and has been reserved for royal use in coronations. Over 50,000 pelts were shipped from the United States for the 1936 coronation of King George VI.

The snowshoe hare accomplishes its color change in another manner, in which only the tip of the hair turns white, while the base remains a grey color (Figure 79). The hare does not have to go through a complete molt to accomplish this color change in the fall. It is interesting to note that arctic hares in the far north do not change color seasonally but remain white during the short arctic summer. The arctic hare is so well adapted to winter that the cost in energy of changing to brown during the short summer exceeds the benefits of permanent adaptation for winter.

The **timing** of color changes is im-

Figure 79. *A white snowshoe hare has been feeding on a snow-covered branch. The grey bases of the hair that show among the white tips indicate that only the tips of the hair change color each winter.*

portant. If the weasel turns white in the fall before winter snows have accumulated, it will stand out against its background. A white ermine displayed on a brown background is easy prey for predators. Similar disadvantages occur in the spring if the weasel, hare, or ptarmigan turns brown before the snow melts. Those animals that can most closely duplicate the timing of the snowpack receive a selective advantage over those animals with poor timing.

Timing may be accomplished through an **endogenous** (internal to the body) **clock** operating on a nearly annual basis. The clock has several purposes. It must provide advance warning that winter is coming, because organisms must start to prepare before the cold season actually arrives. Hiberna-

tors must put on fat, and other animals must change color. The clock also may act as a guide in geographic areas where environmental cues are lacking: it tells the birds at the equator when it is spring and time to migrate north.

The internal clock of natural cycles keeps its own time, and that time does not exactly correspond with the calendar year. The clock keeps the animal in tune with the environment, but it is not exactly synchronized to environmental cues, such as the **photoperiod** (the length of the dark period each night, which changes from season to season). The clock needs flexibility to respond to early or late falls, or early or late springs. Natural rhythms set the clock approximately to the season, but it is aligned by environmental cues. The environmental cues that help to align the clock include photoperiod, temperature, and snowfall.

Timing is a complex phenomenon involving the internal clock and environmental cues. Were the clock to be timed by photoperiod only, the weasel would turn white every year at the same time, regardless of the amount of snow on the ground. Changes in photoperiod trigger changes in **hormones**, which are also influenced by cold and snow. These hormones in turn trigger the changes in hair color. The system is complex and it does not always work exactly; for example, brown weasels can sometimes be seen on white snow (Figure 80). Evolutionary pressures are constantly working to refine the timing for **chionophiles**.

Many legends have grown around discussions of animal preparations for winter and the severity of the coming winter. Some legends refer to the thickness of mammal fur and to the activity of mammals gathering seeds for the winter. Woodsmen, farmers, and others believe that fur thickness predicts coming winter severity. Zookeepers, who maintain and watch animals closely, tell us that fur thickness really reflects weather conditions the previous summer. Hot and dry summers produce light fur coats, and cold, wet summers produce thick, dense fur.

Those who rely on predictions from seed gatherers may be interested to know that detailed studies show food gathering patterns reflect seasonal crop production. If there was a good summer with large seed crops, then the seed gatherers will be very busy. If there was a crop failure, little gathering activity will occur. Starvation may follow crop failures and a mass exodus may even occur. In years of poor seed crops in the north, birds often migrate south.

Figure 80. *Brown weasel on the spring snowpack. The biological timing mechanism has not worked for this weasel as it molted to brown too early in the spring season.*

Dormancy

Other animals prepare for winter by entering a period of **torpor** or **hibernation**. Metabolic rates are lowered, body temperatures drop, oxygen consumption is reduced, and the use of stored fats is almost eliminated. Some of the smallest winter sleepers allow their body temperatures to drop within 1°C of freezing, or even below freezing, as in the case of the Arctic ground squirrel. Larger mammals, such as bears, skunks, and raccoons, lower their temperatures only slightly. Whatever the tactic, though, the animal passes the winter season in a resting state that allows it to conserve needed energy. Animals that hibernate generally have high overwinter survival rates. Cases of hibernating animals dying during severe cold periods are known, however—hibernation is not an absolute escape from winter. In some cases, hibernating animals are vulnerable to predation. Black-footed ferrets prey on hibernating white-tail ground squirrels in their winter nests.

Bears show an interesting adaptation of timing the entrance into hibernation. There is a tendency for the bears to enter their den for the final time in the middle of a snowstorm. This tactic would appear to cover the bear's tracks as it moves to the den. This extra measure of security may be important, because bears have been known to be killed in their dens by other bears.

Food Storage

Some animals store food for winter. Notable for food storage are beavers and pikas. Beavers may **cache** up to 65 kg (143 lbs) of woody material per animal in the mud at the bottom of the pond. The pika, a member of the rabbit order, produces **hay piles**, where it caches the herbs it gathers to dry for the winter. Hay piles may weigh 6 kg (2.7 lbs) and an individual pika may have two to six piles. Scientists have removed hay from these piles, but it did not seem to affect the survival of pika. This would suggest that pika gather more food than they need. However, on Niwot Ridge, Colorado, when experiments created abnormally deep snows, and thereby a late-lying snowpack, survivorship of pika was dramatically decreased. Hay piles, as food sources, may therefore be more important in years of late-lying snowpack and less important in average years.

Those animals that do not store food for winter may increase their body fat. The deer, elk, and moose reach their highest levels of fat accumulation during the early fall. The green, protein-rich diet of summer is stored as fat for winter. Animals preparing for hibernation also increase their fat levels.

Preparations for winter continue through the fall. Some animals build up their food stores as fat, others change colors at the appropriate time, while still others move into their **hibernacula** (dens for overwintering) to wait out winter. Winter eventually arrives at full force and the SCREW factor begins to whittle away at the animal populations.

Winter Severity

The severity of weather in a given winter plays a role in how many animals will survive. Severe winters can have a large impact on population sizes. Scientists have analyzed the severity of winter weather as experienced by populations of moose in the Grand Teton National Park area. Five factors proved critical to moose populations: **temperature**, **snow depth**, **snow density**, **duration of winter**, and **lateness of spring**.

Information on these five factors can be obtained from weather records of the **Teton Science School**, located in the moose-study area of Grand Teton National Park at an elevation of 2,134 m (7,000 ft). Weather records reveal the harsh conditions that moose must survive each winter. On average, temperatures will drop below freezing for 256 days each year, and for 68 of those days the temperature did not go above -17.8°C (0°F).

A deep **snowpack** is common throughout most of the winter, extending the duration of winter conditions (Figure 81). Deep snows (greater than 50 cm) exist for an average of a hundred days each winter. Late snows often perpetuate the snowpack, creating a late spring, when moose are at their weakest. The snowpack is seldom dense enough to completely support the full weight of the moose when walking, because cold temperatures produce light, fluffy snows and unconsolidated **depth hoar** beneath the snowpack.

Moose populations respond to the five critical vectors of winter (the SCREW factor), and harsh years result in decreased numbers of surviving moose. The winters can be ranked ac-

SNOWPACK AT THE TETON SCIENCE SCHOOL

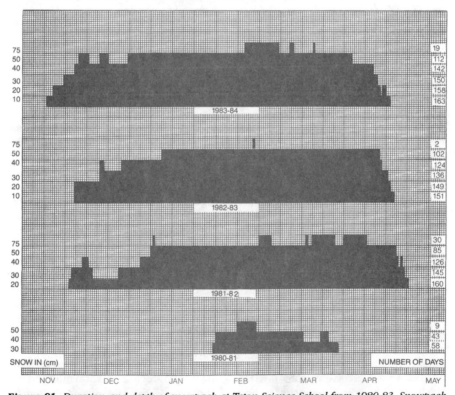

Figure 81. *Duration and depth of snowpack at Teton Science School from 1980-83. Snowpack varied considerably over the time period, with depths reaching 50 cm (19.7 in) each year. In two years, extended periods occurred when the snow was 75 cm (29.5 in). A deep snowpack or extended periods of snow cover is hard on ungulates. The school is located within the study area for moose of Grand Teton National Park.*

cording to severity by the magnitude of impact on moose populations. About one winter out of 35 is extremely severe, about one winter out of 20 is very severe, and just over four winters out of every 20 are above average in severity. Overall, six or seven winters out of every 20 have a heavy impact on the moose population. About one-third of the winters represent challenges to survival and exert selective pressures determining which moose survive.

Winter Kill

The effects of severe winter conditions are reflected in the populations of other animals besides the moose. Many animals die each winter not only from bad weather but also from the combined effects of **malnutrition**, **starvation**, **disease**, and **predation**. Collectively and colloquially, these deaths are referred to as **winter kill**. The rogues' gallery of winter killers includes many problems created by the expanding activities of human beings: fences, domestic pets, snowmobilers and skiers, and car and train accidents. Natural killers include lack of food, disease, predation, and competition. Although it may paint a gloomy picture, we will briefly mention some of the factors not already discussed. It is necessary to review this material to have a full understanding of the impacts of winter on animal populations.

Yarding of animals during the winter often provides better access to food since the trampling of many feet exposes plants for grazing. Numbers also provide additional security against predation. However, these same numbers also produce crowding that is conducive to spreading **diseases** among animals that also may be in a weakened condition because of malnutrition. Pinkeye and lungworm in bighorn

sheep are notable examples of diseases that spread under conditions of crowding. Breaking through **snow crusts** strips the skin from the legs of animals. Bleeding, open wounds provide access for infectious bacteria, besides weakening the animal through blood loss.

Domestic pets, particularly dogs, often take advantage of the reduced mobility of mammals in snow to harass, maim, and even kill them. Even if the dogs do not catch the animal, they cause it to burn off needed fat reserves. Dogs should not suffer all the blame; cats can also successfully prey on medium-sized mammals and birds that are weakened or hindered by winter conditions. Wild animals living near our expanding towns and cities often suffer unfairly in their normal wintering ranges.

Snowmobilers will often chase wintering animals. Although they seldom run them to death, they still deplete animal fat reserves that may be necessary to survive a long winter or a late spring. Surprisingly, though, **cross-country skiers** may cause more damage than snowmobilers. Wild animals tolerate machines used on roads better than they do people. Wild animals do not like to be in close proximity with humans. A person on foot or on skis will spook animals into a run, again depleting necessary fat reserves. A person on a snowmobile does not have the same effect. Perhaps the noise and smell of the machine mask those of the person, or perhaps the combined shape of the person and the snowmobile cannot be recognized as a person. Biologists in **Yellowstone National Park** have long recognized the increased impact of skiers over snowmobilers. In the future, we may see more regulations restricting access by skiers.

Highway systems have proven to be both a boon and a bust for wild animals. The presence of plowed roads, or even just packed trails, provides convenient routes for winter movements. Paved and concrete roads absorb solar energy and melt the snow along their edges. As the snow recedes from the road, grasses and forbs are exposed and provide easy grazing. Animals then move to the road edges to feed, where many are hit by cars. The same phenomenon occurs along railroad tracks. Several years back, a train heading west past Casper, Wyoming, struck a large herd of antelope that was feeding along the edges of the tracks. About 125 pronghorns were killed in the incident.

As much as roads may ease winter movements, fences hinder them. Animals trying to jump barbed-wire fences can become entangled, because the snow offers an unstable surface from which to jump. Once entangled, they die trapped in the wires. Many fences are constructed in such a way as to block animals moving to their winter ranges, or the fences may block movement between the good feeding areas on winter ranges. In 1986, fences constructed in central Wyoming stopped large herds of migrating pronghorn antelope from reaching food sources. Since their use of the winter food source was in direct competition with cattle belonging to local ranchers, the issue of the fences was hotly debated. Eventually, the U.S. Supreme Court decided in favor of removing the fences and allowing the pronghorn continued access to their traditional migration routes. However, the issues of animal versus human rightsin the wake of expanding civilization are not always easily decided.

Many natural processes add to the winter mortality. Differences do exist between human-caused and natural mortality. **Natural mortality** tends to take the weaker animals. The first to die are the young of the year and the old battle-scarred males (Figure 82). The young have not had the time to learn the realities of winter and how to survive. If they are born late or small, they may not accumulate the reserves needed for winter, especially to survive a severe winter. Males have spent most of their energy during the fall trying to breed. Their fat reserves have been greatly depleted. This depletion is very obvious when you see a **harem** bull that has just been ousted from its harem. The bull may be just skin and bones.

Natural selection assures that the fittest animals survive winter kill, but this is not so for **human-caused deaths**. A train or a car does not necessarily select the weakest but tends to causes deaths across all age classes. Deaths due to humans may have the additional impact of unnaturally biasing the genetic makeup of surviving herds.

Detailed data on natural winter mortality is difficult to obtain. Few studies have been able to follow whole populations continuously through normal or severe winters. It is also difficult to find populations controlled only by natural processes and not influenced by humans. Studies in **Yellowstone National Park** have provided considerable insight into the possible magnitude of **winter mortality**.

A herd of 100 to 200 bison have wintered in the Pelican Valley of Yellowstone, probably since prehistoric times. The bison are the only large ungulates that winter in the valley. The winter of 1970-71 was severe in Pelican Valley. Between February and early April, about one-third of the herd (50 animals) died. The spring of 1973 was again a hard time for all Yellowstone animals. Approximately 31 percent of one elk herd, consisting of about 850 animals, died. Forty-five percent of the

Figure 82. *An eagle feeds on an old deer that has succumbed to death early in the winter. This winter-killed animal probably had depleted fat reserves when the winter began.*

deaths were calves, and occurred in the spring. These winter-killed animals succumbed collectively to the forces of severe weather, lack of food, and disease.

Late spring snowstorms can be particularly hard on animals since their fat and food resources are depleted. Perhaps the animals have even started to sense that spring may be near. The young may have been born or at least are near term. Spring snowstorms often bring especially wet and heavy snows. The storms may dump considerable amounts of snow and extend winter by weeks. In 1975, a May 15 snowstorm at Lander, Wyoming, dropped 1 m (39 in) of snow. The deer herds suffered considerably and 90 percent of the herd died. It took many years for the population to return to the previous level.

Predation by carnivores also reduces the number of surviving animals. Studies on elk in Yellowstone show that animals from 1.5 to 7 years of age are rarely victims of predators. Elk that are killed are generally the weaker animals —the young and the old. Predation can remove large numbers from a herd. Sixty-two percent (21) of 34 elk deaths recorded in the spring of 1970 were attributable to predation from grizzly bears coming out of hibernation. Up to 20 percent of lemming populations have been taken by predators during the winter.

Scavengers may often go hungry during the winter and even die of starvation. When a fresh carcass is found, it may be consumed in 24 to 48 hours. Most winters, however, some carcasses go unconsumed or are only partially eaten, because the carcasses are not found by scavengers, the meat is too frozen to chew, or too much carrion exists.

Trapping

Trappers also play a role in reducing the number of animals that survive winter (Figure 83). Although trapping efforts vary geographically, in some areas of North America considerable numbers of animals are taken each winter. In Colorado, the trapping industry is a more than two million dollar business each winter. In some poorer regions, trapping may add substantially to the income and even food supplies of local individuals.

The winter season is the best season for trapping. Yearly acclimation to cold and snow causes the animals to have thick, dense furs known as **prime** skins. Skins become prime in the early winter as the animal completes its **molt**, replacing old hairs and adding new ones. Trappers need to trap the animals before their skins go through much wear and tear, which reduces their value. The best months for trapping vary by species but usually include November through April. The best time may also depend on altitude. Skins from the higher, colder mountain regions come into prime earlier.

Prices also vary by species. Typical prices for muskrat pelt may be as low as $3.00 (U.S.), $7.50 for mink, $30.00 for beaver, $40.00 for coyote, $100.00 for bobcats, and $450.00 for Canada lynx. In general, animals from the regions with the coldest winters produce the best skins. Here is a case where se-

Figure 83. *A local trapper displays skins that he has taken near Lander, Wyoming.*

lection has provided the animal the best protection possible, only to make it more attractive to its main predator—humans.

Trapping may make important reductions in populations of wintering animals. Good trappers strive to harvest their trapping areas utilizing principles of **sustained yield**. Each winter, the trapper leaves behind enough animals to maintain the population and provide for additional harvests next year. We do know, however, that trapping, if uncontrolled or relentless, can cause local extinction of animals.

We have painted a bleak picture of survival for animals in snowy regions. Of the fall population that we started with, up to 28 percent may be lost to hunting, up to 90 percent of the remaining animals may be lost to winter kill, including unknown numbers lost directly to starvation and disease (Table 21). The fall population may be dramatically depleted before spring. But let us remember that these animals evolved with these harsh conditions. Each species, living in the winter country, has a birthrate that allows it to repopulate in the spring. This birthrate has evolved over time to provide the proper number of young to survive the coming winter (Figure 84). Most species in *most* years produce enough young to complete the annual cycle and start over for the next year. The miracle of life offsets the grim realities of winter.

Perhaps the strongest selective pressure of winter has been to evolve reproductive potentials exceeding limitations imposed by the SCREW factor of winter. Spring does arrive!

SUGGESTED READINGS

Arno, S.F., and R.P. Hammerly. 1984. Timberline: Mountain and Arctic Forest Frontiers. The Mountaineers, Seattle.

Casebeer, R.L. 1966. Elk habitat management. Biological Unit Mgmt. Plan, Teton Natl. Forest, Wyoming.

Houston, D.B. 1968. The Shiras moose in Jackson Hole, Wyoming. Tech. Bull No. 1, Grand Teton Nat. Hist. Assoc., Wyoming, Nat. Park Serv., U.S. Dept. Int.

Houston, D.B. 1978. Elk as winter-spring food for carnivores in northern Yellowstone National Park. J. Appl. Ecol., 15:653-661.

Martin, A.C., H.S. Zim, and A.L. Nelson. 1961. American Wildlife and Plants: A Guide to Wildlife Food Habits. Dover Publications, Inc., New York.

Meagher, M. 1971. Winter weather as a population regulating influence on free-ranging bison in Yellowstone National Park. Presented at Amer. Assoc. Advancement Science, Symp. Res. Natl. Parks.

Oedekoven, O.O., and F.G. Lindzey. 1987. Winter habitat-use patterns of elk, mule deer, and moose in southwestern Wyoming. Great Basin Nat., 47:638-643.

Table 21. Processes acting to increase winter mortality. The magnitude of each process is indicated as a percentage.

Process	Magnitude of effect on animal populations
Hunting	3 to 28%
Malnutrition	may be very high
Starvation	may be very high
Disease	may be very high
Winter kill (general)	31 to 90%
Predation	20%, 62% of spring deaths
Trapping	in some cases, large numbers

Figure 84. *The young of the spring are nature's answer to the rigors of life in a winter world. Enough young are born each year to offset population losses during the winter.*

PLANTS AND WINTER

Deep beneath the snowpack, many plants spend the winter wrapped in relative security, and in relative secrecy from inquiring ecologists. Little is known about plants during the winter, since they are largely dormant, and studies tend to begin in the spring when the snow melts. Some plants remain green, some transport their nutrients deep into their roots, some wither but sprout in the spring, some live only as dormant seeds awaiting spring, and some do survive above the snow exposed to the rigors of winter. Whatever the mode of response to winter, plants, as do animals, suffer from the vectors of winter—the **SCREW** factor (Figure 85).

Many frontiers remain in the study of plants during the winter. Most studies relating plants to cold and snow have taken place in arctic or alpine tundra regions. These studies may suffer confounding influences of high altitude or high latitude that might mask the specific influences of winter. Certainly many nontundra plant adaptations to winter may be similar or the same as those in the tundra, but more winter ecology studies are needed concentrating on plants under winter conditions in nontundra regions.

The SCREW factor defines the narrow line of survival for plants during the winter. Only the energy vector is substantially different for plants than animals, since for the most part, plants cannot gain additional energy reserves during the winter. Most of the principles explored for winter survival in animals also apply to plants. We will survey several stresses imposed by SCREW on plants during the winter: changes in photoperiod, lowered temperatures, freezing, desiccation, and mechanical

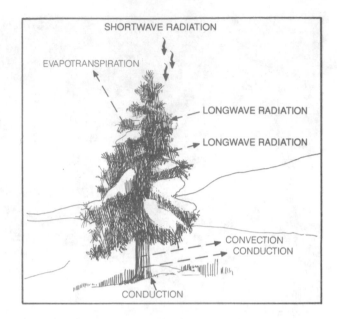

Figure 85. *The energy balance of a plant is controlled by the same energy exchange mechanisms experienced by animals: conduction, convection, radiation, and evapotranspiration, the latent heat of evaporation. Plants also experience energy losses through transpiration which is normally identified as evapotranspiration.*

damage. But first, seasonal acclimation for winter will be considered.

Acclimation to Winter

Since plants do not generate internal heat and are exposed to subfreezing temperatures, they are in danger of freezing each winter. Plants, however, possess the ability not only to resist freezing, but also to become tolerant to the effects of freezing. This ability, known as **hardening**, consists of acclimation to increasingly cold temperatures brought on by winter. The acclimation process is far from being well understood. Weiser (1970, see also Marchand, 1987) provided an excellent overview of the current state-of-knowledge. We will briefly explore hardening.

The details about hardening have been investigated for only a few plant species, and are not known for the vast majority of species. **Population differences** within species are apparent over latitudinal and altitudinal gradients, and little is known about spatial variation within small areas. If, however, we can learn from observation of a closely related phenomena, the turning of the leaves to their fall colors, considerable variation may exist within short distances. When aspen turn yellow in the fall at the **Mountain Research Station** in Colorado, the various **clones** (groups of trees linked by roots), are clearly defined by each shade of yellow or orange. The hillside is a patchwork of colors indicating a variety of individual clones with the same genetic response to the coming of winter. Each clone loses its leaves at a different time, indicating considerable variation in adaptation to the environment.

One of the chemical products important in leaf loss is **abscisic acid**, which is the link to forming the **abscission** layer in the leaf stem. It is this layer that breaks between the leaf stem and the plant stem, allowing the leaf to fall off. As we will see later, abscisic acid is also part of the hardening process. Therefore considerable variation should be expected in the hardening process and additional research may yet identify many other paths that the hardening process may take.

Hardening is a complex phenomenon. Plants exposed to subfreezing temperatures before the hardening process takes place will usually die, as they are incapable of hardening. Freezing resistance tends to increase during the whole hardening process. Hardening may be slowed by **Indian summers** or even be reversed during warm spells or **false springs**.

Hardening occurs in response to environmental changes in the fall, and is a gradual process that may take weeks to complete. Short autumn days are sensed by a **phytochrome clock** in the leaves. Phytochromes are light-sensitive chemicals that induce changes in cellular activity. (Abscisic acid is one such phytochrome.) The phytochrome clock, sensing the shortening of the days in fall, signals the start of hardening and the cessation of the summer's growth.

Stages of Hardening

Hardening appears to be a three-step process, although not all plants reach the third stage (Figure 86). The first stage probably occurs when a **hardiness-promoting** factor is **translocated** from the leaves to the overwintering stem. The identity of this chemical factor is not known, although it is probably a plant hormone; indeed different chemical factors may exist. **Abscisic acid** may be partially or indirectly involved. During this first stage growth ceases, carbohydrates are translocated to the roots, and the permeability of cell membranes increases. Many other chemical changes occur, but scientists do not understand their significance.

By the end of the first stage, plants can tolerate temperatures down to -5 or -10°C (23 or 14°F) without being killed. Water may freeze in the intercellular spaces but will not freeze within the cells (Figure 87). Freezing resistance within the cell is the result of water movement out of the cell to growing intercellular ice crystals. The **cytoplasm** (cellular fluid) is slightly concentrated and has a lowered freezing point because of chemical additions. Stage 1 hardening has reached the limits of its efficiency and further hardening will not occur until triggered by freezing temperatures and frost.

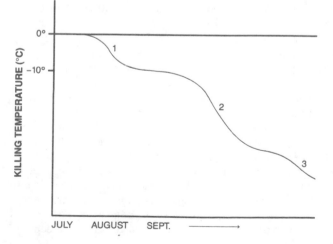

Figure 86.
Diagrammatic representation of the hardening process (after Weiser, 1970). The killing temperature is that temperature below freezing necessary to kill the plant on a given date. The numbers indicate stages in hardening and the level portions of the curve indicate transitions between different stages of the hardening process.

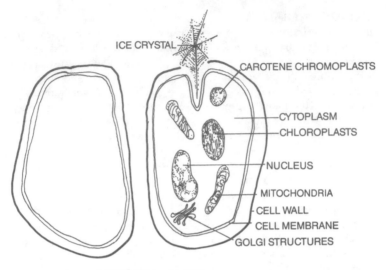

ICE CRYSTAL

CAROTENE CHROMOPLASTS

CYTOPLASM
CHLOROPLASTS

NUCLEUS

MITOCHONDRIA
CELL WALL
CELL MEMBRANE
GOLGI STRUCTURES

LIVING CELL—PLANT

Figure 87. *Microscopic view of plant cells. The cell membrane in plant cells pulls away from the cell wall as dehydration occurs. Small ice crystals puncturing the cell wall push the membrane out of the way without damaging it. Larger crystals may eventually puncture the membrane.*

Stage 2 is characterized by chemical alteration of **membranes**. Reorientation of molecules may occur, increasing the resistance to damage by dehydration. Proteins may be protected from freezing by replacing water molecules with sugar molecules. **Lipid** concentrations may also increase. Stage 2 may confer protection against death by freezing down to a temperature as low as -20 or -30°C (-4 or -22°F).

Little is known about the third stage of hardening, including the number of plant species in which it may actually occur. Buds do not appear to achieve Stage 3 hardening even though it may be found in the stems of the same plant. Stage 3 occurs following exposure to extremely cold temperatures such as -30 to -50°C (-22 to -58°F). A novel method of **cryoprotection**, involving ice formation without crystallization, has been described in **winter-hardened** balsam poplar trees *(Populus balsamifera)*. **Amorphous**

(without a distinct form) **solidification**, also known as **vitrification** or **glass formation**, creates ice masses with smooth rather than sharp edges that would destroy plant cells. It is possible that vitrification occurs during Stage 3. Although vitrification occurred at a relatively high temperature (-28°C, or -18°F), a "three glass" model identified glass transitions in two other intracellular components at -45°C (-49°F) and -70°C (-94°F). Glass formation may help explain the freezing tolerance of some trees down to temperatures of -80°C (-112°F).

Stage 3 hardening probably results from physical processes and is temperature- and-time dependent. Increased resistance to freezing during this stage may result from the decreased thermal motion of molecules in frozen cells. Stage 3 hardening is quickly lost even after only a few hours of warmer temperatures. The degree of hardiness reached during Stage 3 is most dependent on the previous day's temperatures.

Freezing Death of a Plant

A **thermocouple** (small electronic thermometer probe) inserted inside a tree stem as it slowly cools will show **exotherms**, or energy release when ice forms (Figure 88). **Flash freezing** of supercooled water causes sharp spikes of temperature increase. The first exotherm probably occurs when ice crystals form in the nonliving **xylem** cells (cells that conduct water). The second, smaller exotherm probably occurs when ice forms in the micropores and cell walls (Figure 86). Both exotherms occur at about -3 to -10°C (27 to 14°F)

Water freezing inside the plant, but outside the living cell, does little damage to the plant. The living material of the plant is protected inside the **cell membrane**, which is inside the hard cell wall (Figure 87). As ice crystals form external to the cells, water moves from the cell to the ice crystal. Water movement is facilitated by Stage 1 hard-

ening, which increases membrane permeability. Dehydration increases concentration of chemicals within the cell. The increased concentration in the cell lowers its freezing point. In the dehydrated condition, the cell membrane is not rigid and may pull away from the cell wall (Figure 87). Continued growth of intercellular ice draws additional water from the cell, further depressing the freezing point of the cell. Although the growing ice crystal may puncture the cell wall, it does not damage the living cell because the slack cell membrane simply moves away from the sharp point of the ice crystal.

Stage 2 hardening becomes important as dehydration continues. Dehydration eventually would prove harmful to plant compounds, but reorientation of macromolecules and sugar replacement on proteins reduces damage to the cell membrane and cell contents. Vitrification at colder temperatures would prevent ice crystal damage to the cell membrane.

A third exotherm occurs with continued cooling (Figure 88). Freezing of the

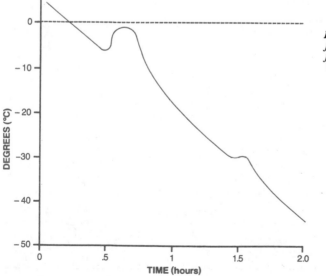

Figure 88. *Cooling curve for a plant stem. See text for discussion (after Weiser, 1970).*

contents of the living cell creates the third exotherm and causes the death of the cell. If enough cells freeze, the plant also dies. Actual death to the cell may also result from mechanical damage to the cell membrane, irreversible dehydration of the membrane and cellular contents, or the accumulation of toxic compounds in the cell. Processes related to ice formation cause the death of the cell, not low temperature itself. The hardening process is summarized in Table 22.

Freeze Resistance and Tolerance

Freeze resistance and tolerance are time-dependent phenomena. Rapid freezing can kill plants that would otherwise survive slow cooling. Abrupt cold spells will kill plants that had been doing well during the winter. These same plants, however, may have been capable of surviving substantially lower temperatures if the cooling occurred at a slower rate, allowing time for further hardening.

Freeze resistance may be reversed during the winter by a warm spell, especially a **false spring**. In 1989, a false spring occurred at the **Mountain Research Station** in Colorado. During January, temperatures were unusually warm, with a six-day mean maximum temperature of 6.4°C (43.5°F). Then in February a severe cold snap followed the first six days. The mean minimum and maximum temperatures for the second six-day period were -29.5 and -7.3°C (-21.1 and 18.9°F). For two nights the minimum temperature was -34°C (-29.2°F). Considerable damage occurred to the **lodgepole** pine (*Pinus contorta*) forests, with needles at the ends of most branches dying and turning red. Presumably this damage resulted from freezing of cells that had **dehardened**

Table 22. Summary of hardening or acclimation in woody plants (developed from Weiser, 1970).

	Spring	Summer	Early Autumn	Late Autumn	Winter
Growth	rapid	slowing	stops	dormant	dormant
Acclimation stage Amount	incapable	slight	first medium	second high	third high
Trigger			short days	freezing temperatures, frost	very low temperatures
Mechanisms producing hardiness			metabolic	metabolic, physical	physical
Hardiness promoting factor			hormone produced in leaves		
Status of resistance	tender	tender	mildly resistant	resistant	extremely resistant
Death from freezing occurs at	first exotherm	first exotherm	second exotherm	third exotherm	third exotherm

Table 23. Freezing resistance of buds of North American trees (after Sakai and Weiser, 1973).

Species		Temperature °C	(°F)
White spruce	*Picea glauca*	-80	(-112)
Englemann spruce	*Picea engelmannii*	-60	(- 76)
Lodgepole pine	*Pinus contorta*	-80	(-112)
Ponderosa pine	*Pinus ponderosa*	-35	(- 31)
Jack pine	*Pinus banksiana*	-80	(-112)
American larch (Tamarack)	*Larix laricina*	-80	(-112)
Larch	*Larix occidentalis*	-40	(- 40)
American white birch	*Betula papyrifera*	-80	(-112)
Balsam poplar	*Populus balsamifera*	-80	(-112)
Cottonwood	*Populus deltoides*	-50	(- 58)
Northern white cedar	*Thuja occidentalis*	-80	(-112)
Subalpine fir	*Abies lasiocarpa*	-40	(- 40)
Douglas fir	*Pseudotsuga menziesii*	-30	(- 22)
Giant sequoia	*Sequoia gigantea*	-20	(- 4)
Live oak	*Quercus virginiana*	- 8	(18)
Magnolia	*Magnolia grandiflora*	-20	(- 4)
Red maple	*Acer rubrum*	-30	(- 22)
Red ash	*Fraxinus pennsylvanica*	-30	(- 22)

due to the false spring. Incidentally, freezing resistance appears to be lost faster than it is gained.

Considerable variation exists in the degree of freezing resistance shown by North American trees (Table 23). Those from southern regions can scarcely survive temperatures a few degrees below freezing, while those from northern regions can survive an incredible -80°C (-112°F). Some trees, if they are first frozen at about -15°C (5°F), can even survive being dipped in liquid nitrogen at -196°C (-321°F).

Biogeographical patterns of resistance to freezing are obvious with three categories of resistance. The first category includes those trees whose freezing resistance approximates the minimum temperature found in the northernmost portions of their range. The live oak and sequoia are examples of trees whose southern ranges suggest that they are limited by adaptation to winter temperatures. The second category includes trees such as cottonwoods, aspen, and spruce, whose freezing resistance far exceeds the limits imposed by minimum temperatures occurring in their ranges. Other explanations must be found for the limits of their northern range. Third is a group of trees that show latitudinal and altitudinal populations with different levels of freezing resistance. For trees like Douglas fir and western hemlock, minimum temperatures appear to force acclimation to low temperatures, but the trees have the plasticity to adapt to a wide range of minimums. Is it possible that Category 3 trees might be more susceptible to false spring events such as that which occurred at the Mountain Research Station?

Response to Low Light Intensity

Many plants pass the winter in a dormant stage, but some are known to continue physiological processes and development in the subnivean environment. Plants active in the winter may be limited by temperature or available light. **Light** is particularly important, since it provides not only the energy source for photosynthesis, but also may signal timing for different developmental stages.

The subnivean environment is a dark home during most of the winter. Early in the winter 30 to 50 cm (12 to 20 in) of snow is sufficient to block light. By early spring, light **transmission** may reach to 2 m (6.5 ft) although **spectral selection** from filtration through the snow will greatly reduce the longer wavelengths, including the red colors. Changes in the quantity and color of light may be very dramatic over the winter season (Figure 89).

Scientists constructed a **snow tunnel** in Franklin Basin, Utah, to study the effect of light in the subnivean environment on plants. The snow tunnel was constructed as a small sunken building with the roof at ground level. The building was reached by a tube through the snow, and contained doors sealed to prevent light entry. Sliding doors in the roof of the tunnel allowed plants to be placed on shelves at the base of the snowpack, beneath glass. Reactions of test plants were carefully monitored to determine the effects of changing light in the subnivean.

Three aspects of light may influence plant activity beneath the snowpack. These include the **quantity of light**, the **timing of light**, and the **quality of light**. Plants can react to very low levels of light. Light-sensitive lettuce seeds in the tunnel **germinated** in response to exposure to light filtering through nearly two m (6.5 ft) of snow. Different species of plants show reduced sensitivity to available light, but wild mustard seeds (*Brassica nigra*) also germinated in response to light beneath the same snowpack, although their seeds required a week of exposure compared to three hours for the lettuce seeds.

Plants may detect the increasing day length (**photoperiod**) beneath the snowpack. The change in photoperiod signals to the plant that it is time to begin development. Cell division and vascular development have been reported in several subnivean plants. Spring beauties (*Claytonia lanceolata*) and snowdrops (*Oregenia linearifolia*) develop leaves and floral parts before emergence from the soil, while still beneath the snowpack. Snowbank buttercups (*Ranunculus adoneus*) flowers will open in the snow. Any advantage that a plant gains by developing beneath the snowpack may add significantly to its survival in the short grow-

Figure 89. Available light under the snowpack drops abruptly in the fall and increases as abruptly in the spring (redrawn from Everden and Fuller, 1972). The fall decrease results mostly from rapidly deepening snow; the spring increase results from increased transmission of the snow as albedo and attenuation change with increased density and water content. The change in the sun's position in the sky (solar angle) also affects light transmission, but is not as influential as the properties of the snow.

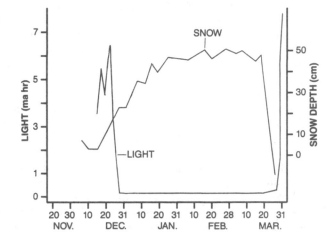

ing season found in many winter regions.

The quality of light changes as the spring snowpack changes. The longer **wavelengths** (reds and far-reds) that have been selectively absorbed during the winter by the snow begin to increase in proportion to the blue wavelengths, with the far-reds showing a greater increase than the reds. Most plants respond to changing photoperiods through a **phytochrome** sensitivity. Phytochrome occurs in a far-red and a red form. The far-red form is the active form and may respond to changes in far-red light intensity signalling the beginning of development.

It is interesting to note that many plants emerging from the snowpack in the spring are red. One of the most common plants of the alpine tundra at the Mountain Research Station, alpine avens (*Acomastylis* or *Geum rosii*) is almost completely red. This plant is very successful in most plant communities, which might be in part because of its ability to take advantage of light transmission through the snow. The red pigments would be able to absorb the greens and blues that passed through the snow all winter.

Response to Lowered Temperatures

Lowered temperatures tend to retard plant activity both above and below the snow. Some processes continue at low temperatures. Since the conversion of far-red phytochrome to its inactive form is slower at low temperatures, plants may be more responsive to its signals at temperatures near freezing. Many species continue development in the subnivean. The plants mentioned above all show cellular activity beneath the snow at temperatures around freezing. Cellular activity leads to leaf greening,

leaf unfolding, shoot development, and flower development. Early development, in turn, offsets the short growing season in winter areas. Additional advantages would accrue to plants that could maintain or prepare for a fast start-up to photosynthetic activity.

Photosynthesis has been detected in some plants in ice and snow. While working in Antarctica, James Halfpenny was able to show that **blue-green algae** frozen in blocks of ice could photosynthesize if exposed to sunlight. Mats of the algae would be trapped in ice cover of lakes by daily freeze-thaw cycles. Reradiated solar radiation would soon form a small hole in the ice. Using a fine, long needle the air in these bubbles was sampled. Bubbles from ice in the sun contained above-normal amounts of oxygen, and bubbles from shaded area contained above-normal amounts of carbon dioxide. The presence of oxygen indicated photosynthesis and the presence of carbon dioxide indicated **respiration**. **Snow algae**, small organisms that live in the snowpack and color it red in the summer, also carry on photosynthesis at temperatures around freezing. Photosynthesis has been detected in higher plants during the winter as well.

Many species of plants remain green during the winter, presenting the possibility that retained **chlorophyll** pigment may allow photosynthesis. It has been demonstrated that blue light increases the synthesis of chlorophyll protein and that chlorophyll is synthesized under the snow. Light penetrating the snow appears to play an important role in maintaining the integrity of the chloroplast and preventing senescence. Plants that can maintain and use retained chlorophyll may then gain an advantage over dormant plants during the winter or early spring.

Let us consider two life forms of

plants that remain green during the winter and therefore have the potential for **winter photosynthesis**. These plants are either **evergreen** or **wintergreen**; that is, they live more than two summers or they start to mature one summer, and finish and die the second summer, respectively. Kinnikinnick (*Arctostaphylos uva-ursi*) is an example of an evergreen herb, and cutleaf daisy (*Erigeron annuus*) is an example of a wintergreen herb.

Winter annuals, plants that germinate one summer, overwinter, and flower and die the next summer, are often wintergreen plants and are also often composed of rosettes of leaves lying nearly flat on the ground. Winter annuals, such as cutleaf daisy and shepherd's purse (*Capsella bursa-pastoris*), have shown the ability to photosynthesize with leaf temperatures less than a degree above freezing. During the winter, leaf temperatures of plants shielded from the wind often may be 10°C (18°F) greater than air temperature due to heating by incoming solar radiation. So even at low air temperatures, the rosette lifeform allows these plants to maintain high temperatures by passive heating.

Three adaptations allow the plant to take advantage of temperatures just above freezing for photosynthesis. First, these plants have very short **start-up times**. After a dark or cold period, they may begin photosynthesis within a few minutes and maximum photosynthetic capability may be reached within 12 minutes. Second, these plants are able to reach maximum photosynthetic capability at lower temperatures (Figure 90). This process is called **temperature compensation**. Temperature-compensated plants not only reach maximum photosynthetic capability at about 10°C (18°F) lower, they are capable of about 45 percent efficiency at temperatures

just above freezing! Third, **light compensation** also occurs, allowing the plant to photosynthesize under low levels of light that would be found in the subnivean environment. Given the temperature and light conditions, these winter annuals will photosynthesize all winter long. Plants that maintain their food-producing mechanisms and that photosynthesize at the beginning of spring will have a considerable head start over winter-dormant plants.

Evergreen conifer trees may not be capable of much photosynthesis during the winter. Measurements for bristlecone pine (*Pinus aristata*) in California at 3,094 m (10,151 ft) indicate that energy loss from respiration generally exceeds energy gain from photosynthesis. Photosynthesis did occur but was not the dominant process. The net loss of energy during the winter was great enough to require approximately 117 hours of photosynthesis during the summer to compensate for winter losses. It is possible that a low amount of photosynthesis during the winter is important in keeping the net energy loss low. It is also possible that under less harsh conditions, photosynthesis would generate a large amount of energy.

The bark of **aspen** trees (*Populus tremuloides*) often appears greenish-yellow. This may be especially obvious on early spring days. The green color is due to the presence of **chlorophyll**, which appears to be synthesized during the winter. Testing with iodine for the presence of starch indicates that the chlorophyll is actively producing carbohydrates during the winter. It has been suggested that the ability of aspen to photosynthesize during the winter may help account for their presence in what is otherwise a conifer-dominated ecosystem.

Plants from algae to flowers appear

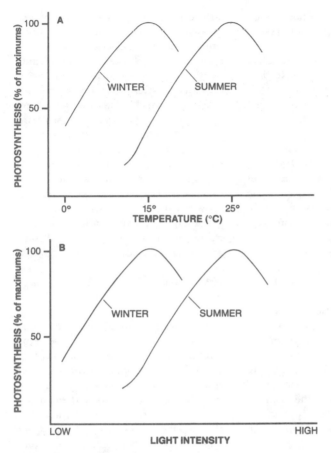

Figure 90. *Temperature (a) and light (b) compensation are shown by winter annual plants. During the winter, plants are capable of maximum photosynthetic activity at lower temperatures and lower light intensities than during the summer.*

to be able to photosynthesize during the winter. This ability may provide a competitive advantage with the arrival of spring. Overwintering dormant plants must gain their advantage by competitive processes later in the summer. Evergreen and wintergreen plants are most apparent in the landscape in the early summer and are replaced by winter-dormant plants later in the summer. Clearly chlorophyll retention and use is a winter-oriented adaptation for survival.

Response to Freezing

Earlier, we discussed the process of acclimation to freezing temperatures and the process of plant death due to freezing. We will briefly consider some response to freezing temperatures. Reversal of the acclimation process followed by cold snaps can result in **winter burn** on conifer leaves and **blackheart** in the stems of deciduous trees and shrubs. **Frost splitting** occurs to tree trunks. During this process, water freezing in tree trunks causes fracturing of trees. Gaps created by frost splitting can range from 5 cm (2 in) to completely shattered trunks. During very cold times in the winter, trees may be heard splitting in the woods. However, frost splitting can occur when a cold snap follows a warm spell during which translocation of water up the trunk has started. Although not studied in detail, frost splitting probably results from dehardening.

Freezing may create another problem for the plant. In order for water to flow from the roots to the crown of the tree, a continuous column of water must exist within the plant. Freezing of the plant stem may cause air bubbles to form in the vascular system, causing the water column to break (**cavitation**). Cavitation occurs in deciduous trees but not in coniferous ones. Apparently the bordered pits in the vascular system of conifers function to isolate freezing sap. The isolation creates a positive pressure, which prevents cavitation.

Response to Desiccation

Plants are also susceptible to damage by **desiccation** during the winter. Desiccation results from excessive drying induced by decreased humidity, increased exposure to radiation, and increased high winds. These factors tend to remove moisture from the plant at the time when the plant is experiencing reduced water absorption from frozen soil.

Plants have evolved a host of defenses to prevent water loss in order to survive the drying conditions of winter. Most water moves through a plant by **transpiration** and is lost through stomates in the leaves or through the **cuticle** covering of the leaf. **Stomates** are openings into the leaf that allow gas and water exchange with the environment. Relative humidity inside the stomatal cavity is high, often around 100 percent, and considerable water loss may occur through the opening. However, stomates remain closed during the winter, preventing water loss. Increased cuticular surface wax also reduces water loss during the winter.

Damage from desiccation is particu-

larly evident at the upper limit of tree growth. Here, under the harsh conditions of winter, desiccation is often a main factor contributing to overwinter death in conifers. Death results from desiccation of leaves on dry sunny days and from **wind abrasion**, which reduces the cuticular wax layer, allowing increased water loss. High winds also increase transpiration. It has been suggested that damage to conifer needles results from predisposition to winter damage associated with poor summer growth conditions. Tests at treeline in Wyoming, however, indicate that the main cause of death is winter exposure and cuticle abrasion.

Response to Mechanical Damage

The physical forces of winter may also cause mechanical stress to plants, resulting in considerable damage. Frost splitting and wind abrasion have already been mentioned. **Soil displacements** resulting from freeze-thaw cycles may damage roots and even tear plants completely out of the soil. Soil displacement, including **needle ice** churning of the soil, influences vegetation succession by keeping patches of ground open to pioneering plants. **Plant upheaval** results from two processes: soil freezing at the surface and needle ice generation, and deep frost penetration and soil heaving (Figure 91).

Primary heaving results from minor cycles of freeze-thaw action that may occur on a daily basis in the spring and fall. Needle ice is formed in saturated soil and elongates vertically to lift small stones and young plants out of the ground. Repeated cycles of needle ice formation "**jack**" the plant out of the ground by increments. If the plant still has its roots deep in the soil, it may return to its former position by **elastic**

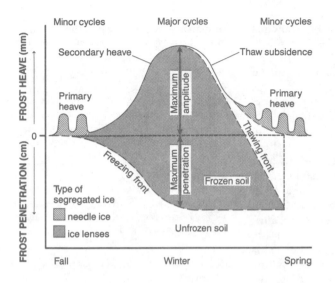

Figure 91. *Schematic diagram of soil displacement resulting from freezing during the winter. Primary heave results from the minor cycles of freezing while secondary heave results from the major cycle of freezing occurring only once each winter. Note the difference in scales on the Y-axis (from Perfect, et al., 1989, with permission from Arctic and Alpine Research).*

recoil when thawing occurs. **Secondary heaving** results from the major cycle of freezing each winter. During the secondary heaving, ice lenses form parallel to the soil surface, causing considerable vertical displacement. The secondary heaving is strong enough to pull fully rooted, mature plants from the soil. Needle ice formation usually occurs in bare, saturated soil, while the major cycle of ice formation also occurs beneath fully vegetated turf. Plant upheaval from either primary or secondary heaving may result in winter plant mortality or may expose the roots so that death results during the summer.

The weight of accumulated snow may be enough to damage plants. **Snow loading** results in branches being stripped from **aspen** trees to heights of 3.7 m (12 ft). Spruce trees, however, seem particularly well adapted to resist the effects of heavy snow. Their branches all slope downward. When the snow becomes too heavy the branches sag and the snow load drops to the ground. This mechanism does not confer complete protection though. In boreal forests, the snow

load will sometimes become uneven and will cause the tree to fall. This opens a gap in the forest, which leads to uneven loads on other trees and the gap continues to increase in size as other trees fall. The new gap provides openings for a new generation of young trees. Uneven loads of snow often deform conifers and aspen in mountainous regions, bending them over to the ground. These plants are not able to function completely during the summer and ultimately die.

Deep snows have another effect. They provide a home for **snow fungi** (*Herpotrichia*). These fungi attack plants, especially conifers, in the spring when temperatures warm up. The filamentous **hyphae** penetrate the needles and twigs, sapping the nutrients from the branches and eventually killing them. Mature hyphae appear as brown shapeless masses on the trees, much as if an animal had defecated on the branch. The snow fungi can only grow in a certain range of snow depths. If the snow is too shallow, fungi won't be present; nor will they if the snow is too deep. Therefore snow fungi kill branches on a tree within a narrow band. Trees whose lower branches have been killed are called "trees with skirts" and can be seen in the **krummholtz** zones on mountain topes. Snow fungi can kill young trees under the right conditions but the fungi is seldom fatal to mature trees.

Plants are subject to the same stresses of winter, as animals. These stresses are characterized by the SCREW factor. Their energy budget differs only slightly from that of animals in that plants are not able to add much energy during the winter. A negative budget results in their ultimate death. Without energy additions, the plants must survive winter and repair any damages that may occur. To survive winter some plants become dormant, others have evolved mechanisms that allow physiological processes to continue, at least at slow rates, during the winter. Little is know about how plants continue their activities during winter and the research field is wide open for the future. This chapter may spark your interest to investigate some of the unknowns about plant survival in winter.

SUGGESTED READINGS

Everden, L.N., and W.A. Fuller. 1972. Light alteration caused by snow and its importance to subnivean rodents. Canadian J. Zool., 50:1023-1032.

Hadley, J.L., and W.K. Smith. 1983. Influence of wind exposure of needle desiccation and mortality for timberline conifers in Wyoming, U.S.A. Arc. Alp. Res., 15:127-135.

Hadley, J.L., and W.K. Smith. 1986. Wind effects on needles of timberline conifers: seasonal influence on mortality. Ecology, 67:12-19.

Hammel, H.T. 1967. Freezing of xylem sap without cavitation. Plant Physiol., 42:55-66.

Hirsh, A.G., R.J. Williams, and H.T. Meryman. 1985. A novel method of natural cryoprotection. Plant Physiol., 79:41-56.

Kimball, S.T., and F.B. Salisbury. 1974. Plant development under snow. Botanical Gazette, 135:147-149.

Perfect, E., R.D. Miller, and B. Burton. 1988. Frost upheaval of overwintering plants: a quantitative field study of the displacement process. Arc. and Alp. Res., 20:70-75.

Pearson, L.C., and D.B. Lawrence. 1958. Photosynthesis in aspen bark. Amer. J. Botany, 45:383-387.

Polunin, N. 1933. Conduction through roots in frozen soil. Nature, 132:313-314.

Regehir, D.L., and F.A. Bazzaz. 1976. Low temperature photosynthesis in successional winter annuals. Ecology, 57:1297-1303.

Schulze, E.D., H.A. Mooney, and E.L. Dunn. 1967. Wintertime photosynthesis of bristlecone pine (*Pinus aristata*) in the White Mountains of California. Ecology, 48:1044-1047.

Richardson, S.G., and F.B. Salisbury. 1977. Plant responses to the light penetrating snow. Ecology, 58:1152-1158.

Marchand, P.J. 1984. Light extinction under a changing snowpack. Pp. 33-38, *in* Winter Ecology of Small Mammals (J.F. Merritt, ed.). Carnegie Museum Nat. Hist. Spec. Publ. No. 10, Pittsburgh.

Marchand, P.J. 1987. Life in the Cold: An Introduction to Winter Ecology. University Press of New England, Hanover, New Hampshire.

Sakai, A., and C.J. Weiser. 1973. Freezing resistance in trees in North America with reference to tree regions. Ecology, 54:118-126.

Weiser, C.J. 1970. Cold resistance and injury in woody plants. Science, 169:1269-1278.

INSECTS AND WINTER

Winter presents different challenges to insects than it does to mammals and plants. True, the insects must face the SCREW factor, but they must do so with a dramatically different makeup. An insect is essentially a liquid-filled box. The liquid is **hemolymph**, the insect equivalent of blood. The internal organs of the insect are free floating in the hemolymph, and the insect's skeleton, an **exoskeleton**, is on the outside of the body. Hemolymph functions to transport nutrients for the body, support organs, maintain hydrostatic pressure, and in some cases even aids in defense. Hemolymph is mainly water. Maintaining a container of water, the insect body, over the course of a winter, requires evolutionary solutions different from those already mentioned.

Strategies for Overwintering

Consider the limitations imposed by the body of an insect. Body size must remain small because of limitations imposed by how much weight an exoskeleton can mechanically support. Small body size limits the distances that an insect can migrate and imposes severe restrictions on thermoregulatory responses to cold. In addition, the small body of the insect contains no **insulation** and insects are **ectotherms**, animals who do not heat their bodies internally (**cold-blooded**). The insect can and does utilize strategies found in mammals and plants (for example, migration and supercooling) but its arsenal of winter defenses contains novel means of protection. General strategies for **overwintering** fall into five categories: migration, dormancy, communal behavior, winter-activity, and physiological escape.

Migration

Insect **migration** involves three strategic alternatives: **horizontal, vertical**, and **selective migrations**. Horizontal insect migrations have only been documented in recent years. Notable for long horizontal migrations are the **monarch butterflies**, which migrate from the continental United States to California, Mexico, and Yucatan (Figure 92). Perhaps yet other species with horizontal migrations will be discovered. Many insects migrate vertically into the ground by digging or following small cracks to deep below the **freezing** or **frost line**. Near Boulder, Colorado, **ladybird beetles** migrate up vertically, concentrating in large numbers to overwinter on the foothills overlooking the vast prairies. Some insects migrate selectively to protected **hibernacula**, including winter homes beneath the bark of trees or in other local, protected spots.

Dormancy

Dormancy is a common strategy, and insects overwinter in many immature stages, including eggs, larvae, and pupae. These overwintering stages are often deposited in or selectively located in protected spaces deep in the leaf litter or under tree bark. Many aquatic and semiaquatic species overwinter in pond and lake mud. Some winter-dormant species, however, spend the winter in very exposed places such as insect **galls** located on willow branches high above the nivean environment. Perhaps most notable for wintering in an exposed area is the **Arctic caterpillar** (*Gynaephora*), which may be found on exposed rocks.

Communal Behavior

Communal behavior is common in the **Hymenoptera** order, in which bees and ants are found in nests of

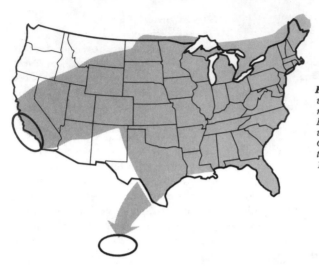

Figure 92. *Breeding and wintering areas of the monarch butterfly. Butterflies migrate to wintering areas in California, Mexico, and in the Yucatan (after Urquhart, 1976).*

thousands. Communal species remain active during the winter, with behavioral responses facilitating response to cold temperature. Honeybees, by their rapid and intense activity, are able to raise the temperature in their hives to prevent freezing damage to the colony.

Winter Activity

Many insects remain active each winter. Aquatic insects continue their activity in streams that remain open. **Stone flies** mature to the winged form, mate, and lay eggs. Small **black flies** (*Capnias*) emerge from streams to crawl over the snow. **Caddis flies** (*Platyphylax*) and **crane flies** (*Helobia hybrida*) mate on warm days in February. **Springtails** (*Podura aquatica*) and **snow fleas** (*Achorutes nivicola*) abound on warm winter days.

Physiological Escape — Cold-hardiness

Perhaps the most exciting story, though, consists of physiologic escapes from freezing that allow winter activity. Insects suffer two types of cold-related fatal injuries during the winter. Mortality due to freezing is well known, but more recently scientists have learned about **nonfreezing fatalities** resulting from exposure to subfreezing temperatures. Insects, much the same as plants, undergo **cold-hardening** with the onset of lowered temperatures. Cold-hardening allows survival from below-freezing conditions and may confer protection for either overwinter or rapid cooling effects. Two types of cold-hardiness are known: overwinter and rapid.

In **overwinter cold-hardiness**, insects commonly achieve protection against freezing down to temperatures of -35°C (-31°F) and, in Alaska, species are known to achieve protection down to -60°C (-76°F). The mechanisms providing overwinter cold-hardiness result from supercooling and insect-manufactured cryoprotectants.

The **freezing point** of **supercooled** water can range down to -41°C (-42°F) as long as it is not moved. Freezing point is dependent on the volume of the water, rate of cooling, and presence of impurities. The smaller the drop of water, the lower the freezing point (Table 24). A 1 mm (0.039 in) drop of water out of the kitchen faucet freezes

Table 24. Relationship between the volume of water and its freezing point. This table assumes household water with its impurities.

Drop mm	Diameter (in)	Freezing Point °C	(°F)
10.000	(0.39)	-18	(- 0.4)
1.000	(0.039)	-24	(- 11.2)
0.100	(0.0039)	-31	(- 23.8)
0.001	(0.000039)	-41	(- 41.8)

at -31°C (-23.8°F) and a similar sized drop of distilled water freezes at -33°C (-27.4°F).

Considerable protection against freezing is available from isolating water into small drops. The body of an insect effectively isolates drops of water. Some drops are intracellular and others extracellular, but all drops are small. Water in an insect body thus can supercool to very low temperatures without freezing. However, if a supercooling strategy is adopted to avoid freezing, then nonmovement is obligatory. Any movement on the part of the insect would cause **flash freezing** and the rapidity of the freezing would cause sharp ice crystals, destroying cells.

Freezing is dependent on impurities in water. The impurities act as **ice-nucleating agents** and initiate the formation of ice crystals. The larger the number of impurities, the more likely the water is to freeze. To achieve a winter cold-hardiness, insects may evacuate their intestinal tracts, removing all contents including impurities that could act as nucleating agents. During hardening, ice-nucleating agents in the tissue may be masked or inactivated by chemical compounds. Proteins have been implicated in this process. Dehydration also appears to influence the supercooling process, because smaller amounts of water freeze at lower temperatures.

Chemicals in the insect act as **cryoprotectants**, that is, compounds that prevent freezing or hinder further freez-

ing once ice crystals form. Cryoprotectants act in three ways: some initiate ice-nucleation, some serve as antifreeze, and some stop or prevent additional freezing.

Those chemicals that initiate **ice-nucleation** are sometimes called **"anti-antifreeze"** because they function to cause freezing in the insect at higher temperatures. The advantage to this strategy is that freezing can be caused outside the cell where it will not harm the cell. Extracellular freezing sets up an osmotic gradient, which removes more water from the cell and increases solute concentrations in the cell. Increased solute concentrations, in turn, prevents intercellular freezing.

Ice-nucleating agents are synthesized by the insect and consist of **proteins** or **lipoproteins**. Nucleating chemicals catalyze extracellular ice-formation at -5 to -10°C (23 to 14°F) causing ice-nucleation in the gut and hemolymph. Synthesis of proteins, which has been studied in **darkling** (*Tenebrionid*) **beetles** is diurnally cyclic and takes from three to six hours to build up.

Other chemicals depress the freezing point and act as a biologic **antifreeze**. Insects synthesize both simple and complex molecular compounds to serve as antifreezes. Simple antifreeze compounds include **sugars**, such as trehalose, and **polyols** (polyhydroxyl alcohols) such as **glycerol** and **sorbitol**. The low-molecular-weight compounds function by increasing the solute content of the cell, resulting in a decrease in the freezing point. Resulting freezing point depression can only go down to about -10°C (14°F). These compounds may also function to stabilize protein structure and membranes against cellular dehydration during freezing.

Complex or high-molecular-weight **proteins** are also synthesized to function as antifreeze. Protein antifreezes function by lowering the freezing point but do not affect the melting point when the insect warms up. Protein antifreezes act to decrease the freezing point another 5 or 6°C (9 or 10.8°F). It has also been suggested that protein antifreezes may stabilize the supercooled state by attaching to the embryonic ice crystal, thus preventing further freezing.

Cryoprotectants often reach high concentrations within insects and are also very pure. Considerable **energy** is required to produce these chemicals and we might expect natural selection to optimize production by using the chemicals for other purposes. Indeed, many of the chemicals serve secondary purposes, which include increasing **energy reserves** and maintaining **osmotic pressure**. Then, too, perhaps the chemicals originally served these purposes and were adapted to act as cryoprotectans. Cryoprotectants are often taxonomically specific, with only certain chemicals being found in related taxonomic groups. Some insect species, however, will utilize more than one type of chemical protection to gain from their additive effects.

In **rapid cold-hardiness**, insects commonly achieve protection against **nonfreezing mortality**. Nonfreezing mortality occurs following rapid exposure to subfreezing temperatures where **supercooling** prevents freezing. Non-

freezing injury is thought to be caused by a phase transition in the lipid membrane, causing the membrane to lose its integrity. Damage may also result from excessive thermoelastic stretching of the membrane. For some species, mortality is not observed until after extended periods of exposure to cold temperatures. Death from long-term exposure has been termed **prefreezing mortality**. For other species, death occurs following short-term exposure and is termed **cold shock**. Rapid cold-hardiness confers protection again both forms of nonfreezing mortality (Figure 93).

Rapid cold-hardiness differs from overwinter cold-hardiness in several ways. Rapid hardiness occurs in all stages of insect life, not simply the overwintering stage. It may occur in feeding and reproducing animals at any time during the year. Rapid hardiness is induced by temperature decreases below freezing and is not photoperiod dependent. The speed of hardening has survival value in polar and alpine regions where nighttime temperatures may become very low (even though it does not get dark in the polar regions, temperatures may lower considerably when the sun is at a low angle at night).

Rapidly formed **cryoprotectants** appear to account for rapid cold-hardening. **Glycerol** has thus far been implicated. Following exposure to two hours of freezing temperatures, glycogen levels will be elevated two to three times. Additionally, elevated levels of **glycogen phosphorylase** have been detected. This enzyme changes stored glycogen into glycerol. Glycerol may prevent injury by stabilizing bilayer- and nonbilayer-forming lipids during cooling.

Even two hours of exposure to near-freezing temperatures can instill considerable rapid cold-hardiness, allowing

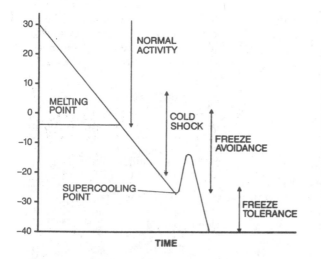

Figure 93. *Insect response to low temperatures. The cooling and freezing curve of the insect body is similar to that of plants with a thermal exotherm indicating the moment of freezing. The types of activity shown on the right are indicative of general ranges. The dividing line between freeze avoidance and freeze tolerance coincides with the supercooling point (after Lee, 1989).*

insects such as adult **flesh flies** (*Sarcophaga crassipalpis*) to survive supercooling down to -10°C (14°F).

Larvae and pupae show similar protection levels if cooling is not too fast. Rapid cold-hardening protects against temperatures as much as 15°C (27°F) above the supercooling point.

Activity Responses to Winter

Insects respond to cooling temperatures in a variety of ways (Figure 93). Normal activities may continue at below-freezing temperatures until the melting point of the insect body fluids is reached. At this point, freezing protection results from **supercooling** body fluids. Since motion causes supercooled fluids to freeze, activity must stop when the melting point temperature is reached. Mortality from cold shock and prefreezing exposure may occur over the range from a few degrees above freezing down to a few degrees above the supercooling point. **Freezing mortality** may occur at any temperature below freezing and different species show differently levels of sensitivity to below-freezing temperatures.

Insect species may be grouped into two categories by the methods they utilize to achieve protection against mortality from freezing. **Freeze-intolerant** or **freeze-susceptible** species avoid ice formation within their bodies (Figure 93) and **freeze-tolerant** species allow ice formation between cells. Both types of species use **supercooling** and **cryoprotectants** against freezing. Only freeze-tolerant species produce **ice-nucleating** agents.

Environmental Synchronization

Insects must react both to cooling in the fall and to daily periods of cooling. The initiation of fall cold-hardening is governed, in part, by a biological clock that responds to a shortening of the **photoperiod**. The beginning of acclimation is also triggered by cooler temperatures in the range of 0 to 5°C (32 to 41°F), which increase the activity of enzymes. Enzyme activities initiate synthesis of **cryoprotectants**. Recent work has indicated interactions between photoperiod and daily cycles of temperature (**thermoperiods**), but more work is needed in this area. Thermoperiod cues may be particularly important to rapid cold-hardening. Acclimation in insects can be quickly reversed by warm temperatures, and cryoprotectants are quickly lost.

A Final Word

The study of insects in the winter provides a fascinating glimpse into a little-known world. Live traps under the snow will reveal more activity than would be expected. Overwintering stages may be collected from galls, under tree bark, and under the snow. When brought into the warm classroom, the rapid loss of acclimation will result in active animals. Stream beds also yield winter-active insects. A refrigerator and a thermocouple can provide exciting and interesting experiments in cold-hardening. It is very easy to investigate the body cooling curve (Figure 93) with the thermocouple.

Insects, housed in their exoskeleton, have evolved mechanisms allowing survival during the winter. They have had to overcome may restrictions placed on them by their diminutive size. Over evolutionary time, they have evolved many interesting and intriguing survival mechanisms. We expect that many more await discovery by the winter ecologist.

SUGGESTED READINGS

Baust, J.G., R.E. Lee, and R.A. Ring. 1982. The physiology and biochemistry of low temperature tolerance in insects and other terrestrial arthropods: a bibliography. Cryo. Lett., 3:191-212.

Lee, R.E., Jr. 1989. Insect cold-hardiness: to freeze or not to freeze. BioScience, 39:308-313.

Lee, R.E., Jr., C.P. Chen, and D.L. Denlinger. 1987. A rapid cold-hardening process in insects. Science, 238:1414-1417.

Lee, R.E., R.A. Ring, and J.G. Baust. 1986. Low temperature tolerance in insects and other terrestrial arthropods: bibliography II. Cryo. Lett., 7:113-126.

Ring, R.A. and D. Tesar. 1981. Adaptations to cold in Canadian arctic insects. Cryobiology, 18:199-211.

Urquhart, F.A. 1976. Found at last: the Monarch's winter home. National Geographic, 150:161-173.

The chrysalis, a type of cocoon, protects a moth or butterfly during its winter sleep.

A view from the top as a cross-country skier carves a telemark turn while skiing down the hill.

4. People and Winter

Just as animals and plants cope with winter, so too must humans. For some, winter is a time of hardship; for others, winter is simply a part of life. Many natives who evolved in cold regions do not consider their existence in a harsh climate to be difficult because of their long heritage of coping with winter. People who depend on the mechanized world often find winter a time to be endured. Increasingly, however, winter is becoming a time for recreation. In this chapter, we explore people out in winter—their perceptions, responses, understanding, and recreation in and about the nivean world. First, we will look at the effects of cold on people and the hazards of being out in the winter. Then, based on our years in the nivean world, we will discuss traveling and camping in winter, including

conserving the white wilderness. Finally, we'll list educational programs for those who wish to pursue being out in winter.

PERSONAL PERCEPTION OF WINTER

As humans, we also experience the forces of the **SCREW** factor. Different individuals, however, may perceive winter differently. Although the terms were originally used as an ecological classification of species, we might even group people as **chionophiles**, **chioneuphores**, and **chionophobes**, for it appears that the human race varies from lovers of winter to those that fear or even hate it. On a given winter day, there will be those who are

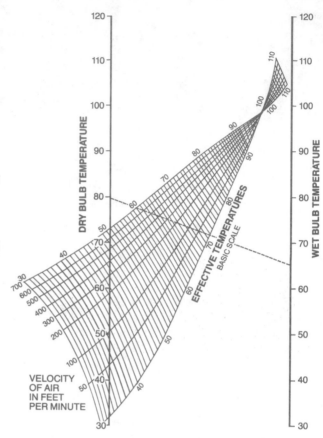

Figure 94. *Nomogram showing the calculation of effective temperature (after Yearbook of the American Public Health Association, 1936). Wet bulb temperatures are taken by wrapping a piece of wet cloth around the mercury reservoir of the thermometer. The effective temperature (dotted line) for a dry temperature of 80°F, wet bulb temperature of 65°F, and a wind speed of 100 feet per minute is 69°F.*

comfortable and those who shiver all day long. Under some conditions, however, almost everyone finds winter uncomfortable and even dangerous.

Scientists have struggled for many years to find a method of describing winter discomfort that was applicable and intuitively understandable to most people. Simple temperature readings do not suffice because many other factors complicate individual perception of cold. We know that the **energy budget** of a person is affected by not only air temperature, but also radiation, conduction, convection, and evaporation effects. In addition, people may wear different amounts and types of clothing, may bear differing amounts of insulating fat, and may differ in their acclima-

tion to cold. Understanding the perception of discomfort during winter has profound implications for health and safety.

In the 1920s, the American Society for Heating and Ventilation Engineers developed the first index of temperature comfort, the **Effective Temperature index** (**ET**) (Figure 94). The ET index defined the degree of warmth perceived by an individual exposed to different combinations of temperature, humidity, and wind. ET was recorded as the equivalent temperature in still, saturated (100 percent relative humidity) air that matched the warmth perception of the sampled conditions. Trained personnel were exposed to different environmental conditions, which they related to standard conditions by moving between control and test rooms.

The temperature index represents an important concept, namely that various environmental conditions could be summarized as an equivalent temperature under standard conditions. The ET index was limited for winter use because its lowest operable temperature was -1.1°C (30°F). In addition, at temperatures below freezing the determination of relative humidity becomes a difficult task in the field.

In the 1930s, scientists defined the components of the **human energy budget**: radiation, conduction, convection, and evaporation. Nude test subjects sitting on copper chairs in enclosed rooms were carefully monitored for energy and moisture exchanges. These experiments defined an **optimal average skin temperature** for comfort of 33°C (91.4°F). To avoid confusion between the conflicting terminology of the heating engineers, medical physicians, and physiologists, scientists defined two important units: the met and the clo. One **met**, or thermal activity unit, is the metabolic heat produced by a person resting in a sitting position under conditions of thermal comfort (50 cal/hr/m² of surface area of the individual). The met unit varies with the size of the individual, but for an aver-

age-sized man, one met is approximately equivalent to the heat generated by a 100-watt light bulb. One **clo** is the necessary resistance offered by clothing to maintain the comfort of the subject under standard conditions. The clo is the unit of thermal insulation and corresponds to approximately the equivalent of everyday clothing, a little less than 0.5 cm (0.2 in) of wool clothing. One clo is defined as the difference in temperature between the skin and the top of the clothing divided by heat flow through the clothing ($0.18°C/cal/hr/m^2$). Standard conditions for these units were considered to be air movement of 10 cm/s (20 ft/min), temperature of 21°C (70°F), and a humidity of less than 50 percent.

One met and one clo are average values, but they provide a general idea of how people respond to environmental conditions. From these empirically derived values it is possible to estimate the optimal temperatures for comfort for a person in normal clothing at various levels of activity (Table 25). The amount of clothing necessary for comfort at different temperatures can also be estimated (Table 26). The U. S. Army Quartermaster Corps has used these figures to estimate the amount of clothing that is necessary to provide for its soldiers for conditions ranging from deserts to polar regions. **Comfort rat-**

Table 25. Optimal temperature for comfort with exercise in normal clothing (after Gagge et al., 1941).

	Resting, sitting		Slow walking		Normal walking		Fast walking	
	°C	(°F)	°C	(°F)	°C	(°F)	°C	(°F)
Activity (met)	1		2		3		4	
Place								
Normal indoors	21.1	(70.0)	14.7	(58.4)	6.1	(43.0)	-19.4	(28.5)
Drafty indoors	23.8	(74.8)	15.3	(59.6)	7.6	(45.6)	-1.1	(30.0)
Normal outdoors	24.4	(76.0)	16.4	(61.5)	8.3	(47.0)	0.6	(33.0)
Windy outdoors	25.3	(77.6)	17.3	(63.2)	9.3	(48.8)	1.7	(35.0)

Table 26. Clothing requirements to maintain comfort under various environmental conditions. Requirements are shown in clo units and in the thickness of wool clothing necessary to maintain comfort. One clo unit or 0.5 cm of clothing is necessary to maintain comfort indoors at 21°C (70°F) (modified from Gagge et al., 1941). Figures shown indicate the maximum amount of clothing needed at a given temperature.

Environmental temperature (normal outdoors)	Resting, sitting		Slow walking		Normal walking		Fast walking	
	clo	(cm)	clo	(cm)	clo	(cm)	clo	(cm)
21°C　(70°F)	1.5	(0.75)	0.7	(0.35)	0.4	(0.20)	0.3	(0.15)
10°C　(50°F)	3.1	(1.55)	1.5	(0.75)	0.9	(0.45)	0.7	(0.35)
1°C　(30°F)	4.7	(2.35)	2.3	(1.15)	1.5	(0.75)	1.1	(0.55)
-18°C　(0°F)	7.2	(3.60)	3.5	(1.75)	2.3	(1.15)	1.7	(0.85)

ings used by Recreational Equipment, Inc. and other outdoor equipment companies traces their origins to these sorts of calculations (Table 27).

Obviously, these rating systems represent averages and include a lot of assumptions. When they are applied to single individuals, care must be taken in interpretation. For example, one individual sleeping in a tent on one ensolite pad with two inches of loft in the sleeping bag will be warm, while another person may be cold. Also, care must be taken when comparing equipment from different manufacturers. Were all the equipment tests conducted in the same way? Did the sleeping test subjects have on clothes, were they in a tent, and how much chocolate did they eat before crawling in? Figures are probably more comparable within one manufacturer's line than between manufacturers. When purchasing insulating items, consider your own temperature perceptions. Are you a cold sleeper or a warm sleeper?

The third **Byrd** expedition to **Antarctica** in 1939-40 provided the testing grounds for determining the dangers of subfreezing temperatures and winds. Paul Siple (1908–1968), a pioneer in the study of the effects of cold on humans, defined the term **windchill** as an index relating heat loss to temperature and wind speed. Windchill has since become a popular index of the perception and dangers of cold temperatures and winds.

Siple and his coresearcher Charles Passel used plastic cylinders filled with water to determine the rate of heat loss for different combinations of exposure to temperature and wind by measuring the time required for the water to

Table 27. Typical comfort ratings for commercially available sleeping bags (after Recreational Equipment, Inc). Notice that the comfort rating is best indicated by the thickness or loft of the sleeping bag, because the weight will vary with the type of insulating material.

Comfort Rating °F	(°C)	Fill Weight lbs	(kg)	Total Weight lbs	(kg)	Loft in	(cm)	Filling
+ 30	(-1.1)	2.0	(0.9)	3.0	(1.4)	3.0	(7.5)	PolarGuard
+ 25	(-3.9)	2.3	(1.0)	3.8	(1.9)	4.0	(10.0)	PolarGuard
+ 20	(-6.7)	3.0	(1.4)	4.0	(2.0)	5.0	(12.5)	PolarGuard
+ 15	(-9.4)	3.0	(1.4)	4.5	(2.1)	5.0	(12.5)	PolarGuard
+ 15	(-9.4)	1.3	(0.6)	3.3	(1.5)	5.5	(13.8)	Down
0	(-18)	1.7	(0.8)	3.3	(1.5)	6.5	(16.3)	Down

Table 28. Windchill equivalent temperatures (°C) calculated according to Siple and Passel (1945) for metric and English units.

Temp (°C)	Wind speed (m/s)							
	Calm	2	4	6	8	10	15	20
5	5	4	-1	-4	-6	-8	-10	-12
0	0	-1	-7	-10	-13	-15	-18	-20
-5	-5	-6	-13	-17	-20	-22	-26	-28
-10	-10	-11	-19	-23	-27	-30	-34	-36
-15	-15	-16	-25	-30	-34	-37	-41	-44
-20	-20	-21	-31	-37	-41	-44	-49	-52
-25	-25	-26	37	-43	-48	-51	-57	-60
-30	-30	-32	-43	-50	-55	-59	-65	-68
-35	-35	-37	-49	-56	-62	-66	-72	-76
-40	-40	-42	-55	-63	-69	-73	-80	-83

Temp (°F)	Wind speed (mph)							
	Calm	5	10	15	20	25	30	35	40
40	40	37	28	22	18	16	13	11	10
30	30	27	16	9	4	0	- 2	- 4	- 6
20	20	16	4	-5	-10	-15	-18	-20	-21
10	10	6	-9	-18	-25	-29	-33	-35	-37
0	0	-5	-21	-32	-39	-44	-48	-51	-53
-10	-10	-15	-33	-45	-53	-59	-63	-67	-69
-20	-20	-26	-46	-58	-67	-74	-79	-82	-85
-30	-30	-36	-58	-72	-82	-88	-94	-98	-101
-40	-40	-47	-70	-85	-96	-104	-109	-113	-116

freeze. They related water freezing to the freezing of human flesh by assuming a neutral skin temperature of 33°C (91.4°F). When skin temperature rises above the neutral point to about 34.5°C (94.1°F), sweating occurs and evaporation reduces skin temperature, so skin temperature is seldom above the neutral point. When skin temperature is below the neutral point a sensation of chill occurs. Therefore 33°C represents the normal skin temperature and the value also corresponds to the **average skin temperature** previously defined. Skin cools at a rate proportional to the difference between skin and air temperatures. The **cooling rate** determined from real data in the field is

$$K_o = (10.45 + 10 \sqrt{V} - V)(33 - T_a)$$

where V is the velocity of the wind in m/s and T_a is the air temperature in °C.

K_o is the total cooling power of the atmosphere. Since Siple was working in the dark of the Antarctic night, his results were in complete shade and without regard to evaporation, because little evaporation occurs at subfreezing temperatures.

Wind increases the cooling rate in a manner defined by the cooling curve. The greater cooling rate caused by increased wind speed equals the same cooling power of a lower temperature with no wind. The lower temperature without wind is the **windchill equivalent temperature** (**WET**) and is the value reported as windchill by the weatherman (Table 28). WET is derived as follows:

$$(10.45 + 10 \sqrt{V_e} - V_e)(33 - WET)$$
$$= (10.45 + 10 \sqrt{V} - V)(33 - T_a)$$

It is important to note here that conditions with no wind rarely exist. The temperature of the human body sets up convective air movement in all but the hottest days of summer. Body temperature alone is sufficient to create wind velocities up to 1.79 m/s (4 mph). Therefore, instead of calculating WET with a wind speed of zero, 1.79 m/s is substituted for V_e, the equivalent wind speed. The resulting equation is

WET (°C) = 33 -
(10.45 + 10 $\sqrt{V}$ - V)(33 - T_a)/22.04

The result of using 1.79 m/s is that under low-wind conditions the WET is greater than the air temperature. Many published tables ignore this fact and list the WET as equal to the air temperature at low wind speeds. Since there is little effect from winds of less that 1.79 m/s (4 mph), this is not a serious problem. Note also that the National Weather Service has modified the constant 10.45 to 10.63. The WETs calculated by this

equation have been presented in various tables and nomograms (Table 28, Figures 95 and 96).

The equation for calculating WET for temperature in degrees Fahrenheit and wind velocity in miles per hour is

WET (°F) = 91.4 -
(.474 + .303 $\sqrt{V}$ - 0.02 V) (91.4 - T_a).

Further research into windchill provided a WET chart that included the influences of clothing, temperature of exposed skin (30°C, or 86°F), activity, ventilation rate, dry and evaporative heat loss from the lungs, and radiative heat loss. The Steadman table (Table 29) shows WET temperatures that are warmer than those derived in the Siple and Passel table (Table 28). General guidelines are provided for the heating effect of sunshine. After considering factors such as solar input, absorptivity of clothing, and heat-transfer coefficients, sunshine effectively raises the air temperature by approximately 14°C

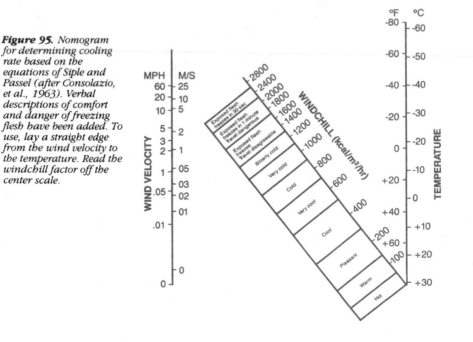

Figure 95. Nomogram for determining cooling rate based on the equations of Siple and Passel (after Consolazio, et al., 1963). Verbal descriptions of comfort and danger of freezing flesh have been added. To use, lay a straight edge from the wind velocity to the temperature. Read the windchill factor off the center scale.

Table 29. Windchill equivalent temperatures (°F) including the effects of solar radiation, humidity, and clothing (after Steadman, 1971).

Temp (°F)	Wind speed (mph)								
	Calm	5	10	15	20	25	30	35	40
30	32	30	25	21	18	15	12	10	7
20	23	20	14	9	5	1	-2	-6	-9
10	13	10	4	-2	-8	-13	-18	-23	-28
0	3	0	-7	-15	-22	-28	-35	-42	-49
-10	-6	-10	-19	-28	-36	-45	-54	-63	
-20	-16	-20	-30	-41	-52	-63			
-30	-26	-30	-42	-55	-68				
-40	-35	-40	-54	-69					

(57.2°F) under nearly calm conditions and by approximately 7°C (44.6°F) in a strong wind.

Steadman also calculated the thickness of clothing required to insulate the body at various WETs (Figure 97). It is apparent that under severe conditions, it is not possible to wear enough clothing to keep warm. Additional activity is necessary to provide metabolic heat for survival. When sitting still, considerable clothing is needed to maintain warmth.

Further testing was done by Siple and Passel to determine the effects of various cooling rates on human flesh. Volunteers, who were warmly clothed but bare-headed, were faced into the wind until a sharp twinge of pain indicated the freezing of flesh. Freezing of flesh occurs when the cooling rate exceeds about 1,200 to 1,400 cal/m²/hr. Further field research has suggested that under most conditions the dangerous value is 1,400. Frostbite may occur in isolated fingers at WETs generating a loss less than 1,400. This occurs because the amount of surface area losing heat from a finger is greater in relation to the volume than for a larger object such as the head. Siple and Passel identified cooling rates that indicate increased health hazards in winter (Table 30).

Many people have criticized the windchill index because it represents human perception of cold by using only two factors, when many other factors obviously contribute to the effects of cold. Others have questioned whether a field-derived index can actually represent the way people feel winter. Two sets of experiments have tested the relationship between cooling rates and perceptions. Students at the University of Saskatchewan were asked to record their perceptions during winter. Broadly, their determination of different sensations of cold corresponded to cooling rates. However, their descriptive terms were warmer for the verbal categories previously listed (Figures 95 and 96) indicating that Canadian students may be more accepting of cold conditions. In a second set of experiments, in Sweden, correlation between descriptive terms and the sensations of people were good. The perception of cold did not differ between men and women.

At the **Teton Science School**, we have tested acclimation to the perception of cold. Students were ranked according to the number of days that their feet had been exposed to cold conditions before the first of January. Test subjects varied from those who had not been out in the cold at all prior to the course to **National Outdoor Leadership School** instructors, who had spent 60 to 90 days in the field

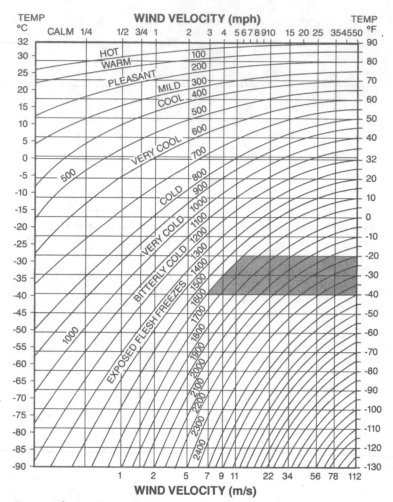

Figure 96. *Graph providing the visual calculation of cooling rate and wind-chill equivalent temperature (WET) for various environmental conditions (after Falconer, 1968). To determine the WET, select the current temperature (in °C or °F). Start on the side of the graph and move horizontally to a point vertically aligned with the current wind speed. Follow the nearest line to the left, then follow that arc downward to the nearest horizontal line intersecting the 7 m/s vertical line. Then go horizontally to the right or left to read the WET. For the example of -20°F and 5mph (darker line), the WET is -40°F. Verbal descriptions of comfort have been added to the chart. Numbers on the center line are windchill losses (kcal/m²/hr).*

prior to the first of January. The student's perception of cold was recorded as their bare feet were cooled under controlled conditions. No difference in perception was detected between "cold-acclimated" individuals and those experiencing their first cold conditions

for the winter. Perception of cold was linked to percentage of body fat. Interestingly, the perception of cold depends on immediately previous conditions. Individuals moving from severe conditions to less severe conditions always perceived the new conditions as

Table 30. Stages of human comfort and freezing of flesh (after Siple and Passel, 1945).

Cooling rate cal/m²/hr	Description of comfort and freezing of flesh
1,400	Exposed flesh begins to freeze. Travel and life in temporary shelters becomes disagreeable.
1,900	Exposed areas of the face freeze within less than one minute. Conditions for travel and living in temporary shelter becomes dangerous.
2,300	Exposed areas of the face freeze within less than 30 seconds.
2,500	Probable average limit of cooling during coldest period of winter.

less harsh than if the progression was from milder conditions.

The **windchill** index will not indicate the exact effect of cold and wind on an individual, but it does provide a relative guide to environmental conditions. It serves the purpose of telling a businessman whether or not to take his overcoat to work or it may tell a mother when to send extra clothes to school with her children. It may serve as a warning of when dangerous conditions exist, and it may be used to indicate minimum clothes needed for different conditions. Although it does not include all factors that influence the energy budget of an individual, the two simply made measurements of temperature and wind provide a lot of information about winter conditions. The index will continue to help people understand their environment and prepare for exposure to severe conditions. Windchill has earned its place in the arsenal of tools available to the winter ecologist.

Since wind-measuring instruments are often not available, we have reproduced a chart for estimating wind velocity from observation of naturally occurring conditions (Table 31).

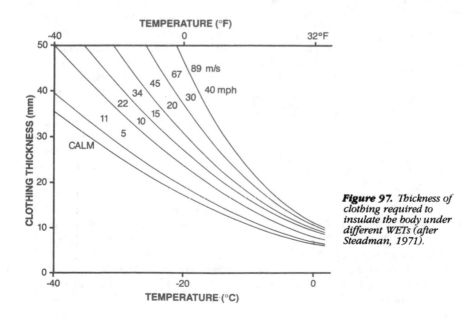

Figure 97. Thickness of clothing required to insulate the body under different WETs (after Steadman, 1971).

Table 31. Estimation of wind velocity.

Indicators	Velocity	
	m/s	(mph)
Calm; smokes rises vertically	0-.5	(0-1)
Smoke shows wind direction	2-3	(4-7)
Small twigs in constant motion	4-5	(8-12)
Snow raised; branches move	6-8	(13-18)
Small trees sway; tents flap	8-11	(19-24)
Large branches in motion; tents billow and strain	11-14	(25-31)
Whole tree in motion; loose snow raises in air	14-17	(32-38)
Twigs break off trees; walking difficult	17-20	(39-46)
Branches break off	21-24	(47-54)
Trees uprooted	25-28	(55-63)

SUGGESTED READINGS

Driscoll, D.M., 1987. Windchill: the "brrrr" index. Weatherwise, June:321-326.

Falconer, R. 1968. Windchill, a useful wintertime weather variable. Weatherwise, December:227-229, 255.

Gagge, A.P., A.C. Burton, and H.C. Bazett. 1941. A practical system of units for the description of the heat exchange of man with his environment. Science, 94:428-430.

Schlatter, T. 1981. Weather queries. Weatherwise, December:266-267.

Siple, P.A., and C.F. Passel. 1945. Measurements of dry atmospheric cooling in subfreezing temperatures. Proc. Amer. Phil. Soc., 89:177-199.

Steadman, R.G. 1971. Indices of windchill of clothed persons. Appl. Meteorol., 10:674-683.

Wilson, O. 1967. Objective evaluation of wind chill index by records of frostbite in the Antarctica. Internat. J. Biometeorol., 11:29-32.

HUMANS AND COLD

Visualize the human body. In simple form, the body consists of a core with extremities attached by stalks. The core is large compared to the extremities; it has a large volume and small surface area. The stalks—the arms, legs, and the neck—are long and cylindrical, relatively small in diameter compared to their length. They have a relatively large surface area compared to their volume. At the tip of each stalk there is an extremity, such as a hand, foot, nose, or ear. These, too, have very large surface areas compared to their volume.

Most of our heat-production equipment lies inside our core. These are the muscles, like chest muscles, diaphragm, torso muscles, back muscles, and upper shoulder muscles. Muscles contribute to the heat production of the torso. Organs, including the heart, lungs, and liver, are also major heat producers. Many large blood vessels in the core can dilate to pool blood, thereby conserving heat in the core.

In the stalks, some heat production occurs in muscles, but there are no organs and very little storage capacity for heat or blood. In the extremities, there is very little muscle to produce heat, and virtually no storage capacity. Heat must be produced in the core. The greatest heat loss occurs in the extremities, because they have large surface areas that lose heat rapidly. Extremities have almost no heat production. Where, then, does their heat come from? The heat that is lost must be transported from the core to the extremities through blood vessels.

Blood vessels and **blood** serve a dual purpose. First, the blood distributes nutrients and oxygen. At the same time, it is used to deliver heat from the core to the extremities. This heat delivery system, the blood flow, is complex. Blood flows through the arteries from the core out to the extremities and back to the heart through the veins. In this system, blood flows through either the middle of the stock or near the surface. In the middle of the stock, blood is insulated from the cold while on the surface it is exposed to the cold. The body has tremendous control over the amount of blood transported between the core and the extremity, and the control of the system is finely tuned. The body can regulate the amount of blood flow to the hands and feet—arteries in the wrists and ankles can constrict, essentially shutting off blood flow to an extremity. Conversely, there are shunts that can be opened up to greatly increase the blood flow. Blood flow can be altered in our extremities by a factor of 10.

The body balances two factors in determining how much blood to send to extremities. First, the core must maintain **thermal regulation**, that is, the center of our body cannot be allowed to become either too hot or too cold. If we are exercising hard and producing a lot of heat, then heat must be dumped to the extremities to get rid of it. The body will open up the blood flow to the extremities. On the other hand, if too much heat loss is occurring, the body will shut down the blood flow to the extremities. The second important factor is the blood supply needs of the local tissue. The feet and the hands need oxygen and nutrients. When oxygen or nutrients are low in these extremities, the blood brings additional

supplies. When the extremities are cold, blood brings more heat. But the core has priority, at least in humans, and its thermal regulatory needs come first. The body allows its extremities to freeze, to suffer frostbite, even to fall off in order to maintain heat in the core.

This is not true of all animals. In the case of the arctic wolf, it appears that the young and the yearlings are more likely to die of hypothermia than suffer frostbite. They do not shut down their blood flow when the core starts cooling off. They maintain enough blood flow to keep their feet from suffering frostbite even at -40°C (-40°F). Navy researchers attempted to use arctic wolves to study frostbite. They hoped to find an animal species in which they could produce frostbite and then learn frostbite prevention measures. However, in experimenting with arctic wolves, they were not able to produce frostbite even when putting the wolves' feet into a dry ice bath. In humans, on the other hand, the constriction of blood flow to repel cold from the core seems to override local needs for oxygen and heat in the extremities, allowing the extremities to suffer injury.

Control of the system is important. The human body's capacity to pump heat through the blood to an extremity is enormous. The capacity is so great that some people have developed the capacity to walk on snow in their bare feet without suffering any problem. Conversely, restriction and constriction are usually used as an attempt to save heat for the core, which has first priority. Control of blood flow can be by restriction in rather large vessels in the stock or constriction of small capillaries near the surface. Often, we apply a sort of tourniquet from the outside, that is, we wear something too tight around the extremity that constricts blood flow.

Travel in Yellowstone National Park. Twelve-person snow coaches are used to transport winter visitors into Yellowstone.

The external tourniquets may be socks or gloves, or even hats.

Even with the capacity to protect the extremities, cold injuries occur every winter. What happens? The obvious conclusion is that, for some reason, sufficient heat was not flowing from the core to the extremity. One of the most common reasons is that the person was not sensitive enough to his own body and applied an external tourniquet. Often the body applies a tourniquet on the inside as well. For some reason the body was constricting blood flow to the extremity.

Perhaps no other animal suffers so much cold injury as do humans. Opossums may be close competitors, however. It is interesting to note the opossum is a more recent newcomer to cold environments than humans. The basic problem may be that opossums (and humans) are subtropical in origin and are better adapted to dumping excess heat than to conserving heat. Although people who are prepared to operate in winter do quite well, it is because we are adaptable and have the experience and background to cope.

This simple picture of the human body does not explain everything about being out in winter. Humans can do more about the environment than plants and animals. We can wrap our bodies in clothing. The core can be protected by layering on rather thick clothing and trapping air. It is not as easy to insulate the stalks (the arms and the legs), and we are all aware of problems of insulating our hands and our feet. Our remarkable system of supply and flow provides first-rate protection against encounters with the cold. We must understand, however, how the body functions and provide extra protection for our bodies during the winter. The next section deals with being out in the winter.

SUGGESTED READINGS

American Public Health Association. Yearbook. 1936:37-84.

Consolazio, C.F., R.E. Johnson, and L.J. Pecora. 1963. Physiological Measurements of Metabolic Function in Man. New York, McGraw-Hill.

Driscoll, D.M., 1987. Windchill: the "brrrr" index. Weatherwise, June:321-326.

Falconer, R. 1968. Windchill, a useful wintertime weather variable. Weatherwise, December:227-229, 255.

Gagge, A.P., A.C. Burton, and H.C. Bazett. 1941. A practical system of units for the description of the heat exchange of man with his environment. Science, 94:428-430.

Gates, D.M. 1972. Man and his Environment: Climate. Harper and Row, New York.

Lewis, H.E. 1971. How men survive the cold. Science J., 7:29.

Schlatter, T. 1981. Weather queries. Weatherwise, December:266-267.

Siple, P.A., and C.F. Passel. 1945. Measurements of dry atmospheric cooling in subfreezing temperatures. Proc. Amer. Phil. Soc., 89:177-199.

Steadman, R.G. 1971. Indices of windchill of clothed persons. Appl. Meteorol., 10:674-683.

Wilson, O. 1967. Objective evaluation of wind chill index by records of frostbite in the Antarctica. Internat. J. Biometeorol., 11:29-32.

OUT IN WINTER

Since the 1930s, there has been a rapid change in the popular impression of winter. The 1932 Olympics at Lake Placid, New York, sparked an increased interest in winter activities in the United States. Troops of the 10th Mountain Division of the U.S. Army returned from World War II to found the modern ski industry in the United States. In recent years, increased leisure time has brought millions of people opportunities to experience the winter world. Each winter millions participate in downhill skiing. An equipment revolution, which provides state-of-science boots, clothes, skis, tents, and so on, reduces many discomforts of winter life. The world's first national park, Yellowstone, opened for overnight use in winter of 1971-72. Significant educational programs in winter camping, survival, and biology began in the 1970s, including those of the **National Outdoor Leadership School** and the **Teton Science School**. The over-snow-machine, often called the **snowmobile**, has introduced thousands, if not millions, to the winter world.

Clearly, there is a need and a demand for winter outdoor education, including training in camping, safety and survival, conservation, and ecology. Each of these topics warrants a book in itself and, indeed, there are many books available. Many educational programs are also available that are oriented to specific aspects of life in the winter. In this section, we will briefly cover camping, safety, and survival; the emphasis will be on humans as organisms in a winter world affected by the SCREW factor. Finally, we will present a list of educational programs that offer opportunities for additional training. We offer an introduction to these topics and we encourage interested parties to attend courses at the listed programs for in-depth education and experience. Knowledge, skills, and equipment for winter continue to improve and educational programs can provide the latest information.

Life in the delightful winter world is not without its hazards to those who venture forth. Proper knowledge and training keep these hazards under control and provide for safe and satisfying winter outings. Here we will concentrate on hazards to the winter enthusiast's health, how to prevent injuries, and how to treat injuries should they occur. Avalanche hazards and avalanche prevention will be stressed.

For many years, we have led students, expedition members, and recreationists with two admonitions. The first is known as the "**6 Ps**." The "6 Ps" stand for **Prior Planning and Promptness Prevent Poor Performance**. The admonition stresses the importance of learning and obtaining the proper training before venturing forth into winter. Implicit within the prior planning is obtaining adequate equipment and learning how to use it. Finally, prior planning implies knowing what to expect for the time of year and the location of the winter adventure. Perhaps the simplest step here includes obtaining the weather forecast before your trip. Look at long-term averages and record conditions and be prepared to meet them. Remember, weather may change quickly, especially in the mountains, and you should plan for the unexpected. Many things must be done before the trip to make a trip safe, but the planning and anticipating is half the fun of each venture.

Promptness plays a particularly important role during the winter. Tardy people are often an aggravation to the other members of their group, but they become a safety hazard in the winter. Standing around outside in the winter exposes trip members to the elements of winter. Waiting is an invitation to exposure injuries, including frostbite and hypothermia. Early starts are often needed to allow adequate time for the trip, including a safety margin at the end of the day to account for the inevitable delays encountered on the trail. Outdoor educators and other trip leaders need to protect their trip members by urging promptness on the part of all members of the trip.

The second admonition is that **mountains don't care**. This is the "Murphy's law" of the outdoors. Simply put, any inadequacies in knowledge, training, equipment, or promptness return to haunt trip members. Bad weather, rough terrain, and short days inevitably expose weaknesses at the worst possible time during a trip. Nature makes no allowances for the inadequacies of people, so winter enthusiasts must be totally prepared for all eventualities. Problems caused by sloppiness in training, equipment, and promptness may not catch up with you on every trip, but each winter many needless injuries and even deaths occur because the "mountains don't care" about your lack of preparedness!

Health and Safety in the Winter

We cannot stress enough the importance of preparation when talking about health and safety in the winter. Following certain general principles will help avoid health and safety hazards.

Preparations

Fuel your furnace. Energetics and nutrition are of critical importance, because internal heat production depends on the food that we carry and eat on winter outings. Everyone should always have an adequate supply of food for the planned length of the outing, plus a bit more. It is always better to carry some food back home than not to have any food when an emergency demands it. Eat whenever possible during the day; don't simply count on three spaced meals. Hourly snacking is recommended. Quick, high-energy foods are important, but the length of the trip or cold weather encountered may demand a large supply of fat-rich foods (see section on *Winter Travel and Camping* in this chapter). If possible, avoid trips when you are in poor health, and when your normal body energies are at a low level.

Maintaining your **water balance** is also critical. Water is lost through heavy exertion in the winter—skiing, snowshoeing, lifting and turning snowmobiles. Considerable amounts of water are also lost to the cold, dry air. Cold air does not hold as much moisture as warm air. When we breathe in cold air, we must warm it up in our lungs, and then we exhale the warm air with an increased moisture content. By this process alone, one to two extra quarts of water may be lost each day, depending upon the level of exertion and amount of breathing.

There is also increased moisture loss from exposed skin, because cool air touches the skin and is warmed, absorbing more moisture. Those who live in heated buildings, especially those with dry skin, are quite aware of the problems of dehydration in winter. The skin may actually feel quite a bit more comfortable the more time you spend outdoors because the outside air is not as drying as the air inside a heated building. Sleeping in a snow shelter is excellent for rehydration, because it is wonderfully humid.

The solution to these problems is to be aware of your hydration level. The easy way is to pay attention to your urine. If you are urinating just small amounts of very dark urine, you are, of course, dehydrated, and need to increase your fluid intake. You may note a slight headachy feeling that comes on with dehydration. One thing to be aware of, for those who are not accustomed to drinking much liquid, is that when you are dehydrated, you often want to put something into your stomach, and you will go for food. If the food is moist, that will help, but if it is dry food, your moisture requirements will not be met.

When you are outdoors in the winter, you need to drink more liquid. That means you have to have water that is not frozen. A simple method is to carry a standard plastic water bottle. Fill it with hot water in the morning and wrap it up in a sock or two. In extremely cold weather, be sure that the water is buried deep inside of your pack, or carry it inside your coat as close as possible to your skin to keep it from freezing. There are some fairly nice thermos jugs available. Both your stomach and psyche enjoy warm tea or some such liquid in the winter. Black tea and honey is a very useful drink in the winter.

A **dehydrated** body is more susceptible to exposure injuries. Therefore, it is important to force yourself to consume adequate water. An adequate water load is in the range of four liters (one gallon) each day. Water becomes more important on longer trips. You can tolerate dehydration if it is only a day trip, but dehydration effects are cumulative on longer trips and lead to greater dangers. Drink lots!

Carry adequate **clothing** and use it. Mother was right when she said "if your toes are cold, put on a cap." Preventing heat loss through the head allows heat to be transferred to the toes. Dress in layers and add layers at the first sign of being cold. Conversely, if you become hot, take off layers.

Carry plenty of **matches**. These may be a life saver if everything goes wrong. Small propane lighters are not as good, as they are often not hot enough to start fires under emergency conditions. Keep a supply of matches in each coat and in your pack. Some day it may pay off.

Consider the length of your trip in your preparations, including selecting food and equipment. Many of the effects of winter are cumulative. You can tolerate one or two nights of -40°C (-40°F) temperatures, but after several nights, moisture starts to accumulate in sleeping bags and clothing. You cannot go home and dry out, so your equipment must be the best to handle these situations. Similarly, your body can tolerate the two nights of extreme cold during a weekend. After several days, however, your nutritional needs will change and more fats are needed. On long, cold winter trips it is not unusual for us to eat butter right off the stick; hot cocoa laced with generous amounts of butter is craved.

Most of the winter, you can get by when you are short of proper energy or equipment. However, you should be prepared for the occurrence of extreme conditions. It is the record extreme that can catch the winter enthusiast unprepared. During the record cold spells of the winters of 1978 to 1980, many skiers and snowmobilers suffered extreme **frostbite** in **Yellowstone National Park** because equipment that would normally have protected them was not adequate. Prepare for the extremes. When you are in a **survival situation**, there is no room for any piece of equipment that is not the very best.

Roy Ozanne demonstrates the effect of small bucket size on rewarming a foot. Water in a smaller bucket is quickly cooled off by the low temperature of the foot, making it too cold to ef-fectively rewarm a frostbitten limb.

Remember, survival situations can occur at unexpected times and from unexpected causes—what will you do if you fall through the ice on a river crossing?

Injuries Common to Winter

The rigors of winter can cause several injuries, which may be grouped into two categories: those caused by exposure to the sun and those caused by exposure to cold. Sun-caused injuries include **sunburn**, **sun bumps**, and **snowblindness**; injuries caused by cold include **frostbite** and **trench foot**.

Sun-caused injuries result from the energetic short wavelengths less than 0.4 μ (Figure 21). In moderate amounts, these rays produce **tanning**, but in ex-cessive levels they damage biological tissue. Those rays between 0.29 and 0.32 μ are particularly dangerous, caus-ing sunburn and snowblindness. Dur-ing the winter, sunburn may be rare be-cause of the low angle of the sun in the sky. As spring arrives, sunburns in-crease as do other sun injuries. Sun in-juries can occur even on cloudy days as atmospheric scattering can increase doses of radiation. Radiation reflected from snow can cause sunburn under the eyelids, on the surface of an open mouth, and in the nostrils. Sun injuries are more likely to occur at higher ele-vations during the winter, because there is less atmosphere to block ultra-violet rays.

Prevention is the key to combating

these injuries. Gloves, hats, and clothing serve to shield the body and should be used whenever possible. Three types of preparations are used to protect against sunburn: oils, sunscreens, and sunblocks. Oils (including creams and lotions), such as baby, olive, and coconut oil, do little if anything to protect the skin and appear to have only cosmetic value; oils when mixed with a sunscreen or sunblock do provide protection. Sunscreens, such as **PABA** (para-aminobenzoic acid), filter out the dangerous rays from 0.20 to 0.32 µ, preventing sunburn but allowing the rays that produce **tanning** to reach the skin. Tanning reduces additional sunburning. Sun blocks, such as titanium dioxide (A-Fil) and zinc oxide (Zincofax cream), completely cut off the dangerous rays, providing protection from burns but preventing tanning.

Sunburn creams and lotions are rated according to a **sun protection factor** (**SPF**) that varies from 2 (minimal sun protection) to 34 (essentially a sunblock). This factor interacts with **minimal erythemal dose**, (**MED**), the amount of sun exposure needed by an individual to cause reddening of the skin. MED is a measure of the tolerance to sunburn. On the average, four times the MED causes sunburn, while eight times causes blistering of the skin. A product with a SPF of 6 allows a person with a MED of 20 minutes to tolerate exposure for two hours, and a SPF of 15 allows exposure for five hours. Care must be taken, however, because sweating or water can wash off the cream. Repeated applications may be necessary.

Individuals show different degrees of sensitivity to sunburn. Recommended protection levels have been devised based on skin type and the ease with which a person sunburns (Table 32). A sunblock or sunscreen with an SPF of 15 or 25 is recommended for body areas that burn easily and are not protected by clothing. Sensitive areas include nose, lips, and ears.

Treatment of sunburn is accomplished by the application of cold, wet dressings; soaking the dressings in boric acid also helps. Solarcaine, Noxema, and other anesthetic creams reduce pain. Extensive or severe sunburn should be treated as a second-degree burn.

Table 32. Recommended sun protection for different skin types (after Wilkerson 1985).

Skin Type	Sunburning and tanning qualities	Other characteristics	Recommend protection (SPF)
I	Burns easily, never tans	red or blond hair, blue eyes, freckles	8-25
II	Burns easily, tans minimally	red or blond hair, blue eyes, freckles	6-12
III	Burns moderately, tans slowly to light brown	red or blond hair, blue eyes, freckles	4- 8
IV	Burns minimally, tans to moderate brown	darker coloration	2- 6
V	Rarely burns, tans to dark brown	darker coloration	2- 4
VI	Never burns	deeply pigmented	none

Little appears to be known about **sun bumps**. Sun bumps are small, clear, liquid-filled bumps that appear on skin exposed to the sun. The bumps tend to be firm and may be painful. Upon rupturing, the sun bumps offer sites for the introduction of infection. Sun bumps can progress to extremely painful open wounds if not prevented or not properly taken care of. Sometimes these bumps are also called **sun poisoning**.

Fair-skinned people are often more likely to get sun bumps. Many individuals exposed to the sun for several days during the winter find these bumps on their skin. Once someone begins to develop sun bumps, they tend to occur again with each new exposure to sun. Sun bumps are a type of hypersensitive reaction to sunlight, in which the sunlight triggers an almost allergic reaction in certain parts of the skin.

Prevention of sun injury involves the use of clothing, sunblocks, and sunscreens with high SPF ratings. Individuals prone to sun bumps find it necessary to completely shade the body with clothing. Lightweight, cheap cotton gloves can be used to protect the hands even under hot conditions. This is probably good advice for anybody, even before problems develop. Most skin does not tolerate the large doses of ultraviolet rays that occur in winter, especially at higher elevations.

Snowblindness consists of eye pain originating from any or all of three mechanisms. First, the squinting muscles become sore when you are in bright sun. Second, the surface of the eye and iris become sunburned. Third, the retina becomes burned.

Snowblindness is particularly dangerous because there is no burning sensation to warn the individual that damage is occurring. The actual symptoms arise six to twelve hours after exposure. First there may be a sensation of dryness or irritation. Irritation may increase until the eyes feel like they are full of sand. Further exposure to the sun makes the problem worse. The eyes are red, the eyelids may be swollen, and excessive tears may form. Exposure to additional light may cause severe pain. Severe cases can result in permanent damage.

Prevention of snowblindness is accomplished by wearing proper sunglasses or goggles. The lens must transmit no more than 10 percent of the radiation below 0.32 μ. Read the labels on sunglasses carefully; many plastic lenses do not offer adequate protection. Glasses should have side shields and the lenses should be large, to prevent fogging. Protection is necessary on cloudy and even snowy days with thin clouds, when side shields are important in stopping reflected ultraviolet rays. If sunglasses are lost or forgotten, some protection may be had by combing long hair over the eyes. In extreme conditions it may be possible to pull a loose-knit stocking cap down over the eyes and look between threads of the yarn.

Little can be done to treat snowblindness. Snowblindness naturally heals in a few days. The eyes should be kept shielded from light. If travel is necessary, use the darkest glasses available. Pain may be relieved by cold compresses. Ophthalmic ointment or drops applied hourly help relieve pain and speed healing. The eyes must not be rubbed.

Do the other creatures that live out in the winter and spend much more time in the bright sun get snowblindness? If not, why not? Do they have more pigment in the retina or in the iris? Not in the least, and certainly no other protection is apparent. Why don't they have problems with snowblindness? Perhaps the animals can tolerate the sun. We don't know; this would make a good research question.

Most humans cannot tolerate the extremely bright sun of very high altitudes in winter. But certainly great individual differences exist as to who will get burned and when. Some evidence suggests that there is the possibility of becoming acclimated to greater levels of sunlight. (We are not advocating trying to acclimate to the sunlight, we are only mentioning it in context of considering the question of how other animals tolerate the sunlight.)

Cold-induced injuries may result from exposure to either wet or dry cold. Dry, cold conditions may lead to frostbite; wet, cold conditions may lead to trench or immersion foot; cold, either wet or dry, may lead to hypothermia. Local cold injuries affecting extremities and exposed flesh include frostbite and trench foot. Hypothermia affects the entire body, especially the central core.

Hypothermia refers to a cooling of the body's core temperature. The problem with hypothermia is that when the organ systems of the body get cold, they do not function very well. This applies to all of the organ systems. Cold nerves and muscles reduce coordination in the hands and feet. The heart muscle is particularly sensitive to being cold—it does not work as well when cold, and starts to function erratically and more slowly. The digestive track shuts down when cold, and does not process food for necessary energy. A cold brain functions sluggishly and irrationally. Cold regulatory centers and regulatory mechanisms malfunction. Overall metabolism slows down, and heat production eventually stops. Continued cooling will eventually produce such a low body temperature that the body cannot reverse the cooling trend. At this point, without outside help, this cooling will lead to death.

Different stages of hypothermia result from lower levels of cooling (Table 33). The normal body temperature is 37°C (98.6°F). In general, a body temperature between 32 and 37°C (90 and 98.6°F) is safe. In this range, the body's protective mechanisms are still intact. Self-help is possible; shivering and the constriction of blood vessels may raise the core temperature and protect against additional heat loss. About 10 percent of the population, however, does not seem to shiver naturally and does not have this protective mechanism. Mental concentration will also stop the shivering mechanism, although

Table 33. Body temperature ranges for symptoms of hypothermia (modified from Wilkerson, 1985).

Body temperature °C	(°F)	Symptoms
37-35	(98-95)	chilly, skin numbness, impaired hand movement, shivering begins
35-34	(95-93)	muscle incoordination, weakness, slow pace, mild confusion, apathy
34-32	(93-90)	muscle incoordination, stumbling, mental sluggishness, slurred speech
32-30	(90-86)	shivering stops, stiffness, inability to walk, incoherence, irrationality
30-28	(86-82)	muscle rigidity, semiconsciousness, dilated pupils, faint heartbeat and breathing
28-	(82-)	unconsciousness, eventual death

For detailed information see Wilkerson (1985).

John Storb in Birkebinder cross-country ski race between Telemark and Hayward, Wisconsin.

scientists don't yet understand why. A collection of symptoms characterize this temperature range and become progressively worse at lower temperatures. At the lower end of this temperature range, definite mental changes occur; motivation is poor, and the victim is irritable and has reduced judgment abilities. Muscles do not work well and coordination is reduced.

A transitional stage exists between body temperatures of 34 and 32°C (93 and 90°F) in which conditions move from safe to very unsafe. Shivering starts to decrease, but the blood vessels still constrict as a means of conserving heat in the core. Once body temperature drops below 32°C (90°F), the protective mechanisms are gone. The person becomes unconscious, shivering stops, and the blood vessels begin to dilate, causing rapid heat loss from the

core to the environment. This is a very dangerous situation. Below 32°C (90°F), a person needs outside help to restore core temperatures.

It is interesting that people can be intentionally cooled to as low as 5°C (41°F) during certain types of surgery and then rewarmed without apparent problems, while in accidental situations, cooling below 25°C (77°F) results in residual impairment, if indeed the person survives at all.

Falling into **cold water** is particularly dangerous, as water conducts heat away from the body about 25 times faster than air. We have actually had situations while crossing rivers, when air temperature was about -30°C (-22°F), when our feet warmed up in our hip waders, because the water temperature was near freezing. However, staying in the water if one falls in is very dangerous, because of the rapid rate at which heat is conducted away from the body by the cold water.

Contrary to popular belief, a person does not die rapidly in cold water. Usually it takes ten to fifteen minutes before the core temperature even starts to drop, and individuals can survive from 30 minutes to two hours in very cold water. If you are around cold water in the winter, do wear extra-warm clothes (wool and polypropylene, for example—not cotton), and wear a life jacket.

Drinking **alcohol** is dangerous in winter because it fools the brain into thinking that the body is warm, and shivering stops. Cooling continues, however, and the core temperature drops at the same rate as when a person is sober. The victim doesn't realize how cold he is, because the brain isn't getting the message.

Other factors often combine to bring on hypothermia. Clothing may be inadequate for the situation. Often wind or rain protection is forgotten or is simply not adequate. Inexperience, miscalculations, and poor decisions prevail over the correct alternatives. Unexpected changes occur in the weather. Storms move in, it begins to rain, the wind starts to blow. People become exhausted, or groups are caught out at night. Incidentally, it is often the highly trained athlete who is more at risk, because his or her body is conditioned to be efficient at ridding itself of heat, and there may be little fat for protection.

Hypothermia is prevented by keeping the core temperature warm. Try to control or limit heat loss from your extremities. Be aware of the condition of others as well as yourself. Be aware of the weather. Be aware of the time. Be prepared, both in knowledge and materials. Wear adequate clothing and have plenty of food available. Be cautious. Stop short of your limits. Keep a re-

serve. Be cautious to avoid accidents. Be fit. Stay dry. See the additional discussion after local cold injuries.

Accidental hypothermia in the outdoors during the winter usually occurs in a previously healthy person. First, recognize symptoms of hypothermia—with luck, before function is greatly impaired. Recognition necessitates paying attention to subtle signs and being suspicious in likely conditions. From our experience, when you suspect that you or someone in the group has hypothermia symptoms, you are usually right. In fact, usually the effects of the cold have been there already for some time. If you are at all suspicious, it is best to take some action.

Talk to the person. If the person is slow to answer, gives unclear answers, or seems out of touch, he or she is probably in the initial stages of hypothermia. Ask the person what day it is or where they are. If the person fails to answer correctly questions such as these, it is definitely time to take action. A more careful check can be made by taking the person's temperature. If you don't have a thermometer, take the temperature by feeling the chest under the clothing. If the chest feels cool, the person is probably in trouble.

Take prompt action. The situation is not going to improve on its own. Since the person is usually exhausted, lighten the load if he or she is hiking or carrying a pack. Head downhill or downwind. Improve the environment that you are in. Provide shelter. Heat the shelter if possible. Consider the person's clothing and decide whether to change some clothing or just add extra clothing. It may also be useful to cover the airway, and have the person breath through a scarf. Certainly cover the skin of the neck and the face.

Do what you can to increase heat production. Give a conscious person hot liquid and some food. Tea with sugar or honey or hot chocolate is excellent. The **theophylline** in tea and the **theobromine** in chocolate stimulate the body's own heat production. **Sugar** in both of these drinks provides an energy source.

If the person is in deep hypothermia (core temperature below 32°C, or 90°F), external heat may have to be added. A person in deep hypothermia has lost the ability to generate enough heat to revive. In the field, the best way to add external heat is to place the naked victim into a sleeping bag with another naked, warm person. The heat from the healthy person's body will serve to revive the victim.

If the victim is unconscious, matters are more complicated. Determine if other injuries are involved and treat them appropriately. Keep in mind that in a winter situation where hypothermia comes on slowly, unconscious persons with a lot of insulation around them (so the heat loss does not continue) will probably be safe until you get them to help. At least the problem will not deteriorate. It is different for someone who falls in cold water—this victim needs to be revived immediately.

There are some problems in treating hypothermia that are not clearly resolved yet. One is the question of **cardiopulmonary resuscitation** (CPR). If you find someone who is unconscious in the cold, and you are not able to detect a pulse, should you give resuscitation or not? If there is a faint pulse, it is usually adequate to keep the person alive. Sometimes if you give resuscitation, you might unintentionally disrupt the heart beat. Breathing may be detected by listening close to the mouth and nose and feeling for warmth from exhalations. If breath is not detected, you should probably provide mouth-to-mouth resuscitation. Chest compres-

sions may be given along with resuscitation, but must be continued until there is help or until the person is clearly able to function alone.

At a base camp or other location where warm water is available, probably the safest thing to do with a victim with no known health problems is to put the person into a warm tub (about 42°C, or 108°F) for rapid **rewarming**. It is probably a good idea to leave the arms and the legs out of the tub until the person is warmed, so that you do not dump the whole lot of cold, acidic blood into the body at one time. Additional health problems, such as a weak heart, might necessitate evacuation to a hospital for rewarming.

If possible, rapid rewarming should be done at a hospital with support in case there are troubles during rewarming. Core temperatures often continue to decline (**afterdrop**) when a person is removed from the situation causing hypothermia. This results from continued momentum from the initial cooling and can result in unconsciousness when the peripheral blood vessels dilate and blood pressure falls. Problems with rewarming also occur because the cold, acidic blood causes the heart to beat erratically when the blood begins to circulate through it. Keep in mind that the hypothermia victim has had a severe injury and should be watched carefully for the next day or so.

Finally, don't give up on a hypothermia victim until the person has been warmed up. In a very cold victim, heartbeat and breathing may not be detectable. The person must be warmed up to give the heart a chance to work again! Remember the admonition among emergency workers, "you aren't dead until you're warm and dead."

Trench foot, also called **immersion foot**, is a local, nonfreezing injury. It usually occurs following prolonged ex-

Each year a few visitors enjoy winter in Yellowstone National Park. Here snowshoers and skiers watch an eruption of Old Faithful geyser.

posure to damp, cold conditions, but not necessarily freezing temperatures. When the extremity is cold enough that the blood supply to the surface is reduced to some extent by the internal tourniquet, there is a chronic shortage of oxygen and nutrients to the tissue of the foot or the hand (usually the foot). A constriction of boots or clothing and immobility (standing around) may facilitate injury, but trench foot can also happen when the boots are loose.

The most sensitive tissues are the nerves, followed by the blood vessels, muscles, bones, and finally the skin. The skin is the least sensitive, but that is where the injury would be first noticed. Trench foot occurs from the inside out: the nerves will be injured first; this will then disrupt the functioning of the extremity, probably letting further injury develop. Usually by the time the person is aware of a problem, there has already been a serious injury to the blood vessels and the muscles beneath the surface of the skin.

Initially, while an extremity affected by trench foot is still **vasal** (blood vessels) **constricted**, it will be cold, pale, and probably swollen. The limb may feel numb and muscle cramping may occur. During the second stage, the **vasodilated** stage, the limb warms and the blood starts to flow freely. The limb becomes red, hot, and painful. This stage may last four to ten days. Muscle weakness will probably occur, sensation will be altered, and there may be ulceration of the skin. Complications may exist for up to six weeks and infection may set in.

Recovery is very slow, taking two to six months. The functioning ability of the extremity may be decreased for years. This may involve loss of sweating ability, extreme sensitivity, and poor circulation. Pigment loss from the skin may also occur.

The single most important factor in developing trench foot is **wetness**— for example, leaving the feet in wet socks for a long period of time. It seems that if feet are dried and put into dry socks each night, they can be wet through much of the day and trench foot will not develop. If dry socks are not available, sleep with your feet in the arms of a dry, wool sweater. The major issue is to pay attention to the feet, not allowing them to be cold and damp for long periods, even though you know they are not freezing. If the feet are wet throughout the day, it is a good idea to change to dry socks at least once during the day, until you know what your system can tolerate. You should definitely change to dry socks at night.

Frostbite is a local, freezing injury, in which ice crystals form in the tissue. Temperatures must be below freezing and injury may occur in seconds or take hours to develop. Initially, the affected part may feel painful, then it usually becomes numb. Once the tissue has become numb, freezing can occur. However, some people do not note the sensation of numbness before frostbite occurs. The severity of the injury depends on the extent of tissue freezing and the method by which the injury is rewarmed.

Three different categories of frostbite are recognized, depending on how deeply the tissue is frozen. The first category, **frost nip**, is mild, and just the very surface of the skin is frozen. The skin appears white and almost waxy during frost nip. Frost nip usually occurs because of extreme cold or high wind. Affected places often include the side of the nose, the ear, the cheek or an exposed hand. The skin quickly recovers with the application of heat—for instance, just a warm hand, a friend's breath, or a warm mitten. Recovery is very much like mild sunburn without blisters. The skin may peel.

The second category, **superficial frostbite**, involves freezing of only the skin; deeper tissues are not affected. The skin appears white and is stiff from freezing. The skin will give to pressure before it is thawed, however, because underlying tissues are not frozen. As thawing occurs, the skin reddens and sensation returns. Blisters and swelling occur within 24 to 36 hours, and a scab forms in about a week. In several weeks, new tissue appears and in two to three months the skin begins to look normal. Actual recovery time of normal skin function may be quite long—up to several years.

The third category, **deep frostbite**, involves freezing of the underlying tissue as well as the skin. The skin appears white and when you push on the frozen area, it feels hard and wood-like. Following thawing, the area remains gray and mottled. The lack of a red skin color occurs because the blood flow beneath the skin is disturbed. The skin may remain numb. Blisters may form on the skin, indicating severe damage, and it is possible to lose the tips of the extremities. Severely damaged parts turn black and will **autoamputate** (fall off) within two to three months.

Frostbite involves three mechanisms of injury. First is an **ischemic** or low-oxygen injury similar to trench foot. When the oxygen supply is low because of vasal constriction, cold disrupts the cell functions, and blood vessels and nerves are injured. Initial injury to the blood vessel leads to additional injury because the injured blood vessels circulate blood poorly. Without proper circulation, tissues freeze. Second, **ice crystals** form between the cells. Crystal formation draws water out of the cells and disrupts cell metabolism. Sharp edges of the ice crystals may directly damage cell structure. Third, upon rewarming, blood returns to damaged vessels and **blood clots** form in damaged vessels. Clotting further decreases blood flow to injured areas. Much of the injury that occurs in frostbite or trench foot happens after the area is rewarmed and blood returns into the damaged vessels, forming clots and obstructing circulation. Areas without blood flow will die if adequate alternate blood vessels for oxygen and nutrient supplies are not available.

Treatment for all local cold injuries is similar. It is most crucial to be aware of possible hypothermia in the field and treat it appropriately if diagnosed. Blood flow will not return to extremities while the whole body is still cool. Hypothermia is a threat to life itself, while the local cold injury is a threat just to the extremity. The main action involved in treatment of local cold injuries is to rewarm the extremity. **Rewarming** procedures are very simple and should be known by everyone who operates in the cold. First, treat hypothermia; second, determine if conditions are safe and appropriate for rewarming or thawing the extremity; third, rewarm the extremity; and fourth, take care of the extremity after it is rewarmed.

Safe and appropriate conditions for rewarming include no threat—absolutely no threat—that the extremity will be **refrozen**. If it is frozen a second time, damage is much more severe. It is better to leave the extremity frozen than to rewarm it and allow it to freeze again. If the victim is far removed from medical help and cannot be transported, it is best use the frozen foot to walk out or ski out on. As soon as the extremity is thawed, it cannot be used and must be treated similarly to a severe burn.

If possible, get the person to medical help before rewarming. If **rewarming** must be done, use a large tub of water. The water should be between 38 and 43°C (100 to 108°F). The temperature must not be warmer than this, because the extremity may be burned. If the water is cooler, warm-up time will be prolonged, and there is a greater chance that blood clots may form. The rewarming period must be as brief as possible. Place the extremity in the water and leave it there until thawed. Thawing will be indicated by flushing, or redness returning as far out to the extremity tips as possible. Once that happens, take the limb out of the water. No benefit is derived from further rewarming.

A large supply of hot water may be necessary for rewarming. If a block of ice is placed in a small bucket, the temperature of that water will decrease quickly. Similarly, the frozen extremity itself can cool the water below the appropriate temperature. Additional water may be added to maintain the appropriate temperature, but avoid getting the water bath too hot. It is advisable to carry a thermometer that is capable of measuring the correct temperature (regular thermometers for medical treatment do not operate in the correct range). If a thermometer is not available, make the water as hot as a noninjured hand can tolerate.

After rewarming, treat the extremity as though it were severely burned. It must be kept very clean to avoid infection. Keep it elevated to improve the circulation. Get immediate medical attention. It is advisable to locate a doctor who has had extensive experience with frostbite. Proper medical treatment may include the use of oxygen and several medicines. Properly cared for, even very bad cases of frostbite can have amazing recoveries.

The treatment of **frostbite** has advanced considerably in recent times and medical doctors consider several factors that the layperson cannot. Medication and oxygen are used during rewarming to try to prevent some of the aftermath injury incurred during and following warming. Drugs reduce coagulation, preventing clot formation and increasing blood flow. Oxygen and intravenous feeding speed healing, while antibiotics prevent infection. Tetanus shots may be given.

Amputation after freezing injury to the extremities is now extremely rare. If there is dead tissue, it falls off on its own. However, recovery may require a considerable amount of time. Increased sensitivity to cold may persist for years. Additional problems include lack of proper sweating functions and pain in the extremities; sometimes arthritis develops later. The victim can only be patient and wait. Future activities in the outdoors must be carefully planned to avoid reinjury.

Several **predisposing factors** often lead to local cold injuries. The environment is usually cold and windy. Often high altitude and moisture are involved, and snow may be present. The person who gets injured often has had low food intake, may be dehydrated, may not be in as good condition as the rest of the party, the person may be wearing cotton clothing, and the feet may be wet. Usually something unexpected happens. Here we are speaking of winter activities, not the things that happen in urban settings, which usually involve alcohol, auto accidents, illnesses such as diabetes, and problems with the elderly we have all heard about. These urban situations require additional solutions. Of the two elements of the environment, the host and the event, it is the host that is the most important. Under similar conditions, only a few people suffer injury; the prepared usually do not.

Prevention of local cold injuries in the winter is a heat regulation problem. First, heat must be produced. Adequate fuel must be present to produce heat. For humans, the fuel is food. Do not short-change yourself on food in the winter. Activity also helps to produce heat. At the same time, the more you move in the cold, the more heat you actually lose to the environment, so there are trade-offs. One effective method is to be active for a while, producing heat in the core, and then curl up in a ball, or stay squatting on your feet. Rest and conserve energy. This is a method Eskimos have used for a long time. When the cold feeling returns, use activity to again warm the body. This may require at least 10 minutes of vigorous activity.

In addition to producing heat, heat loss must be decreased. If the possibility of local cold injury is present, try to keep your core on the verge of being too warm. Do this by having adequate insulation and adequate activity; keep your insulation dry, change it if wet, and avoid materials that take heat away from you, such as cotton. Before you put on or change pants and mittens, prewarm them. Do not take a cold mitten or cold sock out of your pack and put it on. That will instantly induce a constriction response. First, put the sock inside your jacket—or, if you have a warmer friend available, put it against his or her chest, inside the clothing. Once it is warm, put it on.

The third requirement to keep heat available is to avoid becoming exhausted. Exercise must be within the limits that your body can handle. If you are exercising for a prolonged period above about 60 percent of your **aerobic capacity**, you will deplete the ability of your body to keep warm even if

you have extra food on hand. The metabolic machinery is not available to maintain heat production at an adequate rate if you are also exercising at a high rate.

This explains what often happens to individuals in a group. The people who get in trouble are the ones who are not in as good shape as the others. The group is skiing along at the same rate. Individuals with the lowest levels of aerobic conditioning are operating at a higher percent of their capacity. Those who are in better condition want to go for it. Those who are not in the same condition as their companions do not want to slow the others down, so they push themselves. The weaker people are depleting their ability to produce necessary heat. Both groups need to be aware of this problem and avoid it, either by splitting up under different leaders or by just accepting a pace that the slowest person can handle.

Once there is adequate heat available, blood flow (the transport system that moves heat from the core to the extremity) must be maintained. Either external **constriction** or internal constriction may shut down blood flow to the extremities. It takes only slight pressure around the wrist, ankles, calves, or the fingers and toes to reduce the blood supply. A watch band, tight socks, or elastic cuffs on bunting and pile jackets are often tight enough to decrease blood flow. You also must stay hydrated; if you are dehydrated, blood flow will be decreased.

Last, and perhaps most important, be aware of what is happening. Be conservative. If you suspect that something is not going right with you or your companions, stop—do something. What more is there to life than taking care of yourself? Until you are truly comfortable in the outdoors, do not take chances. When something is going wrong, figure out what you need to do. Consider your core: Do you need more food? Do you need more insulation? Consider the blood flow: Is there any possibility something is being constricted? Consider the extremity: Is the insulation damp? Do you need to change mittens or socks? Often all of the above measures are appropriate. There are conditions under which things have gone too far to be self-correcting and then you need an external source of heat. Use little tricks like putting your hands on the back of your neck, in your armpits, or putting your feet on someone else's stomach (Figure 98). Flex your hands and feet to keep circulation going. It is a good idea to keep a dry pair of mittens and socks safely stored in plastic sacks in your pack for emergencies. Avoid getting all your mittens wet during a trip; always keep a pair in reserve.

This has neither been the first nor the last word on cold problems and cold injuries. As with most subjects we have covered here, the message is that we can all develop and keep with us the skill, the experience, the equipment, and the wisdom to keep ourselves safely warm in winter. That does not happen during a short course or from just reading a book, but you can make a start. The knowledge that you are safe is extremely important. A confident and relaxed body performs much better than one that is unsure and fearful. Fear is a real inhibitor of our metabolic processes, our circulation, and our judgment.

Stay tuned to your mental state. It provides the best clues to something going amiss. If you find yourself becoming more irritable or anxious, investigate—see what is the matter. Often this feeling is an early sign of hypothermia or at least exhaustion. If you are getting cold, you must take some action.

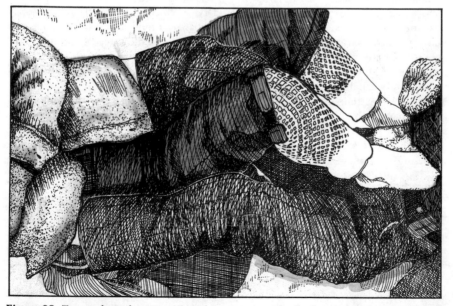

Figure 98. *Two students do a mutual toe warming on each other's stomachs during a particularly cold trip in Yellowstone National Park.*

SUGGESTED READINGS

Jackson, D.D. 1988. Up in the "cold lab" human guinea pigs shiver for science. Smithsonian, December:100-109.

Lathrop, T.G. n.d. Hypothermia: Killer of the Unprepared. Mazamas, Portland, Oregon.

Washburn, B. 1963. Frostbite: What It Is—How to Prevent It, Emergency Treatment. Museum of Science, Boston, Massachusetts.

Wilkerson, J.A., C.C. Bangs, and J.S. Hayward. 1986. Hypothermia, Frostbite, and Other Cold Injuries. The Mountaineers, Seattle, Washington.

Wilkerson, J.A. 1985. Medicine for Mountaineering. The Mountaineers, Seattle, Washington.

Avalanches

Avalanches are a reality that winter enthusiasts must face in many parts of the winter world. Thousands of avalanches occur every winter and many of these threaten winter recreationists. People who frequent areas of possible avalanche danger should become very familiar with their nature. Many excellent training programs and books are available. In this section, we will provide a brief overview of avalanches and make suggestions for avoiding and surviving avalanches. Reading this section should only be considered an introduction to a more complete understanding of avalanches. You will not become an expert on avalanches by reading this section; we strongly urge that readers gain additional training. Several books providing more complete coverage are listed in the bibliography.

The physics of snow avalanches are not completely understood even by the experts and no one can predict avalanches with certainty. From experience, however, many guidelines can be set forth for travel and survival in avalanche country.

Types of Avalanches

Two main types of avalanches occur: loose snow and slab. **Loose snow** avalanches originate from a point on a slope and develop a wider front as they flow downhill. There is little internal cohesion as the snow mass slides. **Slab avalanches** begin at a **fracture line** and a large area of snow slides at once. Slab avalanches do have internal cohesion and large blocks of hard snow may move at once. Slab avalanches often occur when a weak snow layer, such as depth hoar, fails. Avalanches may be either **wet** or **dry** depending on the moisture content of the snow. Wet avalanches tend to occur in the spring or in areas where the snowpack is normally warm and wet. Wet avalanches tend to be slower moving. Dry avalanches can reach great speeds. Avalanches move considerable amounts of snow, and the force of the avalanche may be tremendous.

Avalanches may kill by suffocating the victim, crushing the body, or sweeping the victim off a cliff or into water. Often, it is not a large avalanche that kills, but a small one that sweeps a person into fatal situations. Generally, if a person is buried for more than 30 minutes, he or she has less than a 50 percent chance of survival.

Terrain Factors

The best strategy for survival is to avoid becoming caught in an avalanche. Avalanches can be avoided by understanding where they occur, choosing routes carefully, watching for contributing factors, and practicing good judgement. Four **terrain factors** contribute to the occurrence of avalanches: ground cover, and slope steepness, slope profile, and slope aspect. **Ground cover** that is rough tends to anchor snow. Areas with trees, brush, and rocks provide anchors, while smooth, grassy slopes provide sliding surfaces. Avalanches can begin on slopes with many anchors, however, and anchors may serve as points that weaken the snowpack. The fracture line of slab avalanches occasionally connects between trees and rocks.

Avalanches tend to occur on all **slopes** between 30 and 60 degrees but are most common on slopes between 30 and 45 degrees. They are more rare on slopes of greater or lesser angles. Wet avalanches do occur on slopes of lower angle. On slopes of greater than 60 degrees, snow usually sloughs off without building up dangerous loads.

Avalanches tend to start on the convex **profile** of the slope, with slab avalanches fracturing at a tension zone on the steepest part of the convex hillside. Avalanches can start on concave slopes, but this is more rare.

Avalanche danger varies by season on different **slope aspects**. North-facing slopes are prone to **depth hoar** development because of large temperature gradients. During the colder portions of the winter, avalanches occur more frequently on north slopes. Sun-warmed south-facing slopes are more dangerous in the spring and on very sunny days. Wind tends to pack the snow on **windward** slopes. Generally, there is less snow and it is solid enough not to slide. **Leeward** slopes accumulate snow and form slabs. Often one slab forms on top of another with a smooth sliding surface. Leeward slopes are particularly dangerous.

Existing Snowpack

The existing snowpack, with its accumulation of layers of snow, is important in determining stability. Avalanche danger increases substantially when the snowpack becomes deep enough to cover terrain irregularities serving as anchors. Surface type determines bonding to upper layers. Noncrusty, loose snow provides good bonding. Rough surfaces, such as **wind crusts** with lots of ridges, increase stability. Smooth surfaces, such as sun crusts and ice, decrease stability. A light layer of fresh powder or **surface hoar** frost on a crust is particularly destabilizing. Underlying layers are particularly important. Loose, uncompacted snow or depth hoar provides weak, fracturing layers. Ice layers and internal crusts provide good sliding layers. Hollow zones under slabs are destabilizing as they collapse with additional weight.

Weather

Several weather factors contribute to the likelihood of an avalanche. The **temperature** modulates the rate at which the new snowpack stabilizes. Temperatures around freezing usually stabilize the snowpack quickly. However, temperatures above freezing can lead to wet slides. Colder temperatures cause an existing hazard to continue forming within the snowpack. Decreasing temperatures during a storm produce lighter snows on top and bonding is usually good. However, increasing temperatures during a storm cause a snowpack with poor bonding, and heavier snow on top leads to increased hazard. Cold temperatures along with a wind lead to slab formation, and cold temperatures also increase the rate of depth hoar formation. Both slabs and depth hoar lead to unstable conditions.

Greater **wind speeds** increase avalanche danger by causing slab build-up. Wind speeds greater than 7 m/s (about 15 mph) indicate increased danger. Above 11 m/s (25 mph), extreme caution should be exercised on any slopes showing a build-up. Be very suspicious of leeward slopes.

Most avalanches occur during snowstorms and shortly after the storm passes. Beware when snow falls at a rate greater than 1 cm/hr (about 1/2 in/hr) or 0.6 cm/hr (about 1/4 in/hr) with an accompanying wind. At high **rates of snowfall** the snowpack does not have time to stabilize. When more than 0.25 cm/hr (about 0.1 in/hr) of moisture accumulates in a wet snow storm, danger is also high because of the rapid increase in weight on the snowpack. New snow densities between 0.07 and 0.10 g/cm^3 (7 to 10 percent water content) tend to be stable. Lower densities lead to dry, loose slides and higher snow densities to **slab** formation. **Stellar crystals** of snow, or dendrites, lead to stable conditions. **Graupel**, **needles**, **pellets**, **rime**, and mixed snows tend to be less stable.

Beware of rapid **changes in weather** conditions, especially during a storm. Changes in wind, temperatures, or snowfall may trigger snowpack adjustments. The adjustments may reduce stability.

New Snowpack

Danger signals in a new snowpack include new, added depths greater than 30 cm (12 in) or greater than 10 cm (4 in) with associated winds. Settling of the snowpack may lead to increased stability. A decrease of 15 percent in the total depth of the snowpack indicates stability. The presence of inverted snowcones around trees is a good indicator of settling. The snowcone results from snow sticking to the tree as the snow settles. Settling in lower layers may lead to decreased stability, however, because of the hollows it creates.

Safety Equipment

Obtain the proper safety equipment and training in its use before venturing into avalanche country. All members of the group should be equipped with comparable equipment and be practiced in its use. Recommended equipment includes electronic rescue beacons, avalanche cords, shovels, and avalanche probes. **Rescue beacons** can be obtained from mountaineering stores and, although expensive, are very much worth the cost. The presence of a rescue beacon on a victim dramatically increases the chance of rapid location by survivors. Each beacon both transmits and receives a radio signal. When a victim is buried, survivors turn off their transmitters. Then they use their receivers to follow increasingly stronger signals to the source, where the beacon is attached to the victim. It does take experience to use a beacon, however. Seek training at the store where the beacon is purchased or from a person experienced in beacon use. Ski patrols and avalanche schools are excellent sources for instruction. Remember, practice frequently to hone your skills.

Avalanche cords offer considerably less protection than beacons and are thus often recommended against. Avalanche cords, because of their light weight, tend to float above the moving snow. When the avalanche stops, part of the cord may remain visible to lead rescuers to the victim. Following an avalanche, survivors locate exposed cords on the snow surface and follow them to the victim. Good cords have direction arrows marking the cord about every two meters. Cords are not a substitute for a beacon, but should be used in addition to the beacon. On particularly dangerous slopes, we use all forms of protection that we can get.

Each member of the group needs to

be able to dig out a victim. Snow goes through a sintering process following an avalanche and becomes very hard to dig. At a minimum, each member of the party should be equipped with a backpack **avalanche shovel**. When we are moving with large groups or on long trips we use No. 14 **grain scoops** made of aluminum. If you have to move a lot of snow quickly, backpack avalanche shovels cannot even begin to compete with a grain scoop for efficiency. The grain scoops can also be used for building quinzhees or snow kitchens. Drill two holes in the outside lower corners of the blade of the grain scope for attaching cords to tie the scoop onto the outside of your pack.

Avalanche probes can be bought at stores that specialize in winter equipment. For those who are in the backcountry a lot, it is best to buy ski poles that are probes. In an emergency, the grips come off the poles and they link together to form avalanche probes. Get the longest poles that you can use for skiing; these in turn make longer avalanche probes.

Route Finding

Careful planning of routes will avoid most avalanche danger. If route planning does not allow you to avoid all avalanche danger, consider turning back. Too often, pushing to cross that one risky slope leads to avalanches and deaths.

Study **topographic maps** carefully when planning the trip at home. Woodland overlay maps are best, because *absence* of woodland can imply possible avalanche paths. In general, plan routes that use ridges or broad valleys. Avoid narrow gullies. Timbered areas tend to be safer.

Before leaving on the trip, try to find out about current avalanche danger and the history of the winter's snowpack.

The weather bureau, U.S. Forest Service, ski areas, and mountaineering shops are good sources of information. Some states have avalanche forecasting centers. Also obtain the weather report for the period you will be in the field.

Selection of the route in the field is based on analysis of many clues. An overview of the area may indicate the presence of old **avalanche chutes**. Chutes can be identified by downed trees all pointing in one direction (usually downhill; on the runout side of an avalanche, the chute may be uphill), trees with limbs broken off, V-shaped gullies with no trees, or mounds of snow at the base of gullies. Avalanches tend to run in the same paths time after time. Avoid these areas.

Recent avalanche activity indicates snow instability and areas of instability. **Snowballs** or cartwheels indicate potential for avalanches. Compare north and south facing slopes for signs of recent activity.

Sounds and **cracks** provide other clues about dangerous slabs. Hollow-sounding snow indicates the formation of **slabs**. When the snow cracks and the cracks run, this indicates extremely strong slab formation that is weakly anchored. Avalanches may easily occur under these conditions.

Snow pits should be dug before venturing into new areas. Dig pits frequently during a trip to provide information about changing conditions or conditions that are different in new areas or on new slopes. Consult a book on avalanches for information on how to dig a pit to analyze avalanche danger. Even **hasty pits**—pits dug often with just a ski pole—provide valuable information. Before crossing suspicious slopes, at least run your ski pole down through the snowpack to determine conditions. In particular, look for sliding layers, hollows, and depth hoar.

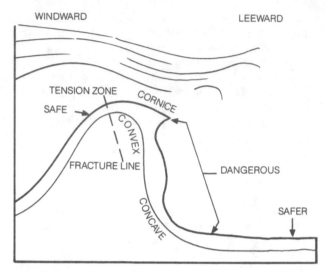

Figure 99. *Cross-section of a hill slope showing safe and dangerous areas for travel.*

Travel routes that take advantage of the terrain. Routes on ridge tops and leeward sides of the slope are safest (Figure 99). Avoid being either above or just below a cornice. Avoid crossing the lower part of an open slope. In the valley bottoms, ski well out into the center. Avoid obvious avalanche paths. If an avalanche path runs out into the valley bottom, ski on the other side of the valley. Use timber or rock outcrops for protection when possible.

Snowmobilers should avoid the lower portions of open slopes. Narrow valleys overhung with **cornices** may be particularly unsafe because the noise from the machines may trigger the cornice to collapse. It is possible to get into a dangerous situation quickly because snowmobiles move so fast. Know your intended route and plan ahead to avoid steep slopes or cornices.

When it is necessary to cross potential **avalanche paths**, stay near the top of the path (Figure 100). Avoid fracture lines in the snow. If you must descend a potential path, go straight down, avoiding traverses. Spend as little time as possible on open exposed slopes.

Cross dangerous slopes *one person at a time*. Other party members should watch from a safe location. Make sure your rescue beacon is turned on and functioning. All members of the party should check their beacons. Prepare your gear for easy removal in case of an avalanche. Undo the waist and chest straps on your pack. Loosen shoulder straps. Take your hands out of the straps on your ski poles. Loosen bindings on skis and snowshoes and undo safety straps on skis. Wear your stocking cap and mittens, and fasten down all your clothing, so that you will have warm clothes on in case you are buried in snow.

Avalanche Survival

If you are **caught in an avalanche**, try to stay on your feet. If you go down, discard all your equipment and try to get out of your skis or snowshoes. Equipment will tend to draw you deeper into the snowpack. It is better to lose some gear and come out on top of the snow. If you are a snowmobiler, you should try to get away

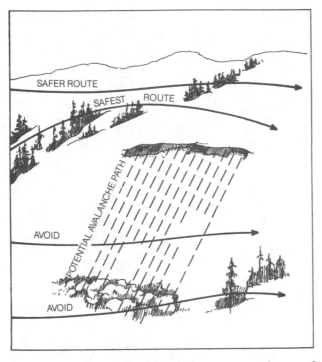

Figure 100. Hypothetical valley showing safe and dangerous routes for travel.

from your machine, otherwise the tumbling snow may push the machine on top of you.

Snow is made from water; try to swim in it. If possible, get on your back with your head uphill. Try to work your way to the edge of the avalanche. When you feel the motion starting to slow down, get your hands near your face. As the snow stops, try to create an **air space** in the snow in front of your face and, if possible, stick a hand towards the surface. Create an air space by shoving snow away from your face with your hands.

Once stopped, try to remain calm and not to waste oxygen. Try to ascertain where the surface of the snow is. If disoriented, spit. Determine which way the spit runs to locate down and up. If possible enlarge your air hole and try to dig a hand to the surface. Do not make great digging efforts, as it uses up air. Do not shout, as sound passes very

poorly out of the snow. Sound travels easily into the snow, however, and you will hear others before they get near you. Wait until you hear rescuers directly above you, then a shout might help. Above all, try to remain calm and wait.

If you are the sole **survivor** of an avalanche, you must do everything you can to find other victims immediately. Do not leave the avalanche area unless help is only a few minutes away. The first 30 minutes are critical to survival. If you are thinking about leaving the area, remember that it takes time to travel to help, time for help to organize, and time to return to the scene. It is usually better to do all you can to rescue the victims unless help is very close.

During the avalanche, watch the **victim**. Mark the last position where the victim is observed, in your mind and against objects on the slope. When the

avalanche is over, immediately go to
that spot and place a marker. If there
were several spots where the victim
was seen, mark them all. Avalanches
tend to flow like water. Use the markers to determine possible fall lines.
Search directly below the last seen
spots. If you have a **rescue beacon**
use it immediately. Conduct a search
using appropriate techniques for the
beacon.

If a beacon is not available, look for
clues on the surface, especially the
lightweight avalanche cord, which may
not be buried deeply. It may be best to
discard skis or snowshoes and work on
foot. Scuff the surface trying to uncover
clues hidden just below the surface. If
this doesn't work, **probe** the snow
below the last-seen point. Working in a
pie-shaped wedge, increase the width
of your search area as you move downhill.

If there are several survivors, send
one or two people for help. It is better
to have as many people searching as
possible, but if there is additional
avalanche danger on the way to get
help, send more than one person. The
people going out should mark the
route so that the rescue party can easily
find their way in. Of course, people
leaving the avalanche site will make ski
tracks on the way out, but rescuers
must be able to identify the correct ski
tracks if there are other skiers in the
area. The sheriff, U.S. Forest Service, or
ski patrol may be able to provide help.
Remaining members of the party
should begin search efforts as outlined
above.

Once a victim is located, proceed
rapidly but cautiously. First, try to uncover the face and provide air. If the
victim is unconscious, **artificial respiration** may be started as soon as the
face is uncovered. Make sure the
mouth and breathing passages are clear

of snow. Be particularly careful while
digging the victim out. The victim may
have suffered broken bones or open
wounds. Back and internal injuries are
common in avalanches. Treat for injuries and treat for shock.

Avalanches are dangerous. If you are
going into the **avalanche country**,
your best defense is knowledge and experience. Obtain additional training
from skilled personnel and read as
much as possible. See the section on
outdoor education for schools that provide avalanche training. The section on
equipment retailers lists companies that
offer avalanche safety supplies.

SUGGESTED READINGS

Armstrong, B., and K. Armstrong.
1986. The Avalanche Book. Fulcrum,
Golden, Colorado.

Fredston, J.A., and D. Fesler. 1985.
Snow Sense. A Guide to Evaluating
Snow Avalanche Hazard. Snow
Avalanche Safety Program, Alaska Dept.
Nat. Resources, Pouch 7-001, Anchor-
age, Alaska 99510.

Daffern, T. 1983. Avalanche Safety for
Skiers and Climbers. Rocky Mountain
Books, Calgary, Alberta.

Fraser, C. 1978. Avalanches and Snow
Safety. John Murray Publishers, Ltd.,
Great Britain.

LaChapelle, E.R. 1985. The ABC of
Avalanche Safety. Mountaineers, Seattle.

Gallagher, D., ed. 1967. The Snowy
Torrents: Avalanche Accidents in the
United States 1910-1966. Alta Avalanche
Study Center, U.S.D.A. Forest Service.

Perla, R.I., and M. Martinelli, Jr. 1978.
Avalanche Handbook. U.S.D.A. Hand-
book 489. U.S. Gov. Printing Office,
Washington, D.C.

Stethem, C.J., and P.A. Schaerer.
1980. Avalanche Accidents in Canada II,
A Selection of Case Histories of Acci-

dents 1943 to 1978, Nat. Res. Council Canada, Vancouver, British Columbia.

Williams, K. 1981. The Snowy Torrents, Avalanche Accidents in the United States 1967-1971. Teton Bookshop Publishing Co., Jackson, Wyoming.

Williams, K., and B. Armstrong. 1984. The Snowy Torrents, Avalanche Accidents in the United States 1975-79. Teton Bookshop Publishing Co., Jackson, Wyoming.

Winter Clothing

In this section, you will find a short discussion of the principles governing the selection of equipment to use in winter. Following this discussion, we have included a list of equipment. Our list is designed to meet the needs of a winter skier on a camping trip in which extreme conditions may be encountered. The list represents the type of equipment we have used on long trips in the western Rocky Mountains and in **Yellowstone National Park**, where camping out at temperatures lower than -40°C (-40°F) is not uncommon. Our list was derived from many years of experience and use by the authors and experience gained at the **National Outdoor Leadership School** and the numerous winter courses we have taught at different programs. The list has stood the tests of time and use by many students and instructors. It balances the need for extra warmth and comfort vs. carrying extra weight on a long ski trip. On a shorter trip, you might wish to carry more socks, for instance. On day trips or trips in areas of milder weather, less equipment may be needed. This equipment list will allow a careful person to survive even the worst winter conditions, including unexpected emergencies like rain in January or falling in a river at -40°C (-40°F). When an emergency occurs, you may not be totally comfortable, but you will survive. The information here could save your life!

Two factors govern selection of clothing for winter trips: **layering** and **proper materials**. A layering system of clothing allows the skier to adjust to warm or cold conditions during the day. It is just as important to avoid sweating as it is to be warm. A single thick parka may provide warmth, but there is no intermediate stage for warmer conditions; you either wear it or you don't. With a layering system, layers are added when it gets colder and taken off when it gets warmer.

Four layers are recommended for a **layering system**: underwear, fair weather clothing, added insulation, and environment-resistant shells. The **underwear** layer really consists of two shells: your intimate items, and the long johns providing insulation. Underpants, undershirts, and bras provide a feeling of comfort and may prevent outer layers from rubbing. Boxer shorts or the old pettipants are helpful for preventing chapping. Tight-fitting underwear often causes chaffing. If these items are made of cotton, they will absorb moisture from sweat and from the air (see below). If you are in survival conditions or if your inner layer is damp, get rid of these items as soon as possible.

Insulating underwear should be smooth, trap dead air space close to the body, and "**breathe**," or **wick** moisture away from the skin. Choose this layer carefully to avoid materials that irritate or are allergenic. Many people like to use the newer polypropylene materials for this layer. Wool is the old standby, but avoid cotton. When conditions warrant, we often simply ski in our long-johns because they wick moisture away from bodies that are working hard. You

A well-dressed ice fisherman enjoys a cold sport (Don Murphy).

may want both lower and upper long underwear, but some prefer to use shirts with buttons that allow the shirts to be opened to provide additional ventilation. This layer must not bind the body or be tight over any blood vessels, such as at the wrists.

Fair weather clothing forms the second layer. These are the items in which you will spend most of your time. A typically mild day with medium to heavy exercise demands that this layer be kept light and thin. The fair weather layer must not bind and should breathe. This layer provides some additional insulation, but not a lot. It also protects against abrasion and snags by tree branches and should shed snow relatively easily. The fair weather layer can be worn with the environmental shell to provide protection from wind or precipitation, or from snow if you fall.

The third layer is the **insulation layer**. Its primary importance is to provide additional dead air space to retain internal heat. The insulation layer becomes important during very cold weather or when stopping for a break on the trail. It should be easy to put on and take off. This layer may actually consist of several thinner shells. Items for this layer should be lightweight and compressible for packing when on the trail. Thick sweaters also work for this layer and a mix between sweaters and jackets or vests should be selected to provide for easy packing, resistance to moisture accumulation (beware of **down** materials, which are useless when they get wet), and weight. Sleeveless vests may be particularly useful because a warm core will send heat to extremities.

The fourth or **environmental layer** provides protection from wind, rain, and snow—in particular wet snow. Two types of garment are used: those that are **wind proof** and those that are **water-resistant** or **waterproof**. A few garments provide both wind and water-proof characteristics. These items should be lightweight and loose fitting. Zippers, which allow additional **ventilation**, are also desirable. Pants with wind bib fronts are becoming popular, since they help prevent snow from going down pants when a skier falls. The additional bib often makes these pants too hot, however. **Wind shells** keep the body protected from wind, but breathe (are porous) and transport condensation through clothing and away from the body. Waterproof clothing that breathes is desirable but expensive. Traditional rain gear is waterproof and does not breathe; because of this characteristic, you can become wet from your own sweat. Avoid plastic rain gear; it tears or fractures when cold and quickly becomes useless. Also avoid ponchos, as the open sides will not provide any protection in high winds. Each person must choose environmental clothing based on balancing cost, weight, and the particular characteristics of the material from which it is made (see below).

Using four layers provides protection greater than the sum of each of the four layers. As layers are added, the area between layers also acts as a dead air space, increasing the insulation. It is very important to choose all layers to be loose and successively larger so that outer layers do not constrict the inner layers. Beware of **constriction zones** on the feet, and around the ankles and wrists. A tight or wrinkled sock, an elastic band in a pair of mittens, or the cuff of a parka may restrict blood flow, causing **frostbite**.

A good winter tactic is to **dress up**. By this, we mean start with the innermost layer and only add layers as needed. It is much easier to put on your wool pants over your long underwear later in the day than to have to stop and take off your wool pants before you can put on your long underwear. Zippered, insulated pants can then be added over the wool pants without having to take things off.

If energy conservation is not a prime requisite, it may be better to be slightly cool during the day. By being slightly cool, the winter person can prevent the build-up of sweat in clothing.

The selection of the proper materials for use in winter relates to the four modes of **energy transfer** that control the energy budget of skiers: conduction, convection, radiation, and evaporation. **Clothing materials** must exploit the properties of energy transfer to protect skiers. Insulation, radiation reflection, wind and water resistance, and other physical properties of the materials must be considered.

Clothing materials **transfer moisture** in different manners. **Cotton** is **hygroscopic**—that is, it absorbs moisture from the air or your body and keeps it in the cloth, resisting drying and thus reducing insulation properties. You can observe this phenomenon when you put on a cotton shirt, a wool shirt with a cotton lining, or climb between clean cotton sheets. All three feel cold from the moisture. The feeling of cold resulting from the collection of moisture can be fatal in the winter. Avoid all cotton for field activities. If you use cotton underwear, as mentioned before, get rid of it in survival situations.

Some materials resist absorbing water; chief among these are the polypropylene products. Wool consists of animal hair with empty cells that trap dead air. The hair can absorb water, but the interior of the **dead air spaces** are dry. Both materials, however, still trap water between fibers. Wool remains slightly warmer for a given thickness because of its internal dead air space.

Both polypropylene and wool **wick** water from wet areas (near your skin) to the dry air. The wicking properties allow both materials to dry from the inside out while in the field. **Polypropylene** appears to wick water better than **wool**. However, to drive the wicking action, energy must be used from the body. Experiments at our **Teton Science School** classes suggested that there is a slightly higher energy loss through polypropylene during the wicking process than through wool (see Figure 118). Polypropylene is desirable when energy loss is not critical, but under extreme **survival conditions** wool may retain more heat as it dries. **Felt** is compressed wool; it works well for insoles and boots.

Insulation results from **dead air space**, areas small enough that air currents will not be set up. Common insulating materials, such as down and wool, and **PolarGuard**, pile, or other synthetics provide effective dead air space but differ considerably in other properties. One centimeter (0.4 inch) of effective dead air space in any of the above materials provides essentially the same amount of insulation, but differs in **weight**, **compressibility**, and **cost**. An inch of down weighs less and compresses more, but costs more than an inch of PolarGuard. If a down item falls in the stream, it cannot be dried out on a trip, whereas the PolarGuard item can. Select insulating properties with careful consideration of your pocketbook and needs. If you live in a wet climate or where long periods of extreme cold will cause moisture to accumulate in your equipment, Po-

larGuard may be the best choice for items such as sleeping bags and even coats.

Wind-resistant materials must completely stop high winds. Tightly woven or coated nylon works well. Parkas made of **nylon/cotton** blends also resist not only wind but water. To determine if a material is **windproof**, use the **breathing test**. Place the material against your mouth and suck in to form a seal. If you can feel air coming through the cloth, it is not windproof. Beware of **plastic**!

Water-resistant materials shed water but will eventually be soaked through. These materials may also tend to breathe. **Nylon/cotton** blends (often called **60/40 cloth**) are both water- and wind-resistant. These materials are acceptable if rain is seldom encountered in cold winter regions.

Waterproof materials pass no water. They can be tested by the breathing test mentioned above or by pouring water onto the cloth. Be aware that since waterproof materials do not pass water, the wearer becomes wet from sweat. Waterproof clothing should not be worn when windproof clothing is needed, because of this quality.

Some materials are waterproof, but still **breathe**. **Gore-Tex** and similar products are made from porous materials in which the pore is small enough to block the passage of water drops, but not small enough to block the passage of water vapor. Vapor from near the body passes through the cloth to the air. The balance between heavy sweating from exercise and high vapor pressures in the outside air may reduce the effectiveness of these materials, allowing the wearer to still become wet. Also, Gore-Tex materials do not work when dirty and consequently may not be as effective on long trips where no means are available to clean the materials.

A common misconception considers that because a material breathes, it will always pass water from the warmer inside to the outside (Figure 101). This may not be true under very cold conditions. Within insulating material of a coat or a sleeping bag, a **temperature profile** is set up which is similar to the profile found in a snowpack. The freezing point of the profile is often beneath the surface of the insulation. Moisture moving from the body condenses and freezes at this point, well within the insulating material. Additional moisture from the air may freeze to the outside of the material. On long, cold trips, it is important to lay sleeping bags out the first thing in the morning to allow moisture and ice to sublimate. As much as

yourself with as much additional insulation as possible. The mylar will stop convection currents, but it also retains moisture, which may lead to wet clothes by morning. Use these products with caution and full knowledge of how they work.

Experience has shown which and how many of each clothing items are needed for different portions of the body. In general, for a winter camping trip, we recommend three layers for feet (includes two pairs of socks and boots), three layers for the legs, three layers for the upper torso, and a stocking cap. Environmental clothing should be available to cover all parts of the body, including gaiters, a face mask, and a windproof covering for the head.

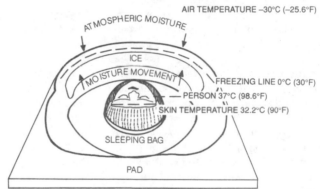

Figure 101. *Cross-section of a sleeping bag showing ice formation during very cold weather.*

1.4 kg (3.1 lb) of body moisture may accumulate inside the insulation of a sleeping bag on a two-week winter trip when it is very cold.

Aluminum-coated **mylar** products (**space blankets**) tend to reduce radiation loss, especially when new. It has been suggested that as they get older, their radiation-retarding properties may be rapidly reduced. These products do not provide insulation and the gain in retained radiant energy may be rather small. Space blankets may serve a purpose in **bivouac** or other emergency situations, but remember to protect

Below, we have listed by category each of the areas of the body and what is needed for protection during a long winter camping trip. Remember—avoid **cotton**!

Feet

• 5 pairs of thick wool socks. Light inner socks (wool or polypropylene) are optional.

• 1 pair of insulated boots. The type with felt liners are very good. Sorels are good but heavy, and equivalent non-Sorel brands, such as boots made for snowmobilers, which have felt liners and nylon covers, may be cheaper and lighter. Dacron or down booties with nylon overboots also work well. Boots with rough bottoms prevent sliding into bad positions during the winter. Be sure to sleep with your boots inside your sleeping bag when it is really cold to prevent them from freezing.

• 1 pair of ski boots. Ski boots should be big enough for two pairs of thick socks without binding the toes. Oftentimes the toes of the boot are not high enough for two pair of socks. In this case, a felt insole and one pair of socks may keep your feet warm. If you have cold feet while wearing two pairs of socks, try one pair and felt insoles. Again, sleep with your boots if it is really cold.

• 1 pair of gaiters. Avoid gaiters that are completely waterproof, as your legs will sweat in them when it is warm (having only the lower half waterproof is a good alternative). Gaiters should be rugged so that the edges of skis or snowshoes will not cut them. Obtain gaiters that have both zippers or snaps and a Velcro closure. Zippers often fail on trips and the backup closure is important. Gaiters that have a complete, under-the-foot bottom add considerable dryness and warmth beyond that offered by other gaiters. For serious winter use, gaiters that have add-in insulation offer extra comfort.

Legs

• 1 pair of long underwear. Light underwear can be worn daily and heavy ones kept in the pack for extreme conditions.

• 1 pair of wool pants. In addition to regular stores, these may be bought at military surplus outlets and at garage sales. Another pair of wool pants may be substituted for long underwear as long as you can wear both pairs together, one on top of the other.

• 1 pair of insulated "ski pants." Make sure the leg zippers allow room for pulling on the pants over your ski boots.

• 1 pair of wind pants. Make sure the legs are large enough to fit over all your other clothing without constricting.

• 1 pair of waterproof pants (optional). These are nice to have for digging snow caves, but you may get wet anyway from your sweat.

Underwear

• 3 changes. Remember, if things get bad, take off any cotton underwear that you are wearing. Silk is nice for preventing chapping but provides little insulation.

Upper Body

• 3 layers minimum. Shirts or sweaters. Shirts are a good choice in that they can be unbuttoned for ventilation.

• 1 insulated coat. Lightweight coats are good and down may be useful here. Pockets on the inside, about waist-high, are helpful to keep boots in from the time you get up in the morning until you are ready to ski. When the weather is very cold, your body heat prevents your boots from freezing.

• 1 wind shell.

• 1 waterproof coat. Nice to have for digging snow caves, but you may get wet from your own sweat.

Hands

• 3 pairs of mittens. Avoid gloves as your main source of insulation. Gloves separate the fingers, making each finger individually responsible for maintaining its own warmth. Remember the small mammals and let your fingers huddle together to stay warm in a mitten. Gloves are colder than mittens.

• 1 pair of nylon over-mittens. Avoid

Students using hip waders to cross the Snake River in Wyoming.

leather and military cotton, as they quickly get wet and freeze.

• 1 pair of glove liners. These gloves, called **anticontact gloves**, serve to prevent fingers from freezing to cold objects, especially metal, when you have removed your mittens. Silk and nylon gloves are nice but provide little insulation. Light wool or polypropylene gloves may serve the purpose better as they keep your fingers warm while doing chores.

Head

• 1 cap. Use an insulated hat that covers the ears or a heavy stocking cap.

• 1 wind shell. This shell may be a nylon cover or a hood on your wind parka.

• 1 face mask. Face masks made for snowmobiling or downhill skiing are excellent. A balaclava, which serves as a hat and a face mask, is good. A scarf may substitute under bad conditions.

Daypack

• 1 pack. Make sure that your daypack is large enough to carry all your items. It is better to have a bag that is too large and have extra room.

Sleeping Bag

• 1 bag. If conditions are at all wet or if you anticipate very cold conditions, a synthetic bag (PolarGuard for example) is recommended. It will dry from the inside out should it get wet. Only experienced campers should use down bags in the winter, as they will not dry in the field. A winter bag should have at least 15 cm (6 in) of loft. Lay it on the floor and measure its

height. To get 15 cm (6 in) of loft requires about 1.8 kg (4 lbs) of synthetic
material and 1.4 kg (3 lbs) of down.

• 1 sleeping pad. Get a full length
pad for winter use. Therm-a-Rest pads
are excellent but expensive. Closed-cell
foam pads work well and they are waterproof. Some pads, however, crack at
cold temperatures. The white ensolite
pads will shatter; the light-blue ones
will not. As soon as you get up in the
morning (if you are moving from a
camp) roll your pads up and pack them
while they are still warm and pliable.

• 1 ground cloth. This is not needed
if your pad is waterproof. If you are
sleeping directly on the snow, get a
ground cloth that is wider than the
sleeping pad.

• 1 bivouac sack. An optional item,
but nice for sleeping in snow caves, as
no matter which way you roll, you will
not come in contact with the snow. Get
a bivouac sack that breathes, or make
one. A coated nylon bottom with a
Gore-Tex top works excellently.

Miscellaneous Items:

• Toiletries: toothbrush, toothpaste,
comb, disposable tampons with a Zip-
loc plastic bag. Avoid soap during your
trip as it takes the protective oils out of
your skin that cannot be replaced in
winter. Washing with snow is very effective. We do not carry toilet paper but
use snowballs instead (see conservation
section).

• Skin: sunburn prevention cream,
lip salve.

• Light source: small flashlight or
headlamp. Lithium batteries work best
in the cold, followed by Duracell brand
alkaline batteries.

A final hint: Keep one pair of mittens
and two pairs of socks tightly packed
and sealed in a plastic bag at the bottom of your pack. These are indispens-
able if an emergency arises and, otherwise, a delight for the last day of the
trip.

Finally, a short story to illustrate the
effectiveness of this equipment list.
During the 1978-79 winter, I (JCH) led a
National Outdoor Leadership School
course of 17 students from Old Faithful
in **Yellowstone National Park** on a
ski trip out to the south entrance of the
park. During the next two weeks, 11
out of 14 nights were colder than -40°C
(-40°F). One night my thermometer
recorded -57°C (-70°F), the lower limit
for an alcohol thermometer. This was
the coldest winter in the recorded history of Yellowstone Park. In Jackson
Hole, Wyoming, the Wort Hotel burned
its wooden furniture in the fireplace to
keep the guests warm. All students and
instructors were equipped as outlined
above, and on about half the nights we
built snow shelters and campfires. The
other half of the nights we spent in our
tents. Our group suffered no frostbite,
even though numerous cases of serious
frostbite were recorded in the park
from other recreationists that winter. *Be
prepared*.

Winter Travel

Many modes of travel are used
during the winter and we will not try to
speak directly to each type. Whether
your travel is by skis, snowshoes,
snowmobiles, cars, or 12-person snow-
coaches into Yellowstone, there are
some general guidelines that may be of
use to you who venture out during the
winter season.

The most important of the guidelines,
of course, are the **6 Ps**: Prior Planning,
Promptness Prevent Poor Performance.
The 6 Ps urge the traveler to do everything to be prepared. Perhaps the first
tool of preparedness is knowing what
to expect. Do a little research ahead of

Winter travelers cross the Oxbow bridge over the Snake River, Grand Teton National Park.

time to learn the average weather conditions for the time of the year when your traveling will occur. A good atlas will provide climate maps, and travel services such as the AAA Auto Club will provide climate conditions for the traveler. As the date nears for your trip, watch the weather reports on television. Call the U.S. Weather Bureau for up-to-date weather forecasts. Flight services at the local airport may also be of service for weather reports. Understand the type of weather that is being predicted for the dates of your trip. Plan and dress accordingly.

Select your equipment to match the expected conditions and possible extremes. If travel is in your **private vehicle**, see that it is equipped for emergency breakdowns. During the winter keep a sleeping bag and extra food in the car. An extra set of cold-weather clothing, including boots, should also be stowed in waterproof containers in the car. Beside the normal emergency repair equipment and flares, it is wise to carry a large snow shovel and tire chains. Leave a set of waterproof matches in the glove compartment. In an emergency, the seats of the car may provide insulation or material that can be burned to provide heat. Above all, in a blizzard, stay with your car. Run the engine for short periods of time only and make sure that the exhaust pipe is well vented to prevent **carbon monoxide poisoning.**

If you are traveling on public conveyances, carry extra food and clothing. Public transportation is usually not equipped to protect passengers in the case of a winter breakdown, and delays often leave the passenger hungry. Try not to trust public transportation companies to transport your most important winter gear; carry it with you if you can.

Winter hikers, skiers, snowshoers, and snowmobilers should heed the above cautions. In addition, check your local sources of avalanche prediction (these may be the U.S. Forest Service or state or private agencies) for avalanche warnings. If you are in an area unfamiliar to you, consider hiring a local guide, since he or she will know the area and its local weather and avalanche patterns. Travel with others when possible and leave information about your route and expected return time with someone responsible. It is also helpful to leave information on the type of vehicle you'll be driving and its license number.

Winter Camping

Winter camping can be a source of great pleasure if you have the proper equipment, training, and planning. Several books are available that provide background on equipment, meal planning, packing, traveling, and camping in the backcountry (see *Suggested Readings*). Here we will cover snow shelters, especially as they relate to an organism—a person—living under the snow.

Natives of the cold regions have developed three types of snow shelter, depending on the snow conditions where they live. Where conditions form hard but level snowpacks, **igloos** have been the shelter of choice. In regions where snowpacks form deep drifts, **snow caves** are favored. In regions of shallow and loose snowpacks, natives build **quinzhees** using **sintered** snow piles. Each type of snow shelter has similar properties of insulation and provides similar protection (Elsner and Pruitt, 1959). We often use quinzhees and their derivatives because they can be made under a wide variety of snow conditions.

Quinzhees

The quinzhee is a snow shelter developed by the Athabascan Indians. In their home country snows are soft and fluffy, and are seldom very deep. The shelter they developed takes advantage of these characteristics. The basic quinzhee consists of a small mound of snow built and hollowed out by the winter camper (Figures 102 and 103).

To build a quinzhee, stand in the center of an open area and trace a circle around yourself with a ski pole or stick. The circle should be 2.5 m (8 ft) in diameter (Figure 104). Then exit the circle and pile snow into the center of the circle until the mound reaches a minimum of about 1.25 m (about 50 in). If the snowpack is shallow, snow will have to be brought from a distance. (The good thing about a quinzhee is that it can be built in very shallow snow, which then only has to be brought from farther away.) Use shovels, snowshoes, skis, pots, or pans to help pile the snow. As you are piling, break up any snow lumps. If it is very cold, or if the snow contains **depth hoar**, try to pack down the snow on the pile so that it will sinter. If possible, avoid depth hoar for your quinzhee, as its unstable nature prevents the quinzhee from setting up well.

Piling the snow has mixed the relatively wetter snow from near the ground with drier upper layers. Movement also frees moisture and spreads it among crystals. The snow moved to form the quinzhee is then left to **sinter** for around two hours, allowing the free moisture to freeze and snow crystals to bond. Longer times may be required for sintering depending on snow conditions. If it is very cold, below -18°C (0°F), more than two hours may be necessary. Icy snow or depth hoar conditions also require longer. The sintering process allows moisture between the snow crystals to bind the crystals together into a higher density and a stronger snow.

Once set up, the inside can be hollowed out. We enforce certain safety rules during the digging-out process. There must always be someone outside to help the person inside should the quinzhee collapse. Quinzhees become very stable with time and we have seen one collapse only during the digging-out process. Since there is little snow in a quinzhee, the digging person could probably get out without help, but why take a chance? The outside person can also pass the snow removed from the inside away from the door to facilitate digging.

Thickness of the wall varies with location and can be determined from Figure 103. In general, the wall at the base should be at least 30 cm (12 in) wide and at the top 20 cm (about 8 in) wide. In between, the wall tapers in thickness. Before digging, select several handfuls of twigs. Break these twigs to the appropriate length and shove them into the snow pile to tell the digger on the inside when the wall is thin enough. With practice a person can learn to dig out a quinzhee without sticks for reference.

The digging process starts by making an opening the size needed for the door. Learn to dig with as big a shovel as possible; skilled campers can use No. 14 **grain scoops**, which speed the process. Snow is removed in a manner to keep the inside cavity in a dome shape (Figure 105). This is important, because digging straight into the mound creates a flat roof that will collapse the quinzhee. Although snow is porous, you should make an **air vent** in the top of the cave. This is particularly helpful if cooking is done within

Figure 102. *Scooping out the inside of a quinzhee, a type of snow shelter originated by the Athabascan Indians.*

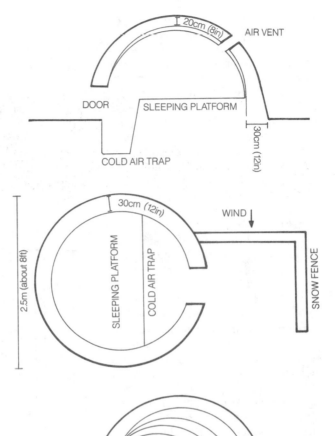

Figure 103. *Cross-section of a quinzhee showing shape, dimensions of the wall, a sleeping platform, and a cold air trap.*

AIR VENT

20cm (8in)

DOOR SLEEPING PLATFORM

30cm (12in)

COLD AIR TRAP

Figure 104. *Floor plan of a quinzhee showing sleeping platform, cold air trap, and snow fence.*

30cm (12in)

WIND

2.5m (about 8ft)

SLEEPING PLATFORM

COLD AIR TRAP

SNOW FENCE

Figure 105. *Cross-section showing the progression of the roof shape while digging out a quinzhee. The domed structure must be maintained during the complete excavation process.*

the snow cave; an air hole allows steam to escape easily. The vent can be made by pushing a ski pole or similar object through the ceiling.

Indians living in regions with a shallow snowpack first remove all the snow down to the ground before building a shelter. We have found that if the snowpack is deep, it is warmer to sleep on a snow shelf (Figure 103). By not digging down to the ground in a deep snowpack, you can also avoid disturbing the **depth hoar** and causing the shelter to

collapse. In deep snow country, we first stomp down the snow in the circled area with our feet to collapse as much of the depth hoar as possible. Then we pile the snow and sleep on stomped platforms.

Once the quinzhee is dug out, it can be improved by adding a **platform** for sleeping, cutting a **cold air trap**, cutting a **snow block** for closing the door (or place a pack in front of it), and building a **snow fence** outside the door (Figures 103 and 104). The cold air trap is a pit cut deep in the floor of the snow shelter. It allows cold air to settle and warmer air to occupy the upper reaches of the shelter. The trap allows residents to sit while cooking, placing their feet down into the trap. Candles or stoves will quickly increase the internal heat, making the quinzhee a warm place to sleep. Following a night of use, the quinzhee becomes extremely strong. We commonly have six or more students stand on a quinzhee to demonstrate its strength. The thermal properties of a quinzhee are explained in the next chapter.

The quinzhee type of construction lends itself to building large and complex structures. The basic two-person quinzhee can be enlarged to a luxurious structure with a high roof and more space. It is simple to make it big enough for about four people. We have built two-story quinzhees and a quinzhee arch large enough to drive cars through. Designs more practical for housing several people in the field (Figure 106) can be made by joining several quinzhees together. On trips when the weather is bad, let the imagination run wild and spend a day constructing creative quinzhees. We have even had an 2.5 m (8 ft) high moose-shaped quinzhee. Large quinzhees are fragile while they are being excavated; work carefully. Quinzhees are ideal class exercises and can provide playground fun while teaching important survival skills.

Over time, the roof of the quinzhee will sag into the center. Warmer temperatures, lots of use, heat from candles and cooking speed this process. Simply pile more snow on top and carve off the roof from the inside. The fill and carve process will enable the use of a quinzhee all winter.

Snow Caves

Snow caves, like quinzhees, are a

dugout shelter, but snow caves count on redistribution of the snow by the wind. To build a snow cave, find a slope where the wind has created a pile of snow. Sometimes small, safe snow **cornices** may be used to advantage. If possible, find a place where there is a continuous slope below the proposed entrance to the cave (Figure 107). This will allow the snow shoveled from the inside to fall downslope, facilitating digging. Digging a snow cave is

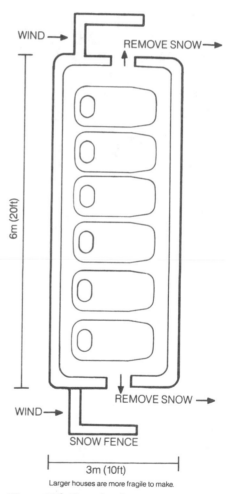

Figure 106. Floor plan for a six-person quinzhee. The quinzhee is dug from both ends at the same time.

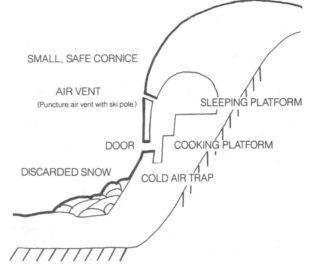

Figure 107. *Cross-sectional view of a snow cave, showing a platform for sleeping and a cold air trap.*

SMALL, SAFE CORNICE

AIR VENT
(Puncture air vent with ski pole.)

SLEEPING PLATFORM

DOOR   COOKING PLATFORM

DISCARDED SNOW   COLD AIR TRAP

the same as digging a quinzhee. Follow safety procedures. We sometimes use a nylon tarp or rain fly to pile snow onto and then pull it out from our large snow caves.

Again, elaborate snow caves may be constructed. Many different types and designs are common. Refer to a good book on winter camping for other ideas. The basic snow cave can be improved easily. Sleeping and cooking platforms make living easier. A cold air trap may be added at the door. If the roof sinks, add more snow to the top and carve out the inside.

Igloos

Igloos were developed by the Eskimos to take advantage of the wind-packed, level snow that occurs in the arctic regions. The Eskimos cut blocks of snow, which they use as building blocks to fashion an igloo. To build an igloo, find a hard-packed surface that will support your weight when walking on it. If the snow is too soft, it is possible to pack the snow and let it harden before cutting blocks. A **snow saw** is

useful for cutting blocks and can be obtained from outdoor equipment stores. Alternatively, a large knife or small shovel may be used.

Traditional igloos were made by cutting blocks of snow about 76 x 25 x 7.5 cm (30 x 10 x 3 in). These blocks were tapered to cause the igloo to spiral in towards the center (Figure 108). When snow conditions are softer, wider and smaller blocks may be made and placed on their wide, flat side. The smaller blocks are about 30 x 25 cm (12 x 10 in) with the dimension of the third side being determined by how soft the snow is. The third side may vary from 7.5 to 25 cm (3 to 10 in); larger blocks are needed when the snow is soft.

Begin by marking a circle the desired size of the inside of the igloo. One person gets inside the circle and another person passes the snow blocks. The first ring of blocks is tapered (Figure 109) to cause the igloo to spiral to the center. Hint: in soft-snow country, place a few handfuls of snow between the existing wall and new blocks. This snow will sinter and help hold the wall

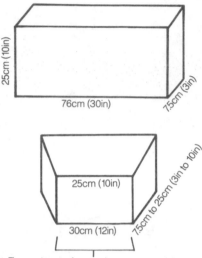

Figure 108. *Diagram showing how to cut blocks for an igloo. The more traditional method uses narrow blocks placed on edge (a); a modified method for softer snow uses wide blocks placed on the flat side (b). Trim the inside edge (c) so that the blocks slope inward.*

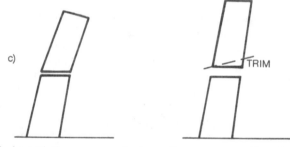

Tapered to conform to the curvature of the wall.

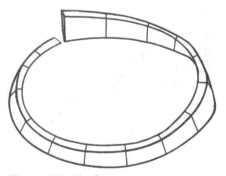

together. Blocks are added until the sides dome in to form the top. The top block is carefully placed using help from the inside and outside. Before placing the block, estimate its shape and carve a special block to shape for the keystone of your igloo. Next, carefully carve a door to let the inside person out. Chink any cracks between blocks with powder snow. Occasionally, igloos do collapse when placing the final block, so do this carefully. The igloo will set up to be very strong.

Living in Snow Shelters

Here are some hints for safety while sleeping in snow shelters: Always make sure that you punch an air vent through the shelter wall. It will prevent the ac-

cumulation of gas, especially when cooking inside. Always take your shovel inside at night. A blizzard may cover the entrance to your tunnel; we

Figure 109. *The first ring of snow blocks in an igloo is tapered to cause the igloo to spiral into the center.*

have known of a couple of snow shelters that were buried by avalanches.

The final touch to winter camping is the **snow kitchen** or cooking pit. The kitchen consists of a pit with shelves for the stoves and food supplies, and for sitting. A fire pit may even be placed on one side. A recessed kitchen protects campers from winds and provides a pleasant place for congregating. Let your imagination go; be inventive with interior designs.

Construct the kitchen simply by digging down into the snow. A No. 14 **grain scoop** works well for this chore. Tables, benches, and shelves are cut into the walls. Patting the snow will help it to set up, providing a solid surface for sitting. Place your sleeping pad on the benches to provide additional warmth while sitting. Walls of the kitchen may have recesses cut underneath them to allow the user to stand close by, allowing the toes to be under the snow.

Designate different areas for food, supplies, stoves, fuel storage, and sitting. This segregation of articles will help prevent items from becoming lost. Cutting shelves into the walls is helpful if a lot of fresh snow is falling. This prevents the snow from covering small or even large items. Each night all items should be stored in place, because snowfall during the night may cover things left out. Domed, small niches may be cut for candles. A niche will serve as a reflector, using the candlelight more efficiently.

A trick for **water storage**: snow that has been melted, or fresh, unfrozen water can be stored in the snow during the night with little freezing. If the water is cold, it helps to warm it slightly on the stove first. Warm water is placed in a covered pan in the snow and covered by additional snow. The place at the edge of the kitchen is marked so it can be found in the morning even if considerable new snow falls. The insulation provided by the snow will trap heat in the water and

Students work in a kitchen dug down into the snow. A table has been constructed for the stove and students watch from the recessed shelter of the pit.

keep the water from freezing even on very cold nights. Morning operations are speedier when it is not necessary to melt snow for cooking water.

Fill stoves away from the kitchen and candles. A word of warning: white gas vapors can be ignited by a candle located a considerable distance away. Always make sure that you are far from sources of flame when opening a fuel bottle—this includes making sure that there are no lingering flames on your stoves. Many people have been injured and many camping trips have been tragically ruined by exploding fuel bottles.

SUGGESTED READINGS

Antell, S. 1980. Backpacker's Recipe Book. Pruett, Boulder, Colorado.

Bower, D. 1969. Manual of Ski Mountaineering. Sierra Club, San Francisco.

Cary, B. 1979. Winter Camping. Stephen Greene Press, Brattleboro, Vermont.

Elsner, R.W., and W.O. Pruitt, Jr. 1959. Some structural and thermal characteristics of snow shelters. Arctic, 12:20-27.

Hampton, B., and D. Cole. 1988. Soft Paths. Stackpole Books, Harrisburg, Pennsylvania. Available through the National Outdoor Leadership School, Box AA, Lander, Wyoming 82520.

Nordic World Magazine. 1975. All About Winter Safety. World Publications, Box 366, Mountain View, California.

Pallister, N., and T. Cunningham. 1978. NOLS Cookery. National Outdoor Leadership School, Lander, Wyoming.

Petzoldt, P. 1974. The Wilderness Handbook. W.W. Norton, New York.

Richard, S., D. Orr, and C. Lindholm. 1988. NOLS Cookery. National Outdoor Leadership School, Lander, Wyoming.

Rutstrum, C. 1968. Paradise Below Zero. Collier Books, New York.

Simer, P., and J. Sullivan. 1983. The National Outdoor Leadership School's Wilderness Guide. Simon and Schuster, New York.

Wilkinson, E. 1986. Snow Caves for Fun and Survival. Windsong Press, Box 1484, Denver, Colorado 80201.

Winter Conservation

Those of us who love the nivean world have learned to **conserve** its beauty and its resources. We ask that others who enter this world do likewise. The winter world demands special care to guard against pollution. Our experiences have taught us many techniques for traveling and camping, which we wish to share.

Travel quietly, so that all may enjoy the silence of winter. If you use vehicles, make sure that effective mufflers are installed. Sounds travel great distances over expanses of snow. Snow machines should use only designated routes so that all backcountry travelers can enjoy the silence of the world beyond the roads. Skiers, too, should travel quietly. Loud parties and blasting radios or cassette players have no place in a quiet world.

Animals also like the silence. Snow machines, even though they are noisy, are more tolerated than are people. Evidently animals have not learned to associate the machines with danger, whereas the presence of humans on foot tends to displace animals. Whatever the reason, respect the fright or flight distance of animals by not getting too close. Respect their privacy. Animals are a resource that must be conserved. In many winter areas, the human impact on animals is now being managed, and we can reduce potential problems by careful consideration of animal rights.

Travel discreetly, so that all may enjoy untouched scenes of winter. Single trails through open fields are more pleasing to the eye than a spaghetti maze of tracks. If selecting slopes for snow machine or telemark practice, pick slopes that are out of sight of major travel routes.

Visual pollution takes many forms. The bright colors of winter clothing and camping gear provide an important safety margin, but try to camp out of sight, back away from the open meadows. Don't discard even biodegradable items. Winter cold prevents degradation and animals don't always eat discarded food. Orange peels are particularly offensive, as animals tend not to eat them.

Though snowfall may cover your visual pollution signs during the winter, you can't count on the occurrence of a snowfall. In popular areas, shovel snow over signs of your activities, destroy your **snow shelters**, and fill in your **cooking pits**. Snow shelters and **kitchens** may be left for other winter travelers, if they are well out of the line of travel or line of scenic view. Unsightly stains should be covered by shoveling snow on them before leaving.

Good **trail etiquette** provides a track that is pleasing to all who follow. Place ski tracks about shoulder width apart. Trails get narrower as more people pass over them, and narrow trails will trip people with wider boots. It is better to make the trail slightly wide than too narrow. When stepping onto or off of the trail, completely lift your feet and step to a platform that is parallel to the trail. Avoid skiing off at an angle, as this produces diverging ruts that may trip a skier who is moving fast. On slopes, step off the trail to the downhill side, so that if you fall you will not destroy a well-packed trail. When you fall, remember to fill in your **sitzmark**, the hole your body and pack leave in the snow on impact. Stomp good, wide platforms for all kick turns. Leave the trail completely to go to the bathroom.

Selection of **winter campsites** is governed by many of the same rules as in the summer. Choose sites that are well away from open water and streams, to avoid pollution of water sources. Avoid **widow makers**—dead trees that winter winds may blow down on your tents. Consideration also must be given to what will be beneath the snow when it melts in the spring. Avoid potentially embarrassing situations such as fire pits located on top of the snow but over buildings or the parking lot of the summer camping area.

Fires are a delight on winter trips, but some areas are so heavily traveled that fires are not allowed. Fires should not be built where wood collecting will leave obvious scars. Winter campers can create wood collection lines: they have broken every branch off the trees up to as high as they can reach while standing on the snow. These may be very unsightly in the summer. When possible, carry fuel and use stoves so you will not need to collect firewood in the winter.

When building fires, collect your wood from locations away from the trail and scenic views. Beware of broken limbs; these are dangerous near your campsite, where skiers may be poked in the face. Place your fire pit carefully. Avoid situations in which the pit may melt through the snow and create damage at the snow/soil interface. Remember that the ashes will melt down to the soil in the spring, so avoid locations where the they may offend summer travelers.

Food wastes will not decompose during the winter and may lie frozen until spring melts. Try to eat all food, cleaning your utensils thoroughly. While camping in the winter, we avoid using plates and instead use large cups. The cup provides heat when hands are wrapped around it. In addition, mixing and drinking hot beverages from the eating cup will help to wash it out. We avoid dish soap, because it is often hard to provide adequate rinsing. Utensils are washed only with boiling water as we make the beverages. If there is some "dish water," it is poured in one hole in the snow near the cooking spot. This hole is covered when leaving. **Toothpaste** and toothpaste water are also poured into this hole.

Prior planning can reduce the amount of waste that a winter camp may generate. This is important because it is easy to lose things on the kitchen floor, especially when snow is falling. Before the trip, take **wrappers** off of candy and packaged foods, and avoid ties for **plastic bags** (a simple, loose overhand knot is adequate). Incidentally, cutting cheese and meats into chunks before the camping trip is an excellent safety measure to avoid cutting fingers when trying to split frozen food. Carry out all waste, including the wax from your candles, **ski wax**, and ski wax wrappers.

Latrines are placed using the same guidelines as in summer—DDPP, or depth, drainage, privacy, and proximity. Choose a relatively flat area with vegetation where feces and urine will not run into the water supply. Choose a spot that offers privacy, but is conveniently close enough to camp that it will be used. If possible, do dig a latrine in the ground. The action of freezing and thawing, along with spring bacterial **decomposition**, will speed the breakdown of feces. Shallow burial is best, because cold soil temperatures deeper in the ground may delay bacterial decomposition. When possible, avoid latrine placement solely in snow as it is best to have some contact of feces with the ground to promote decomposition. Ground contact facilitates bacterial action.

When the snow is so deep that the latrine cannot be placed in contact with

A camp robber (Canada jay) feeds on a bit of trash left by a careless winter visitor.

the ground, it is better for each person to make personal **cat holes**. A new cat hole should be made each time. Large concentrations of feces and urine will freeze into a compact mass that may not decay for extended periods into the summer. Kick snow over urine stains.

We avoid **toilet paper** during the winter. Even the supposedly biodegradable brands do not degrade well at cold temperatures. There is nothing more unsightly than finding a tree draped with toilet paper when the snow melts in the spring. Instead of toilet paper, we use **snowballs**, and pieces of ice. While this may sound cold, it is an effective means of personal hygiene, and more comfortable than you might think. Wash your hands with snow following use of the latrine. If toilet paper is used, unfold it and burn it with a match. **Sanitary napkins** and **tampons** should be sealed in plastic bags, frozen, and carried out. They do not burn well. It has been suggested that packing them with crushed aspirin or teabags reduces odor problems.

These practices have proven very effective over many years of use and with many students. However, field conservation is dynamic and practices change as more is learned about the effects of different procedures.

Some techniques prove to be less effective in certain areas. Keep up-to-date on the latest in techniques by contacting local outdoors people and instructors. An excellent reference book for year-round camping techniques is Soft Paths, available through the **National Outdoor Leadership School**.

Most important—"Let no one say it, and say it to your shame, that all was beauty before you came."

SUGGESTED READINGS

Hampton, B., and D. Cole. 1988. Soft Paths. Stackpole Books, Harrisburg, Pennsylvania. National Outdoor Leadership School, Box AA, Lander, WY 82520.

Winter Educational Programs

Table 34 lists the **winter educational programs** of which we are aware. The list is certainly not exhaustive. It simply shows those programs that we know have recently conducted classes in either winter ecology or winter outdoor activities. If you know a school or a program that is not on this list, please write and we will include it in the next printing. This is the best way we know of bringing together all those with a love of winter. We hope that this will serve as the beginning of a winter activities directory. Send additions to:

A Naturalist's World
P.O. Box 8005, Suite 357
Boulder, CO 80306-8005

Table 34. Winter Ecology Courses and Winter Outdoor Activities Programs

Alaska Avalanche School
State Department of Natural Resources
Division of Parks and
    Outdoor Recreation
Pouch 7-005
Anchorage, AK 99510
(907) 276-2653

American Avalanche Institute
Box 308
Wilson, WY 83014
(307) 733-3315

Aspen Center for Environmental Studies
Box 8777
Aspen, CO 81612
(303) 925-5756

Center for Northern Studies
Wolcott, VT 05680
(802) 888-4331

Cloud Ridge Naturalists
Overland Star Route
Ward, CO 80481
(303) 459-3248

Colorado Outward Bound School
945 Pennsylvania
Denver, CO 80303
(303) 837-0880

Four Corners School of
    Outdoor Education
East Route
Monticello, UT 84535
(801) 587-2859

Keystone Science School
Box 38
Keystone, CO 80435
(303) 468-5824

Mountain Research Station
University of Colorado
Campus Box 450
Boulder, CO 80309
(303) 586-2371

National Outdoor Leadership School
P.O. Box AA
Lander, WY 82520
(307) 332-6973

Rice Creek Field Station
State University of New York at Oswego
Oswego, NY 13126
(315) 342-0961

Rocky Mountain Biological Laboratory
P.O. Box 519
Crested Butte, CO 81224
(303) 349-7231

Rocky Mountain Nature Association
Rocky Mountain National Park
Estes Park, CO 80517
(303) 586-2371

Teton Science School
Box 68
Kelly, WY 83011
(307) 733-4765

W.K. Kellogg Biological Station
Michigan State University
3700 E. Gull Lake Drive
Hickory Corners, MI 49060
(616) 671-5117

The Yellowstone Institute
Box 117
Yellowstone National Park, WY 82190
(307) 344-7381 ext. 2384

Yosemite Institute
Yosemite Association
P.O. Box 230
El Portal, CA 95318

Students measuring environmental variables including wind, radiation, and temperature during a winter storm, Teton Science School.

5. Experiencing Winter

Ecological processes become more apparent with investigation of the winter environment. A few field exercises will serve to illustrate how life proceeds in the winter. These experiments will also introduce the student and winter enthusiast to hidden intricacies of **survival** in a cold environment. We suggest seven field experiments for your education and enjoyment. These experiments may be combined with classes for a minicourse about winter ecology.

These field exercises were chosen to provide background in the properties of snow, life under the snowpack, human perceptions of winter, insulation of the human body, and human damage to the winter environment. The experiments, which may be used individually, tend to build on each other. Together, the series of experiments forms a symposium on the ecology of winter. We suggest that all experiments be completed, with students then presenting their results with posters at an oral symposium; suggested data presentation formats are shown. Finally, a list of equipment manufacturers that can provide equipment suitable for the experiments and outdoor activities is provided. You may need to review the material throughout the book to aid in your interpretation of results.

All field exercises should be carefully monitored by an adult. At no time should exercises be continued if extreme discomfort or danger exists from environmental conditions. Proper clothing and equipment should always be available for all participants. Remember the **6 Ps**.

WINTER FIELD EXPERIMENTS

Field Exercise 1
The Snowpack:
Its Temperature Profile

Purpose:
- to demonstrate differences in snow density
- to demonstrate differences in snow crystal structure and metamorphosis
- to demonstrate temperature differences within the snowpack
- to calculate the insulating properties of the snow

Equipment needed: One snow survey kit consisting of layer markers (tongue depressors or plastic markers for garden plants), a known-volume snow cutter, a snow classification chart, a metric ruler, good scales, and a digital thermometer. Long-stem thermometers will work, but their low level of accuracy severely limits interpretation.

Preparations: Select a site for **snow pit** study and draw an east-west trending line on the snow (Figure 110). All sampling will be done from the north side of the line so that the face of the pit is in the shade. Dig a pit to ground level. At one end of the pit dig a small vault to store instruments in the shade and out of the way. Always place instruments in the vault so that they are not lost or buried by fresh falling snow.

Procedures: Smooth off the north-facing side of the pit so that you have a straight wall for sampling. Push a knife

or credit card down the snowpack; be sensitive to changes in density of the snow to identify the main layers. At each layer boundary, insert a layer marker. Remember, it is hard to sample a layer thinner than your snow cutter. If there is a thin ice layer, you may improve your estimates by including snow on each side in a sample of a thin layer. We have provided a sample data sheet for help in collecting data (Figure 111). Check each category to make sure that all types of data have been collected.

Determine and record the top of each layer in the snowpack, measuring up from the ground. Also measure and record the middle of each layer. When graphing the data, the point for representing where the data were collected is the middle of the layer.

Record the temperature in the center of each layer in the snowpack. Do this chore immediately after determining layers and work quickly so that air temperatures do not change temperatures in the snow.

Next, record the density of each layer in the snow. First, weigh a plastic bag and record the weight. Then insert the cutter into the center of each snow layer and take a known volume of snow out. Be careful not to pack the snow into the cutter and be sure the cutter is completely free of snow when you remove it. Place the snow in a plastic bag and weigh it. Subtract the bag weight from the filled bag weight to get the weight of the snow. Divide the snow weight by the volume to obtain the density. Density must be recorded in g/cm^3 for later calculations.

Using a snow classification chart, determine and record the type of snow crystal in each layer. Use either the **LaChapelle** or **Colbeck** system for classification of snow on the ground. The LaChapelle system is most com-

Figure 110. Students from Teton Science School digging snow pits in Grand Teton National Park (Marsha Benning).

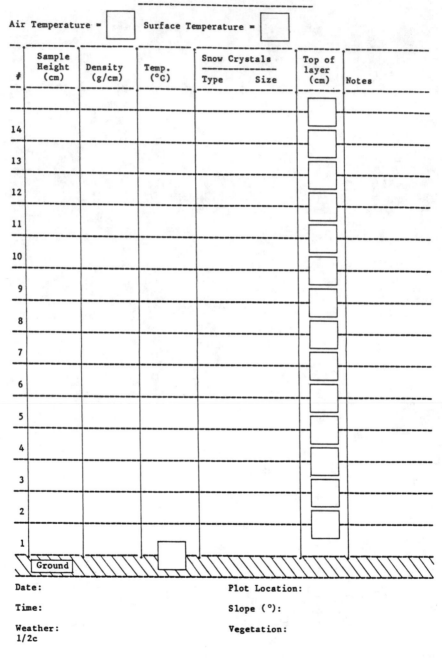

Figure 111. *Data collection sheet for a snow pit survey.*

mon. Measure crystal size, especially **depth hoar** crystals.

Finally, calculate the **thermal index** for the snowpack. It must be calculated for each layer; total the figures to get the final result. Also calculate the greatest thermal gradient within your snowpack.

Discussion: Layering should be present in the snowpack (Figure 112). Layers approximately represent individual snowstorms but tend to disappear as time passes. Major weather events such as rainstorms, hot days, and **surface hoar** formation may form distinct layers.

Snow density should increase deeper in the snowpack, until significant depth hoar formation starts. Layers with depth hoar have lower densities and are unstable. The crystals may fall out of the wall because of a lack of cohesiveness.

A steep temperature gradient will be present in all but **isothermal** snowpacks. The snowpack should be warmest near the bottom and coldest near the top for most of the winter. In the spring this trend may bend in the middle, with warmer temperatures occurring near the top.

The **thermal index** indicates the effective insulation of the snowpack. A value of greater than 150 to 200 indicates that maximum buffering against air temperature changes has been achieved. The temperature gradient indicates the probability of depth hoar formation; larger gradients will predict greater amounts of depth hoar. Gradients greater than 0.1°C/cm are needed for depth hoar formation. Depth hoar present at temperature gradients of less than this probably indicate a recent change in the temperature profile. The depth hoar has not had time to change to a new crystal type.

The most interesting snowpack temperature field exercise is to compare snow pits in several places. Different aspects and slopes may be used, or pits may be dug in different communities, perhaps in an aspen grove and in an open meadow. If possible, mark your snow pit locations and use them from year to year for comparison.

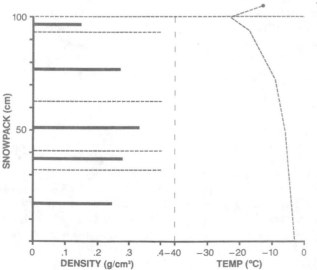

Figure 112. Attributes of a snow profile. Five layers are apparent, as is the history of the snowpack. The upper layers are newer and have not gone through temperature gradient (TG) metamorphism. The top two layers still have low densities (density bars) but the next two layers have become dense through equitemperature (ET) metamorphism. Density bars show that the lower layers have undergone TG metamorphism resulting in a lower density. Temperature at the ground/snow interface is -3°C (27°F). The temperature at the snow surface, -24°C (-11°F), has not yet warmed up to that of the warmer early morning air.

Field Exercise 2
The Snowpack: Its Structure and Thermal Properties

Purpose:
- to demonstrate buffering of atmospheric temperature changes at the ground/snow interface
- to demonstrate the speed with which cold temperatures pass through the snowpack

Equipment needed:
- 5 to 10 thermocouples or 3 to 10 long stem thermometers
- digital thermometer for thermocouples.
- 1 data logger (if possible)

A **thermocouple** is a bimetallic wire soldered at one end. Different temperatures generate differing amounts of electricity, which are read by an electrical meter and translated into temperatures. Thermocouples are very accurate and cheaper than **thermistors**, which do the same thing.

Preparations: Label the end of the lead of each thermocouple with masking tape and a permanent-ink black marker, numbering them, beginning with 1. Calibrate thermometers in an ice bath by placing them in a large bowl of water full of ice cubes. Each thermometer should be set to read 0°C (32°F) or, if the thermometers cannot be adjusted, a record should be made of each thermometer and how much it deviates from freezing. Use the deviations to connect data when it is analyzed.

Tape thermocouples to a wooden dowel or bamboo pole at 15-cm (6-in) intervals starting with one thermocouple at the bottom. Make sure you know which thermocouple is at what height on the pole. Push the pole into the snowpack with the leads extending

above the snow surface. The height of the thermocouple probe on the pole should be written on the label that is above the snowpack. A **data logger** may be used to gather readings or a volunteer must visit the site every two hours.

If thermometers are used, a snow pit must be dug. Shield the pit from sun and stick the thermometers into the wall of the pit at 15-cm (6-in) intervals. Keep the pit as small as possible. Put a covering over the snow pit to prevent heat exchange. This method will not be as satisfactory as the first because temperatures in the pit may eventually influence the thermometer readings. This method does work for a short period of time, though; the temperatures are most accurate from early morning to noon.

Procedures: Record the snow profile temperatures, preferably every hour for 24 hours. At the minimum, record the temperatures from before sunrise to about noon. Graph the results out for at least three heights in the snowpack: one height near the top, one in the middle, and one at the ground/snow interface (Figure 113).

Discussion: The temperature at the shallowest probe (near the snow surface) should show the most variability, while the deepest thermometer recordings should not vary much over 24 hours. The ground/snow interface should be relatively buffered against air temperatures changes.

Figure out how long it takes the cold pulse from the coldest night temperature to move down through the snowpack to ground level. Twenty-four hours of data are needed to do this successfully, but data taken at two-hour intervals during the night will be adequate to provide an estimate. The snowpack buffers against great magni-

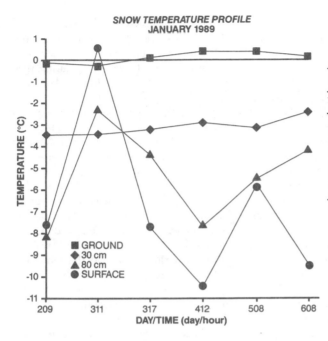

SNOW TEMPERATURE PROFILE
JANUARY 1989

Figure 113. Snow temperature profile for January 2 to 6, 1989. Surface temperatures fluctuated widely over the time period but ground temperatures remained near freezing. The snowpack effectively dampened the air temperature changes. Heights are measured from the ground/snow interface up.

tudes of change as well as against the speed with which changes reach the ground. Dig a **snow pit** at the test site (Field Exercise 1) and compare data from the two exercises. See Schmid (1984) for an advanced discussion of dampening of thermal fluctuations by the snowpack.

Field Exercise 3
Snow Properties:
Building a Quinzhee

Purpose:
- to demonstrate the ability of snow to set up (sinter)
- to demonstrate density changes in disturbed snow
- to demonstrate the strength of snow
- to develop winter camping and survival skills

Equipment needed:
- Two large shovels, such as alu-

minum No. 14 grain scoops and a small backpacker's snow shovel.
- Waterproof pants and parka may be helpful.
- Several handfuls of twigs for marking the wall thickness.

Preparations: Select a suitable site. This site should be close to where others are sleeping. If data is to be recorded using a data logger, the site should be close to an electric outlet and heated room; see discussion in Field Exercise 4.

Procedures: See the directions in the previous chapter for making a quinzhee. Plan your day so that you can pile the snow and come back later to dig it out. Digging the quinzhee out should take one to two hours. Do most of the work with the large shovels and trim the insides with a small shovel.

After the quinzhee has set over night, sample the snow density by the procedure used in Field Exercise 2. Consider the quinzhee one layer of snow. Measure its thickness and density, and calculate the thermal index.

Discussion: Once the quinzhee has set over night, the **density** should be between 0.25 and 0.40 g/cm³. The **thermal index** should be about 70 to 130 depending on the thickness of the walls. Compare this density and thermal index to the snow profile that you did in Field Exercise 1. The snow is harder and denser than that found in normal snowpacks. The refirnification process has increased the tensile strength of the snow. The strength may be tested by having several people carefully crawl onto the structure. Do *not* bounce, but crawl carefully—the quinzhee should support several people. You may not want to test its strength until after you have completed Field Exercise 4! The thermal index will be lower than the normal snowpack, but still sufficient to start providing protection to the occupant during a night's stay. Record the wall thickness, its density, and thermal index for later reference in Field Exercise 4.

Field Exercise 4
Life in the Subnivean:
A Night in a Quinzhee

Purpose:
- to demonstrate the comfort of life in a quinzhee
- to experience life in the subnivean
- to calculate the energy cost of a night in the subnivean

Equipment needed:
- 6 thermocouples (if possible)
- 1 data logger (if possible)
- 1 roll of first aid tape or other sticky tape
- 1 sleeping bag
- 1 sleeping pad
- 1 volunteer

Preparations: Construct the quinzhee as in Field Exercise 3. Make sure that you construct a door cover or use a backpack to cover the entrance during this experiment. Place the sleeping bag and pad inside the quinzhee.

Prepare the quinzhee by placing the probes as illustrated (Figure 114). All wire can be run to a data logger kept in a building adjacent to the quinzhee or the data logger may be kept in the sleeping bag to keep it warm. Set the data logger to record data every hour. If a data logger is not available, a digital thermometer may be used. The volunteer needs to use an alarm and awaken every two hours to read the temperatures at the probe positions. Each probe may have to be individually plugged into the thermometer to read it.

Wires or sticks may be used to hold the thermocouples at the top of the roof and on the ceiling. One thermocouple should be taped to the outside of the sleeping bag on top of the area where the volunteer's chest will be. One thermocouple should be taped to the inside of the sleeping bag in the same position as the outside thermocouple. This thermocouple can be omitted if there is a shortage of thermocouples. Body core temperature may be obtained by placing a thermocouple in the rectum. If doing this, carefully wrap the thermocouple in first aid tape. The last thermocouple should be taped to the bottom of the sleeping pad below the area where the volunteer's chest will be.

Procedures: Have the person enter the sleeping bag at about 10:00 pm and stay in it until about 7:00 am. In the morning collect the data from the data logger or from notes made by the volunteer reading the digital thermometer. All temperatures must be in centigrade

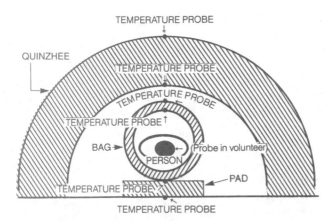

Figure 114. *Cross-section of a person sleeping in a quinzhee to show the placement of thermocouples (temperature probes).*

for the equations to work. If the data are collected from a Fahrenheit thermometer, translate to centigrade before analyzing the data. Graph the data as in Figure 115.

The **energy loss** for a night in a sleeping bag is estimated by splitting the problem into two parts and making the necessary calculations. First, calculate the heat loss to the ground and then the heat loss to the air.

Heat loss to the ground is through the sleeping pad, a slab of insulation. The equation for heat conducted through a slab is

$$Q = \frac{k\,A}{PD}\,(TT - TB)$$

where Q is the **heat flux** (cal/s), k is **thermal conductivity** (cal/s cm³ °C) with an estimated value for a sleeping pad of 0.000087, A is area of the body, PD is pad thickness, TT is temperature at the top of the sleeping pad (°C) and TB is the temperature at the bottom of the pad (the pad/snow interface). Area (A) is calculated by obtaining the average body width (ABW) and multiplying

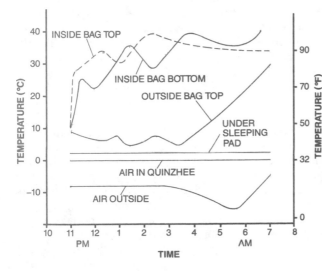

Figure 115. *Temperature record for a night in a quinzhee. Early in the morning, the outside air temperature dropped to -15°C (5°F). The air temperature inside the quinzhee remained relatively constant at about freezing, as did the temperature under the sleeping pad. Even though the outside temperature dropped very low, temperatures inside the bag and outside the bag were relatively warm. Considerably thermal advantage was gained by being inside the quinzhee protected by a sleeping bag.*

body width times height, all in cm.

$$ABW = \frac{\left(\begin{array}{c} \text{width (across ankles)} \\ + \\ \text{width (across shoulders)} \end{array} \right)}{2}$$

A = ABW x height

The final answer is in calories lost per second through the bottom of the pad. A typical person with the following dimensions has a heat flux (Q) of about 7.4 cal/s through the sleeping pad to the ground.

Pad conductivity = 0.000087
Height = 185 cm
Shoulder width = 45 cm
Ankle width = 15 cm
Pad thickness = 2 cm
Pad temperature at top = 34°C
Pad temperature at bottom = 3°C

Second, heat loss to the air is through half of a hollow cylinder. The equation for heat conducted through half a hollow cylinder is

$$Q = \frac{\pi \, k \, H \, (TI - TO)}{\ln (RO \, / \, RI)}$$

Where π (pi) is a dimensionless constant (3.14159), k is **thermal conductivity** with an estimated value for a down sleeping bag of 0.000046, H is the height of the person, TI is the temperature inside the bag, TO is the temperature outside the bag, RO is the radius from the center to the outside of the bag, RI is the radius to the inside of the bag, and ln is the natural logarithm. The inside radius (RI) is calculated by dividing the average body width (ABW), an estimate of body diameter, by 2. The outside radius (RO) is equal to RI plus the thickness of the sleeping bag (cm). The final answer is in calo-

ries lost per second through the top of the sleeping bag.

For the typical person listed above with the following additional dimensions, the heat flux (Q) is about 1.2 cal/s through the sleeping bag to the air.

Bag conductivity = 0.000046
Sleeping bag thickness = 15 cm
Outside radius = 30 cm
Inside radius = 15 cm

Total **heat flux** is 7.4 + 1.2 cal/s or 8.6 cal/s. The total heat flux for an eight-hour night is calculated by multiplying by 60 s/min by 60 min/hr by 8 hr for 247,680 cal/night. This is the equivalent of 248 **nutritional calories** or 248 kcal per night.

Discussion: It is important to design your experiment to be as similar to the one diagrammed as possible. Deviations may affect the energy calculations. Energy losses on a winter night should be about 248 kcal per night. The **energy cost** of sleeping in a good winter sleeping bag in a quinzhee is about 0.85 Snickers bars per night (248/290 kcal). The protection (insulation) offered by the sleeping bag and quinzhee is adequate to substantially reduce energy loss during the night. Imagine the extra energy needed if the quinzhee were not there—or better yet, test it.

An interesting variation on this project is to have someone sleep with more than one pad beneath the bag. To test the effect of extra **insulation** beneath the person, remove or add pads during the night to see the difference. The sleeping bag is compressed under the body and adds little to the insulation. Under the body, sleeping pads that do not compress are most important. Compare the effect of adding insulation to the top of the sleeping bag versus adding more pads underneath the person.

The **energy loss** through the quinzhee may be calculated from the inside and outside temperature probes. Treat this problem as half a hollow sphere:

$$Q = \frac{4\pi \text{ k RI RO (TI - TO)}}{\text{RO - RI}}$$

Use a conductivity (k) of snow as 0.00064 (Elsner and Pruitt, 1959). You may wish to compare the results with snow temperature profiles and their thickness, density, and thermal index values.

Field Exercise 5
Cold Effects on the Body:
A Cooling Curve for a Foot

Purpose:
- to understand personal sensations of cold
- to determine how exposed portions of the body react to the cold
- to construct a cooling curve for a foot

Equipment needed:
- 2 thermocouples per volunteer
- 1 digital thermometer
- 1 watch with a second hand
- 1 roll of first aid tape
- warm clothing for volunteers and recorders
- 1 large cardboard box for each volunteer
- chairs to sit on
- a shaded place outdoors to sit
- note pad for each volunteer

Preparations: Establish an experimental area where volunteers can sit in the shade. For each volunteer, there should be a chair and a cardboard box big enough to surround a foot so it does not touch the sides of the box. The box is placed directly in front of the chair so that the volunteer can sit on the chair with his or her foot in the box. The box protects the foot from drafts.

Prepare the volunteers inside where it is warm. Thoroughly clothe each volunteer except for one **foot**, which will be covered with socks that are easy to remove once the experiment starts. Make sure the volunteers have caps and warm coats. The only portion of the body that we wish to have cold is the one foot.

Tape two thermocouples to one foot of each volunteer. One thermocouple should be placed on the tip of the big toe and one in the arch of the foot. Place the tape so that the thermocouple is held tightly against the foot, but not in a manner that restricts circulation. The tape should not run around a toe or the foot; use only short pieces placed flat along the skin surface. If you have a third thermocouple available, tape it in between the big toe and the second toe.

Assign volunteers to their chairs, and provide them with note pads. Other people will help with data collection. (It is not feasible to do more than about three volunteers per run of this field exercise.) Assign a timer and provide a watch. Assign one person to switch thermocouple leads in the thermometer, and another person to read the thermometer. Also assign one person to be a data recorder (Figure 116).

Procedures: Lead volunteers outside quickly and seat them on the chairs. Have each volunteer take the socks off the foot to be tested (test only one foot) and place the foot in the cardboard box. The volunteer must not move except to make notes! The timer calls out the time every 30 seconds. Every 30 seconds, the volunteers

Date _____   Location _____

Name _____   Name _____   Name _____

Time
1 _____   _____   _____
2 _____   _____   _____
3 _____   _____   _____
4 _____   _____   _____
5 _____   _____   _____
6 _____   _____   _____
7 _____   _____   _____
8 _____   _____   _____
9 _____   _____   _____
10 _____   _____   _____
11 _____   _____   _____
12 _____   _____   _____
13 _____   _____   _____
14 _____   _____   _____
15 _____   _____   _____
16 _____   _____   _____
17 _____   _____   _____
18 _____   _____   _____
19 _____   _____   _____
20 _____   _____   _____
21 _____   _____   _____
22 _____   _____   _____
23 _____   _____   _____
24 _____   _____   _____
25 _____   _____   _____
26 _____   _____   _____
27 _____   _____   _____
28 _____   _____   _____
29 _____   _____   _____
30 _____   _____   _____

Cooling rate calculations:

	Person 1	Person 2	Person 3
Beginning temperature =	_____	_____	_____
Ending temperature =	_____	_____	_____
Difference in temperatures =	_____	_____	_____
Elapsed time =	_____	_____	_____
Cooling rate =	_____	_____	_____

The cooling rate is the difference in temperatures divided by the elapsed time.

Figure 116. *Data sheet for cooling curves for three volunteers. This sheet may be used for cooling curves of bare feet. When the experiment is over, the cooling rate for each volunteer is calculated by dividing the difference between the beginning and ending temperatures by the elapsed time.*

should make notes about how their toes feel, but they should not talk.

At every 30-second interval, the thermometer reader reads the temperature on each thermocouple, and one person switches the leads to make this possible. The thermometer reader calls out temperatures to the recorder.

Continue the experiment until the cooling curves start to level out as temperatures become more stable or until the volunteer wishes to stop. Never continue the experiment on any person whose toe temperatures have dropped below 2°C (35.6°F).

After the experiment, graph the **cooling curves** for each individual (Figure 117).

Discussion: Different individuals will perceive different **sensations** as their toes begin to cool down. The feelings also develop at different temperatures. Two stages of sensation are particularly important. The first is the feeling of **pain** that occurs roughly at 10°C (50°F). The second is the **loss of any feeling** of cold or pain. Once feet no longer sense cold or pain, **frostbite**

can occur without the person being aware of damage being inflicted. In the field, it is all right for a person to feel cold or pain in the feet, but once sensation is lost, stop and immediately rewarm the feet or hands. Experienced winter personnel do not worry about cold feet, but merely tolerate them. Once sensation is lost, however, immediate rewarming action is taken.

Compare the cooling effect of the well-insulated foot with the one that is exposed to the cold to understand the importance of proper insulation during the winter. Consider how quickly the exposed foot cooled compared to the insulated foot.

Compare cooling curves for different volunteers. Speculate on differences between genders and differences between those whose feet have been exposed to cold several times previous to the experiment and those who have had no cold exposure.

Cooling rates may be calculated for comparisons. The main control on cooling is the **fat content** of the person. An interesting variation on the exercise is to match individuals by their

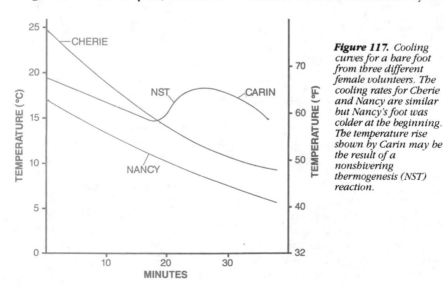

Figure 117. Cooling curves for a bare foot from three different female volunteers. The cooling rates for Cherie and Nancy are similar but Nancy's foot was colder at the beginning. The temperature rise shown by Carin may be the result of a nonshivering thermogenesis (NST) reaction.

body fat content. A **fat-o-meter** can be obtained from scientific supply houses, such as Edmund Scientific, for making this comparison.

Field Exercise 6
Insulation to Protect the Body: Choosing the Best Socks

Purpose:
- to examine the insulating properties of various materials
- to demonstrate the effect of water on energy transfer

Equipment needed:
- several pairs of clean socks of various materials, including cotton, polypropylene, thermax, wool
- 2 water bottles for each pair of sock to be tested
- a cork for each bottle with a hole in the center
- a thermometer for each bottle
- 1 large pot for heating water
- 1 large pot for cold water
- 1 pair of vernier calipers are helpful

Preparations: Measure the thickness of socks and try to place them in comparable combinations. For instance, two pairs of thin cotton socks may equal the thickness of one pair of polypropylene socks. Place a test combination of socks on each bottle. Make a duplicate set of bottles for each sock combination to be tested, as each set will be tested under wet and dry conditions. Place all thermometers in the corks and have them ready to go. Heat a large pot of water to about 37°C (98.6°F).

Procedures: Quickly pour water into each bottle without wetting the socks. Cork bottles and set them aside. One duplicate set of bottles then should be immediately immersed in the cold water for wet condition testing. Place

all bottles outside in the shade (Figure 118). Record the temperatures of each bottle every minute until the cooling curves have begun to level off.

Graph the wet and dry temperatures on two different graphs (Figure 119). Give each sock material line a different color. **Cooling rates** can be calculated for the steepest part of each curve for comparisons.

Discussion: Comparisons should only be made between socks or combinations of socks of similar thickness. **Cooling curves** for dry socks will not differ too much, but cotton will probably have a slightly faster cooling rate. The wet socks will cool substantially faster than dry socks. There should be dramatic differences in cooling rates between materials under wet conditions.

Discuss the importance of careful selection of materials for winter use based on the material's ability to retain heat. It is also important to realize that socks on feet are never dry. All feet, contrary to what some believe, sweat each day. The accumulation of sweat inside insulated ski or snowmobile boots is considerable. Your feet are always wet from perspiration in winter, so use the best material available for insulation.

Field Exercise 7
Human Damage to the Snowpack: Skiers and Snowmobilers

Purpose:
- to demonstrate compaction of the snowpack by human use
- to evaluate the magnitude of the damage to snowpack insulation

Equipment needed:
- snow pit survey kits

Figure 118. *A student at Teton Science School conducts an experiment to test insulation properties of different types of socks (Doug Frisbie).*

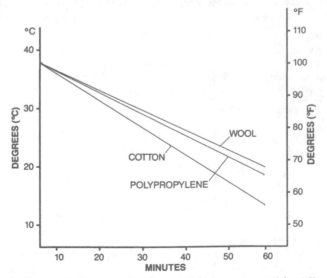

Figure 119. *Cooling curves for wet socks. The raw data were corrected for differences in sock thicknesses by dividing the temperature readings by the ratio of the sock being tested to the thinnest sock. Wet wool and polypropylene socks have similar properties, but wool is a slightly better insulator when wet.*

Preparations: Locate an area frequented by snowmobilers and skiers. Select places where there have been a single pass and multiple passes each by skiers and by snowmobilers. If needed, tracks may be made the day before for testing. However, it is best to have tracks that have accumulated over the winter so that time-specific changes may be apparent in the snowpack.

Procedures: Dig a long snow trench that cuts through the edge of each of the four types of disturbance so that part of the trench is under the disturbance and part of it is in undisturbed area. The undisturbed area will serve as the control comparison to the disturbance. In each pit, sample the snow profile as in Field Exercise 1. If the complete experiment is done, there should be eight snow profiles with a disturbance and control for single pass skier, single pass snowmobile, multiple pass skier, and multiple pass snowmobile sites.

Determine if the control snow profiles of all four trenches are similar. If they are similar, a comparison can be made directly between the disturbed areas. Graph the control area data versus the disturbed area data to show the effects of compactions (Figure 120). Also graph the data so that comparisons are apparent between disturbed areas (Figure 121). Calculate **thermal indices** and the greatest **temperature gradients**.

Discussion: Disturbed areas will show considerable more **compaction** than undisturbed controls. However, compaction should be attenuated in the lower portions of the lower snow profile and the bottom layers may not even be affected. Compaction decreases thickness, thereby decreasing **insulating** power (thermal index) and increasing the temperature gradient. Increased temperature gradients lead to more **depth hoar** formation. However, disturbance from extensive daily passes may keep a depth hoar layer from developing. Depth hoar may also develop at a hard or ice layer caused by the disturbance. The ground will probably be

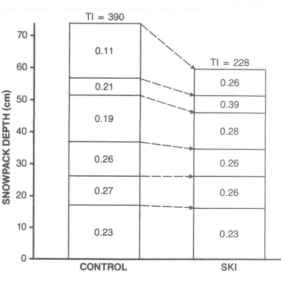

Figure 120. *Comparison of control snow pit data to that of the test site. A single cross-country skier had skied over the test site. Note the total compaction caused by the skier. Less compaction occurs in the lower layers, which are protected by the tensile strength of the snow. Also note the increase in the density (boxed figures) caused by the skier. One pass of the skier reduced the thermal index from 390 to 228.*

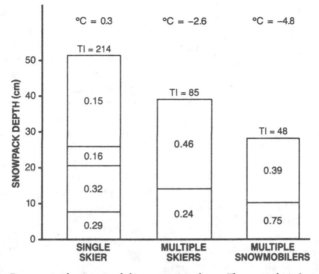

Figure 121. *Damage to the snowpack by recreational use. The control pit (not shown) had a thermal index of 226 and a depth of 54 cm (21.3 in). The temperature at the ground/snow interface under the control was 0.5°C (23.9°F). Substantial decreases in the thermal index have caused low ground/snow interface temperatures and freezing of the soil beneath the repeated use areas. Repeated use by snowmobiles has increased the snow density to 0.75 g/cm³ producing an ice layer above the ground. We could not ascertain how many skiers or how many snowmobilers had used each test site, so the graphs should not be used for comparisons. They provide examples of the magnitude of the possible impact. Snow density is shown under each thermal index figure.*

colder beneath the disturbed track indicating loss of the buffering capacity of the snowpack (decreased thermal index).

It is interesting to note that oftentimes **skiers** may do more damage than snowmobilers to the snowpack because their narrow skis cut deeper in to the pack. Also, the **foot load** on the skis may be greater than that on the snowmobile. **Snowmobiles** have a wide track which spreads the weight out, so there is less weight per unit of area. Furthermore, snowmobiles will pass a given point faster than skiers.

In most situations, the activities of people serve to construct underground "fences" of hard snow which reduce **subnivean** habitability and restrict subnivean travel. Repeated daily use of the same trails makes the trails hard down to the ground surface, and prevents the

development of a depth hoar layer which would let animals pass beneath the trail. If the habitat area is large compared to the disturbed area, underground snow fences may not be a significant impact to the subnivean world. However, if the habitat area is small, if it is home for rare species, or if the disturbance activity is not constricted to narrow paths, the impact may be substantial and damaging to subnivean overwinter survival.

SUGGESTED READINGS

Birkeland, C.W., and J.C. Halfpenny. 1987. Winter ecology. Science Teacher, 54:42-46.

Porter, W.P., and D.M. Gates. 1969. Thermodynamic equilibria of animals with environment. Ecol. Monogr., 39:227-244.

Schmid, W.D. 1971. Modification of the subnivean microclimate by snowmobiles. Proc. Snow and Ice in Relation to Wildlife and Recreation Symp. Feb. 11-12, 1971. Iowa State Univ., Ames, Iowa.

Schmid, W.D. 1984. Materials and methods of subnivean sampling. Pp. 25-32, *in* Merritt, J.F. (ed.) Winter Ecology of Small Mammals. Carnegie Mus. Nat. Hist., Spec. Publ. 10.

THE ECOLOGY OF WINTER: A SYMPOSIUM

When completed, this series of field exercises represents an in-depth look at winter ecology that will serve to integrate the student's knowledge of the processes affecting life in a nivean world. We use this package of experiments to foster knowledge about the scientific research process. Initially, students are encouraged to develop hypotheses for each project and to test these by research. The final step in the scientific process is the presentation of results. Presentation is done at an afternoon or evening symposium.

Students are divided into groups to plan presentations and to make posters. One group should be designated for each of the field exercises. Students are encouraged to design their presentations to include the following subdivisions: introduction (purpose and hypotheses), methods, results, and discussion. Spokespersons are selected for each section. Posters are utilized for explanations. Sometimes students show real innovation in their poster preparation. Posters are made from rolls of newsprint and colored markers.

One person functions as the master of ceremonies and serves to maintain the train of thought through the whole program. Each experiment builds on the previous one and adds to the knowledge of the group. Experiments are interlinked to form a total picture of an organism (in this case the human) living in a **nivean world**. The following outline serves as a reminder of the interconnectedness of exercises.

Properties of snow
    its temperature profile
    its structure and thermal properties
    building a quinzhee
Life in the subnivean
    a night in a quinzhee
Human perceptions of winter
    a cooling curve for a foot
Insulating the human body
    choosing the best socks
Damage to the subnivean
    skiers and snowmobilers

We hope that you have fun with this minisymposium on the ecology of winter.

RESEARCH EQUIPMENT FOR WINTER ACTIVITIES

The recent availability of specialized equipment lends enjoyment to research in the winter. Specialized types of equipment are listed first with the name of the retailer (Table 35). Names and addresses of retailers follow (Table 36). Contact retailers for a catalog of available equipment.

Table 35. Equipment retailers listed by type of equipment.

Data loggers
  Campbell Scientific, Inc.
  LI-COR, Inc.
  OMNIDATA International, Inc.

Fat-o-meters
  Edmund Scientific

Magnifying glasses, rulers, calipers
  Ben Meadows Company
  BioQuip Products
  Carolina Biological Supply Company
  Forestry Supply
  Markson

Outdoor Equipment
  Alpine Research, Inc.
  Cabela's
  Campmor
  Eastern Mountain Sports (EMS)
  Eddie Bauer
  Great Pacific Chouinard
  International Mountain Equipment,
    Inc.
  Madden
  Recreational Equipment, Inc. (REI)

Snow pit survey kits and related items
for snow research
  Alpine Research, Inc.
  Hydro-Tech
  Life-Link International, Inc.
  Strong Stitch Fabric Products
    Company

Snow shovels
  Life-Link International, Inc.
  Check hardware stores for grain
    scoops

Stick-on marking tape for skis
  Flormel

Thermometers, thermocouples, other
temperature devices
  Ben Meadows Company
  Carolina Biological Supply Company
  Cole-Parmer Instrument Company
  Digitar
  Edmund Scientific
  Forestry Supply
  Koolatron Corporation
  Markson
  Omega Engineering, Inc.
  Taylor
  Testotherm, Inc.

Table 36. Equipment Retailers.

Alpine Research, Inc.
1930 Central Avenue, Suite F
Boulder, CO 80301
(303) 444-0660

Ben Meadows Company
—Headquarters
3589 Broad Street
P.O. Box 80549
Atlanta (Chamblee), GA 30366
(800) 241-6401

Ben Meadows Company
—Western Division
2601-B West Fifth Avenue
P.O. Box 2781
Eugene, OR 97402
(800) 547-8813

BioQuip Products
P.O. Box No. 61
Santa Monica, CA 90406
(213) 322-6636

Cabela's
812 13th Avenue
Sidney, NE 69160
(800) 237-4444

Campbell Scientific, Inc.
815 West 1800 North
P.O. Box 551
Logan, UT 84321
(801) 753-2342

Campmor
810 Route 17 North
P.O. Box 997-F
Paramus, NJ 07653-0997
(800) 526-4784

Carolina Biological Supply Company
2700 York Road
Burlington, NC 27215
(800) 334-5551

Cole-Parmer Instrument Company
7425 North Oak Park Ave.
Chicago, IL 60648
(800) 323-4340

Digitar
3465 Diablo Avenue
Hayward, CA 94545
(800) 678-3669

Eastern Mountain Sports (EMS)
One Rose Farm Road
Peterborough, NH 03458

Eddie Bauer
Fifth & Union
P.O. Box 3700
Seattle, WA 98130-0006
(800) 426-8020

Edmund Scientific
101 E. Gloucester Pike
Barrington, NJ 08007-1380
(609) 573-6250
(609) 547-3488

Flormel
510 First Avenue
P.O. Box 110
West Haven, CT 06516
(800) 356-7635

Forestry Supply
205 West Rankin Street
P.O. Box 8397
Jackson, MI 39204-0397
(800) 647-5368

Great Pacific Chouinard
P.O. Box 90
245 West Santa Clara
Ventura, CA 93002
(805) 653-5781

Hydro-Tech
4658 NE 178th Street
Seattle, WA 98155
(206) 362-1074

International Mountain Equipment, Inc.
Box 494, Main Street
North Conway, NH 03860
(603) 356-7013

Koolatron Corporation
—56 Harvester Avenue
Batavia, NY 14020
(716) 343-6695

Koolatron Corporation
—27 Catharine Avenue
Brantford, Ontario
Canada N3T 1X5
(519) 756-3950

LI-COR, Inc.
Box 4425
Lincoln, NE 68504
(402) 467-3576

Life-Link International, Inc.
P.O. Box 2913
1240 Huff Lane
Jackson Hole, WY 83001
(800) 443-8620

Madden
2400 Central Avenue
Boulder, Colorado 80301
(303) 442-5828

Markson
10201 South 51st Street
Phoenix, AZ 85044
(800) 528-5114

Omega Engineering, Inc.
One Omega Drive
P.O. Box 2669
Stamford, CT 06906
(800) 826-6342

OMNIDATA International, Inc.
P.O. Box 3489
Logan, Utah 84321
(801) 754-7760

Recreational Equipment, Inc. (REI)
P.O. Box 88125
Seattle, WA 98138-0125
(800) 426-4840

Strong Stitch Fabric Products Company
1415 East 3045 South
Salt Lake City, UT 84106
(801) 484-9436

Taylor
Thermometer Corporation of America
280 Cane Creek Road
P.O. Box 1349
Fletcher, NC 28732
(704) 684-5178

Testotherm, Inc.
6 Emery Avenue
Randolph, NJ 07869
(201) 989-8872

Index

Page numbers in boldface
refer to figures and tables.

Abortion, 142
Abrasion. *See* Wind abrasion
Abscisic acid, 164, 165
Abscission, 164
Absorption, 61, 62
Absorptivity, 123
Acclimation, 66, 164, **168**
Acidity, 89
Activation. *See* Energy, activation
Activity, 118, **118**, 134, 178, 181, 262
Acute heat production. *See* Heat
Adaptation, 65, 66, **78**, 103
Adenosine triphosphate (ATP), 92
Adrenal system, 111
Advection, 34
Aerobic capacity, 212
Afterdrop, 207
Air: air space, 219; dead air space, 34,
    224; cold air trap, 233; vent, 231,
    233, **235**
Albedo, 58, **59**
Alcohol, 206
Algae, snow, 49, 171; blue-green, 171
Allen's rule, 70
Amino acid, 93, **96**
Ammonia, 114
Amorphous solidification, 166
Angle, solar. *See* Solar angle
Antarctica, 188
Anticontact. *See* Gloves, anticontact
Antifreeze, 105, 106, 179; alcohol, 107
Anti-antifreeze, 179
Antlers, shedding, 152
Aphelion. *See* Orbit
Arousal, 113
Artificial respiration, 207, 220
Aspect. *See* Slope
Aspen, 172, 175
ATP. *See* Adenosine triphosphate
Attenuation, 58, 59, **59**
Autoamputation, 210
Autumnal overturn. *See* Overturn
Avalanche, **218**, **219**; chute, 217; cord,
    216; country, 220; dry, 214; loose
    snow, 214; path, 218; probe, 217,
    220; shovel, 217; slab, 214, 217; sur-
    viving, 218; types, 214; wet, 214

Bacteria, 141
Basal metabolism. *See* Metabolism
BAT. *See* Brown adipose tissue

Bear, 116
Beetle: darkling, 179; ladybird, 177
Behavior, **135**; index, **78**
Bergmann's rule, 70
Bilayer. *See* Lipid
Biochemistry, 65, 88-90, 92, 94, 97
Biological clock, 79, 154, 165
Biosynthesis, 94
Bivouac, 225
Black body, 29, **30**
Black box, 62
Blackheart, 173
Blood: clot, 210; flow, 126, 209
Body, **204**, 226, 255, 258. *See also* Size
Bond, 32, 90, 91, 97, 195; covalent, 91,
    91, 97, 120; electrostatic, 101; hydro-
    gen, **92**, 101; hydrophobic, 96; strong,
    91; weak, 92, **92**, 97
Boundary layer, 125
Boreal Institute for Northern Studies, 5
Breakthrough, **63**, 78
Breathing, 221, 224; test, 224
Brown adipose tissue (BAT), 110
Browsing, **133**, 140, **141**; induced resis-
    tance, 143
Budget. *See* Energy budget, Mass budget
Buds: foliar, 142; staminate, 142
Butter. *See* Oil
Butterfly, 177, **178**, **183**
Byrd expedition, 188

Cache, 156
Calorie, 32, 254
Camping, 230
Campsite, 239
Carbohydrate, 41, **85**
Carbon, 90; dioxide, 32, **83**, 84; monox-
    ide poisoning, 230
Cardiopulmonary resuscitation (CPR),
    207, 220
Carnivores, 72
Casting antlers, 152
Cat holes, 241
Catalyst, 97, **98**
Caterpillar, Arctic, 177
Catkin, 142
Cave, snow. *See* Snow cave
Cavitation, 174
Cell. *See* Membrane, **101**, **166**
Celsius. *See* Temperature
Center for Northern Studies, 7
Centigrade. *See* Temperature
Chemical defenses, 142
Chemical energy. *See* Energy, chemical

Chemical reaction. *See* Reaction
Chest height, 76, **77**
Chion, 73
Chioneuphore, 74, 185
Chionophile, 75, 155, 185
Chionophobe, 73, 185
Chipewyan, 38
Chlorophyll, 82, **84**, 91, 143, 171, 172
Chloroplast, 102
Chronic heat production. *See* Heat
Chronic response. *See* Response
Classification, ecological, 73; *See also*
    Snow, classification
Clo, 187, **188**
Clock, evolutionary, **17**; biological. *See*
    Biological clock; phytochrome. *See*
    Phytochrome clock
Clone, 164
Cloth: cotton, 223, 225, **259**; down. *See*
    Down; Gore-Tex, 224; mylar, 225;
    nylon/cotton, 224; PolarGuard, **188**,
    224; polypropylene, 224, **259**; plastic,
    224; 60/40, 224; space blanket, 34,
    225; wool and felt, 224, **259**
Clothing, **118**, **193**, 200, 221; fair
    weather, 222; material, 223
Colbeck, **45**, 246
Cold, 12, 66, 88, 97, 98, 100, 103, 194,
    222, **225**, 255; cold air trap, 233;
    cold-blooded, 177; shock, 180, **181**;
    water, 205
Cold hardening. *See* Hardening
Collagen. *See* Protein
Color, 60, 61, **154**, **155**; phase, **20**, 21;
    change, 153
Comfort rating, 187, **187**, **193**
Compaction, 260
Compensation: light, 172, **173**; tem-
    perature, 172, **173**
Conduction, 33, **33**, 126
Conductivity, thermal, 52, **53**, **54**, 124,
    125, 253, 254
Conservation, 238, **240**
Constriction, 209, 212; zone, 223
Contractile protein. *See* Protein, con-
    tractile
Convection, 33, **33**, 125
Cooking pit, 239
Cooling curve, **167**, **181**, 255, 257, **257**,
    258, **259**
Cooling rate, 189, **190**, **193**, **256**, 257,
    258
Coping, 68, **77**, **78**
Cornice, 218, 234
Cortisol, 109
Cortisone, 111
Cost, **113**
Cotton. *See* Cloth, cotton

Covalent. *See* Bond
Cp. *See* Heat, specific
Cracks, 217
Criteria, selective, 16
Critical period, 79, 80
Cross-country skier. *See* Skier
Crust: melt-freeze, 49; snow. *See* Snow
    crust; wind, 49, 215
Cryoprotectant, 179-181
Cryoprotection, 166
Crystal. *See* Ice; damage 174
Cuticle, 174
Cytoplasm, 165

Data: collection, **248**, **256**; logger, 250
Deaths, human-caused, 155
Decision tree. *See* Winter response tree
Decomposition, 140
Dehardening, 168
Dehydration, 101, **166**, 200
Density, 50, **50**, **53**, **54**, 60, **60**, **82**,
    249, 250, **260**, **261**; critical, 61;
    vapor. *See* Vapor
Depth hoar. *See* Hoar, depth
Desiccation, 174
Detritivores, 86
Diet, **141**, **151**; switching, 140, 151
Discretionary energy. *See* Energy, dis-
    cretionary
Disease, 146, 158
Diurnal cycles, 47
DNA, 89, 94, 95
Dominance, 153
Dormancy, 72, 112, 156, 177. *See also*
    Hibernation
Down, **188**, 222
Dress up, 223
Duration of snowpack, 17, **157**

Ecology, 1, **2**, 3, 4, 73; causal, 2; com-
    parative, 2; descriptive, 2; experimen-
    tal, 2; theoretical, 2
Ectotherm, 177
Elastic recoil, 174, 175
Elastin. *See* Protein
Electrostatic bond. *See* Bond
Elephant trap, 2
Emissivity, 123
Endogenous, 154
Endosperm, 142
Endotherm, 104
Energetics, 131
Energy, 25, 26, 66, 90, **98**, 118, **118**,
    135, 180; activation, 96, **98**, **100**;
    allocation strategy, 134; balance, 34,
    35, 65, **129**, **136**, **137**, **164**; budget,
    35, **35**, **113**, **120**, **122**, 186; budget,
    human, 187, 254; cost, 254; chemical,

25, 32, 90, 119, **119**; electrical, 25; gravitational, 25; loss, **253**, 255; kinetic, 25, 45, 46; potential, 25; radiant, 25, **29**; reserve, 180; solar, 32; storage, 90, 91; surface free, 41; thermal, 25, 28, 88, 120; transfer, 32, **33**, **130**, 223; synchronization, 181
Enzyme, 91, 96, 97, **98**, 103, 104
Epinephrine, 109
Equipment, 262
Equitemperature metamorphism. *See* Metamorphism
Ermine, **20**, 21, **155**
Erythemal dose, minimal (MED), 202
Evaporation, **33**, 34, 120, 126
Evergreen, 172
Evolutionary time. *See* Time
Exoskeleton, 177
Exotherm, 167
Extinction coefficient, 59, **60**

False spring. *See* Spring
Fat, 91, 93, 94, **94**, 102, 107, **113**, **160**, 257; animal, 94; saturated, 92, 94, **95**; unsaturated, 92, 95, **95**, 107
Fatality, nonfreezing, 178
Fatty acid, 94, **94**, 96, **97**, 141
Fat-o-meter, 258
Feeding, **154**; deterrent, 142; group, 137; supplemental, 141, 152
Feet, 225, 255, **256**, **257**, 158
Feeling, loss of, 257
Fermentation time, 132
Firn mirror, 49
Firnification, 45
Firnspiegel, 49
Fish, 105
Flea, snow. *See* Snow, flea
Flexibility, 99
Flooding, 80
Fly: black, 178; caddis, 178; crane, 178; flesh, 180; stone, 178
Food, 86, **87**, **113**, **119**, **120**, **127**, 138, 140, **141**, 142, **151**, 156, 240; web, **87**
Foot load, 75, **75**, 76, **76**, **77**, 261
Foraging cessation, 136
Forb, 140, **141**
Fracture line, 214
Freeze: avoidance, **181**; intolerance, 181; resistance, 168, **169**; susceptibility, 181; tolerance, 168, 181, **181**
Freezeout, 79
Freezing, 105, 167, 173, **190**; line, 177; point, 178, **179**
Friction, 125
Frog, 105
Frost: hoar. *See* Hoar frost; line, 177; nip, 209; rime, 46; splitting, 173

Frostbite, 65, 101, 102, 200, 201, 209, 211, 223; deep, 210; superficial, 210

Gall, 107, 177; moth, 107
Ghost tree, **10**, 11
Glacier fire, 49
Glass formation, 166
Gloves, anticontact, 227
Glucose. *See* Sugar
Glycerol, 94, **94**, 96, 106, 179, 180
Glycogen, 93, 105
Glycogen phosphorylase, 180
Glycoprotein, 106
Goldfinches, 110
Goldenrod, 107
Gore-Tex. *See* Cloth
Grain: scoop, 217, 231, 237; size, 60, **60**
Grand Teton National Park, **133**, 138, **139**, **157**, **229**
Granivores, 86
Grazing, 140
Ground cover, 215
Group feeding. *See* Feeding
Grouse, 142
Growth, 71, **118**, 119; compensatory, 143; form, kinetic, 45, 46

Habitat, 136
Hardening, 65, 66, 80, 164, 165, **165**, 168, **168**, 178, 180
Hardiness-promoting factor, 165
Harem, 159
Hay-pile, 156
Head, 227
Heat, **120**, **122**; balance, 120, 121; exhaustion, 121; flux, 53, 253, 254; latent heat of evaporation, 126; latent heat of vaporization, 34; sensible, 34; specific (Cp), 28
Heaving: primary, 174, **175**; secondary, 175, **175**
Health, 199
Heme, **96**, 99
Hemoglobin, 90, 93, 95, 99, 105
Hemolymph, 177
Herbivores, 72, 86, 142
Heterothermy, 71
Hibernacula, 156, 177
Hibernation (*See also* Dormancy, Torpor), 112, **113**
Hibernation induction trigger (HIT), 115
Hiemal threshold, 79
Highway, 158
HIT. *See* Hibernation induction trigger
Hoar: frost, **12**, 47 (*See also* Frost); cave, 47; crevasse, 47; depth, 43, **44**, 46, 47, 55, 157, 215, 231, 233, 249, 260; surface, 47, 215, 249

Hormones, 89, 155
Hourglass of darkness, **16**
Humans, **193**, 194, 255, 258
Hunting, 145, **145**, **146**
Hydrogen, 90; saturation, 94 (*See also* Fats)
Hygroscopic, 223
Hymenoptera, 177
Hyphae, 175
Hypothalamus, 111
Hypothermia, 65, 204, **204**

Ice, **40**, **54**, **62**; crystal, **101**, 106, **166**, 210; crystal formation, **92**, 101, **101**, 106, **225**; layer, 48; lens, 48, 80; needle. *See* Needle ice; nucleation, 106, 179; water, 47
Igloo, 230, 235, **235**
Index. *See* Behavior index, Morphological index, Snow-coping index, Stability index, Thermal index
Indian summer, 164
Insectivores, 134
Insolation, 14, **16**, 23, **24**, **25**, 58, 131, 224
Insulation, 125, 137, 177, 224, 254, 258, **259**, 260
International Snow Classification System, 40, **41**
Inuit, 38, **39**
Ion pump, 32, 93, 102
Ionization, 101
Ischemic, 210
Isoenzymes, 105
Isotherm, 12, 249
Isothermal, **83**, 138; point, 55, 80

Jack, 174

Kelvin. *See* Temperature
Ketones, 114
Kilocalorie (kcal), 32
Kinetic form. *See* Growth
Kitchen. *See* Snow kitchen
Kleptoparasitizing, 137
Krummholtz, 176

LaChapelle, **45**, 176
Lactose. *See* Sugar
Latent heat of evaporation. *See* Heat
Latrine, 240
Layer. *See* Boundary layer; environmental, 223; insulation, 222
Layering, 47, 48; system, 221
Life functions, **118**
Light, 59, **61**, 82, **83**, 169, **170**, **173**; absorption of, 61, 62; color of, 61, 62; compensation. *See* Compensation,

light; quality, 170; quantity, 170; scattering of, 61; transmission, 59, **60**, 170
Lignin, 143
Lipid, 89, 96, 166; bilayer, 96, **97**, 166
Lipoprotein, 93, 179
Load, foot. *See* Foot load
Load, snow. *See* Snow load
Location, 137
Lodgepole pine, 168
Longwave. *See* Radiation, longwave

Macromolecule, 89
Maintenance, 118, **113**, **118**, **127**
Malnutrition, 132, 158
Map, **139**, 217
Margarine. *See* Oil
Mass, 132; budget, 118-121, **122**
Matches, 200
MED (minimal erythemal dose). *See* Erythemal dose
Melanin, 123
Melting point, 92, **181**
Melt-freeze: crust. *See* Crust; layer, 48
Membrane, 89, 96, **97**, **101**, 102, 166, **166**, 167
Met, 187
Metabolism, 119, **119**; basal, 67
Metabolic rate, resting, 133
Metamorphism, 41; constructive, 43, **44**; destructive, 43, **44**; equitemperature (ET), 43, **44**; melt-freeze, 45; pressure, 45; temperature gradient (TG), 43, **44**
Migration, 146, **147**, **148**, **149**, **150**, **151**, 177, **178**
Minimal erythemal dose (MED). *See* Erythemal dose
Mitochondria, **101**, **106**, 109
Modulation, 105
Moisture transfer, 223
Molting, 153, 161
Moose, **77**, **78**, **129**, 132, **133**, **150**, **157**, **163**
Mortality: freezing, 181; natural, 159; nonfreezing, 180; prefreezing, 180; winter, 159, **162**
Mountain Research Station, 5, 7, 164, 168
Mountains don't care, 199
Movement, 93
Mt. Rose sampler, 138
Mt. Washington, 12
Muscle, 93
Mylar. *See* Cloth

National Elk Refuge, 138, **139**, 142, 149, **149**, **150**

National Outdoor Leadership School, 7, 191, 198, 221, 228, 241
Natural history, 2
Needle ice, 47, **48**, 80, 174, **175**
Neonate, 140
Nivean environment, 73, **83**; intranivean, 73, 79, **83**; subnivean, 73, 79, **83**, **85**, 86, **87**, 252, 261; supranivean, 73, 75, **75**, **78**, **83**; world, 262
Nonshivering thermogenesis (NST or NTG), 108
Norepinephrine, 111
NTG. *See* Nonshivering thermogenesis
Nucleating agent, 38
Nucleus, 102
Nutrition, 131, 254

Oil, 94; neatsfoot, 107
Omnivores, 133
Orbit, **23**; elliptical, 24; aphelion, 24; perihelion, 24
Organelles, 89
Organization, 89
Overturn, thermal: autumnal, 79; vernal, 80
Overwinter, 177, 178; period. *See* Period
Oxidation, 92
Oxygen, 86, 90, 105

PABA, 202
Papyriferic acid, 143
Pelage, 153
Penetration, 58, **60**
Perihelion. *See* Orbit
Period: critical. *See* Critical period; fall, 79; overwinter, 80
Permafrost, 47, 53
Ph, 89, 101
Phase change, 100. *See also* Color phase
Phenol, 142
Phosphate, 96; phosphofructokinase (PFK), 115
Photon, 26
Photoperiod, 83, 154, 170, 181
Photosynthesis, 91, 171; winter, 172
Phytochrome, 171; clock, 165
Pinosylvin methyl ether (PME), 143
Pit: hasty, 217; snow, 53, 217, 246, **247**, **249**, **260**, **261**. *See also* Cooking pit
Planning, 198
Plant, 163; upheaval, 174
Plastic: bags, 240; *See also* Cloth
Plasticity of snow, 50, **51**, **53**
Platform. *See* Sleeping platform
Poisoning, carbon monoxide, 230
PolarGuard. *See* Cloth
Pollution. *See* Visual pollution

Polyol, 179
Polypropylene. *See* Cloth
Population, 144, 145, 164, **163**; census, **145**
Potassium, 93, 102
Predation, 158, **162**
Predisposing factor, 211
Preparation, 199
Pressure, osmotic, 180
Prime skin, 161
Prior Planning, Promptness Prevent Poor Performance (6 Ps), 198
Probe, temperature, 253
Profile. *See* Slope
Protein, 91, **96**, **97**, 179, 180; collagen, 93; contractile, 93; elastin, 93; informational, 94
Protochlorophyll, 82
Protozoan, 141

Qali. *See* Snow
Quinzhee, 230, 231, **232**, **233**, **234**, 251, 252, **253**

Radiation, **24**, **25**, 26, **30**, 33, **35**, **62**, 66, **127**, **129**, **130**; cooling, **36**; longwave, 26, 31, **36**, 123; shortwave 26, 29, 123; solar (*See also* Sun), 14, 23, **27**, **30**, 123; terrestrial, 26, **27**; thermal, 31
Rain, freezing, 49
Rapid cold-hardiness. *See* Cold
Rate, 96, **99**, 100, 105, 216
Reaction, 96, **98**, **99**, 100
Recruitment, 132
Reflectance, 58
Refrozen, 210
Repeatability, 18
Reproduction, 71, **118**, 119
Rescue beacon, 216, 220
Respiration, 171; cellular, 92
Response, 67, 169, 173, 174, 181; physiological, 108; qualitative, 104; quantitative, 103; tree. *See* Tree
Resting metabolic rate. *See* Metabolic rate
Return. *See* Time
Rewarming, **201**, 207, 210, 211, **213**
Rimming, 40, 216; *See also* Frost
Ripening, 80
RNA, 94
Rocky Mountain National Park, 13
Rocky Mountain Biological Laboratories, 7
Route, 217
Rumen, 140
Ruminant, 140

Rumination, 140
Runoff channel, 49

Safety, 199, 216
Sanitary napkin, 241
Sastrugi. *See* Snow
Scavenger, 160
SCREW factor (snow, cold, radiation, energy, and wind), 66, **68**, 131, 160, 163
Seasonality, 18, 23, **23**, **24**
Selection: of winter sites, 136; food, 138, 140; location, 137; spectral. *See* Spectral selection; site, 136
Sensations, 257
Shape, 32, 88, 131, 163
Shovel. *See* Avalanche, Grain scoop
Sinter, 49, 230, 231
Site, 136, 140
6 Ps, 198, 228
60/40 cloth. *See* Cloth, 60/40
Size, body, 70, 132
Sitzmark, 239
Ski wax, 240
Skier, 158, **184**, **205**, **208**, 258, 261
Skin temperature, average, 187, 189
Sleeping bag, **225**, 227; platform, 233, **233**, **235**
Slope, 215; dangerous, **218**; leeward, 215; windward, 215
Snickers bar, 91
Snow, 8, 14, 38, **53**, **54**; algae. *See* Algae; block, 233; cave, 230, 234, **235**; classification of, 38, **39**, 40, **40**, **41**, **42**, **44**, **45**, **46**, 50, 66; crust, 76, 158; density. *See* Density; depth, 156; falling, 38, **41**, **42**; fence, 233; flea, 4, 178; flies, 4; fungi, 175; kitchen, 237, **237**, 239; language, 38, **39**; load, 75, **75**, **76**, 175; mold, 85; on ground, 41, **44**, **45**; properties, 50, 251; pit. *See* Pit; qali, 38, 40; sastrugi, 38, **39**; saw, 234; shelter, 230, 236, 239; sugar, 43; temperature profile. *See* Temperature; tunnel, 170; water content of. *See* Water; wet, 45
Snowball, 217, 241
Snowblindness, 31, 201, 203
Snowcover; disappearance, **19**; formation, **18**
Snowfall: mean annual, **15**; rate, 216; record, 14
Snow fence. *See* Snow
Snowflakes, 38; columns, 40; germ, 40; graupel, 40, 216; needle, 40, 216; pellets, 216; rime, 216; spatial dendrites, 40; stellar, 216
Snowmobile, **196**, 261

Snowmobiler, 158, 218, 258
Snowpack, **56**, **57**, **58**, **59**, **61**, 157, **157**, **170**, 215, 216, 250, 258, **260**
Snow-coping index, 76, 77, **78**
Sodium, 93, 102
Soil displacement, 174, **175**
Solar, **16**; constant, 30; radiation, 26
Solidification, 166
Sorbitol, 179
Sound, 217
Space blanket. *See* Cloth
Spectral selection, 61, **61**, 170
Spectrum: electromagnetic, 26, **27**; visual, **27**, 61
SPF. *See* Sun
Spicule, 45
Spring, 80, **163**; ephemeral, 83; false, 165, 168; lateness of, 156; runoff, 80
Springtail, 4, 178
Stability index (SI), 81
Starvation, 65, 158
Stefan-Boltzmann, 30, 123
Stevenson screen, 11
Stomate, 174
Storage, **118**, 119, **120**
Strategy. *See* Coping
Subdominants, 153
Structure, 93, 95, **96**, 250
Sublimation, 43, 47
Subnivean. *See* Nivean
Sugar, 32, 92, 179, 207; glucose, **91**, 93, 106
Sun, 14, 23, **30**; crust. *See* Crust; poisoning, 203; protection factor (SPF), 202, **202**
Sun bump, 203
Sunburn, 201
Supercooling, 46, 106, 178, 180, 181
Supersaturation, 47
Surface-to-volume ratio, 69, **69**, 133
Survival, 200, 218, 224, 245
Survivor, 219
Sustained yield, 162

Tampon, 241
Tanning, 201
Temperature, **13**, **19**, 28, **39**, 81, 88, **95**, 97, **100**, **119**, **127**, **130**, 156, 171, **204**, 215, **253**; average low, 12; celsius, 28; centigrade, 28; compensation. *See* Compensation; dependent, 100, 103; effective (ET), 186, **186**; gradient (*See also* Metamorphism), **45**, 53, 260; killing, **165**; inversion, 13, 35, **36**; Kelvin, 28; optimal **187**; profile, 53, **54**, **56**, **57**, **58**, 225, 246, **249**, **251**; radiant, 128; record low, 12, **12**; skin. *See* Skin; sky, 128; stability, **83**;

transient, 70; windchill equivalent (WET), 189, **189**, **191**, **192**, **193**
10th Mountain Division, 5, **6**
Terpene, 142
Terrain factor, 214
Terrestrial radiation. *See* Radiation
Teton Science School, 5, **35**, **54**, **56**, 157, **157**, 191, 198, 224, **243**, **244**, **247**, **259**
Theobromine, 111, 207
Theophylline, 111, 207
Thermal (*See* Conductivity, Radiation), **122**, 124, 250; index (TI), 81, **82**, 138, 249, 252, 260, **260**, **261**; memory, 55; neutral zone, **119**; overturn. *See* Overturn; regulation, 71, 195; transfer, 123; wavelengths, 31
Thermistor, 250
Thermocouple, 167, 250, **253**
Thermoperiod, 181
Thermoregulatory penalty, 135
Threshold, hiemal. *See* Hiemal threshold
Thyroid adrenal system, 111
Time: budget, **135**; evolutionary, **17**, **68**, 147; return, 19; scale, 103; start up, 172
Timing, 14, 17, 112, **151**, 153, **155**, 170
Toilet paper, 241
Toothpaste, 240
Torpor, 72, 122. *See also* Hibernation
Trail etiquette, 239
Trailing, 77
Translocation, 165
Transmission, 59, 170
Transpiration, **164**, 174
Transport, 93, 98
Trap. *See* Air, cold
Trap, elephant. *See* Elephant trap
Trapper, **161**
Trapping, 161
Travel, **218**, **219**, 228, **229**, 238
Tree, spruce, **21**; decision tree. *See* Winter response tree
Treeline, **49**, 147
Trench foot, 201, 207
Triterpene, 142

Underwear, 221, 226
University of New York at Oswego, 7
Unsaturated fat. *See* Fat

Valve, 102
Vapor, 38, **39**; density, 126; pressure, 43
Vectors of winter. *See* Winter
Vehicle, 230

Ventilator shaft, **83**, 85
Verglas, 47
Vernal overturn. *See* Overturn
Victim, 219
Viscosity, 50, 101
Visual pollution, 238
Vitrification, 166

Warm, 108
Warm-blooded, 104
Waste, 240
Water, 80, 101, 205; content, 50, **52**; ice, 47, **92**; storage, 237
Waterproof, 223
Water-resistant, 223, 224
Wavelength, **27**, **35**, 60, 171
Wax. *See* Ski wax
Weather, 215; change, 216; winter, 37
Weight, 224
Wet, 209
WET. *See* Temperature, Windchill
Wicking action, 221, 224
Widow makers, 239
Wind, 34, 66, **129**; abrasion, 174; crust. *See* Crust; highest maximum, 14; shell, 223; speed (velocity), **14**, **194**, 215
Windproof, 223, 224
Wind-resistant, 224
Windchill index (*See also* Temperature), 14, 188, **190**, 193
Winter, 1, 23, **23**, 37, 65, 67, 74, 112, 152, 163, 181, 185, 198, 201, 221, 228, 230, 237, 241, 245, 246, 262; aggregation, 133; annual plant, 172; burn, 173; duration, 156; ecology of interior Alaska, 7; educational programs, 241; ground, 147; kill, 136, 144, 158, **160**, **162**; range, 145, **151**; response tree, 67, **68**, **169**; survivorship, 152; vectors of, 65, 66 (*See also* SCREW factor)
Winter-active, 86, **87**, 178
Wintergreen, 82, 172
Winter-social, 133
Winter-solitary, 134
Wood frog. *See* Frog
Wool. *See* Cloth
Wrappers, 240

Xylem, 167

Yard up, 75, 136
Yarding, 141, 158
Yellowstone National Park, **10**, **48**, **51**, 53, 138, 142, **149**, 158, 159, **196**, 200, **208**, **213**, 221, **227**, 228

LENGTH

INCHES (in)

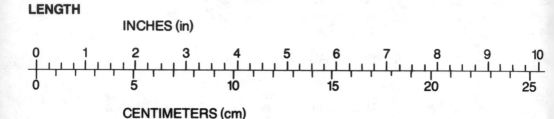

CENTIMETERS (cm)

FEET (ft)

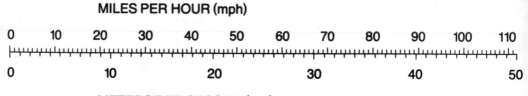

METERS (m)

SPEED

MILES PER HOUR (mph)

0 10 20 30 40 50 60 70 80 90 100 110

0   10   20   30   40   50

METERS PER SECOND (m/s)

TEMPERATURE

DEGREES KELVIN (K)

233 243 253 263 273 283 293 303 313 323 333 343 353 363 373
|｜｜｜|
-40   -30   -20   -10   0   10   20   30   40   50   60   70   80   90   100

DEGREES CENTIGRADE (C)

DEGREES FAHRENHEIT (F)

-40 -30 -20 -10 0 10 20 30 40 50 60 70 80 90 100 110 120 130 140 150 160 170 180 190 200 210
|｜｜|
-40   -30   -20   -10   0   10   20   30   40   50   60   70   80   90   100

DEGREES CENTIGRADE (C)

MASS

OUNCES (oz)

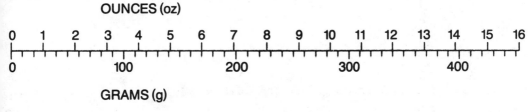

GRAMS (g)

POUNDS (lb)

KILOGRAMS (kg)